THE

VISIGOTHIC CODE

(*FORUM JUDICUM*)

TRANSLATED FROM THE ORIGINAL LATIN, AND EDITED BY

S. P. SCOTT

Author of "Through Spain" "History of the Moorish Empire in Europe'
Member of the Comparative Law Bureau of the American Bar Association

Lex est magistra vitæ
I–II–2

BOSTON
THE BOSTON BOOK COMPANY
1910

The Riverdale Press, Brookline, Boston, Mass.

TO

MY FELLOW MEMBERS

OF THE COMPARATIVE LAW BUREAU

IN THE HOPE THAT IT MAY PROVE AN ACCEPTABLE CONTRIBUTION

TO THE LITERATURE OF THE NOBLE SCIENCE OF THE LAW

THIS TRANSLATION

OF ONE OF THE MOST VENERABLE MONUMENTS OF JURISPRUDENCE

IS DEDICATED

EDITOR'S PREFACE

It was well said by Gibbon that "Laws form the most important portion of a nation's history," for from them, more impartially than from any other source, we derive information of the customs, virtues, vices, political ethics, faults, follies, and religious prejudices of a people. Especially is this true of the Visigothic Code. In it are depicted the traditions and history of a race which, originally nomadic, with unprecedented rapidity became stationary; and, from being for ages subject to institutions formed by the desultory acts of tumultuous assemblies, often dictated by caprice and enmity, in less than two generations acknowledged obedience to a government partly imperial, partly theocratic. In the annals of no people so recently barbarian, is to be found more marked and substantial progress, from the primitive surroundings of pastoral and predatory life, to the tastes, the laws, the refinements, and the social usages of civilization.

An analysis of the Visigothic Code may be made under three heads: historical, descriptive, comparative. Its story is practically that of the Gothic monarchy in Spain. In the variety and scope of its provisions; in the skilful adaptation of its canons to the purposes of ecclesiastical supremacy; in the care with which it preserves the distinctions of caste; in the accuracy and conciseness of its maxims defining the principles of equity; in the elaborate, yet simple, arrangement of its judicial system; in the thoroughly philosophical spirit that pervades the greater portion of its pages; it is radically different from, and, in many respects superior to, all other collections of legal enactments of ancient or mediæval times.

It is far more instructive and suggestive than a chronicle. Nowhere have the purposes of the law been more ably stated than in its terse and expressive phraseology. It proclaims the sentiments of a lofty morality. It appreciates the true object and end of legislation. In its stern and inflexible disregard for the arrogant claims of superior wealth and station, it assured to the most lowly the administration of impartial justice.

The Goths, a branch of the Indo-Germanic race, from which the Caucasian of modern times is descended, and whose habitat once extended from Western Europe to the great plains of Central Asia, seem to have wandered farther, and to have changed more materially, as regards their laws, customs, and religious belief, than other tribes of migratory barbarians. Distinct from the Germans, or Teutons, they have, nevertheless, often been confounded with them; a fact due to their nomadic tendencies, personal appearance, and general habits of life. The similarity which characterized the vast hordes, or vagrant multitudes, which issued in ancient times from the *officina gentium*, has been the cause of much confusion in the more or less fanciful accounts of classic annalists and historians. The coincidence of numerous terms of the Gothic language with those of Sanscrit, and the identity of many roots of words in both languages, have established the origin of the Goths to be Indian, and not Scandinavian, as was once generally supposed. It is related by Herodotus, that Darius, a thousand years before Christ, repelled from the confines of the Persian dominions, across the Danube, a great migration of barbarians, moving and living on horses and in chariots. This people, known as Scythians in antiquity, were the ancestors of the modern Slavs, and kindred of the Goths. Driven back by the Persians, they, with others who followed them, distributed themselves over Northern Europe, whence, in time, they descended to overwhelm, with their numbers and their valor, the decadent and tottering Roman Empire.

The original Goths were typical savages. They had practically no political organization; dressed in skins; disdained all labor; showed no mercy to their enemies; killed their parents, when they became old and infirm; had few religious ideas; worshiped a drawn sword as a divinity; were filthy in their personal habits; and recognized only the law of the strongest. From such unpromising progenitors was derived the race destined to be, in large measure, the lawgivers of Europe.

The Visigoths, in the course of conquest firmly established in Gaul and Spain, and everywhere victorious over the Romans by arms, were, in their turn—as inevitably happens under similar circumstances—both enervated and subjugated by the arts of luxury and peace. Despite their surroundings, they, for a long period, preserved their ancient habits and traditions. For more than a century they went about half-clad and unkempt, as they had done on the shores of the Euxine and the Baltic, to the astonishment and disgust of the polished Roman provincials, who had inherited the luxurious tastes, courteous manners, and artistic conceptions of Greece and Italy. To the last, they wore long hair as a badge of sovereignty; a barbarian custom which first became known to the Romans, when the city was saved by Marius from the invasion of the Cimbri and Teutons. In the early days of their domination in the West, the laws of the Goths, like those of all other unlettered races, were based upon custom and oral tradition. They carried with them in all their migrations the same principles which had guided them in distant countries, and under a far different political and climatic environment. Many of their rules and customs were never abrogated, and eventually constituted no unimportant part of their Code. Under new conditions of government and society, changes became necessary in their jurisprudence. Roman laws, generally subjected to modification, and rarely adopted *in toto*, were incorporated into their statutes. Never, however, was servile obedience, without remonstrance, offered to despotic authority. Their government was strictly one by law. The Crown, long elective, and unsuccessfully attempted to be made hereditary within a quarter of a century of the Saracen invasion, while at first bestowed by the votes of the entire people, ultimately became dependent upon the choice of the clergy. The Throne and the Altar were thus closely connected, and, to a certain extent, necessary to one another. The bishops, having the power of election, and likewise of deposition, exercised unbounded influence over the king, who was indebted to them for his throne. On the other hand, the sovereign had many opportunities for granting favors and privileges to the ecclesiastical order, a prerogative which he did not hesitate to frequently exercise. Ecclesiastical supremacy, however, rarely countenanced oppression in the early ages of the Gothic monarchy. The Visigoths, in common with others of their race, professed the Arian heresy, whose adherents, unlike their successors, the Catholics, were never noted for bigotry or intolerance, and, as a rule, never accepted a point of religious faith or discipline without free and careful deliberation and debate. The omnipresent sacerdotal order, basing its claims upon Divine precept and example, discouraged, with unfaltering persistency, the tyranny of the Crown. The coronation oath of the king was long and minute and abounded in promises to support and defend the interests of his subjects. When invested with the insignia of royalty, he was admonished "*Rex ejus eris si recta facis; si autem, non facis, non eris.*" "Thou shalt be king so long as thou dost do right; but if thou do not do right, thou shalt no longer be king."

The legal and political events of the Visigothic domination are written in the annals of its ecclesiastical councils, which designate the chief events of every reign. These were of three kinds, national, provincial, diocesan. Of the national councils there were nineteen in all; one of which was held in the fifth century, two in the sixth, and sixteen in the seventh; all, after the sixth council, being held at Toledo, which gave to that venerable city vast and permanent prestige and influence in the affairs of the hierarchy and the kingdom. The national councils assembled at the order of the king, who also presided over them; and this prerogative, strange to say, was assumed and exercised, without remonstrance from Christian prelates, by the emirs of Moorish Spain. These ecclesiastical convocations which have been frequently referred to as the first representative popular assemblies of Europe, were very far from deserving that title. While, originally, the laity were admitted to their deliberations and participated, to some extent, in the discussion of secular matters, the clergy, at all times, were supreme in power, as they were superior in learning and eloquence. By degrees, laymen were excluded; the secular element lost its influence; there was no representation, even theoretical, either of the nobility or of the people; the sovereign was but the presiding officer of the assembly; legislation was wholly inspired by the priesthood; and the authority of the clergy became absolutely paramount. The State became synonymous with the Council; the theory of popular representation had vanished; and, while the monarch still assumed the name and state of royalty, the government of the once independent and liberty-loving Goths was, in fact, purely and essentially theocratic, and the clergy, from being teachers, advisers, and pious mediators, were now the absolute rulers of the Peninsula. This predominance, progressive from the very beginning, was felt and acknowledged in everything, whether of greater or minor importance, which affected the welfare of the kingdom. Although the bishops sometimes imposed upon the weakness of their kings, their rule was, in the main, beneficent; and the theocratic character, which they imparted to the government, elicited the respect of the nobility, and the reverence of the people. These wise and pious legislators contributed, by their tact and piety, to the thorough fusion of the victorious and subjugated races. They confirmed the royal power. They stifled conspiracy, and suppressed rebellion. They crushed the treasonable aspirations of many a daring aspirant to the throne. The truculent impulses of the barbarian rabble, never entirely extinguished, were quietly, but effectually, restrained by their judicious display of gentleness, firmness, and devotion. By anointing the sovereign with holy oil, at his coronation, they confirmed his title, and instituted a ceremony which came to be regarded as essential to the royal accession. As they possessed a monopoly of the meagre knowledge of the age, they enjoyed an immense advantage over all other classes, which they did not hesitate to employ, by every available means, for the maintenance and perpetuation of their authority.

Thus, under the Arian system, the government of the clergy was, all things considered, highly salutary. With the conversion of the nation to the Catholic communion, the organization of the hierarchy was little altered; but a far different spirit animated the legislative assemblies. Heresy was punished by the most barbarous laws. The Jews, whose wealth and intelligence had long been conspicuous in the Peninsula, were made the subjects of legal enactments especially devised to deprive them of their property and their liberty. Every expedient was employed to bring them within the pale of the Church. Authority over them was vested in the priesthood, and where a Jew was tried for a criminal offence, it was provided that an ecclesiastic should always be present. Such Jews as refused to profess Christianity were subjected to the most stringent and harassing regulations. They were placed under the constant supervision of spies. Exorbitant taxes were levied upon them, and, in addition to their own, they were compelled to pay those of their apostate brethren. They were not permitted to testify in the courts, to sue, or to defend an action at law, unless the adverse party was one of their own sect. Under the pretence of loans, enormous sums were wrung from their unwilling hands. By means of frivolous pretexts and false accusations, they were frequently reduced to servitude. The laws even went so far as to prohibit them from entertaining thoughts relative to the customs and observances of their sect. Yet, under all these oppressive restrictions, the Hebrews prospered. They were the wealthiest class in the kingdom, and well understood how to employ their riches for their own preservation and profit; while the heavy penalties prescribed for the bribery of judges and other officials, indicate how common and widespread was the influence of such corruption. The extraordinary intelligence and information of the Jew rendered his advice and assistance always acceptable, and often indispensable, to the ignorant and profligate noble; services which were often requited with open protection. Nor was this tolerance and partiality confined to the laity. Not only were the clergy often remiss in enforcing the laws against the Hebrews, but the Code specifically and significantly prohibits their intimacy with Jewish women. In certain offences where punishment was meted out to them for breaches of the law, they underwent the Biblical penalty of being stoned to death; and this was inflicted by certain of their brethren, who, it appears, were appointed for that very purpose, and were recompensed for their treachery with the property of their victims. The persecution of the Hebrew under these atrocious laws, exercised indirectly a great influence upon the destinies of Europe. The Jews of the Peninsula had long entertained intimate relations with their co-religionists of the northern coast of Africa; the oppression under which they languished; the confiscation of their property; the seizure of their children; their enforced proselytism; and the prospect of the ultimate annihilation of their race, tightened the bonds of union existing between them and their African brethren; established an understanding between itinerant traders and the Moorish conquerors of the West; and thus invited and accomplished the Mohammedan conquest of Spain. The most drastic of these regulations against the Jews were enacted under the reign of Ervigius, in the latter part of the seventh century; and, less than forty years afterwards, the whirlwind of Saracen invasion swept the Visigothic monarchy from the face of the earth.

The cruel and unrelenting pursuit of the Jews, commanded by the Visigothic Code, was the foundation of the Spanish Inquisition and its diabolical procedure. From it were derived many of the dogmas, tortures, and penalties, of that awful tribunal; with the exception, that what was once only directed against a single sect, was destined eventually to include the votaries of every heresy. That the descendants of a nation renowned throughout all antiquity as ardent lovers of liberty, should, in a few short generations, be transformed into the most merciless of persecutors, is one of the most remarkable political anomalies to be met with in history. Even San Isidoro, referring to driving the Jews to baptism, and into enforced communion with the Church, declared indignantly that it was "*non secundum scientiam;*" a remark which, made under the reign of Sisibutus, in the beginning of the seventh century, is one of remarkable significance, as emanating from a Father of the Church, in an age of almost universal ignorance and religious prejudice.

The Hispano-Gothic church was absolutely independent of Rome. The supremacy of the pope was not recognized, and, in all the annals antedating the Reconquest, there is no mention of an appeal to the Holy See on questions of government, ceremonial, or doctrine. The bold and haughty spirit of the Basques and Iberians, animated the ecclesiastics of both the Arian and Catholic churches of Spain. Before the Saracen conquest there were no archbishops. The metropolitans, or bishops of the principal churches, were equal in rank in the hierarchy, until the national councils began to be regularly held in the sixth century; when, gradually, by common consent, Toledo became the seat of the Primacy, a distinction which it has ever since maintained. The dominance of the priesthood in the government, once established, advanced with prodigious strides. In the eighth Council of Toledo, seventeen nobles and fifty-two bishops sat; in the sixteenth Council, held fourteen years afterwards, there were in attendance sixteen palatines and counts, and seventy-seven prelates, and, with this preponderating ratio of ecclesiastics, the authority and importance of the latter naturally increased. The morals of the clergy in that age, while far from being blameless, were not subject to the reproach which they so justly incurred from the profane and ribald poets and novelists of subsequent times. Their influence over the people was unbounded, and their popularity, for the most part, well deserved. Their intervention in behalf of the oppressed effectually curbed the ferocious instincts of the monarch and the noble. The criminal, pursued to the doors of the church, or to the foot of the altar, could not be removed from their sacred precincts without the consent of a priest, or a bishop; and the mere fact that he sought refuge in the House of God rendered him exempt from the death penalty, no matter how grave the character of his offence might be. To the bishop was granted the right of supervision over the conduct of the judge, when the latter exceeded his powers, or rendered decisions manifestly in violation of justice. The Goths, the most plastic and obedient of proselytes, regarded their spiritual advisers with peculiar respect and veneration. They were their guides, their protectors, their benefactors. Nor was the potent influence of the clergy in the maintenance of justice and right, confined to the lower orders. They pronounced anathemas against treason; excommunicated pretenders to the throne; curbed the ambition and greed of marauding nobles; compelled the reverence of aspirants to the royal office; and exacted from the king, who was often their creature, the deference and submission which they considered due to their sacred office and authority.

The people of the Peninsula, while apparently attached to the Arian heresy, evinced little steadfastness in faith with the appearance of orthodox Christianity. Confident in their power, and well aware that no monarch would venture to promulgate an edict menacing their supremacy, or, in any way, conflicting with the privileges of the Church, the priesthood did not require, as an essential condition of its validity, that every law should be confirmed by the voice of a council. Consequently many regulations were established by the sole authority of the king; and this privilege, at first merely a concession, came, in due time, to be considered and accepted as a royal perogative. The appeal to the sovereign instead of to the pope, further strengthened the authority of the throne; but never, at any time, was the king permitted to forget to whom he owed his election and his title; and that the same power which had raised him to that exalted position could, at any time he violated his coronation oath, depose him, and reduce him again to the subordinate and comparative y obscure position, from which ecclesiastical favor, aided, perhaps, by his own talents and ability, had raised him.

This circumstance, alone, shows the primitive state of society under the Visigothic domination; a state largely due to the simplicity of popular manners; the spirit of inherited traditions; the enjoyment of intellectual pre¨minence by a single class, in its turn, favorable to the overwhelming growth of sacerdotal power.

The Visigoths were different from other barbarians, in that, in legislation and the management of their civil affairs, they manifested a sense of humanity, and a genuine philosophy, rarely to be found even among nations that are thoroughly civilized. They intermarried with the conquered race. Under their system all persons were equal before the law. The distinction between citizen and foreigner, as defined by the *Jus Civile* and the *Jus Gentium* of Roman jurisprudence, was repudiated. The punishment for crime was graded according to the wealth of the offender, rather than according to the rank and station of the party injured. Children of both sexes could inherit alike the property of their parents; a measure of undoubted justice, but in direct contravention of the laws governing the descent of property in most of the countries of modern Europe. The slave being merely a thing, an injury to him was rated according to his commercial value. His rights were, however, carefully guarded against the abuse and cruelty of his master. When emancipated, his freedom was either absolute, or burdened with certain restrictions by the terms of which he and his family forever owed loyalty and obedience to his former owner, and were, in turn, entitled to the advice and protection of the latter and his descendants.

The love of freedom, as with all migratory races, was strong in the hearts of the Visigoths.

Always obedient to the Church and to their king, they, nevertheless, stubbornly resisted every encroachment upon their ancient rights and liberties. The throne, originally elective, was not as far removed from the body of the people as it was in other nations; for any person of the pure blood of the Goths who had never entered the cloister, or been sentenced for some crime by a court, and who was eminent for great qualities or distinguished services, could aspire to the supreme power. At the time of the monarch's accession, justice, honor, truth, piety, faith, and mercy, were diligently inculcated, to be ever observed as virtues most appropriate and becoming to the royal office. At the same time, fearful penalties were denounced against all princes who violated the coronation oath; and, during the ceremony, these penalties were repeated aloud by all persons present, both ecclesiastics and laymen. Subsequent to the seventh century, when Catholicism was adopted, the generous and noble spirit which had hitherto pervaded the councils of the kingdom, was supplanted by a fierce intolerance, and the king was obliged to bind himself to the relentless extirpation of heresy. The sovereign was treated with much less consideration under the Gothic system, than under those established by other peoples in ancient or in modern times. Regal supremacy, while necessarily invested with much importance in time of war, on the other hand, in time of peace had comparatively little significance. Not until the reign of Leovigild, in the latter part of the sixth century, did the Gothic kings assume the outward marks and insignia of royalty. They did not differ in dress or general appearance from their subjects, nor was a conspicuous place reserved for them in the assemblies of the people; all classes were entitled to address their sovereign with familiarity; and, still retaining in his manners and demeanor the traces of his barbaric origin, he seemed rather the elective magistrate of a republic (which to all intents and purposes he was) than the supreme ruler of a great and powerful nation. The right of primogeniture, derived from feudalism, and omitted from the Salic Law, was likewise unknown to the Goths. A monarch, in the same manner as a private individual, could only transmit to his heirs the personal property which he, in his turn, had acquired by his talents, or inherited from his ancestors. Like the chieftains of the Ostrogoths and other barbarians, who considered long, blond hair a badge of royal authority, he assumed the title of Flavius, from the Latin *flavus*, as indicative of this august and highly prized distinction.

With the fusion of races the identity of the Goths was speedily and completely lost. The military spirit to which they were indebted, not only for their civil and political organization, but also for their integrity as a people, and for their preservation as well, disappeared. In former times, and for ages after their occupation of the Spanish Peninsula, that spirit which was their most distinguishing trait, and the most prominent one which they possessed in common with the Germans, was, by degrees, imperceptibly weakened, and finally lost in the premature decadence of an entire nation. The servile spirit of the Roman colonist and slave, whose sense of independence had been crushed by centuries of oppression, now asserted its predominance over the bold and active sentiments of the hardy soldiers who had overrun and conquered Europe. Under the Visigothic polity there was no pay for military service, and the glory and adventure held out by a campaign, were not considered a sufficient recompense for its hardships. Formerly, the Goths paid their soldiers only in time of war, and, during peace, the army was supported by taxes. The Feudal System, originally derived from the *emphyteusis*, or perpetual lease, of the Roman law, with its rule exacting military service for the possession of a fief, had not yet been established. The unconquerable repugnance of the Visigoths to war caused them to avoid, under every imaginable pretext, extending their aid to their rulers in times of either conquest or invasion. They refused to protect the person of their monarch, or defend the frontiers of their country. The nobles and wealthy landowners persistently violated the law requiring them to bring into battle one tenth of their slaves, thoroughly armed and equipped. The ninth book of the Code contains stringent regulations against such delinquents as, under various pretences, sought to evade the service in the army, due from them and their dependents; and it was said that, at one time, half the able-bodied population of the Peninsula had, by reason of their refusal to obey those regulations, rendered themselves liable to the dreadful penalties which they imposed. In this fact alone is significantly disclosed, not only the thorough deterioration of the once valiant Gothic race, but one cause of the amazing and unprecedented success of the Saracen power. The Mohammedan squadrons, impelled by the mighty force of fanaticism, could not be withstood by a mob of ill-treated peasants and effeminate nobles, disunited by faction, without reverence for their king, or love for their native land; in whom the martial spirit of their ancestors had long been supplanted by the ignominious passions of cruelty and avarice; where their leaders served under fear of the confiscation of their property, and the rank and file were driven into action with the scourge.

The original Visigothic laws, wholly based upon oral tradition, were first reduced to order and committed to writing by Euric, at Arles, in the latter half of the fifth century. This collection is unfortunately lost, but many of its provisions were incorporated into the Visigothic Code, although, no doubt, subjected to important and numerous modifications in the course of centuries. At the beginning of the sixth century, Alaric II. promulgated the *Breviarium Alaricianum*, a body of laws compiled mainly from the Codes of Justinian and Theodosius, which collection was the source of the subsequent Lombard and Bavarian Codes. From the two compilations of Euric and Alaric, under the reigns of Kings Chintasvintus and Recesvintus, 649–652, was formed the *Forum Judicum*, or Visigothic Code; the most remarkable monument of legislation which ever emanated from a semi-barbarian people, and the only substantial memorial of greatness or erudition bequeathed by the Goths to posterity. Like the Roman works on jurisprudence it is divided into twelve books, sub-divided into titles and chapters. The language in which it is written is monkish Latin, a barbarous jargon, extremely difficult to translate, and vastly different from the polished idiom of Tacitus and Cicero. Its examination discloses many discrepancies, variations, ambiguities, and contradictions, unquestionably due to the ignorance of the various transcribers; a fact which is not surprising when the imperfect knowledge and defective education which prevailed in Spain during the seventh century, are considered. There is no mention of the *Forum Judicum* during the Saracen domination, except that it is known to have been preserved by the Moors; and as Christians were permitted the use of their own laws, where they did not conflict with those of the conquerors, upon the regular payment of tribute, it may be presumed that it was the recognized legal authority of Christian magistrates during the period that Spain remained under the Moslem sceptre. When Ferdinand III. took Cordova in the thirteenth century, he ordered the *Forum Judicum* to be adopted and observed by its citizens, and caused it to be rendered into Castilian. This translation, which is usually appended to the Latin version, is incomplete, incorrect, and unsatisfactory. It contains many omissions and substitutions; the meaning of the sentences, in many cases, is not even approximately given; the proper names seem to have originated in the fertile imagination of the monkish translator; and, not infrequently, interpolations, derived from some unknown source, have entirely usurped the place of the original text.

In considering the general details of the Visigothic Code, one of the striking and suggestive features which presents itself is the inculcation of exalted precepts of honor, probity, and justice, and, at the same time, the acceptance and adoption of a belief in the basest and most grovelling forms of superstition. Upon the same page where the duties to be observed between man and man are set forth with a perspicuity and a piety worthy of all praise, appear laws denunciatory of divination and sorcery. With all its imperfections, however, it presents us not only with noble and accurate conceptions of justice, but indirectly gives us, as well, a faithful and picturesque representation of the gradual, but constant, advancement of a people. Unlike other Codes which preceded and followed it, it is deficient in regularity of classification and division, and, in that respect, signally differs from the Institutes of Justinian, whose arrangement was almost literally followed by Blackstone in his Commentaries on the Laws of England. The irreconcilable character of many of its enactments; the identity of penalties for offences of a widely different gravity and nature; the enunciation of the most sublime principles of morality, side by side with mandates requiring the infliction of tortures whose inhumanity would almost appal a savage; the absence of ordeals and the wager of battle, so frequently appealed to in that and following ages, as proofs of guilt or innocence; are, in addition to those previously referred to, among the most prominent characteristics of this extraordinary compilation. The array of one caste against another, a practice which has never failed to destroy a government and degrade a people, is conspicuous everywhere. The court was regarded rather as a place of execution than the seat of the rendition of justice; the judge rather an avenger of injury, than the representative of the law and the guardian of social order. The words *ultio* and *ulciscor*, constantly recurring in the Code, disclose only too plainly the vengeful sentiments of the legislator. In common with all barbarians, and likewise with the majority of civilized men, force, with its consequent inconvenience and suffering, was the only idea which appealed strongly to the Gothic mind, and the moral and deterrent influence of legislation was almost entirely lost sight of.

In the arrangement of the Visigothic Code, the oldest laws, that is, those based upon the unwritten observances of ages, are without any evidence of the time of their adoption; such as are derived from Roman sources are designated *antiqua*, or ancient; the edicts of kings are promulgated under the royal title, a distinction indicative also of those which were exclusively enacted by the national councils.

In an age of ignorance and degeneracy a body of laws enacted and compiled by a semi-barbarous people, was necessarily largely dependent upon the maxims and precedents of such as had preceded it. The harsh, and often cruel, provisions of the Twelve Tables and the Civil Law, were greatly softened in the Visigothic Code. By the terms of the Roman *Nexum*, a debtor hypothecated himself as security for his obligation, forfeiting his liberty in case he failed to fulfil his contract; and thus, as is also declared by the Bible, "the borrower was servant to the lender;" a custom absolutely prohibited by the *Forum Judicum*. The relations of patron and client were essentially different under the Roman and Gothic dominations. At Rome, the condition of clientage could not be renounced; in Gothic Spain a freedman, or *libertus*, had the right to leave his patron and select another, provided he previously surrendered all the property he had received from his benefactor; the obsequious behavior of the Italian client often degenerated into abject servility, which was regarded with gratification by its object; while among the Visigoths nothing was exacted by the patron for his favor but the practice of obedience, and the manifestation of gratitude. The rules governing the control of public lands did not differ greatly under the civil administration of the two races; in the Peninsula, two-thirds of the conquered domain, in accordance with the usual custom of barbarians, became the property of the State by right of conquest; and the remaining third was abandoned to those who had been vanquished in the appeal to arms. The *Lex Talionis*, a prominent feature in the history of all nations in the early times of their formation, while known to have existed at Rome from the reign of Numa, and which appears with such frequency in the enactments of the Visigothic Code, was unquestionably borrowed by the authors of the latter from the institutions of Moses, in accordance with their theocratic prejudices and predilections. According to Roman ideas, a person unquestionably guilty of crime, and caught *in flagrante delicto*, was not entitled to a trial, which was considered superfluous, and his punishment could be inflicted then and there; a principle also frequently acted upon by the Visigoths.

This famous Code consists of laws emanating from four different sources: first, those based on ancient Gothic customs; second, such as were adopted from the Roman jurisprudence; third, the acts of ecclesiastical councils; fourth, edicts of kings, promulgated at different times, according to the various exigencies that arose; all of which seem to have had equal validity. One of the most remarkable characteristics of this collection is the maintenance of the principle of legal responsibility, irrespective of wealth, rank, or dignity. Every precaution was taken to prevent the interference of the sovereign with the magistracy and the tribunals, in instances where the royal power might be improperly exerted to pervert the course of justice; and where the judge, yielding to superior influence, rendered an unjust decree, that decree was declared to be void. In cases where an appeal was taken to the throne, the king, in the consideration of the questions brought before him, was admonished to strictly observe the forms and principles of equity, and to render his decision accordingly. While the judge derived his authority from the Crown, he was in fact, independent of it; and, equally removed from the voice of popular clamor, unlike the elective magistrates of the tribunals of antiquity, was under no obligations to the populace. The sacerdotal legislator, never unmindful of his own interests while defining the rights of the people, was, nevertheless, himself subject to the secular power. While this was the case, however, a great distinction existed between the punishment inflicted for practically the same offences upon the clergy and the laity, with the advantage entirely upon the side of the former. The penalties usually imposed upon ecclesiastics for breaches of the law were fines, penance, and monastic seclusion; and their sacred office was a safeguard against the horrible and degrading punishments from which even the highest nobility were sometimes unable to escape. In this undisguised leniency, and practical exemption from severe judicial sentences, may be discerned the germ of the "benefit of clergy," carried to such lengths, and productive of such manifold injustice and abuse, in mediæval times.

The theocratic principle animating the Visigothic Code is conspicuous in almost all its chapters. The pious and significant maxim, "*Omnis potestas a Deo,*" pervades it from beginning to end; in the preambles, which recite the reasons for the enactment of the laws; in the body of the latter, which appeal to

Divine sanction for their promulgation; in the penalties, which breathe the ferocious sentiment of the ordinances of the Pentateuch. Many of the latter are copied almost verbatim from the Bible. Recalcitrant Jews were stoned to death. Adultery was the only cause for which divorce was permitted. In the long, elaborate, and frightful oath which Jews, apostatizing to Christianity, were compelled to take and subscribe, everything that was most reverenced by them and could be considered most binding, was borrowed from the Old Testament, and, supplemented by appeals to, and confessions of, Christian doctrine, invoked the direst maledictions upon the heads of all who, either tempted by ambition or influenced by hypocrisy, violated their vows, the impressiveness of which was increased by every circumstance of solemnity, superstition, and power. In the contest for ascendency, the Church possessed the advantages of thorough organization and submissive obedience of inferiors, of reverence for alleged celestial origin, and of unity of language; advantages never, in any former age, enjoyed to such an extent by any other society, political, or religious; and which, inspiring respect among all classes, founded upon a solid and enduring basis the magnificent fabric of her authority and grandeur.

The innummerable details relating to the infringment of the rights of property show that many abuses must have previously existed. The great number of laws designed for the protection of agriculture, indicate the importance with which it was considered by a people who, but a few generations before, had been shepherds and predatory vagabonds. The Visigoths were the first of the nomadic barbarians of the North to acknowledge the privileges and responsibilities attaching to the occupation of a permanent and limited domain. The offences of trespass, and forcible entry and detainer, are clearly and explicitly set forth. Severe penalties are denounced against all who deface, remove, or in any way interfere with, established landmarks. Questions relating to transfers, devises, partition, leases, land belonging to the state, boundaries, disputes concerning the ownership of real-property, and title by adverse possession, are discussed and determined with an ability and an accurate conception of the principles of equity, most remarkable for that age. While enjoyment of liberty was theoretically the unquestioned right of every person except the slave, the limits of castes and classes, adopted, for the most part, from the Roman polity, were strictly defined. Notwithstanding minute and often voluminous provisions, designed for the protection of the people, oppression by the rich and powerful was not unusual, and was sedulously provided against. Cruelty, and persecution of the weak, could be practised by no one, no matter how exalted his dignity, without reprobation and punishment. The interference of individuals of rank in the trial of causes, and their obstruction of the process of the law—evidently a common practice, and a source of endless trouble in former times — is repeatedly prohibited; and every attempt was made to preserve the courts from external influence, and insure the justice and impartiality of their decisions. An appeal could be taken from the decision of the judge to the governor of the city, from him to the governor of the province, and from the latter to the king. Where a person was too poor to incur the ordinary expenses of litigation, he could appeal directly to the bishop; who, as the protector of all within his diocese, was authorized to settle their claims and disputes, and enjoined to interpose his good offices to prevent the exercise of injustice and injury. Founded upon the strict principles of morality which everywhere should control the conduct of mankind, the precepts of the Visigothic Code present a strong and remarkable analogy to those which govern the proceedings of modern judicial tribunals. A contract made under duress, or vitiated by fraud, was void. A principal was liable for the act of his agent, where the latter was known not to have exceeded his authority. A master was responsible in damages for injuries committed by his slave. .Guardians were held to strict accountability in the treatment of their wards.

The rights and disabilities of minors are clearly and definitely stated. The legal incapacity of insane persons, excepting during lucid intervals, when publicly recognized to be in possession of their faculties, is declared. The questions of *lis pendens*, *res judicata*, judgment by default, and vendors lien, are treated in much the same way as in modern treatises on those subjects. The laws of inheritance, and the descent of estates, are explained at great length, and with a minuteness corresponding to their importance and effect upon social and domestic life. The relations of husband and wife are exhaustively discussed; no marriage was valid without a dowry, which was given by the husband; the amount was proportioned to the wealth and position of the latter; and a sum in excess of that established by law could not be bestowed through affection, or exacted by improper influence. Patrimonial estates, in the possession of widows, could not be alienated without the consent of a council of relatives; a provision which was, for centuries, the law in Portugal. In the penal legislation of the Code there is a curious mingling of the barbarous and the civilized. The compounding of crimes was permitted by law. The amount of damages to be assessed, like the penalty for the offence, was estimated according to the dignity and possessions of the culprit. The law of retaliation was sanctioned and enforced in cases where the injury was of a personal character; and, in support of this barbarous custom, the authority of the Bible was constantly invoked. The inhumanity of the punishments imposed is another striking indication of the survival of barbarism. Decapitation was the ordinary sentence for capital crimes. The penalty for arson was death by fire. Branding, maiming, scalping, and castration were inflicted for offences not deemed of sufficient gravity to require the imposition of the extreme penalty. Blinding, probably the most cruel of all, though abolished by the Code of Justinian, had been retained by the degenerate Greeks of the Byzantine Empire, from whom the Visigoths acquired it. Scourging was frequently inflicted; the number of blows varied from fifty to three hundred; they were almost always given in public; and even a judge who had been guilty of misconduct in office, was liable to the lash, symbolical at once of suffering and disgrace, and only surpassed in infamy and horror by scalping with fire, or decalvation. Torture, though authorized by law, was sparingly used. Under the Roman system it could only be inflicted upon slaves; the Visigoths, however, countenanced its exercise where the crime sought to be discovered by its means was one implying great moral turpitude; but it was solely employed as a method of eliciting evidence, and never as punishment for crime. With a people so jealous of their liberties, false imprisonment was naturally regarded as one of the greatest of wrongs;

while, on the other hand, few penalties are more common than that involving the forfeiture of freedom. Informers, another institution of Byzantine treachery and deceit, were encouraged, and, where they were not participants in illegal acts, were substantially rewarded for their suspicious and ignominious services. The recognition of malice prepense, and criminal intent, especially in cases of homicide, reveals a just perception of the responsibility attending the commission of crime, rare, indeed, among nations just emerging from barbarism, and quite at variance with other provisions asserting the existence of witchcraft, charms, and incantations. Under the Visigothic polity, a crime is expressly declared to die with its author, where he underwent a capital penalty; no blame or reproach attached to his family or his posterity, where they were not implicated in his guilt; and the sweeping and unjust law of attainder, which confiscated the property, and branded the descendants of an offender with infamy, for centuries in force in England, was unknown to the more equitable and indulgent system of the Visigoths.

We are ignorant of the details of the procedure followed by the Visigothic tribunals. They had, however, their summonses and other writs of various kinds, their pleadings, arguments, depositions, appraisments, judicial opinions both oral and written, appeals and executions. The proceedings were conducted with due solemnity; the most assiduous care was exercised to insure the integrity of the magistrate; the rules of propriety were strictly enforced; exhibitions of contempt were punished with exemplary severity; and even a person of the highest rank, if guilty of marked disrespect to the judge, or participating in any unseemly demonstration, was unceremoniously ejected by the bailiffs. By the enforcement of such measures, the courts were not only invested with a proper dignity and importance, but their impartiality was established and secured; and all, even including the people of the lower classes, came to regard these tribunals as fountains of equity, and the protection and mainstay of their liberties. They were almost continually open; the judges had but few hours of rest or recreation; they were made responsible, in both person and property, for a proper determination of the causes brought before them; their remuneration was fixed by law, and was independent even of royal favor; and the crimes of oppression and bribery, when committed by a magistrate, were made the subject of some of the most savage enactments in the *Forum Judicum*, including degradation from office, forfeiture of property, scourging, decalvation, exile, slavery, and death.

The employment of compurgators under the Visigothic system was an important and popular one. Their number is not stated, and does not appear to have been limited, but originally it consisted of twelve. The probable predecessor of our system of trial by jury, this institution was derived from the Saxons, and was, without question, of remote antiquity. The oath, under other systems of jurisprudence, rarely employed in purgation of crime, was frequently resorted to by the Visigothic magistracy, as it formerly had been under the primitive legal procedure of the Germans. An accused party, if he had hitherto borne a good character, was entitled to establish his innocence by this means; a proceeding which could be confirmed and accompanied by the affidavits of his friends, neighbors, and kinsmen, who, being persons best acquainted with his character and habits, came into court, and swore to their belief in his innocence. No testimony was offered in their presence, and no arguments were made before them, as with the modern jury. With more correct notions of the requisites and effect of legal evidence than their German predecessors, the Visigothic courts did not admit the intervention of compurgators, except under circumstances where competent proof had failed to conclusively establish the guilt of the accused. It is a curious fact that their services were enlisted by criminals and litigants in the courts of England until comparatively recent times. At first limited to criminal prosecutions, their introduction was subsequently extended to various civil actions, and especially to those brought for the recovery of debts; and, recognized by the Canon Law, compurgators were sworn in England as late as the reign of Elizabeth. This remarkable institution, which bears so plainly the impress of ecclesiastical influence, appealing to the piety and superstitious fears of the ignorant, evinces, by the surprising vitality which it exhibited, its peculiar adaptation to the purposes of legal procedure in the age when it prevailed.

While members of the sacerdotal order were, to a certain extent, subject to secular justice under the Visigothic polity, the reverence with which they were universally regarded, the great power they exerted over the institutions of the kingdom, and their superior intelligence, which with the ignorant of all classes, invested them with mysterious powers, rendered their appearance in courts of law most infrequent.

The history of the Visigothic monarchy, especially after its adoption of Catholicism in 587, is, therefore, as has already been remarked, closely interwoven with that of the Visigothic Church. The Crown possessed little real authority. The complete and universal municipal organization, instituted by the Romans, had disappeared with the Gothic occupation. Civil and judicial officers, although appointed by the Crown, were subject to ecclesiastical supervision; not only in the parish and the diocese, but in the tribunals of justice, in the most intimate relations of domestic life, in the determination and settlement of secular disputes, and even in the presence of the throne. The influence of the priest increased in the same ratio in which that of the soldier declined. It reached its climax at the time of the Saracen invasion, when, to all but the most discerning eye, the rule of the Church seemed destined to endure through many centuries, and its civil and political power appeared impregnable. The illusory character of this apparent greatness was soon to be exhibited. Two years after the last of the Gothic kings ascended the throne, the Moorish armies were in possession of the Spanish Peninsula.

The enactments of the Visigothic Code, from their promulgation to the present day, have been never entirely abrogated by the legislative powers of Spain, and, as the foundation of the national judicature, many of its precepts and its rules still maintain their original force and power in the legal and ecclesiastical tribunals of the Spanish Peninsula. During the Moslem domination, their authority was unquestioned in the different Christian kingdoms of the North. The voluminous compilation, known as *Las Siete Partidas*, published by Alfonso el Sabio in 1348, was largely borrowed from the *Forum Judicum*. Charles III. in 1788, expressly declared that the provisions of the latter had never been repealed by subsequent statutes, and ordered that they should prevail in a contest involving the law of inheritance, where the property of a deceased monk was claimed both by his monastery and his relatives, in the royal chancery court of Granada. Not only are some of these laws still recognized as binding in the Peninsula, but they were long used in Southern France, and the capitularies of the early kings of that country bear unmistakable internal evidence of their derivation from this same source.

The Castilian version of the Visigothic Code, notwithstanding its coarseness, its ambiguities, and its errors, is still most useful for the purposes of the philologist and the historian. It displays the beginning and the development of the noble and elegant Spanish idiom, from its origin, full of barbarisms, down to its perfection of today; from the crude and awkward expressions of the chronicle and the missal, to the perspicuous and polished diction of Calderon, Mendoza, and Cervantes. We detect in its labored and awkward sentences the corrupt Latin of the times when classic purity was lost, and the Romance languages had not yet been formed; an epoch of transition, abounding in abbreviated words and crabbed expressions, curious etymology, phrases constructed with little regard to the rules of syntax, incorrect quotations from Scripture, provincial peculiarities of construction and nomenclature, archaic terms, whose meanings are now forgotten, words of purely Arabic derivation, the names of animals and objects, then, for the first time, introduced into Castilian,—much of it confusing, yet all instructive in revealing the customs and prejudices of a people, and depicting the various gradations accompanying the formation and growth of a language.

Such are our obligations, legal, historical, ethical, philological, and economic, to the Visigothic Code. Its harsh, inelegant style, its repetitions and absurdities, its incoherence, its superstitions, and its savage treatment of heretics, may well be forgotten in the services it has rendered to mankind. All modern systems of government are infinitely indebted to it, for it forms to-day the basis of the jurisprudence of a large portion of the civilized nations of the earth. A great number of the principles it inculcates would reflect credit upon any legal treatise, human or divine. Its translation into Castilian aided, more than any one literary work, to invest with beauty, grace, and symmetry, what is now one of the most magnificent and sonorous languages spoken by the tongue of man. It has delineated, with a fidelity not to be found in tradition or chronicle, the state of a society, remarkable in its characteristics, still devoted to barbarian customs, yet evincing sentiments and impulses usually only to be encountered under conditions of the most advanced moral and intellectual development.

Prefixed to the Code, yet clearly indicating by their position and contents that they have properly no more right to be included in it than scores of other products of ecclesiastical legislation to be encountered in the canonical compilations and ancient chronicles of Spain, are ten pages of decrees and fragmentary ordinances of various Councils, purporting to relate to the election of kings and their duties, but which, in reality, are mainly taken up by edifying homilies, invocations of the Deity, and fulminations against such as venture to dispute the divine authority of the Church. These pages fairly swarm with repetitions, anachronisms, and absurdities; their diction is far more barbarous and perplexing than even that of the Code itself; and their general features strongly suggest that they may have been inserted by some ignorant monk, zealous for the superior privileges of his order. For these reasons, as well as because much of what they contain is repeated in the body of the work, they have been omitted.

The translation of this ancient body of laws has been a laborious undertaking, and one to which little assistance has been afforded by the obscure Castilian version. Equivalents for many of the Latin terms do not exist in English. Some passages are of doubtful significance, others absolutely unintelligible. In not a few instances, the text is so involved that only paraphrases can be employed. Despite these serious obstacles, in the treatment of the subject, I have endeavored to observe, as far as practicable, the spirit of the original, and have preferred to render the words and expressions literally—where this can be done—rather than to make use of the terms of modern legal phraseology.

PHILADELPHIA, May 1, 1908.

CONTENTS.

BOOK I.

CONCERNING LEGAL AGENCIES.

TITLE I.—*The Lawmaker.*

TITLE II.—*The Law.*

BOOK II.

CONCERNING THE CONDUCT OF CAUSES.

TITLE I.—*Concerning Judges, and Matters to be Decided in Court.*

TITLE II.—*Concerning Causes.*

TITLE III.—*Concerning Constituents and Commissions.*

TITLE IV.—*Concerning Witnesses and Evidence.*

BOOK III.

CONCERNING MARRIAGE.

TITLE I.—*Concerning Nuptial Contracts.*

TITLE II.—*Concerning Unlawful Marriages.*

TITLE III.—*Concerning the Rape of Virgins, or Widows.*

TITLE IV.—*Concerning Adultery.*

BOOK IV.

CONCERNING NATURAL LINEAGE.

TITLE I.—*Concerning the Degrees of Relationship.*

TITLE II.—*Concerning the Laws of Inheritance.*

BOOK V.

CONCERNING BUSINESS TRANSACTIONS.

TITLE I.—*Ecclesiastical Affairs.*

TITLE II.—*Concerning Donations in General.*

TITLE III.—*Concerning the Gifts of Patrons.*

TITLE IV.—*Concerning Exchanges and Sales.*

BOOK VI.

CONCERNING CRIMES AND TORTURES.

TITLE I.—*Concerning the Accusers of Criminals.*

BOOK VII.

CONCERNING THEFT AND FRAUD.

TITLE I.—*Concerning Informers of Theft.*

TITLE II.—*Concerning Thieves and Stolen Property.*

TITLE V.—*Concerning Forgers of Documents.*

TITLE VI.—*Concerning Counterfeiters of Metals.*

BOOK VIII.

CONCERNING ACTS OF VIOLENCE AND INJURIES.

TITLE I.—*Concerning Attacks, and Plunder of Property.*

BOOK X.

CONCERNING PARTITION, LIMITATION AND BOUNDARIES.

TITLE I.—*Concerning Partition, and Lands Conveyed by Contract.*

BOOK XI.

CONCERNING THE SICK AND THE DEAD, AND MERCHANTS WHO COME FROM BEYOND SEAS.

TITLE I.—*Concerning Physicians and Sick Persons.*

TITLE II.—*Concerning Those who Disturb Sepulchres.*

TITLE III.—*Concerning Merchants who Come from Beyond Seas.*

BOOK XII.

CONCERNING THE PREVENTION OF OFFICIAL OPPRESSION, AND THE THOROUGH EXTINCTION OF HERETICAL SECTS.

TITLE I.—*Concerning the Exercise of Moderation in Judicial Decisions, and the Avoiding of Oppression by Those Invested with Authority.*

LAWS OF THE JUDGES.

BOOK I.

CONCERNING LEGAL AGENCIES.

TITLE I. THE LAWMAKER.

I. What the Method of Making Laws Should Be.

We, whose duty it is to afford suitable assistance in the formation of the laws, should, in the execution of this undertaking, improve upon the methods of the ancients, disclosing as well the excellence of the law to be framed, as the skill of its artificer. The proof of this art will be the more plainly evident, if it seems to draw its conclusions not from inference and imitation but from truth. Nor should it stamp the force of argument with the subtlety of syllogism, but it should, with moderation, and by the use of pure and honorable precepts, determine the provisions of the law. And, indeed, reason plainly demands that the work be performed in this manner. For, when the master holds in his hand the finished product, in vain is sought the reason for its having been impressed with that particular form. On subjects that are obscure, reason eagerly seeks to be informed by examination; in matters, however, that are well known and established, action alone is required. Therefore, when the matter in question is not clear because its form is unfamiliar, investigation is desirable; but it is otherwise in affairs known to all men, where not speculation, but performance, becomes essential. As we are more concerned with morals than with eloquence, it is not our province to introduce the personality of the orator, but to define the rights of the governor.

II. How the Lawmaker Should Act.

The maker of laws should not practise disputation, but should administer justice. Nor is it fitting that he should appear to have framed the law by contention, but in an orderly manner. For the transaction of public affairs does not demand, as a reward of his labors, the clamor of theatrical applause, but the law destined for the salvation of the people.

III. What Should be Required of the Lawmaker.

First, it should be required that he make diligent inquiry as to the soundness of his opinions. Then, it should be evident that he has acted not for private gain but for the benefit of the people; so that it may conclusively appear that the law has not been made for any private or personal advantage, but for the protection and profit of the whole body of citizens.

IV. What the Conduct of the Lawmaker Should Be in his Daily Life.

The framer of laws and the dispenser of justice should prefer morals to eloquence, that his speech may be characterized rather by virtuous sentiments, than by elegance of expression. He should be more eminent for deeds than for words; and should discharge his duties rather with alacrity than with reluctance, and not, as it were, under compulsion.[1]

V. How the Lawmaker Should Impart Advice.

He should be mindful of his duty only to God and to himself; be liberal of counsel to persons of high and low degree, and easy of access to the citizens and common people; so that, as the guardian of the public safety, exercising the government by universal consent, he may not, for personal motives, abuse the privileges of his judicial office.

VI. What Manner of Speech the Lawmaker Should Use.

He should be energetic and clear of speech; certain in opinion; ready in weighing evidence; so that whatever proceeds from the source of the law may at once impress all hearers that it is characterized by neither doubt nor perplexity.

VII. How the Lawmaker Should Act in Rendering Judgment.

The Judge should be quick of perception; firm of purpose; clear in judgment; lenient in the infliction of penalties; assiduous in the practice of mercy; expeditious in the vindication of the innocent; clement in his treatment of criminals; careful of the rights of the stranger; gentle toward his countrymen. He should be no respecter of persons, and should avoid all appearance of partiality.

VIII. How the Lawmaker Should Comport Himself in Private and Public Affairs.

All public matters he should approach with patriotism and reverence; those concerning private individuals and domestic

[1] It must be remembered that under the Gothic polity, the legislator, invariably a member of the ecclesiastical order, was frequently called upon to exercise the exalted functions of the judge. In some instances, the two officials had concurrent jurisdiction; in others, the bishop was authorized to decide questions of law and fact in the absence of the magistrate. Especially was this the case where the interests of the Church were, in any way, concerned. Hence arises the apparent confusion of the duties of legislator and judge, in this and other chapters of the Visigothic Code.—[ED.

controversies he should determine according to his authority and power; so that the community may look up to him as a father, and the lower orders of the people may regard him as a master and a lord.

He should be assiduous in the performance of his duties so that he may be feared by the commonalty to such a degree that none shall hesitate to obey him; and be so just that all would willingly sacrifice their lives in his service, from their attachment to his person and to his office.

IX. What Instruction it is Fitting that the Lawmaker Should Give.

Then, also, he should bear in mind that the glory and the majesty of the people consist in the proper interpretation of the laws, and in the manner of their administration. For, as the entire safety of the public depends upon the preservation of the law, he should attempt to amend the statutes of the country rather than the manners of the populace; and remember that there are some who, in controversies, apply the laws according to their will, and in pursuance of private advantage, to such an extent that what should be law to the public is to them private dishonor; so that, by perversion of the law, acts which are illegal are often perpetrated, which should obviously be abolished through the power of the law itself.

TITLE II. THE LAW.

I. *What the Lawmaker Should Observe in Framing the Laws.*
II. *What the Law Is.*
III. *What the Law Does.*
IV. *What the Law Should Be.*
V. *Why the Law is Made.*
VI. *How the Law Should Triumph over Enemies.*

I. What the Lawmaker Should Observe in Framing the Laws.

In all legislation the law should be fully and explicitly set forth, that perfection, and not partiality, may be secured. For, in the formation of the laws, not the sophisms of argument, but the virtue of justice should ever prevail. And here is required not what may be prompted by controversy, but what energy and vigor demand; for the violation of morals is not to be coerced by the forms of speech, but restrained by the moderation of virtue.

II. What the Law Is.

The law is the rival of divinity; the oracle of religion; the source of instruction; the artificer of right; the guardian and promoter of good morals; the rudder of the state; the messenger of justice; the mistress of life; the soul of the body politic.

III. What the Law Does.

The law rules every order of the state, and every condition of man; it governs wives and husbands; youth and age; the learned and the ignorant; the polished and the rude. It aims to provide the highest degree of safety for both prince and people, and, in renown and excellence, it is as conspicuous as the noon-day sun.

IV. What the Law Should Be.

The law should be plain, and not lead any citizen to commit error or fraud. It should be suitable to the place and the time, according to the character and custom of the state;

prescribing justice and equity; consistent, honorable, worthy, useful, and necessary; and it should be carefully noted whether its provisions are framed rather for the convenience, than for the injury, of the public; so that it may be determined whether it sufficiently provides for the administration of justice; whether or not it appears to be contrary to religion, and whether it defends the right, and may be observed without detriment to any one.

V. Why the Law is Made.

Laws are made for these reasons: that human wickedness may be restrained through fear of their execution; that the lives of innocent men may be safe among criminals; and that the temptation to commit wrong may be restrained by the fear of punishment.

VI. How the Law Should Triumph over Enemies.

Domestic peace having been once established and the plague of contention having been entirely removed from prince, citizen, and the populace, expeditions then may be made safely against the enemy and he may be attacked confidently and vigorously, in the certain hope of victory; when nothing is to be anticipated or feared from dissensions at home. The entire body of the people being prosperous and secure, through the influence of peace and order, they can set forth boldly against the enemy and become invincible, where salutary arts are aided by just laws. For men are better armed with equity than with weapons; and the prince should rather employ justice against an enemy than the soldier his javelin; and the success of the prince will be more conspicuous when a reputation for justice accompanies him, and soldiers who are well governed at home will be all the more formidable to a foe. It is a matter of common experience, that justice, which has protected the citizen, overwhelms the enemy; and that those prevail in foreign contests who enjoy domestic peace; and while the moderation of the prince insures temperance in the enforcement of the law, so the united support of the citizens promotes victory over the enemy. For the administration of the law is regulated by the disposition and character of the king; from the administration of the law proceeds the institution of morals; from the institution of morals, the concord of the citizens; from the concord of the citizens, the triumph over the enemy. So a good prince ruling well his kingdom, and making foreign conquests, maintaining peace at home, and overwhelming his foreign adversaries, is famed both as the ruler of his state and a victor over his enemies, and shall have for the future eternal renown; after terrestrial wealth, a celestial kingdom; after the diadem and the purple, a crown of glory; nor shall he then cease to be king; for when he relinquished his earthly kingdom, and conquered a celestial one, he did not diminish, but rather increased his glory.

BOOK II.

CONCERNING THE CONDUCT OF CAUSES.

TITLE I. CONCERNING JUDGES AND MATTERS TO BE DECIDED IN COURT.

I. *When Amended Laws should come in Force.*

II. *The Royal Power, as well as the Entire Body of the People, should be Subject to the Majesty of the Law*

III. *It is Permitted to No One to be Ignorant of the Law.*

IV. *The Business of the King shall First be Considered, then that of the People.*

V. *How the Avarice of the King should be Restrained in the Beginning, and How Documents Issued in the Name of the King should be Drawn Up.*

VI. *Concerning Those who Abandon the King, or the People, or their Country, or who Conduct Themselves with Arrogance.*

VII. *Of Incriminating the King, or Speaking Ill of Him.*

VIII. *Of Annulling the Laws of Foreign Nations.*

IX. *No One shall presume to have in his Possession another Book of Laws except this which has just been Published.*

X. *Concerning Fast Days and Festivals, during which No Legal Business shall be Transacted.*

XI. *No Cause shall be Heard by the Judges which is not Sanctioned by the Law.*

XII. *When Causes have once been Determined, at no Time shall They be Revived; but They shall be Disposed of according to the Arrangement of this Book: the Addition of Other Laws being One of the Prerogatives of the King.*

XIII. *It shall be Lawful for No One to Hear and Determine Causes except Those Whom either the King, the Parties by Voluntary Consent, or the Judge, shall have Invested with Judicial Powers.*

XIV. *What Causes shall be Heard, and to what Persons Causes shall be Assigned for a Decision.*

XV. *Judges Shall Decide Criminal as well as Civil Causes.*

XVI. *Concerning the Punishment of Those who Presume to Act as Judges, who have not been Invested with Judicial Power.*

XVII. *Concerning Those who Ignore the Letters of the Judge, or His Seal, Calling Them to Court.*

XVIII. *Where a Judge Refuses to Hear a Litigant, or Decides Fraudulently or Ignorantly.*

XIX. *Where a Judge, either through Convenience to Himself, or through Want of Proper Knowledge, Decides a Cause Improperly.*

XX. *Where a Judge, either through Deceit or Cunning, imposes Needless Costs upon Either, or Both the Parties to a Suit.*

XXI. *What, First of All, a Judge should be Familiar With, in order that he may Understand a Case.*

XXII. *Where the Integrity of a Judge is said to be Suspected by Any One of Honorable Rank, or where a Judge presumes to render a Decision Contrary to Law*

XXIII. *How a Judge should render Judgment.*

XXIV. *Concerning the Emoluments and the Punishment of the Judge, and of the Bailiff*

XXV. *Everyone who is Invested with Judicial Power shall Legally bear the Title of Judge.*

XXVI. *Every Bond which is Exacted by a Judge, after an Unjust Decree, shall be held Invalid.*

XXVII. *An Unjust Decree, or an Unjust Interpretation o the Law, Prompted by Fear of the Throne, o Made by Order of the King, shall be Invalid.*

I. When Amended Laws should come in Force.

In assigning their place to laws which have been amended, we have considered it proper to give them the most important rank, for, as clearness in the laws is useful in preventing the misdeeds of the people, so obscurity in their provisions interferes with the course of justice. For many salutary edicts are drawn up in obscure and contradictory language, and are instrumental in promoting the controversies of litigants; and, while they should put an end to chicanery, they, in fact, give rise to new sophisms and abuses. For this reason, therefore, litigation increases; disputes between parties are encouraged; the judges become undecided, so that, in attempting to dispose of false claims and charges, they are unable to form definite conclusions, as all seems perplexed and uncertain. And because all questions which arise in suits at law, cannot be disposed of in a few words, except those which have been determined in our presence; we have decided that certain laws should be amended in this book; that doubtful matters should be made clear; that profit should be extracted from those things that are evil; clemency from those that are mortal; clearness from those that are obscure; and that perfection should be given to those that are incomplete; whereby the people of our kingdom, whom our peaceful government alone restrains, may be checked and controlled, hereafter, by the aid of said amended laws. And therefore, these laws as amended, and approved by us, and our new decrees, as set forth in this book and its titles, as well as such as may be subsequently added, shall be enforced from the second year of our reign, and the twelfth Kalends of November, and shall be binding thereafter upon all persons subject to our empire, irrespective of rank. Those laws, however, which we have promulgated against the offences of the Jews, we decree shall be valid from the date when they were confirmed by us.

THE GLORIOUS FLAVIUS RECESVINTUS, KING.

II. The Royal Power, as well as the Entire Body of the People, should be Subject to the Majesty of the Law.

The Omnipotent Lord of all, sole Founder and Provider of the means of human salvation, ordered the inhabitants of the earth to learn justice from the sacred precepts of the law. And, because the mandate of Divinity has been thus imposed upon the human race, it is fitting that all terrestrial creatures, of however exalted rank, should acknowledge the authority of Him whom even the celestial soldiery obey. Wherefore, if God should be obeyed, justice should be highly esteemed, which, if it were thus esteemed, would be constantly practised, as every one loves justice more truly and ardently when a feeling of equity unites him with his neighbor.[1] Willingly, therefore, carrying out the Divine commands, let us give temperate laws to ourselves and to our subjects; laws such as we and our successors, and the whole body of the people, may readily obey; so that no person of whatever rank or dignity may refuse to submit to the power of the law, which the necessity and will of the King has deemed it proper and salutary to inculcate.

[1] Preambles, such as the above, which are of frequent occurrence in this body of laws, show unmistakably its ecclesiastical origin, and the theocratic principles, which, at all times, dominated those who framed it. The Mosaic Code alone, among those of great antiquity, is constantly pervaded by similar religious sentiments; which, emanating from the high authorities of the Church, undoubtedly exerted great and beneficial influence over an ignorant and superstitious people. Such additions to legal enactments would seem strangely out of place at the present day.—[ED.

FLAVIUS RECESVINTUS, KING.

III. It is Permitted to No One to be Ignorant of the Law.

All true science declares that ignorance should be detested.[1] For while it has been written, "he need not understand who desires to act with propriety," it is certain that he who does not wish to know, despises an upright life. Therefore, let no one think that he can do what is unlawful because he was ignorant ot the provisions of the laws, and what is sanctioned by them; for ignorance does not render him innocent, whom guilt has subjected to the penalties of the criminal.

FLAVIUS RECESVINTUS, KING.

IV. The Business of the King shall First be Considered, then that of the People.

God, the Creator of all things, in his arrangement of the human form, placed the head above the body, and caused all the different members of the latter to originate from it, and it is, therefore, called the head; there being formed the brightness of the eyes, by which all things that produce injury can be discerned; there being born also the power of intelligence, through which the members connected with, and subject to, the head, may be either controlled or protected. For this reason it is the especial care of skilful physicians to provide the remedies for the head before treating the other members of the body; which, indeed, may not be thought unreasonable, when properly explained; because, if the head should be healthy, it is reasonable to suppose that the other members can be readily cured. For if disease attacks the head, health cannot be imparted by it to the members

---

[1] The first sentence of this chapter is directly at variance with the maxim subsequently inculcated with such diligence by the Church of Rome; through the rigid enforcement of which it long maintained its despotic empire, and which it still regards as one of the most important sources of its power: "Ignorance is the mother of Devotion."

It may be conjectured from the above, that the familiar legal axiom, "*Ignorantia legis neminem excusat*," already ancient, and well established in the seventh century, is probably as old as the law itself.—[ED.

which are constantly being wasted by weakness. The most important duties of the prince are, therefore, the preservation of health and the defence of life; so that the proper method may be adopted in the conduct of the affairs of the people; and while the health of the king is cared for, the preservation of his subjects may be the better maintained.

THE GLORIOUS FLAVIUS RECESVINTUS, KING.

V. How the Avarice of the King should be Restrained in the Beginning, and How Documents Issued in the Name of the King should be Drawn Up.

Earthly greatness appears the more sublime when compassion for our neighbors is displayed; and, therefore, it should be the duty of every monarch to pay more attention to the safety of his subjects than to his own personal advantage. For the greater the number of his subjects, the greater the benefit to be derived by him from them; as, however much the king may desire to profit by his individual efforts alone, there is little to be gained therefrom. Hence, the well-being of the people, whose bounds are not defined by the will of one, but affect the prosperity of all, is directly concerned. Wherefore, that the favor of the prince may not seem to be manifested rather in words than in deeds, he should be attentive to the unspoken wishes of his subjects; and thus unsolicited compassion may often effect what otherwise crowded assemblies would hardly be able to obtain.

For the reason that, in former times, the unbridled greed of princes despoiled the people of their possessions, and the wealth of the state was persistently wrung from the misery of its citizens; as we have already given laws to the subject, we deem it in accordance with the teachings of the Holy Spirit to place restraints upon the exactions of the prince. Hence, after sincere deliberation, as well for our own glory as for that of our successors; God being our mediator; we decree that no king shall, by any means, extort, or cause to be extorted, any documents whatever in acknowledgment of any debt, whereby any person can unjustly, and without his consent, be deprived of his property. And, if by the free will of any one the king should receive a gift, or should openly profit by any transaction, the character of the transaction or contribution should be clearly set forth in the document; by which means either the influence of the prince or the fraud of his accomplice may be readily detected. And, if it should appear that the document had been exacted from any one against his will, either the dishonesty of the prince shall be atoned for, and he shall cancel his corrupt contract, or, if he should be dead, the document shall be declared void as against him from whom it was extorted, or his heirs, and this shall be done without delay.[1] But the ownership of property whose acquisition is free from all suspicion, shall vest absolutely in the prince, and be his own forever. And whatever disposition he wishes to make of any of these things, he can make according to his judgment. But as sincerity and truth confirm all matters of this kind, whenever any documents are made for the advantage of the prince, the witnesses who have attested those documents shall be carefully examined, and if no indication of corrupt or forcible influence by the prince is apparent, or should any fraud in the execution of the document be detected; according to these circumstances the instrument shall either stand as properly made, or, having been proved to be illegal, it shall be declared void.

---

[1] The Visigothic Councils, whose authority was presumed to emanate from Heaven, and whose alleged sacred character invested also, to a certain extent, the monarchs elected by them, presumed to legislate for all coming time. Instances often occur where future kings are declared to be bound irrevocably by the acts of their predecessors, and by the decrees of the collected wisdom and piety of the nation, represented by the ecclesiastical assemblies of Toledo. Despite the solemn adjurations of prince and prelate, however, few kings hesitated to repeal or abolish the laws of their ancestors, when those laws either offended their prejudices, or interfered with their ambition.

The manifest injustice and iniquity now recognized by nearly all civilized nations as attaching to *ex post facto* laws, were not appreciated by the Visigothic legislator, or sovereign. Laws were frequently made retroactive, and were enforced with great severity in cases affecting questions of religious belief, as well as in those relating to the rights and privileges of the Crown.—[ED.

Similar arrangements concerning lands, vineyards, and bodies of slaves shall be observed, even when such disposition has been made of them verbally and in the presence of witnesses. In regard to all property that has been acquired by princes since the time of King Chintilanus, or that hereafter shall be acquired by others; and whatever property a king has left, or shall leave undisposed of, when it is proved to have been acquired by the head of the government; we decree that it shall belong to his successor in the kingdom, and he shall have the power to dispose of it according to his pleasure. But property obtained from relatives, or inherited from parents, shall descend to his sons, or, if he have no sons, to his legitimate heirs, as their rights may appear, or as they are acknowledged by the laws of succession: but if it should happen that he has left undisposed of any property inherited from his parents or his relatives, or derived from any contribution, or obtained by any legal contract; it shall belong, not to the successor of the kingdom, but to the sons or heirs of him who has thus acquired it. For whatever the prince is known to have possessed before his accession to the throne, either as his own property, or gained through honorable transactions with others, he shall have absolute power to dispose of according to his will, and his sons shall have full right to its inheritance; but, if he should have no sons, such property as he did not dispose of, shall descend to his lawful heirs. This law shall apply solely to, and shall be observed in, the affairs of the prince, and shall be forever enforced, and no one shall ascend the royal throne before making oath that he will observe it in all its details.

Whoever, either through an insurrection of the people, or by secret machinations, shall attain to supreme power, shall, with all his adherents, be accursed, and shall be excommunicated from the society of all Christians; and every Christian who shall have any intercourse with him shall undergo the same condemnation and pay the same penalty. And if any one holding an office in the royal palace, shall, through malice, criticise this law, or evade it in any way, or murmur against it; or shall have been convicted of having openly condemned it; he shall be deprived of all his employments and privileges, shall be stripped of half of all his possessions, shall be forcibly restrained of his liberty, and be excluded from the society of the palace. Any one in holy orders who has shared his offense, shall undergo the same confiscation of his property.

FLAVIUS CHINTASVINTUS, KING.

VI. Concerning Those who Abandon the King, or the People, or their Country, or who Conduct Themselves with Arrogance.

The extent to which the country of the Goths has been afflicted by domestic strife, and by the injuries caused by deserters and their abominable pride, is not generally known; yet it is evident in the diminution of the population; and these disturbances are the source of more trouble to the country than enterprises against the enemy. Therefore, that such contemptible conduct may be abolished, and the manifest crimes of these transgressors may no longer go unpunished, we have decreed by this law, which shall prevail through all ages, that whoever, from the time of King Chintilanus of sacred memory, until the second year of our reign, has deserted, or shall desert to the enemy; or shall repair to any foreign country; or even has wished, or shall wish, at any time, to act with criminal intent against the Gothic people; or shall conspire against his country; or, perchance, has attempted at any time to conspire against it; and has been, or shall be captured or detected in the commission of any of these offences; and if, eithei from the first year of our reign has attempted, or, hereafter, any one within the limits of the country of the Goths shall attempt, to foment any disorder, or cause any scandal to the detriment of our government, or of the people; or, what is unworthy to be even mentioned, may have seemed to have plotted our death or injury, or shall hereafter plot against subsequent kings; or has appeared, or shall appear, to manifest, in any way, the intentions of a traitor; whoever shall be found guilty of all of these crimes, or of any one of them, shall undergo sentence of death; nor shall any leniency be shown him, under any condition, except that his life alone may be spared through the considerate pity of the prince. But this shall not be done until his eyes have been put out, so that he may not see the wrong in which he wickedly took delight, and may henceforth drag out a miserable existence in constant grief and pain. The property of such atrocious criminals shall belong absolutely to the king, and whoever he bestows it upon shall possess it in security forever; and no succeeding king, at any time, shall presume to review the cause, or shall interfere, in any way, with this sentence. But, as many are found who, having been implicated in these, and in similar wicked designs, and have fraudulently transferred their property to the Church, or to their wives, or to their sons and friends, or to other persons; or have secretly conveyed said property to foreign countries, in order that they may claim said property, and demand its possession thereafter; when, in fact, none of said property has been alienated, and the papers evidencing its transfer are fraudulent, making false representations under an appearance of truth; therefore, we have decided to abolish this most iniquitous fraud by the decree of this law; so that, wherever documents have been drawn up with a manifest intention to wrong or deceive, any property owned by a person who has been convicted of such criminal practices shall be confiscated for the use of the royal treasury; and it is hereby declared that all such property above mentioned shall be at the disposal of the king, and he shall hereafter do with it whatever his judgment dictates, but whatever other provisions relating to a fraud of this description are contained in other laws, are hereby confirmed in all their force.

All persons to whom pardon has been granted by preceding kings are expressly excepted from the penalties of this decree; and if, through motives of humanity, the king should wish to bestow anything upon a criminal, it should not be taken from the property belonging to the malefactor, but must be obtained from such other source as it may please the king; and it shall be only lawful for him to give an amount equal to the twentieth part of the inheritance of the criminal.

THE GLORIOUS FLAVIUS RECESVINTUS, KING.

VII. Of Incriminating the King, or Speaking Ill of Him.

As we have forbidden all persons to either plot treason, or to institute violence against the king, so it shall also be unlawful to either accuse him of crime, or utter maledictions against him. For the authority of the Sacred Scriptures does not permit evil to be spoken of one's neighbor, and declares that he who curses the prince, is an offender against the people. Wherefore, whoever shall accuse the prince of crime or shall utter curses against him, and, instead of humbly and respectfully admonishing him as to his life, shall boldly insult him with pride and contumely; or, in order to degrade him, shall refer to him in ignominious, base, and injurious language; if the offender should belong to the nobility or to a family of high rank, no matter whether he is a member of the clergy or of the laity, as soon as he has been detected and convicted, he shall forfeit half of all his property, which the prince shall have the privilege of disposing of according to his pleasure. If, however, he should belong to the lower classes, or those without dignity and position, both his property and his person shall be at the absolute disposal of the king. And even should the king be dead, these same provisions shall apply to whoever dares to defame his memory.[1] For the living vainly cast the darts of slander against the dead, who, having departed this life, cannot be affected by abuse, or influenced by criticism. But, for the reason that he is evidently insane who heaps detraction upon one who cannot comprehend it; the slanderer shall receive fifty lashes, and his presumption shall be silenced. But the privilege is given freely to all, while the prince is either living or dead, to discuss all matters

---

[1] Considering that the crown was elective; that the monarch was only "*Primus inter pares*," and that the subject had apparently the right to sometimes admonish his sovereign of his errors, a relic of the sturdy independence which characterized all northern barbarians; the doctrine of *lesè-majesté* seems to have early acquired great importance among the Visigoths, judging from the severe penalties visited upon those guilty of the offence.—[ED.

pertaining to any cause he may have before the legal tribunals and to use such arguments as may be proper and right, and obtain such judgment as he may be entitled to; for, by this means, we endeavor to establish reverence for human dignity, as well as to maintain faithfully the justice of God.

FLAVIUS CHINTASVINTUS, KING.

VIII. Of Annulling the Laws of Foreign Nations.

We both permit and desire that the laws of foreign nations shall be studied for the sake of the useful knowledge that may be obtained from them, but we reject and prohibit their employment in the business of the courts. For although they may be couched in eloquent language, they abound in difficulties; and so long as the methods, principles and precepts contained in this body of laws suffice for the purposes of justice, we are unwilling that anything more be borrowed, either from the Roman laws, or from the institutions of foreigners.

THE GLORIOUS FLAVIUS RECESVINTUS, KING.

IX. No One shall presume to have in his Possession another Book of Laws except this which has just been Published.

No one of our subjects, whosoever, shall presume to offer to a judge as authority, in any legal proceeding, any book of laws excepting this one, or an authorized translation of the same; and any person who does this shall pay thirty pounds of gold to the treasury.[1] And if any judge shall not at once

---

[1] The coins principally in use among the Visigoths were those of the Byzantine Empire at that epoch, as follows:—Gold, The *Libra*, or pound, twelve ounces in weight, and divided into seventy-two *Tremisæ*, or twenty-four *Siliqæ;* and Silver, The *Libra*, containing twenty *Solidi*, and the *Solidus*, containing twenty *Denarii* of copper. The smaller coins, of which there were many, were those of ancient Rome, and of the Eastern Empire.

The *Libra* of gold was worth $368, and the one of silver worth $88, or, at the present value of money, $4,048, and $968, respectively.

destroy such a prohibited book when it is offered him, he shall undergo the above named penalty. But we decree that those shall be exempt from the operation of this law, who have cited former laws, not for the overthrow of ours, but in confirmation of causes which have previously been determined.

THE GLORIOUS FLAVIUS CHINTASVINTUS, KING.

X. Concerning Fast Days and Festivals, during which no Legal Business shall be Transacted.

No litigation shall be commenced on Sunday, for religion should take precedence of all legal matters, and upon that day no one shall presume to subject another to annoyances either for the trial of a case, or for the payment of a debt; nor shall any person be permitted to bring a suit at Easter; that is, for fifteen days, the seven which precede the celebration of that festival, and the seven which follow it. The days of Christmas, of the Circumcision, of the Epiphany, of the Ascension, and of Pentecost shall be observed with the same reverence; and, in like manner, during the harvest festivals, from the fifteenth Kalends of August, to the fifteenth Kalends of September, the same pious conformity shall be required. But in the province of Carthage, by reason of the constant ravages of the locust, we decree that the harvest festival shall be celebrated from the fifteenth Kalends of July to the fifteenth Kalends of August; and, on account of the vintage, from the fifteenth Kalends of October to the fifteenth Kalends of November.

This provision we decree shall be obeyed by all; so that, during these festivals, no one may be summoned to court, or

---

The *Solidus* ($56 gold, and $44 silver,) was the standard coin in circulation.

The gold *Tremisa* was the only coin struck by the royal mints during the Visigothic domination. Heavily alloyed, rude in design, and coarse in execution, these clumsy medals disclose the primitive conditions of the numismatic art of the period, being notably inferior to the contemporary examples of Byzantine coinage, themselves far below the artistic models of ancient Rome.

The severe fines imposed under the Visigothic Code, and whose non-payment generally involved the alternative of perpetual servitude, often caused the financial ruin of the offender.

subjected to prosecution, unless the suit in which he is concerned has already been brought before the judge. For there can be no reason, if the action should still be undecided, that he who has been sued should be placed at any disadvantage on account of holidays. And if either of the parties is a person of credit and honor, he may depart the court, under his promise to return. But if he should be of doubtful faith, he shall provide securities for such time as is necessary; either until the cause has been decided, or until the judge shall appoint a time for it to be heard. An exception should be made, however, against those who have committed a crime punishable with death, who may be arrested upon any of the hereinbefore mentioned days, and kept in close custody, until Sunday or the above-named festivals shall have passed, when they shall be subjected to the vengeance of the presiding judge. The harvest or vintage festivals shall, in no way, interfere with the punishment of criminals and malefactors worthy of death. But the law shall not hold him excusable who, not yet having been brought into court, knows that he shall eventually be summoned there, and who, concealing himself for the rest of the time, appears in the presence of him to whom he is liable, only on the festival days aforesaid, thinking that, through no process of the law, he can be held until the cause is heard; such a person we decree shall be placed under restraint until the case of plaintiff shall have been disposed of. And if there should be any one concerning whose good faith there may be suspicions, and who cannot find security, he shall remain in custody, until, the holidays having expired, the cause in which he has been summoned shall be decided. And if any one shall presume to act contrary to the decree of this law, and shall come to the judge with a complaint upon the days which are prohibited, as aforesaid, he shall be scourged in public with fifty lashes.

XI. No Cause shall be Heard by the Judges which is not Sanctioned by the Law.

No one has a right to hear a cause which is not authorized by the laws; but the governor of the city or the judge, either in person, or by their messengers, may cause both parties to appear before the king, that the matter may be disposed of at his discretion; and, after this promulgation, such decisions shall have all the force of law.

FLAVIUS RECESVINTUS, KING.

XII. When Causes have once been Determined, at no Time shall They be Revived; but They shall be Disposed of according to the Arrangement of this Book: the Addition of Other Laws being One of the Prerogatives of the King.

Whatever legal proceedings have heretofore been begun, but remain unfinished, we decree shall be disposed of according to these laws. But those causes which, before these laws have been amended by us, have been legally decided, that is, according to the tenor of the laws which prevailed previous to our reign, shall under no circumstances whatever be revived. But, if the judgment of the prince should approve it, and conditions require it, he shall have the right to add other laws, which shall have the same validity and force as those now in existence.

THE GLORIOUS FLAVIUS RECESVINTUS, KING.

XIII. It shall be Lawful for No One to Hear and Determine Causes except Those Whom either the King, the Parties by Voluntary Consent, or the Judge, shall have Invested with Judicial Powers.

It shall be lawful for no one to decide causes unless authorized either by the mandate of the prince, or by the consent of the parties evidenced by an agreement made in the presence of three witnesses, and attested by their seals or signatures. If those, however, who have received from the king authority to preside in court, or those who exercise judicial functions either through the appointment of magistrates or judges, should delegate their powers in writing to others who are properly qualified, the latter shall have the same power in determining or settling affairs pertaining to their offices, as the judges themselves, or the other officials from whom they received their commissions.

THE GLORIOUS FLAVIUS RECESVINTUS, KING.

XIV. What Causes shall be Heard, and to what Persons Causes shall be Assigned for a Decision.

While deputies are permitted to render judgment in certain criminal and civil cases, they must not presume to release criminals under the sentence of the law, but shall see that said sentence is duly executed; and those who choose such deputies, should solemnly impress upon them that, during their absence, they should act with moderation and decide with justice.

THE GLORIOUS FLAVIUS RECESVINTUS, KING.

XV. Judges Shall Decide Criminal as well as Civil Causes.

The judges shall have all of the business of the court under their control, as they have full authority to dispose of all criminal and civil business. But Defenders of the Peace cannot dispose of other causes than those which the royal power has permitted them to determine. The Defender of the Peace is he who has been appointed by the royal authority for the sole purpose of settling legal disputes between the parties.

FLAVIUS CHINTASVINTUS, KING.

XVI. Concerning the Punishment of Those who Presume to Act as Judges, who have not been Invested with Judicial Power.

No one shall presume, either by decree, or by means of a bailiff, to either imprison or oppress any person, in any way, in a district over which he has not been appointed, or where he has no judicial authority, unless by the order of the king, or by agreement of the parties, or under instructions of a governor or a judge, in accordance with what has been stated in a former law relating to the appointment of judges. And, where a non-appointed judge, as aforesaid, is guilty of usurpation, and unlawfully presumes to do things that are prohibited; as soon as this fact shall come to the knowledge of the governor of the province, whether he is acting in his own proper person, or by a deputy, he shall cause the illegal act to be punished; and the magistrate who has thus exceeded his authority shall pay a pound of gold to him whose rights have been affected, if insult or injury have alone been committed. But if said person who has illegally assumed judicial functions, shall boldly deprive anyone of any property, or order it to be done, he shall not only make restitution, but shall be compelled to surrender an equal amount of his own property to the party injured. And if any judge shall appoint his own slave, or the slave of another, to transact any legal business, the judge who appointed him shall render full satisfaction to the law for whatever injustice said slave shall commit. Any bailiff who, acting under the orders of such an usurper of judicial authority, shall arrest or imprison any one, or remove any of his property, shall be scourged with a hundred lashes, and, in this way, shall pay the penalty of his insolence.

FLAVIUS CHINTASVINTUS, KING.

XVII. Concerning Those who Ignore the Letters of the Judge, or His Seal, Calling Them to Court.

When application has been made to the judge by a plaintiff, he may compel the other party to come into court, either by means of a letter or by his seal, in this manner, to wit: that the messenger of the judge shall offer the letter or seal to him who has been summoned, in the presence of respectable witnesses. And if, after having received said summons, he should either delay, or refuse to appear, he shall forfeit five golden *solidi* to the plaintiff, on account of his delay or refusal, and five more to the judge on account of contempt. But if he should not have the means to pay this fine, he shall, for each offence, receive fifty lashes in the presence of the judge, but they must be so inflicted as to place upon him no permanent mark of infamy. But if he should only be guilty of contempt, and should not have the means wherewith to render satisfaction, he shall receive thirty lashes, without further penalty. And if he who has been sued shall declare, before he receives punishment from the judge, that he has, in no way, been guilty of delay or contempt, and shall be unable to prove this fact by witnesses, and shall make oath that, at no time, has he been guilty of contempt as aforesaid, he shall be exempt from the condemnation and punishment hereinbefore mentioned. But if any bishop, relying upon the privileges of the sacerdotal order, shall ignore the summons of the judge, and neglect to give security for his appearance, he shall, without delay, be compelled, either by the presiding judge, or by the governor or lord of the province, to pay a fine of fifty *solidi:* of which sum the judge shall receive twenty *solidi*, on account of contempt, and the plaintiff the remaining thirty. But if any priest, deacon, clerk, or monk, after receiving the letter or seal of the judge, should delay to answer either in his own person or by a representative, or should continue obstinately in contempt, he shall undergo the punishment hereinbefore mentioned, according to the provisions of the law relating to the laity; and if he should not have the means to pay his fine, the bishop may be notified, that he may have the privilege of paying the same for him, if he so desires. But if he should be unwilling to do so, the bishop must bind himself by oath, in the presence of the judge, that he will place the above-named person under such restraint that he shall be compelled to fast continuously for the space of thirty days, and shall only receive each day at sunset, a little bread and water; that, by this means, his contumacy may be punished in a proper manner. It shall always be in the discretion of the judge, that if it should be evident that, either through age or sickness, a severe sentence could not be endured; the judge shall not inflict the extreme penalty upon any one belonging to any rank of the clergy, or upon a layman; but the illness or age of the offender being taken into consideration, he may impose such a penalty that the person in contempt may not thereby undergo either great weakness or exhaustion, or death. Any one who refuses to obey the mandate of the judge, and conceals himself, so that the judge cannot easily find him, and does not present himself in court within four days after the appointed time, but presents himself upon the fifth day, shall not be subject to the sentence of this law. In like manner, if any one who, at the time, is distant more than a hundred miles, should appear upon the eleventh day after the appointed time, he shall not undergo the penalty of this law. And also, if he who is distant two hundred miles, should present himself in court on the twenty-first day after he has been summoned; he shall be free from punishment under this law. And a similar regulation shall prevail where the length of the journey is still longer. And, finally, if he to whom reasonable time has been given, should purposely delay, and does not appear, upon the last day prescribed by law, the judge shall at once grant the prayer of the plaintiff; and if, subsequently, the other party should appear in court, and the twenty-first day shall have passed, he shall be fined twenty *solidi* of gold. And if he that is distant more than a hundred miles, should exceed the term of eleven days, he shall be liable to a fine of ten *solidi:* of which the judge shall reserve for himself half, and the other half shall be given to the plaintiff. But if sickness should prevent one who is summoned from appearing; or if he should be hindered by an inundation; or his paths across the mountains should be obstructed by snows; this must plainly appear; and the truth must be established either by credible witnesses, or by the oath of the party himself.

FLAVIUS CHINTASVINTUS, KING.

XVIII. Where a Judge Refuses to Hear a Litigant, or Decides Fraudulently, or Ignorantly.

If any one should file a complaint against another before a judge, and the latter should refuse to hear him, or deny him the use of his seal, or, under different pretexts, should delay the trial of his cause, not permitting it to be heard, through favor to a client or a friend, and the plaintiff can prove this by witnesses, the judge shall give to him to whom he has refused a hearing, as compensation for his trouble, a sum equal to that which the plaintiff would have received from his adversary by due course of law; and he who brought the suit may have it continued until the time appointed by law;

and, when it comes before the court for trial, he shall receive the judgment to which he is entitled. But if the plaintiff should be unable to prove either the fraud or undue procrastination of the judge, the latter shall make oath that he, through no malice, nor through favor or friendship, has delayed the hearing, and, by reason of this oath, the judge shall in no manner be deemed guilty.

The judge shall be permitted, for two days in every week, or every day during the noon hour, to desist from holding court, and to repose in quiet at home. But, for the remaining time, he shall attend to the business of his office, and, without any unnecessary delay, determine such matters as may be brought before him.

XIX. Where a Judge, either through Convenience to Himself, or through Want of Proper Knowledge, Decides a Cause Improperly.

If any judge should render judgment for the sake of gain, and direct that any one should be treated with injustice, he who has been benefited by the decision of the said judge shall make restitution. And the judge himself, who has thus acted contrary to the precepts of equity, shall surrender to the losing party the same amount of his own property, as he has ordered him to be deprived of; that is to say, that in addition to the restitution that has been made, he shall, in satisfaction for his improper conduct, give to him whom he unjustly condemned, a sum equal to that which was disposed of by his decree. But if he should not have sufficient property wherewith to make amends, he shall be deprived of all that he is known to possess, and shall be delivered as a slave to him to whom he is indebted, or, after having been exposed in public, he shall receive fifty lashes. But if he shall have rendered an unjust judgment through ignorance, and can declare under oath that he has done this only through want of knowledge, and not through partiality or cupidity, or for the sake of profit, his judgment shall be invalid, and he himself shall not be considered guilty.[1]

[1]Nothing in the whole system of the Visigoths is more remarkable than the care with which they attempt to preserve the integrity of the judiciary. It is not impossible that the notorious corruption attend-

FLAVIUS CHINTASVINTUS, KING.

XX. When a Judge, either through Deceit or Cunning, Imposes Needless Costs upon Either, or Both the Parties to a Suit.

It is part of our duty quietly and carefully to admonish judges not to subject litigants to unnecessary delay, or impose heavy costs upon them. But, if it appears that, through craft or cunning, a judge has so delayed matters that one or both parties have suffered injury, he shall be compelled to refund to them all costs that have been incurred after eight days from the time the action was begun; the facts having been established under oath. But if either through illness or from considerations of public utility, the judge should be prevented from performing his duties, he shall not subject the litigants to delay, but shall dismiss them at once, and shall appoint a time for the hearing of the cause.

XXI. What, First of All, a Judge should be Familiar With, in order that he may Understand a Case.

In order that he may be perfectly familiar with a case the judge should first interrogate the witnesses; then he should examine the documents, if any there be; and, that the truth may the more certainly be determined, the oaths of the parties should finally be taken with all due reverence. The true investigation of justice demands that written instruments should take precedence over everything else; and that neces-

---

ing the dispensation of justice by the Roman tribunals, in the days of the decadent Empire, may have prompted the drastic legislation against judicial misconduct which is so prominent a feature of the Code. The penalties in extreme cases are but little inferior in severity to that said to have been imposed by Cambyses; who flayed a corrupt judge, and placed his skin in the judgment seat, as a suggestive warning to his successors. It may well be presumed that, in the face of such punishment, the acceptance of bribes was not a common vice among the Visigothic magistrates. The latter did not receive regular salaries, but were paid according to the work they performed; a regulation which would appear, in some instances, rather calculated to encourage, than to suppress litigation.—[ED.

sity alone justifies the administering of oaths to the parties. But in those cases where there is no documentary evidence, or other proof, or where the judge shall not be able to decide without it, the parties to the suit shall be sworn.

FLAVIUS CHINTASVINTUS, KING.

XXII. Where the Integrity of a Judge is said to be Suspected by Any One of Honorable Rank, or where a Judge presumes to render a Decision Contrary to Law.

If any one should declare that he suspects the integrity of either a judge, a governor, a vice-governor, or any other official, and demands access to his superior, or shall even allege that he has suspicions of that superior himself, he shall not be subject to delay on this account, especially if he should be poor. But those who decide the case shall do so with the bishop of the diocese, and their opinions and judgment shall be reduced to writing, and be signed by them; and he who has declared that he suspected the judge, should he desire to bring a suit against him, after judgment has been rendered in the case in question, shall have the right to summon that judge to appear before the king. And if a judge or an ecclesiastic should be convicted of having decided wrongfully in any cause, the property of which the complainant has been deprived shall be restored to him, and an equal quantity of property shall be given him by way of satisfaction, by those who are proved to have rendered an unrighteous judgment. And if anyone should lodge an unjust complaint against a judge, and it should appear that the cause in question has been properly decided, the accuser shall undergo the same penalty which the judge would have suffered. And if he should not have the property wherewith to make amends, after having been exposed in public he shall receive thirty lashes in the presence of the judge himself.

If anyone, however, should allege that he possesses information which relates to the interests of the Crown, access to our presence shall not be denied him.

FLAVIUS CHINTASVINTUS, KING.

XXIII. How a Judge should render Judgment.

If the lawsuit is important, or matters involving the ownership of valuable property are in question, the judge shall, in the presence of both parties, make two copies of the decree, which shall be exactly similar in text and signature, and each party shall be given one of them. But where affairs of minor importance are concerned, only such things as have been testified to in favor of him who prevailed, shall be reduced to writing by the judge. He who has been defeated shall be entitled to a transcript of the decree and of the testimony of the witnesses, should he desire it. But if the party who has been brought into court in any case, shall declare in the presence of the judge that it is not necessary for the plaintiff to introduce any evidence, the judge shall put the decree in writing, and confirm it with his signature, however insignificant the action may be, in order that the matter may not, under any circumstances, be brought up again in the future. But if, under an order of the court, one party should offer witnesses, and, at the time that their testimony is to be heard, the other party should absent himself without the knowledge of the judge, the testimony of the witnesses shall be received, and what they have established by their evidence shall be given in writing, under seal, to him who produced them. It shall not be lawful for him who fraudulently left the court to afterwards offer any evidence in the case, but he shall have the privilege, before the death of any witness who has testified against him, to adduce any reasonable accusation against him, which shall be heard by the judge; and if the accused witness should have been manifestly guilty of perjury, his testimony shall be rejected. And if, after such examination, all the witnesses should be impeached but one, he who has offered the testimony, must produce other witnesses to prove his case, within the space of three months. But, if he is unable to find any, the property in question shall remain in the possession of him who formerly held it. The judge shall always keep copies of the judgment which he has rendered, to prevent a renewal of any controversies in the future.

FLAVIUS CHINTASVINTUS, KING.

XXIV. Concerning the Emoluments and the Punishment of the Judge, and of the Bailiff.

There are some judges who, on account of cupidity, and in violation of the provisions of the law, presume to reserve for themselves the third part of the property involved in the causes which are brought before them; wherefore, we now decree by the present law, in order to effectually abolish this practice, that no judge shall accept more for his trouble, after the case has been properly considered and decided, than has been fixed by a former law, to wit, twenty *solidi*. If any one should fraudulently attempt to extort more than this sum, he shall lose the entire compensation which he would have lawfully received; and also, because he has unjustly appropriated more than twenty *solidi*, contrary to the provisions of the law, he shall pay double that amount to him from whom he directed it should be taken. And likewise, because we are aware that certain bailiffs who busy themselves in the affairs of others, receive greater compensation for their labor than they deserve; we also decree by this law, that no bailiff who is employed in any lawsuit, shall have more than ten *solidi* for his fee. And if any one should presume to extort more than this established amount, he shall not only lose his legitimate fee, but also he shall restore to the person from whom he received it, double the amount which he has extorted. The fees of both judge and bailiff shall be paid by the party against whom judgment is rendered; and if a case should occur where a settlement cannot be made, the legal compensation of the judge and the bailiff shall be required of both parties. The same rule shall apply to a debtor who did not return upon the appointed day, the money which he has borrowed; as well as to one who unjustly retains the property of another; and also, in cases of partition, where both parties demand their rights from the judge, it shall be required of each of them, that he pay to the court his portion of the fees aforesaid. And, likewise, where no crime has been proved; or no contempt, unlawful possession, or indebtedness have been established; this provision shall be in force, and the fees of the judge and the bailiff shall be paid by both parties.

In cases of partition, where one of the parties causes unnecessary delay; as soon as the fact shall come to the knowledge of the judge, he may exact his fee and that of the bailiff from him who has delayed to assert his claims within the specified time. If any corrupt bailiff should fail to execute an order of the judge, when the property involved is worth an ounce of gold, or less, the bailiff shall pay to him who is entitled to the judgment, a *solidus* of gold; and where the property is worth more, he shall pay for every ounce, a *solidus*, on account of his delay. And if the property in question should be worth more than two ounces, and not more than a pound of gold, said bailiff shall receive ten lashes, and the number of lashes shall increase with the number of pounds of gold.

If the cause or the party is of minor importance, and the bailiff must travel to perform his duties, he shall be entitled to two common horses, from the plaintiff, in addition to his fees. But if the cause should be important, and the party of high rank, the bailiff shall not be entitled to demand more than six horses for the purpose of his journey.

FLAVIUS RECESVINTUS, KING.

XXV. Every one who is Invested with Judicial Power shall Legally bear the Title of Judge.

As the remedies of the law are applied in many ways, it is decreed, that a duke, count, vicar, deputy, and any other official, who, either by the royal order, or by consent of the parties, has been, or shall be, selected to determine questions of law; or any person of whatever rank invested with the legal right to preside in court; as well as all to whom has been delegated the power to decide causes; shall be invested with the name of judge, and shall be entitled to the rights, and subject to the liabilities of that office, whether these relate to the emoluments or the penalities attaching to the same.

XXVI. Every Bond that is Exacted by a Judge, after an Unjust Decree, shall be held Invalid.

We occasionally find that justice is distorted, and deprived of its proper force, by unjust judges; and see injustice, confirmed by their decrees, prevail in its stead. And, indeed, certain judges after they have rendered unjust decrees, cause one or both the parties to bind themselves in writing, in order that the wrongful judgment that has been rendered may not at any time thereafter be remedied; but where such a transaction is not fair and honorable, but entered into with the manifest intention of oppressing any one whose cause is just, the matter may be reviewed; and all obligations relating thereto shall be declared invalid, and not, in any way, authorized by law.

FLAVIUS RECESVINTUS, KING.

XXVII. An Unjust Decree, or an Unjust Interpretation of the Law, Prompted by Fear of the Throne, or Made by Order of the King, shall be Invalid.

Sometimes the influence of power defeats the ends of justice, and although it often prevails, it is certain that it always inflicts injury; for, when the abuse of authority once causes oppression, it never permits the restoration of justice to its original integrity. Therefore, as judges through fear, or at the command of princes, sometimes decide questions contrary to law, for the sake of the peace of our kingdom we have determined to cure two diseases with one remedy; declaring that when it should have been discovered that any document has been drawn up, or any judgment rendered, not according to justice or to the established laws, but by the command or through the dread of the king, then that which is evidently contrary to justice and to the laws shall be void; and those who have rendered the judgment or have caused it to be rendered, shall receive no mark of infamy, nor be subjected to any punishment whatever; and any judge shall be immune from the penalties of the law, if he will swear that he has decided wrongfully, not through his own depravity, but on account of royal compulsion.

FLAVIUS RECESVINTUS, KING.

XXVIII. Concerning the Power, conferred upon Bishops, of Restraining Judges who Decide Wrongfully.

We direct the ministers of God, to whom the Divine authority has been committed to remedy the misfortunes of oppression and poverty, that they admonish, with paternal piety, such judges as oppress the people with unjust decrees, by which means such wrongs may be remedied. But if any magistrate, invested with judicial functions, has either decided unjustly, or has imposed a wrongful sentence upon any one, then the bishop in whose diocese this has been done, shall summon the judge who is alleged to have acted unjustly, and shall render a just decision, sitting along with him, in the presence of ecclesiastics, or other persons of respectability But if the judge, moved by perversity, refuses to correct the iniquitous judgment given by him, after the bishop has exhorted him to do so, then the bishop shall have the privilege of reviewing the case, and of rendering judgment alone; and the wrongful decision of the judge, subsequently set aside by him, as well as his own decision, shall be committed to writing, and be deposited among the records of the court. The bishop shall so act toward the party who has been oppressed, and liberated by him from that oppression, that truth may be established and confirmed by our authority If the judge should prevent the party whom he has oppressed from appearing before the bishop, he shall forfeit two pounds of gold to the king.

FLAVIUS CHINTASVINTUS, KING.

XXIX. The Judge, when Inquired of by a Party, should be able to give a Reason for His Decision.

Every judge is hereby admonished that if a demand is made upon him by any one, he shall give the reasons, in their proper order, for the decision he has made; and this he shall do, either in the presence of the governor of the city, or of those whom the governor has chosen to represent him. And if the matter has been brought before the king, those judges whom the king shall appoint for the purpose, shall decide the cause, without the presence of the bishop and the other judges. And if, after the action has been brought to an end, either before the bishop or before the governor, either of the parties should present himself, a second time, with the royal order, he who heard or decided the cause in the first place, must account for his conduct to those who have been specially appointed judges by the royal decree; so that in case he should be found to have rendered an improper decision, he may give satisfaction therefor to the plaintiff before the law. And if the plaintiff shall have filed an unjust complaint, he shall be condemned to suffer the legal penalty prescribed for the same.

FLAVIUS RECESVINTUS, KING.

XXX. Concerning the Punishment of Judges wno Appropriate the Property of Others.

While it is evident that judges have been appointed for the purpose of remedying evils, some of them, on the other hand, with all the insolence of power, attempt to attack those very things which, according to the principles of equity, they ought to defend. For, once invested with authority, some judges do not hesitate to assume illegal control over the property of others; and do not fear, under almost any pretext, to subject them to unreasonable expense in the exercise of official tyranny. Henceforth, any judge who shall take any property belonging to another, contrary to an order of court, or in violation of law, or shall injure said property in any way, shall be condemned to suffer the same penalty which he, acting in his judicial capacity, would have imposed upon any one guilty of the same offence.

FLAVIUS RECESVINTUS, KING.

XXXI. Concerning those who Treat the Royal Order with Disdain.

Any freeman who shall have been convicted of having disobeyed the royal summons, or shall have been proved to have acted in such a manner that his duplicity is apparent, and shall say contrary to the truth, that he has neither seen nor received the summons; if he is a person of noble birth, he shall pay three pounds of gold to the treasury; but, if he should not have sufficient property to pay this fine, he shall receive a hundred lashes with the scourge, without any degradation of rank. But if he should have been prevented from travelling by sickness, tempest, inundation, or snow, or by unavoïdable trouble of any kind, and this should be established by the testimony of reliable witnesses, he shall not be considered guilty of disobedience to the royal order, or be liable to any punishment, as it is evident that the delay was the result of manifest necessity.

XXXII. How the Judge should Inquire into Causes by the Ordeal of Hot Water.

We are aware that many persons assert that they have received injuries at the hands of freeborn citizens; and it is our opinion that torture should be applied in such instances, where an amount exceeding three hundred *solidi* is involved; and we now declare this to be a salutary measure, and decree that whenever crime has been committed by any one, where a small amount of property is concerned, the ordeal by hot water be instituted by the judge; and should the accused appear to be guilty, the judge shall not hesitate to put him to the torture, and after confession has been obtained, he shall inflict upon the criminal the sentence of the law provided in such cases. If, after the test, he should prove to be innocent, his accuser shall incur no reproach whatever. This test shall also be applied to suspicious persons who present themselves in court to give testimony against others.[1]

---

[1] This chapter does not appear in the Castilian translation. It is the only instance in the Visigothic Code where any ordeal is permitted as a means of obtaining evidence of crime. The other ordeals, subsequently so popular during the Middle Ages, and employed not only in proceedings before judicial tribunals, but also by the clergy to establish the existence of demoniacal possession, do not seem to have been practised by, or even known to, the Visigoths. Nor did they ever appeal to the wager of battle, so congenial to the spirit of the pugnacious barbarian, and which afterwards became one of the institutions of the age of chivalry and feudalism.—[ED.

TITLE II. CONCERNING CAUSES.

FLAVIUS RECESVINTUS, KING.

I. No One can Refuse to Answer because the Plaintiff has Never Presented his Claim to Him.

No one can interpose a defense to the action of any plaintiff by saying that the latter has no right to bring a suit, because he has not made formal demand upon him for his claim, unless he can show that the time within which the suit may be brought, has expired.

FLAVIUS CHINTASVINTUS, KING.

II. The Court must be Disturbed by no Clamor or Tumult.

The court shall not be disturbed by any tumult or clamor whatever; those who have no interest in the case shall be compelled to withdraw; and only such as are known to be concerned in the proceedings shall come into the presence of the court. But if the judge desires spectators to be present, he can permit it, in case he should wish to confer with them about the case. But if he should be unwilling, no one shall be allowed to enter the court room, either to aid one party by improper suggestions, or to interpose objections to the conduct of the other, whereby either party may be unnecessarily annoyed. And if any one, having been admonished by the judge to be silent, should not obey, nor desist in his attempts to aid either party, and should, in defiance of this warning, continue to interfere, he shall be compelled to pay ten golden *solidi* to the judge. And if he should still persist in his conduct, he shall be unceremoniously ejected from the court.

III. Where there are Many Litigants, Two may be Chosen who shall have Power to carry on the Suit.

If the litigants are more numerous on one side than on the other, both sides, in turn, shall select from their number, parties to carry on their case. For all ought not to participate in the conduct of the action, but, as we have said, those chosen by both sides should alone appear in court, so that all noise and confusion may be avoided.

FLAVIUS CHINTASVINTUS, KING.

IV. Both Parties may be Compelled by the Judge, or the Bailiff, to be Present in Court on the Day when the Case is to be Heard.

Often, through the negligence of the judges or the bailiffs, when security is not required of the parties, one or the other of them unnecessarily suffers inconvenience or injury. For when one party is present in court, and the other is absent, no little expense is often incurred by the former. Therefore, we decree that all judges, and all upon whom judicial power has been conferred, whenever the time arrives in any suit for the giving of security; or when a cause is about to be heard, or settlement to be made; both parties, that is the plaintiff as well as the defendant, shall be required to give bond, that, upon the day appointed for trial, either in person, or by representatives, they shall be present in court, in order that the case may be heard, or the claim otherwise disposed of; and if either party should refuse to come, and absent himself upon the appointed day; or if sickness, or any accident during his journey, should prevent him from coming; and he should not communicate the fact to the judge or his attorney; and should not appear in court within the time prescribed by law, and the case should be delayed on that account; he shall pay the amount of the bond to him before whom he entered into the obligation. And if either the judge or the bailiff should neglect to exact security from both parties, as aforesaid, and, while compelling one party to give bond should excuse the other, he shall pay out of his own property, a sum equal to that for which he wished to make him liable whom alone he placed under bond. And if, to the injury of either party, the judge or the bailiff should restore to one the undertaking which he had exacted from the other, or should destroy or conceal it, he shall pay him on account of whom the bond was executed, out of his own property, a penalty equal to that which was inserted in the bond.

He who brought the suit may then insist that it be carried on without further delay. The penalty, although declared in the bond to be payable to the judge or the bailiff, shall not entirely belong to them; but, after the case has been decided, they shall be entitled to half of said penalty, and the other half shall be given to the party who gains the suit.

V. Those whose Affairs have been brought before a Tribunal for a Decision, shall, under no Circumstances, enter into a Compromise before the Case has been Decided.

If cases are not permanently disposed of by the temperate decision of the judge, not only do great difficulties arise in settling the disputes of litigants, but the course of justice is often interfered with, through the irreconcilability of adverse claims; for many persons, after they have brought their disputes before the royal tribunal to be finally determined, in order to avoid the legal penalty for their conduct, settle, by agreement between themselves, the cause which they have brought to the hearing of the king. Lest, therefore, any party by means of such a fraud may escape the justice of the court, we decree, by this law, that whoever, hereafter, shall apply to the royal tribunal for the determination of his case against another, shall, under no circumstances, absent himself, or make any compromise with his adversary, but shall prosecute the cause already begun until the king shall have given a decision in the matter. And, if either plaintiff or defendant should neglect to carry on the action before the king, or before those whom he has chosen to hear it, or should enter into any arrangement with the other party, each shall pay to the Crown the sum which he who filed the petition, could have obtained, had he gained the suit; and whatever shall be thus obtained by the king in this proceeding he can dispose of at his pleasure. All those shall be liable to a similar penalty, who seek to have their disputes settled by a judicial decision, and, after the cause has been begun, refuse to proceed with it and presume to compromise with one another.

The judge and the bailiff shall have the right to divide the aforesaid penalty between them. But if the parties should not have sufficient property to pay said penalty, each shall receive one hundred lashes with a scourge, and the judge shall terminate the suit forthwith. We decree, however, that those shall be free from the operation of this law to whom the royal mandate was especially directed, as well as those whom the judge, who heard the cause, shall have dismissed, after a settlement has been effected with his consent.

FLAVIUS CHINTASVINTUS, KING.

VI. Both Parties shall be Required to Furnish Testimony.

Whenever a cause is heard, both parties, that is, plaintiff as well as defendant, shall be required to produce evidence, and the judge shall decide which side is entitled to a decree. But if, after the testimony has been taken, the truth does not appear to have been established, the defendant shall declare under oath that the property in question, if any has been demanded of him, has never been, and is not now, in his possession, and that he is not aware of any reason why he should be sued, and that he truly does not know that he has done anything to render him liable, in any way, to the party who complains of him, and after the defendant has thus made oath, the plaintiff shall be compelled to pay him five *solidi.*

FLAVIUS RECESVINTUS, KING.

VII. Concerning the Journey which any one Compels an Innocent Person to Make.

All those whose innocence is established, should be free from injury, and exempt from annoyance by unprincipled men. Henceforth, whenever any one shall cause another to be wrongfully summoned before the king, or brought, without cause, before a court; as soon as it has been proved that the claim of the plaintiff was not well founded; if the party has, in obedience to a summons, been compelled to come fifty miles, or less, he shall receive from the plaintiff five *solidi*, on account of the unjust demand by the latter. If he has been forced to come a distance of sixty miles, the unjust plaintiff shall pay him six *solidi;* and so on, the number of *solidi* increasing at the rate of one for every ten miles; and, for the distance of one hundred miles, ten *solidi* shall be given by said plaintiff to him who has been subjected to annoyance and trouble; and thus the number of *solidi* shall increase as aforesaid, in the ratio of five for every fifty miles, and ten for every hundred miles; the amount of pecuniary satisfaction being always proportionate to the length of the journey.

FLAVIUS CHINTASVINTUS, KING.

VIII. Where any one Residing in the District of one Judge has a Cause of Action against a Party Living in the District of another Judge.

If any freeman or slave has a cause of action against anyone residing outside of the province in which he lives, and within the jurisdiction of another judge, the judge of the district to which the plaintiff belongs shall send a letter under his signature and seal, to the other judge, and direct him to hear the cause of the complainant, without delay; and if he should neglect or deny this request, then the judge in whose district the plaintiff resides, shall seize as much of the property belonging to the judge to whom he sent the letter, as the sum amounts to, concerning which the plaintiff brought the suit; wherever he can find said property in his jurisdiction; which property, however, must not be delivered into the possession of the plaintiff. And he who receives it shall hold it, so that, when the case has been disposed of, the costs and expenses may be paid out of the income derived from the same. If the judge who, on the reception of the letter from the other judge, refused to hear the cause of the plaintiff, should afterwards conclude to do so, such property of his as was seized by the former judge, shall be restored to him without delay; but none of the amount which has been expended for reasonable costs shall be returned. And if, after the case has been decided according to the rules of justice, the judge shall be found to have lost anything by reason of the unjust demands of the plaintiff, then the latter shall make full restitution to the said judge, and shall be compelled to pay him in addition, an equal amount from his own property. And if that judge who was the cause of the delay, has no property, in the jurisdiction of the other judge who notified him, wherewith to reimburse the plaintiff, the latter judge may seize the property of the former, wherever he can find it, even when it is not in his jurisdiction; or he may deliver to the plaintiff a memorandum under his seal, in which the amount of the sum involved is set forth, by authority of which the plaintiff may have the power to seize said property.

If one whose property was illegally taken for a debt should complain of this to the king, the judge, or the governor; a judge convicted of unnecessary delay in hearing the case, shall pay all damages incurred, and four times their amount besides, out of his own purse. But if a creditor should privately accept from his debtor, a sum equal in value to the amount of property involved, the judge cannot be required to give satisfaction as above stated. If the judge who was notified should hear the cause of the plaintiff without delay, and should find that there is no justice in his claim, he must send a copy of the decree in writing, carefully made out, and signed with his hand and sealed with his seal, to the judge by whom he has been notified, as hereinbefore stated. And if, after the decision, the wrong-doing of him who made the claim should appear; if he is a freeman, he shall pay double the amount of the property involved, that is, a sum equal to what the other party lost, and as much more. Any slave who shall have been detected in the commission of such acts, shall receive one hundred lashes with the scourge; shall be scalped as a mark of infamy; and shall at once restore the entire amount of property which he had seized, as security.[1] And all concerned in the seizure, if they are slaves, and did so willingly, shall each receive a hundred lashes; but if they are freemen, they shall restore to the owner as much as they are proved to have taken from him, without the sum usually given as indemnity by him who has been convicted of having acted wrongfully in similar cases.

IX. Concerning Those who Venture to Defend the Suits of Others.

Whoever has recourse to a person of high rank or influence, that, through his aid in court, he may be able to oppress his adversary, shall lose his case, even though his cause be just; and as soon as the judge perceives that any powerful person is interfering in a case, he shall order him to desist. But if

---

[1] "*Decalvatio*" was one of the most dreaded punishments sanctioned by the Visigothic laws. The tonsure was itself considered degrading, among a people who attached the highest importance to a luxuriant growth of hair, even when, as a distinctive mark of their calling, it was undergone by ecclesiastics; and shaving the head, in the execution of a judicial sentence, was often regarded as an indelible mark of infamy. There were several degrees of this punishment, all of which did not entail the same suffering and disgrace. In some cases, the hair was cut in the form of a cross; in others, the head was entirely shaved. He who was "*turpiter decalvatus*," was scalped, and had the skin entirely stripped from his head above the ears; a practice surpassing in barbarity that peculiar to the American Indian. It was not unusual, in the infliction of this cruel penalty, to include a portion, or even all, of the skin of the forehead; thereby horribly disfiguring the victim for life.—[ED.

the said person should defy the judge, and, obstinately resisting, should refuse to leave the court, or to cease interfering with the proceedings, the judge shall have authority to fine him two pounds of gold, one of which shall be for his own benefit, and the other for the benefit of the party injured by the said powerful adversary, and the latter shall be violently thrown out of court. Any freeman or slave who refuses to desist from interference with the business of the court, after having been warned by the judge, shall receive fifty lashes with the scourge, in public.

FLAVIUS CHINTASVINTUS, KING.

X. No Freeman shall Refuse to Answer the Slave of another in Court.

In order that insolence may be the more easily punished, the law regards excuses as superfluous. Sometimes freemen do not hesitate to injure the slaves of others, and then refuse to answer the petition of a slave in court; declaring that they should not be compelled to answer any one from whom they cannot collect damages, if they should chance to be victorious. But lest, through this delay, the slave himself should unjustly suffer injury; though his master should be distant fifty miles, or any objection should be made by his master on account of his employment at the time; after due deliberation, we hereby decree that a hearing shall be denied to no one. If, however, a slave should assert that he has any claim of his own, or any business to transact in court on behalt of his master or mistress, he against whom he files a complaint, shall straightway be compelled to appear and answer; and, in the end, make such compensation as is authorized by law, if he be vanquished by the slave; but if the slave is unable to prove what he has adduced, then the freeman shall declare under oath that he has no knowledge of, nor has in his possession, the property to which claim is made; nor has done, nor has caused to be done, any of those things of which he is accused. And, after this oath has been taken, the slave or the freeman, as the case may be, must not delay to make amends for filing his unjust complaint. But if, in the settlement of these damages, where the claim is for a small amount, it should appear that his master is only worth ten *solidi*, the slave shall be compelled to pay only half the penalty, that is to say, two half *solidi*. But if it should appear that the master of the slave is distant less than fifty miles, his slave cannot bring an action against any freeman, unless the master is unable, in person, to be present in court; or should send a letter, written in his own hand, and signed with his signature, authorizing the slave to appear for him, by the latter as messenger to the judge.

If the slave, acting on behalf of his master, should cause him any injury, either through fraud or neglect, or should lose the case, it shall be lawful for the master to have it reviewed, either upon his own application, or upon that of a lawful representative, and have it justly decided by the testimony of such witnesses as he may be able to produce.

TITLE III. CONCERNING COMMISSIONERS AND COMMISSIONS.

I. *Princes and Bishops should not Conduct their Cases in Court in Person, but through their Subjects or Subordinates.*

II. *The Judge must inquire of a Litigant, whether the Suit brought by Him is his Own, or that of Another.*

III. *He who cannot Conduct his Cause Himself must give Written Authority to his Attorney.*

IV. *Torture shall, in no Case, be inflicted upon Persons of Noble Birth who are acting as Representatives of Others; and, In what way a Freeman of the Lower Class, or a Slave, may be subjected to Torture.*

V. *If He who has Appointed an Attorney Suffers Delay, he can Revoke his Commission.*

VI. *It shall not be Lawful for a Woman to Act as an Attorney, but She may Conduct Her Own Case in Court.*

VII. *The Constituent shall receive the Benefit, and bear the Loss, resulting from Proceedings Instituted by his Attorney.*

VIII. *If a Representative should die, his Heirs shall be entitled to his Fees.*

IX. *What Persons those in Power, and those that are Poor may appoint to Conduct their Cases.*

X. *Those who have Charge of the Royal Treasury, when the Suit is brought for its Benefit, have authority to appoint whom they wish to represent them.*

FLAVIUS RECESVINTUS, KING.

I. Princes and Bishops should not Conduct their Cases in Court in Person, but through their Subjects or Subordinates.

As it is the office of persons in power to decide questions of law, and as, in many instances, they should not be needlessly subjected to the annoyances resulting from litigation; therefore, if either the king or a bishop should have a lawsuit with any one, he may select a personal representative to whom the transaction of the business shall be intrusted; for the reason that it would seem an insult to the dignity of persons of such high rank, if those of a lower class should contradict their evidence in court. And again, if the king should choose to personally assume the conduct of his case in any matter, who is there who would dare to contradict him? Therefore, lest the fear of royal power should suppress the truth, the case should be conducted, not by the king, but by some of his subjects.

II. The Judge must inquire of a Litigant, whether the Suit brought by Him is his Own, or that of Another.

The judge must, in the first place, make inquiry of a litigant whether he is conducting his own case, or that of another. He shall also be asked whom he represents; and, after the judge has decided the case, he shall include in the decree him by whose order the action was prosecuted, and, in addition, he shall receive a copy of the authority of the representative, to be filed with the record of the judgment. And it shall be lawful for the defendant to examine the commission given by the plaintiff, in the presence of the judge, so that he may know, without doubt, for what reason he was brought into court, as well as ascertain the contents of the order granting the authority.

III. He who cannot Conduct his Cause Himself, must give Written Authority to his Attorney.

If any one is unable to conduct his own cause, or is unwilling to do so, he must appoint a representative, by an instrument in writing, under his own hand, confirmed by the seals and signatures of witnesses. And if any such representative should be guilty of collusion with his adversary, so that he is defeated, he shall pay to his principal, as much of his own property as the latter has lost, or as much as he ought to have obtained. But it shall not be lawful for a slave to conduct any case whatever, through the commission of another, unless on behalf of his master or mistress, or of the Church, or of some poor person, or under the commission of the royal treasury. If, through either the neglect or misconduct of the judge, or through the perjury of a witness, the provisions of this law should not be carried out, then it shall be the duty of the king to enforce the same.

FLAVIUS CHINTASVINTUS, KING.

IV. Torture shall, in no Case, be inflicted upon Persons of Noble Birth who are acting as Representatives of Others; and, In what way a Freeman of the Lower Class, or a Slave, may be subjected to Torture.

No person of noble rank shall, under any circumstances, be put to the torture by authority of a commission given to another. It is, however, hereby permitted that any freeborn person of low rank who is poor, and has already been convicted of crime, may be tortured under such a commission; but only when the principal gives authority in writing to do this, signed by him, and attested by three witnesses, which shall be entrusted for delivery, to a freeman, and not to a slave. And if he should cause the torture to be inflicted upon an innocent person, the aforesaid principal is hereby admonished, that he has incurred the penalty of the law which is found in the sixth book, first title, second chapter; wherein it is stated for what things freeborn persons are to be put to the question. It is lawful for other criminal causes to be prosecuted under commission; and, as has been said above, tortures may be applied to a freeman by the representative of another who is also free. And it is granted by the law to a freeman or a slave, to subject a slave to torture, with this provision, to wit: that if either torture or injury should be inflicted upon an innocent person, the principal shall be compelled to give complete satisfaction, under the instructions of the judge. Nor is he to be discharged who received the commission, until either the principal may be produced in court, or shall make amends according to law. And whoever desires to inflict the torture, having received authority to do so under a commission, shall be compelled by the judge to give bond.

V. If He who has Appointed an Attorney Suffers Delay, he can Revoke his Commission.

He who conducts a case as the representative of another should proceed with it as rapidly as possible; and if he is dilatory, and the case which should have been prosecuted with alacrity, is retarded unnecessarily, or is fraudulently postponed, the principal may have recourse to the judge. And if he who receives the commission to conduct the case should, through malice or corruption, cause delay for ten days after he has received the order of the judge to proceed with the same, the adversary or the judge being present, then the principal can either conduct the case himself, or appoint any one else whom he may select, to conduct it for him.

ANCIENT LAW.

VI. It shall not be Lawful for a Woman to Act as an Attorney, but She may Conduct Her Own Case in Court.

No woman can conduct a case under the authority of another, but she is not forbidden to transact her own business in court. Nor can a husband conduct the case of his wife without authority from her; and, indeed, he should protect himself with such an instrument in writing, that the wife may not repudiate the whole proceeding; and if she should repudiate it, the husband shall undergo the penalty to which he is liable who presumed to conduct a case without the authority of his wife. And if the husband should lose a case which he prosecuted without the order of his wife, her rights shall in no way be prejudiced; and she can afterwards either prosecute the case herself, or can authorize any one she wishes to do whatever is proper in the matter. And if the case should justly go against the husband, and the wife should believe that the adversary who prevailed should again be sued; and, after the second trial, it should be apparent that her husband was not unjustly beaten in the first trial, the wife shall render satisfaction as prescribed by law, not only to the judge who first heard the case, but also to the other party whom she brought into court for the second time.

ANCIENT LAW.

VII. The Constituent shall receive the Benefit, and bear the Loss, resulting from Proceedings Instituted by his Attorney.

He who authorizes a case to be conducted by another as his attorney, shall enjoy the profit, or endure the loss resulting from the same, according to the circumstances; and he who carried on the action in compliance with his instructions, and exerted himself faithfully in the performance of his duty, shall not be deprived of his commission by his constituent; nor shall the latter be permitted to afterwards transfer the conduct of the case to another; because it is unjust that he who is known to have labored faithfully in the business which he has undertaken, should be deprived of his reward. He who is about to assume the conduct of a case should have an understanding with his constituent beforehand, and ascertain what amount he is to receive as a recompense for his services after the cause has been decided. And if he who conducted the case shall neglect to deliver to his constituent, within three months, any property which came into his hands under the decree, he shall lose the compensation for his services which he would otherwise have received; and shall be compelled by order of court to deliver to his constituent, whatever he was entitled to under the decision.

VIII. If an Attorney should Die, his Heirs shall be entitled to his Fees.

Where any person authorizes another to conduct a case for him, and dies before it is heard, said authority shall determine; and if he who received it should be surprised by death before the cause is heard, then also the order addressed to him before his death shall have no validity. But if the cause has been heard and energetically prosecuted through his diligence, and yet, for some reason or other, it was not entirely concluded, or some payment should remain to be made before final settlement; and if the case has been prosecuted as far as he who was commissioned to conduct it should have carried it; then, his heirs shall be entitled to receive from the constituent whatever compensation their ancestor would have been entitled to.

FLAVIUS CHINTASVINTUS, KING.

IX. What Persons those in Power, and those that are Poor, may appoint to Conduct their Cases.

It shall not be lawful for any one who selects an attorney to conduct his case, under any circumstances, to appoint a person who is more powerful than himself, so that the capacity to oppress, or terrify, may be greater than his own. For if a powerful person should be involved in a lawsuit with one who is poor, and is unwilling to conduct it himself, he cannot appoint any one else to carry it on but one of equal standing with, or perhaps inferior to, the other party. But, on the other hand, if a poor man chooses, he may select as his attorney any one of equal rank and power with his adversary.

FLAVIUS CHINTASVINTUS, KING.

X. Those who have Charge of the Royal Treasury, when a Suit is brought for its Benefit, have authority to appoint whom they wish to represent them.

Nothing should be done rashly in matters relating to the royal treasury. And whenever it appears advisable to proceed against any one on behalf of the treasury, he who is charged with that duty shall have the right to conduct the case before either the governor of the city, or the judge. If, however, he should happen to be absent from the place where the business is to be transacted, or should be prevented by any accident, or even should be unwilling to appear in his own person, he shall have the unquestionable right to appoint any one he chooses, to bring an action in which the public interests are involved.[1]

---

[1] The mutual relations and liabilities of principal and agent, and constituent and attorney, seem to have been well defined among the Visigoths. The attorneys, "*assertori*," referred to in the Code, were, in reality, attorneys-in-fact. Strictly speaking, lawyers (although the *assertor* appeared in court, and, to some extent, exercised the

TITLE IV. CONCERNING WITNESSES AND EVIDENCE.

---

functions of an attorney-at-law) did not exist among the barbarians who had migrated from the Euxine and the Danube, and by whom members of the legal profession were looked upon with both suspicion and hatred. It is said that Alaric, by way of mockery, cut out the tongue of a distinguished Roman advocate who fell into his hands. In the Visigothic tribunals each party stated and argued his own case; and, where an attorney was appointed, every precaution was taken to prevent the exertion of that insensible, but none the less weighty, influence which everywhere attaches to the possession of superior wealth, rank and power. The effect of written instruments delegating authority to agents of various kinds, was also well understood, and their validity was insured by the attestation of reputable witnesses. —[ED.

FLAVIUS CHINTASVINTUS, KING.

I. Concerning Persons who are not Permitted to Testify.

Murderers, malefactors, thieves, criminals, poisoners, ravishers, perjurors, or those who are addicted to the practice of sorcery or divination, shall under no circumstances be permitted to testify.

II. Witnesses shall not Testify except under Oath; Where both parties offer Witnesses which should be Believed; and Where a Witness Testifies Falsely.

The judge, as soon as the cause is heard, the witnesses having been sworn according to law, shall render judgment. No witnesses shall be permitted to testify without having first been sworn. If evidence should be offered by both sides, its weight shall be duly considered, and the judge shall determine on which side it preponderates.

If any one, after having been warned by the judge, should refuse to testify concerning any matter within his knowledge; and should either say that he does not know the facts, and hesitates to take the oath, or should suppress the truth through favor to any one, or through bribery; if he is a person of noble rank, he shall not be permitted to give testimony afterwards in any cause in court, nor shall his testimony be taken in any proceeding whatever. But if he who refuses to testify, should be an ordinary citizen, or a person of inferior rank, he shall be considered infamous, and shall receive a hundred lashes; because it is no less criminal to suppress the truth, than to commit perjury.

FLAVIUS CHINTASVINTUS, KING.

III. Where a Witness Testifies Orally, and Written Evidence Contradicts Him.

Whenever a witness testifies to something contrary to what is contained in any document, which he is known to have signed, although he may directly contradict the text of the document, the latter shall be preferred as evidence. But if witnesses should testify that the document offered is not valid, he who introduced it must confirm it by the testimony of witnesses; and if he cannot prove it by them, and by the production of other documents, the judge must require the witness who denies that it is in his hand, to write a similar document, in order that the truth may be the more readily established. And the judge shall make every effort to find other documents which may be compared with the one in question. And if all these efforts should fail, he shall not delay to make the witness swear that he had never signed the document; and if, afterwards, in any way it should become evident, that the latter had lied for the purpose of suppressing the truth, he shall be branded with the mark of infamy; and, if he is a person of high position, he shall be compelled to pay, by way of satisfaction, to the person affected by his false testimony, double the sum which the latter would have lost.[1] But if he is a person of inferior rank, and has not sufficient property wherewith to make amends, he shall never again be allowed to testify, and shall receive a hundred lashes with the scourge.

In regard to the two credible witnesses, whose evidence the authority of a former law declared should be received as sufficient; it must be required, not only that they should be reputable, that is, unquestionably freemen, but also of honorable rank and possessed of property. For care must be taken lest any one oppressed by poverty, and unable to bear his privations, should, without due reflection, perjure himself.

---

[1] Branding was a penalty rarely imposed under the Visigothic system, and was deemed especially infamous on account of it being reserved for crimes involving unusual turpitude. He who was "*notatus infamia*" was deeply burned upon the forehead with a red-hot iron, which left an ineffaceable scar. Few offences were more detested by the Visigoths than perjury.—[ED.

FLAVIUS CHINTASVINTUS, KING.

IV. A Slave shall not be Believed unless He Belongs to the Crown; and When Royal Slaves shall be Believed.

A slave is not to be believed at all if he should try to prove any one else guilty of crime, or if he should endeavor to implicate his master in any offence. And even if he should be subjected to torture, and should confess what he has done, still he must not be believed; an exception, however, being made in the case of such slaves as have been transferred to the royal service, and are deservedly honored with the offices of the palace; that is to say, the chiefs of the grooms, of the fowlers, of the silversmiths, and of the cooks; or any besides these who are superior to them in rank or position. Moreover, to any slaves who are well and favorably known to the king, and who have never been guilty of depravity or crime, permission is granted by the law to testify, as well as to persons who are freeborn. But it must not be thought that other slaves in the royal service can be called as witnesses, for no credit shall attach to any of them, unless the king should especially authorize their testimony to be taken.[1]

---

[1] There were various degrees of slavery recognized by the Visigoths. Slaves in the service of the Crown were often highly educated and accomplished for that age; exercised important and responsible employments at court; enjoyed many privileges, and were exempt from many restrictions ordinarily attching to the servile condition. They were rather serfs than bondsmen; and could themselves own, and, under certain conditions, dispose of, slaves: a singular anomaly which could hardly exist, for any length of time, in a thoroughly civilized state. While the Roman master, under the law, was invested with absolute control over his slave, even to the extent of putting him to death, the Visigoth could exert no such irresponsible power. The worst features of the Roman System, rendered necessary where slaves existed in immense numbers, were rejected by the Visigoths, who displayed, in this instance, far more humanity than their polished and corrupt predecessors. Among them the Roman legal axiom, "*Partus sequitur ventrem,*" did not exclusively prevail; as the children followed the condition of the father as well as that of the mother. In both the Roman and the Visigothic codes the slave was considered as devoid of all personality; and was merely a chattel, with which debts and other

FLAVIUS CHINTASVINTUS, KING.

V. A Witness shall not give His Testimony in Writing, but Orally; and How Testimony should be Given.

Witnesses shall not give testimony by letter, but present, in person, they shall be required to tell the truth, as far as lies in their knowledge. Nor shall they testify concerning foreign matters, but only concerning those which they know to have taken place under their own eyes. But if the witnesses, or their relatives, or friends, should either be oppressed with age or infirmity, or resident in a foreign or distant province, and should think that their testimony should be taken, and if all those concerned in the case are not residents of the same province, they shall assemble in that province, where he who is the highest in rank among the parties lives, and, either in the presence of the judge of the district, or of those whom he shall select, and those interested having been duly summoned, shall give their evidence under oath. Any other proceeding relating to such matters shall be void and of no effect in law.[1]

---

obligations could be discharged, as with any other article of portable property. The *servus idoneus*, or slave of superior rank, was distinguished for his ability and integrity, or for the confidence reposed in him by his master; the *servus vilis* was ignorant, debased, and frequently criminal. In the infliction of penalties, a distinction was made between the individuals belonging to these two classes, and always in favor of the former. Freeborn persons who, by the sentence of the law, were reduced to slavery, a common occurrence under the Visigothic system, and a penalty from which tyrannical and corrupt judges were not exempt, were designated *mancipia*. Slaves belonging to the Church were generally of a high order of ability and trustworthiness, like those who were the property of the Crown. The owner was made liable in damages for any injury committed by his slave; as the latter not being a person, and still less a free agent, was legally presumed to be under the control of his master, who, consequently, was responsible for his acts. The Visigothic Code in comparison with others, protects the rights of slaves with great impartiality, and often treats their minor offences with marked indulgence.—ED.

[1] This is probably the first instance on record, of a law authorizing the taking of depositions. It will be observed that no provision is made for the service of notice on the other party to the suit. The art

FLAVIUS CHINTASVINTUS, KING.

VI. Concerning Those who give False Testimony.

If any one should give false testimony against another, and be detected, or should acknowledge his crime; if he is a person of rank, he shall give as much of his own property to him against whom he testified falsely. as the latter would have lost by his evidence, and he shall never again be permitted to testify in court. If he is a person of inferior rank, and does not possess the means wherewith to make amends, he shall be delivered as a slave to him against whom he testified falsely. But the cause shall by no means be lost by reason of such false testimony, unless the truth shall have been established otherwise; that is, either by a lawful and approved witness, or by just and legal documents in writing. If any one should corrupt another, either by a gift, or by fraud, and should thereby induce him to perjure himself, then, as soon as this fact shall become apparent, the instigator of the crime who aimed at the injury of another, as well as he who was induced by avarice to swear falsely, shall undergo the penalty of forgery

FLAVIUS CHINTASVINTUS, KING.

VII. Concerning Those who are Proved to have given False Testimony; and Concerning the Space of Six Months in which a Witness may be Declared Infamous. It shall not be Lawful to give Testimony concerning One who is Dead.

The wickedness of those who give false testimony is not limited to this offence merely, but attempts to add another

---

of cross-examination does not seem to have been either recognized, or practised, by the Visigothic tribunals. The rigid investigation by the judge, who examined all witnesses, was presumed to be amply sufficient to elicit the truth.—[ED.

[1]In the words of the text, "*pari simul sententia falsarii teneantur.*" Subornation of perjury was, as will be seen from the above, placed in the same category with perjury. The penalty for the latter crime varied with the social status of the culprit, from the loss of the fourth of his property, to scourging, and perpetual servitude. See Book VII, Title V, Chapter II.—[ED.

crime to that of perjury. And, therefore, because such detestable criminals are condemned to death by the Divine Law, we decree that those whom judicial authority has proved to have given false witness against their brethren, shall henceforth not be permitted to testify, as they have already been declared worthy of death, not by human, but by the Divine decree. And if any one should give evidence in court concerning any matter in dispute, and the case should be gained by his testimony, and this witness should subsequently declare that he had given false testimony in the first place, and should then testify in such a manner that his former evidence shall be overthrown; he having been influenced by friendship, or fear, or by a gift from that party against whom he formerly testified; we decree by this new law, the old one still remaining in force, that the testimony of said witness shall not be entitled to credit; and that the cause in which he perjured himself shall not be lost by reason of his testimony, unless it happens that the judgment shall be reversed by the introduction of more reliable, legitimate witnesses, or by means of properly verified documents; so that it may be proper to have a rehearing of the case, and a second decision, as hereinbefore stated. If a party desiring to accelerate the progress of his case should produce a witness in court, and his adversary being present, the latter should declare that he cannot offer anything to contradict said witness, the matter in question shall be settled by the judge in favor of him whose witness has testified. We, however, grant the privilege to the party who declared that he did not know what he could adduce to contradict the witness, to discover, if possible, within six months, the means of contradicting him, and to remedy the defects of his case. But if, within six months, he cannot impeach this witness, and establish his infamy in court, no further time shall be given him in which to do so, or to introduce other witnesses in his behalf; and whatever has been proved by the aforesaid testimony, shall remain established for all time. And, on the other hand, if he who has the right to impeach the aforesaid witness within six months, shall be able to prove his assertions within the appointed time, and if he can thereby establish the infamy of said witness, it shall be lawful for the said party to produce evidence to contradict any witness who is living. But if it should be proved that any witness who formerly testified, is dead, no testimony to impeach him shall be given. Nor shall the testimony of a living witness, in contradiction of one who is dead, ever be taken; excepting in the case of a lawful and manifest instrument in writing, in which he who is dead, confessed, over his own signature, that he was guilty of crime, or that he has been rendered publicly infamous by the sentence of a court of justice. And these statements concerning the infamy which renders any one incompetent to testify in court are sufficient. But if a debt is due from a person who is dead; or if he is accused of wrong; it shall be lawful for a party, according to another law, to prove, either by a competent witness, or by a legal document, either the existence of the debt or the commission of the wrong; and to obtain such redress as he may be entitled to.

FLAVIUS CHINTASVINTUS, KING.

VIII. Concerning Those who Induce Others to give False Testimony, or Encourage the Slaves of Others to Seek their Liberty.

Any one convicted of having induced another to give false testimony against a freeman, shall pay the same amount to him whom he attempted to injure by that false testimony, as the latter could have justly obtained by a judgment in court. But if a witness, asked by another to testify, is known to have given false testimony against a freeman or a liberated slave, and the latter has been reduced to servitude by his evidence, and he who introduced the witness shall not have been convicted of the fraud; the witness himself is to be subjected to the penalty hereinbefore stated; that is, he shall be liable to him whom he wished to injure by his testimony, for the full sum involved in the suit. And if he should not have the means to make amends, he shall be delivered over, with all his property, to the party he attempted to defraud, to forever serve him as a slave. We hereby decree that the same penalty shall be inflicted upon those who have been convicted of giving false testimony in order to liberate the slaves of others; or who, by their schemes, have manifested an intention to deprive freemen of their liberty.

FLAVIUS CHINTASVINTUS, KING.

IX. In what Causes Slaves can Testify.

What relates to the general benefit of the public must not be neglected in our decrees, nor shall the facility for committing crime be such, that any person may think that he is exempt from the operation of the law. Since, therefore, when an affray takes place among freemen whereby death results, and no freeman is present who can give evidence of the crime, slaves may testify; so that it may be ascertained from their evidence how the homicide was committed. But for the reason that, under other circumstances, the course of justice would be obstructed; as, for instance, when the accused freeman shall be some distance away, or, if at hand, should not be recognized; therefore slaves shall be permitted to testify when no freemen were present, or those who were there are implicated in the affair in question. But slaves shall not be allowed to give testimony in other cases, nor in matters of great importance, but only in such as are comparatively insignificant; as those involving the title to lands, vineyards, or buildings, which are of lesser moment, and concerning which disputes often arise between heirs or neighbors. A slave shall also be believed in matters in which he is personally interested; as, for instance, if he should be seized by others, or be illegally detained by them, and also where another slave has escaped; on his statement, when true, the former may be returned to his master; and by reliable information imparted by a slave, any dispute which has arisen on account of the ownership of another, may be ended. Nevertheless, slaves shall be considered unworthy of credit, unless they are known to be innocent of all crime, and are not grievously oppressed by poverty; and their testimony can, under no circumstances, be received to contradict that of freemen; unless, as has been hereinbefore stated, it should happen that a homicide has been committed.

FLAVIUS CHINTASVINTUS, KING.

X. Concerning Those who Bind themselves in Writing, not to give True Testimony in the Causes of Others.

We are aware that many persons are in the habit of entering into obligations in writing, binding themselves to promptly give evidence in their own behalf, or in that of their friends; but to furnish no information in case any one else should bring a suit against them. And because it is well established that they are contrary to truth and equity, all judges shall have the power to at once examine such contracts, cancel them, and inflict a hundred lashes on all who are mentioned in them. Yet that this punishment may not fix upon said persons any mark of infamy, it is granted to them by this law, that they shall afterwards have the right to testify, and that their liberty shall, in no way, be restrained.

FLAVIUS CHINTASVINTUS, KING.

XI. At what Age Minors can Testify.

It is hereby decreed that after a boy or girl has reached his or her fourteenth year, they shall be competent to testify in any case in court.

XII. A Near Relative, or a Kinsman of a Party to a Suit, cannot give Testimony against a Stranger.

Brothers, sisters, half-brothers, uncles, aunts, or their children, also grandsons and granddaughters, shall not be permitted to give evidence in court against strangers; unless relations belonging to the same family should have lawsuits among themselves, or there should not be any other freeman who can testify in the case.

TITLE V. CONCERNING VALID AND INVALID DOCUMENTS; AND HOW WILLS SHOULD BE DRAWN UP.

I. *What Documents are Valid in Law.*
II. *No Witness shall Testify as to the Contents of a Document of which He is Ignorant.*
III. *Concerning the Drawing Up of Contracts, and Other Legal Documents.*
IV. *Neither Children, nor Other Heirs, shall contest the Final Disposition of Property by their Ancestors.*
V. *Concerning the Penalties to which those are Liable who attempt to Repudiate their Written Contracts.*
VI. *Contracts and Agreements made by Slaves are Invalid, unless Ordered by their Masters.*
VII. *Concerning Dishonorable and Illegal Contracts.*
VIII. *No One shall be Liable in Person or Property, under the Terms of any Contract, where Deception has been Practised: nor shall He be Liable to any Penalty provided by the same.*
IX. *Every Obligation, or Contract, which has been Extorted by Force, or Fear, shall be Void.*
X. *What Contracts entered into by Minors shall be Valid.*
XI. *How Wills shall be Drawn Up and Proved.*
XII. *How the Wills of those who Die during a Journey shall be Proved.*
XIII. *A Will must be Published in the Presence of a Priest, or of Witnesses, within Six Months.*
XIV. *Concerning the Comparison of Handwriting, where Doubt attaches to any Document.*
XV. *Concerning Holographic Wills.*
XVI. *Concerning the Comparison of Documents, and the Infliction of Penalites prescribed by Wills.*
XVII. *No Testator shall be Permitted to Dispose of Property in One Way in the Presence of Witnesses, and in Another by a Written Will.*

FLAVIUS CHINTASVINTUS, KING.

I. What Documents are Valid in Law.

All documents which have been drawn up for a year and a day, and are known to have been executed according to law; or which are confirmed by the seals or signatures of the parties, or of witnesses; shall be deemed valid. Such documents also, as any person, on account of sickness, was unable to sign, but requested witnesses to affix their signatures thereto, in his presence, shall be equally valid. And, also, where any one is requested to affix his seal or signature to a document, instead of the party himself; it shall be valid only under the condition that if the maker of said document should recover from his illness, and desiring that that which has been thus attested be irrevocably established, should confirm it by his own signature, then it shall have complete validity. If a testator should die after making a will attested by another, as aforesaid, he who was called as a witness shall see that the will is proved by him within six months, as provided by another law.

FLAVIUS EGICA, KING.

II. No Witness shall Testify as to the Contents of a Document of which He is Ignorant.

Where any one is asked to witness a document of any kind, he must not sign it before he has read it, or has heard it read. And if he should do so, and then attempt to testify concerning what he has done negligently, his evidence shall not be received, because he was ignorant of the contents of the paper to which he affixed his signature; nor shall the document be valid, because its authenticity has not been established by legal proof.

ANCIENT LAW.

III. Concerning the Drawing Up of Contracts, and Other Legal Documents.

All contracts and agreements, which have been properly and lawfully reduced to writing, provided they have been published for a year and a day, shall be thereafter unalterable.

ANCIENT LAW.

IV. Neither Children, nor Other Heirs, shall contest the Final Disposition of Property by their Ancestors.

It shall not be lawful for a son, or other heir, to contest the just and legitimate provisions of the will of an ancestor, because it is presumption in him who attempts to nullify the acts of his ancestors.

V. Concerning the Penalties to which those are Liable who attempt to Repudiate their Written Contracts.

He who repudiates a contract, or obligation, lawfully and properly executed, unless some more powerful person compelled him to do so by force; and afterwards, before the cause is heard, shall pay the penalty prescribed by the said contract, or obligation, then the latter shall be valid. And any contract or obligation, properly drawn up between the parties, even if it contains no penalty, shall under no circumstances, be altered or cancelled. And whatever things are set out in writing in contracts or obligations, shall be perfectly valid; and especially if a party has drawn them up himself, and they have reference to any indebtedness incurred by him.

FLAVIUS CHINTASVINTUS, KING.

VI. Contracts and Agreements made by Slaves are Invalid, unless Ordered by their Masters.

Honor and justice both demand that, where slaves enter into contracts in writing, or in the presence of witnesses, and not by the order of their masters, such contracts shall be void.

VII. Concerning Dishonorable and Illegal Contracts.

We hereby decree that any contract or obligation, entered into by any person whomsoever, which is injurious and unlawful, shall be void.

VIII. No One shall be Liable in Person or Property, under the Terms of any Contract, where Deception has been Practised: nor shall He be Liable to any Penalty provided by the same.

The practices of wicked and depraved men should always be opposed by the authority of the law. For the reason, therefore, that the avarice of designing persons often fraudulently ensnares others, and induces them to enter into contracts whereby their liberty and their property are lost, such transactions are hereby absolutely prohibited. And whenever a contract is entered into, the penalty for its violation shall not be more than double the amount involved; or triple the amount, if a sum of money be in dispute. But, under no circumstances shall a person be permitted to pledge all his property or his person for the debt of another, because it is manifestly unjust that any one should be ruined personally and financially on account of such indebtedness; and therefore, any obligation or contract made in violation of this law, shall be void and of no effect.

IX. Every Obligation, or Contract, which has been Extorted by Force, or Fear, shall be Void.

Any contract which a person of high or low rank has extorted by force or fear; that is, if he who makes it has been put in prison, or threatened with violent death, or undergone any punishment, or any indignity whatever, or suffered injury of any kind, in an attempt to compel its execution; then any obligation or agreement made under such circumstances shall be void.

FLAVIUS RECESVINTUS, KING.

X. What Contracts entered into by Minors shall be Valid.

Minors under fourteen years of age who wish to dispose of their property by will, or in any other manner, whether in writing, or in the presence of witnesses, shall not be permitted to do so, unless in case of serious illness, or impending death. But if they should be impelled by necessity, as aforesaid all minors who are more than ten years of age, have full liberty to make such disposition of their property as they may desire. If, however, they should recover from their illness, whatever they have done shall be void; unless, being ill a second time, they should confirm what they have previously done; or, having reached their fourteenth year, they should have full authority to act for themselves in all matters in which they are interested. All persons who are insane from infancy, or indeed from any age whatever, and remain so without intermission, cannot testify, or enter into a contract, and, if they should do so, it would have no validity. But such as have lucid intervals, shall not be prohibited from transacting business during those periods.

FLAVIUS RECESVINTUS, KING.

XI. How Wills shall be Drawn Up and Proved.

The last will of a dying person, whether it be signed by his hand and those of witnesses, or confirmed by the seals and signatures of all parties; or even if the testator could not write, or attach his seal, and some one else be requested by him to affix his signature, or seal, instead of his own, along with those of lawful witnesses; or if the wishes of said testator should only be expressed verbally, in the presence of others; where any one of the methods above stated is adopted, the will shall be valid in law. But care must especially be taken that those wills which are executed according to the first and second regulations, that is, such as are signed by the testator and witnesses, or confirmed by the seals of either of these parties, shall be published in the presence of an ecclesiastic within six months, as has been provided for in another law. And if it should happen that the maker of the will, who should have signed it, attaches his seal, the witness who has signed the will, must establish the fact by oath, and explain why the testator attached his seal. But those wills that are executed under the third provision hereinbefore stated, that is, where a competent witness subscribed it at the request of the testator, shall be considered valid if published within six months. And he who signed the will instead of the testator, and the witnesses who had been requested by the latter to be present, shall make oath concerning these facts, before the judge, and shall swear that there was no fraud in the execution of the will signed by them, but that it was drawn up according to the wishes of the testator himself, and that they appeared at his request, and thus the act of the agent of the testator who subscribed the will in his stead shall be proved and confirmed. But a will made verbally, in the presence of witnesses, which the testator, being in extremity, was not able to put in writing, shall be fully proved if the witnesses who heard it, and appeared at the request of the testator, should confirm by oath, in the presence of the judge, within the space of six months, what the testator had declared; and this oath must be signed by the judge as well as by the witnesses. And when the affair shall have been fully settled, the witnesses shall receive for their trouble the thirtieth part of the property of the defunct; but only in money, conveyances, and books, which otherwise would belong to the heirs. The witnesses must, within six months, serve notice upon those who are interested in the settlement of the estate, of the disposition of the same made by the testator.

If any of the witnesses should neglect to carry out the provisions of this law within the appointed time, they shall be liable to the penalty of forgery; excepting, however, they should be able to prove that they had been prevented from performing their duty within the six months aforesaid, either through the fraud or deception of others, or by the royal order; under which circumstances no blame shall be attached to them.

FLAVIUS CHINTASVINTUS, KING.

XII. How the Wills of those who Die during a Journey shall be Proved.

If any one should die while on a journey, or on a public expedition, if there should be no freeman with him, he may write his will with his own hand. But if he does not know how to write, or if, from weakness, is unable to do so, he may communicate his wishes to his slaves, whose good faith must subsequently be established by the bishop and the judge. And if the said slaves, at no time previously, have been guilty of fraud, their statements shall be received and reduced to writing, sworn to, and attached by the signatures of the bishop and the judge; and afterwards, if confirmed by the royal authority, they shall be valid.

FLAVIUS CHINTASVINTUS, KING.

XIII. A Will must be Published in the Presence of a Priest, or of Witnesses, within Six Months.

A written will must be published within six months, either in the presence of a priest, or of witnesses. And if any one should suppress a will through fraud, he shall be compelled to pay as much out of his own property to the beneficiaries of said will, as they are entitled to according to its provisions.

FLAVIUS CHINTASVINTUS, KING.

XIV. Concerning the Comparison of Handwriting, where Doubt attaches to any Document.

Documents of every description, where he who made them and the witnesses to the same are dead, and in which the signature of the former and the attestation of the witnesses appear, when brought into court to be verified, may be proved by comparison of their seals and signatures with those of other documents; and the proof shall be sufficient in this investigation, if the seals and signatures of three or four other documents, when introduced, shall be evidently those of the parties in question. But if the documents aforesaid shall not have been published within the time prescribed by law, they shall be invalid.

FLAVIUS CHINTASVINTUS, KING.

XV. Concerning Holographic Wills.

It happens frequently, through necessity, that the solemnities of the law cannot be complied with; and where the locality is such that witnesses cannot be found, by whom any one may have his will subscribed according to the regulations required by law, the testator may write those things in his own hand which he desires to have done; provided it be specifically stated, what he intends to dispose of, or what business he wishes any one he may select to transact; the day and the year being both given in the instrument. And when the will has been written, the testator himself shall sign it; and if said will should come into the possession of him for whose benefit it was made, or into that of his heirs, within thirty years, it must be presented to the bishop or the judge within six months thereafter. The bishop and the judge—three other documents having been produced in which the signature of the testator appears—shall then determine, by comparison of all these documents, whether the will which the testator wrote with his own hand is genuine or not, and if it should become evident that it is genuine, then the bishop, or the judge, or other reputable witnesses, shall confirm the same by their signatures, and, in this manner, the said holographic will shall be fully proved and established.

FLAVIUS RECESVINTUS, KING.

XVI. Concerning the Comparison of Documents, and the Infliction of Penalties prescribed by Wills.

As we should not, where it is proper to do so, refuse salutary remedies to those who are in distress, so we should justly impose censure where irrational contention occurs. Hereafter, when any dispute arises concerning the will of an ancestor, which appears to have been drawn up justly and legally, and according to obligations which have been incurred; if any interested party to whom the will is shown, should say that he does not know that it is true, he who has produced it must immediately swear that no fraud or mutilation has been made therein at any time, by him, or by any one else, so far as he knows; but that it still remains just as the testator executed it. Then he who refused to accept it shall be forced to swear that he does not know that said will is authentic, and does not recognize it, and is not aware that it has been legally drawn up, or that the seal or signature of the maker is genuine. Then search must be made by both parties, among the effects of the deceased, for instruments in writing; so that, by comparison with the seals and signatures of other documents, it may be properly established, whether the matter alleged is true or false. Then, if documents of the testator should not be found, by comparison with which the will in question can be proved, he who introduced the will shall make diligent inquiry, wherever he can, for other papers of the testator, by comparison with which he may prove the will in question. And if, after all these efforts, the truth should not be ascertained, he who introduced the will, even if he had summoned witnesses from a distance, must pay all expenses; and he who refused to accept it, shall not be liable to any penalty whatever. But in such cases, if he who declared the will to be fraudulent, did so, not for the sake of truth, but solely for the annoyance of the other party, and to compel him to summon witnesses, and incur expense, in order to establish the genuineness of the will; then he who introduced the will, must prove by witnesses that it is true and unmutilated; and he who, through an unjust contention, has caused annoyance and expense to his adversary, must pay the amount of the penalty mentioned in the will. But if he has not sufficient property, after an estimate has been made of the same, to pay the sum which the testator prescribed, or openly refuses to pay said penalty, he shall be forced to surrender to him whom he has wronged, all that he would have inherited from the testator. We decree that this law shall apply to the wills of parents alone; because we see that sons or grandsons very frequently are involved in unjust disputes with one another. This exception, however, is made, that if a will shall be found to be, in any way, opposed to the laws, any one is free to dispute its validity.

FLAVIUS CHINTASVINTUS, KING.

XVII. No Testator shall be Permitted to Dispose of Property in One Way in the Presence of Witnesses, and in Another by a Written Will.

The evidence, either oral or written, by means of which the proof of a bequest from one person to another is established, and which should be true and manifest, is often rendered doubtful; so that the intentions of the testator, concerning the gifts and other matters set forth in his will, can with difficulty be determined; for the reason that while he has made certain statements in his will, he has made others, of a directly contrary character, secretly, in the presence of witnesses.

Thus, by reason of this duplicity, it is evident that there are practically two wills; for clearness and honesty are excluded, where one thing is published openly, and another secretly stated in the presence of witnesses.

And, where any one who has executed a document conveying property of any kind to another, by gift or sale, shall be found to have made a different disposition of said property before a witness, than he did in writing; he shall pay the penalty prescribed in the document to him upon whom this deceit has been practised; and, in addition to this, he shall never be permitted to recover what he has surrendered.

Nor shall any witness be allowed to testify concerning anything which is not contained in a will; so that, hereafter, all temptations for dispute having been removed, whatever is found to be the manifest and lawful tenor of such documents may not be brought into dispute, through the machinations of a corrupt witness.

This law shall have equal force with those already promulgated.

If he who offers a will is of such rank and power that the said will appears to have been rather exacted by, than offered to him, and this fact can be proved, then the will shall be declared invalid; and the property disposed of by it shall be distributed among the heirs according to law.[1]

---

[1] A large part of the preceding Book has been borrowed from the Roman jurisprudence, and some of it is older than the Twelve Tables. It is hardly necessary to remark that the intelligence and experience of semi-barbarians are unequal to the task of the framing, construction, and execution of enactments relating to the enforcement of civil obligations, and the testamentary disposition of property, as set forth in these chapters. The power to distrain, referred to in Chapter VIII as effecting the property of a surety for a debt, is a remedy whose origin antedates all history. It was the *pignoris captio* of the Romans, among whom it was a summary proceeding, undertaken without previous application to a judicial tribunal. It was supplemented by the *manus injectio*, or seizure of the person of a debtor or wrongdoer; followed by his subjection to hard labor, and often to cruel treatment, until the unpaid claim was satisfied, or the tort he had committed, had, in the opinion of the injured party, been sufficiently punished. This form of execution was much used by the Visigoths, and its severity was somewhat modified by their laws; but while its most oppressive features were eliminated, enough remained to render the proceeding liable to great abuse.

The rules relating to the execution, attestation and proof of wills and other legal documents, contained in the *Forum Judicum* were, for the most part, derived from the Codes of Theodosius and Justinian. The provisions governing nuncupative and holographic testaments are very similar in all these collections. The will made by a traveller or a soldier, while on a journey or absent in the service of the government, is merely the *peculium castrense*, or military will of the Roman legionary. Codicils, introduced by the laws of Justinian, were unknown to the Visigoths.—[ED.

BOOK III.

CONCERNING MARRIAGE.

TITLE I. CONCERNING NUPTIAL CONTRACTS.

THE GLORIOUS FLAVIUS RECESVINTUS, KING.

I. Marriage shall not be Entered Into without a Dowry.

Marriage is recognized to have greater dignity and honor, where the dowry is given before the nuptial contract has been entered into in writing. For where the dowry has been neither given, nor stated in writing, what expectation can there be of future conjugal dignity, when propriety does not confirm the celebration of the marriage, nor the honorable obligation of the written contract accompany it?

FLAVIUS RECESVINTUS, KING.

II. It shall be as Lawful for a Roman Woman to Marry a Goth, as for a Gothic Woman to Marry a Roman.

The zealous care of the prince is recognized, when, for the sake of future utility, the benefit of the people is provided for; and it should be a source of no little congratulation, if the ancient law, which sought improperly to prevent the marriage of persons equal in dignity and lineage, should be abrogated. For this reason, we hereby sanction a better law; and, declaring the ancient one to be void, we decree that if any Goth wishes to marry a Roman woman, or any Roman a Gothic woman, permission being first requested, they shall be permitted to marry. And any freeman shall have the right to marry any free woman; permission of the Council and of her family having been previously obtained.

III. Where a Girl Marries against the Will of her Father, while she is Betrothed to Another.

Where anyone is betrothed to a girl, either by the consent of her father, or of any near relative in whom authority in these matters is vested by all, and the girl, in defiance of the wishes of her father, desires to marry another than him to whom she has been betrothed; this we decree shall under no circumstances be permitted. But if the girl, against the will of her father, should have fled to him who was her choice, and should have married him, both shall be delivered into the power of him to whom, with her father's consent, she had previously been betrothed. And if her mother, or brothers, or other relatives, should grant her wishes, and give her to him whom she has chosen, against the will of her father, those who have plotted this shall pay a pound of gold to whomever the king may direct. Nor shall the act of the parties be valid, but both of them, as has hereinbefore been stated, shall be delivered up, with all their property, to him to whom the girl had already been betrothed. And we decree that this law shall be observed where the father shall have made arrangements concerning the marriage of his daughter, and the amount of the dowry has been agreed upon, and her father dies before the marriage has been concluded; in such a case the girl shall be given to him to whom she had been contracted by either her father or her mother.

FLAVIUS CHINTASVINTUS, KING.

IV. Where a Gift is made by way of Pledge, a Nuptial Contract cannot be Rescinded.

Since we have treated of things that are past, we consider it eminently proper to discuss and determine those that are to come. For the reason that there are many who, disregarding the betrothal, fail to complete the nuptial contract; we deem it proper to abolish this abuse, that no one may delay a marriage according to his will. Therefore, we decree, from this day, that when the ceremony of betrothal has been performed, either between the parents or relatives of the parties, or in the presence of witnesses, and the ring shall have been given or accepted as a pledge, although nothing may have been committed to writing, the promise shall, under no circumstances, be broken. Nor shall it be lawful for either party to change his or her mind, if the other is unwilling to consent; but if all the provisions relating to the dowry have been carried out according to law, then the marriage shall be celebrated.

FLAVIUS RECESVINTUS, KING.

V. Women Advanced in Years shall not Marry Young Men.

The law of nature is framed in the direct hope of progeny when the nuptial contract is entered into with all due solemnity. For if a marriage takes place between persons who are incompetent, either through age or some personal defect, to properly perform their marital duties, how can their offspring be other than dwarfed or deformed? For that cannot be perfect whose origin is defective. We sometimes see persons who, not observing the laws of nature, but induced by avarice, dispose of their children in marriage so improperly, that neither the age, rank, or morals of the parties concerned, are considered by them. For though men have received their name from the fact that they control women by their superior strength; some, in violation of the laws of nature, give the priority to women, when they unite females of advanced age with boys who are little more than children; and thus, for the sake of gain, and through unwise delay, encourage the commission of vice by the former. Therefore, that an end may be put to practices whose results are unfavorable to future generations, we now decree, that, hereafter, women shall always marry men who are older than themselves, and a marriage under other circumstances shall not be valid, if either of the parties should object. A space of time, not longer than two years, shall be permitted to elapse from the day of betrothal to the day of marriage; unless a longer period shall be agreed upon by the parents or relations, or by the parties themselves, if they are of age. But if, after the contract has been made, it is determined by common consent to defer the date of the nuptials; or if one of the persons should fail to be present, through necessity, this may be done; but the marriage shall not then be deferred longer than two years more. And if a second time, or several times, it may be desirable to prolong the interval, it shall only be for a period of two years; otherwise, the marriage contract, though made in writing, and accompanied with the delivery of the dowry, shall not be valid. If any one unnecessarily or arbitrarily should protract the time, and violate the marriage contract, he shall be liable to the penalty which is contained in it, and the contract shall still remain in force. Any woman who has had one or more husbands, shall after the death of those husbands, be permitted to marry any man of proper age who has never been married before, or who has had one or more wives already deceased.

FLAVIUS CHINTASVINTUS, KING.

VI. What Property the Dowry shall consist of.

As disputes concerning the dowry often arise between parties contemplating marriage, it is a matter of common advantage that no doubt should hereafter be possible under this our law. Therefore, we decree and declare, that the following law shall be perpetually observed hereafter, to wit: that if any one of the nobles of our palace, or of the principal personages of the Gothic nation, should demand in marriage for his son either the daughter of another, or the widow of any one; or if any one should choose for himself a wife, of the aforesaid rank; no person shall pay, or bind himself to pay, as the dowry of the girl or woman, more than the tenth part of his property. But if it should happen that a parent should wish to give the dowry for the benefit of his daughter-in-law, he can then give as said dowry, the tenth part of the property which his son would inherit from him in case of his death; and, in addition, he must give ten young men and ten young girls, and twenty horses: or, in ornaments, as much as would amount in value to a thousand *solidi*. And the wife shall have absolute liberty to dispose of this property if she should not leave any sons; and if she should die intestate, this donation shall go to the nearest heirs of the husband.

It shall not be lawful for the parents of the girl, or for the girl herself, or for any woman, to ask more as a dowry from the bridegroom, than is provided for by this law; and, as was permitted by the Roman laws, the girl, or the woman, may give to the bridegroom as much out of her own property as she herself has demanded of him, should she desire to do so. If the bridegroom should promise in writing, or bind himself by oath, at the time of the marriage, to give a larger sum than is permitted by this law, he is hereby fully authorized to take possession of all over and above said sum, whenever he chooses. But if it should happen that, through reverence for his oath, or, as often is the case, through negligence, he should be unwilling to revoke or appropriate the surplus amount which he had given to his bride, or should refuse to do so; as it is not proper that, through the carelessness of one, injury should be inflicted upon the many; therefore, when the parents of the bridegroom, or his relations, shall become aware of the facts, they may deprive the bride of all over and above the sum above mentioned as legal; and this they may do as a matter of right, and without prejudice. If, however, the husband, when a year has passed since the marriage, should wish, through affection for his wife, to make her a present of any kind, he shall have full liberty to do so. But not within the space of a year shall the husband give to the wife, or the wife to the husband, any present whatever, except the dowry hereinbefore mentioned; unless either of them should be attacked by grievous illness, and be in imminent danger of death.

In regard to others who desire to make marriage contracts, we deem it proper, and so decree; that whoever is known to possess ten thousand *solidi*, shall give to his bride as a dowry, as much as a thousand *solidi* out of all his possessions. And he who has only a thousand *solidi* shall, in the same proportion, give a hundred as a dowry.

This law relating to the dowry shall be observed, without controversy, in all matters great and small. Given and confirmed on the second day of the Ides of January, and the third year of our reign.

ANCIENT LAW.

VII. The Father shall Exact and Keep the Dowry of his Daughter.

The father shall have the right to demand and keep the dowry of his daughter. If the father or mother should not be present, then the brothers, or the nearest relatives, shall receive the dowry, and deliver it untouched to their sister.

ANCIENT LAW.

VIII. In case of the Death of the Father, the Disposition of the Children, of Both Sexes, in Marriage, shall belong to the Mother.

If the father should be dead, the right to dispose of the children of both sexes in marriage shall belong to the mother. If the mother also should be dead, or if she should have married a second time, the brothers shall have the right to select the husbands or wives for the other children. But if any of the brothers should not be of age, which is indispensable when their brother or sister is to be disposed of in marriage; then the paternal uncles shall have that authority. Where a brother is of full age, and declines the advice of his relatives, he shall have the power to marry without their consent. But if a suitor, equal to a sister in rank, should seek her in marriage; then her uncle or her brother should consult with the other relatives as to whether said suitor shall be accepted, or rejected, by common consent.

IX. Where Brothers Defer the Marriage of their Sister, or Where a Girl Marries beneath her Station.

If the brothers of the girl should put off her marriage, with the expectation that she, taking refuge with her intended husband, may lose what she would have inherited from her father according to law; and they should repulse her suitor two or three times; the girl, as soon as the deceit of her brothers becomes evident, should she deem that her suitor is her equal in birth, shall then receive from her brothers whatever property she is entitled to inherit from her parents. But if, on the other hand, her brothers should do nothing to affect the rights of their sister, but only cause delay in order to provide her with a husband more worthy of her; and she, forgetful of her modesty, and disregarding her rank, should marry a man inferior to her in station; she shall lose what she would have inherited from her parents, whether that inheritance has been divided or not, but she shall still have the right to inherit from her brothers and her sisters, and from any other relatives.

FLAVIUS CHINTASVINTUS, KING.

X. Where the Items of a Dowry, relating to any kind of Property, are reduced to Writing, it shall not be Contested.

When any one is desirous of contracting marriage, either in his own behalf, or in behalf of his son, or of any other relative; he shall have a right to dispose of, as a dowry, any of his own property; or any given him by the king; or any he has acquired legally, in any way whatsoever. And whatever has lawfully been stated in writing to be a dowry, by any person, shall be valid, as such, in every respect.

TITLE II. CONCERNING UNLAWFUL MARRIAGES.

ANCIENT LAW.

I. Where a Woman Marries within a Year after the Death of her Husband.

If any woman, within a year after the death of her husband, should marry another, or commit adultery, the children by her first marriage shall receive half of her property; or, if there are no children, the nearest heirs of the deceased husband shall receive half of her property, by order of the court. We have especially prescribed this penalty lest the woman, having been left pregnant by her husband, and desiring to enter into a second marriage, should destroy her unborn offspring. We decree, however, that those only shall be exempt from the operation of this law, who marry within the prohibited time under order of the king.

II. Where a Freeborn Woman Marries a Slave, or her own Freedman.

If a freeborn woman should commit adultery with her own slave, or freedman, or should marry him; as soon as this has been proved, she shall be put to death; and both adulterer and adulteress shall be publicly scourged before the judge, and burned. And whenever any judge shall be convinced of the commission of such a crime, and shall learn that any mistress has married her slave, or her freedman; he shall at once cause them to be separated, in order that the sons of her former husband, or those of his relatives entitled to it by legal succession, may obtain possession of her property. But if heirs, to the third degree, should be wanting, then all her property shall belong to the royal treasury; for it is not proper that the children born of such a marriage should be heirs. And the woman, whether she be a virgin or a widow, shall be liable to the penalty hereinbefore mentioned. But if she should take refuge at the altar, and claim the privilege of sanctuary, she shall be given by the king to whomever he chooses, to serve him forever as a slave.

III. Where a Freeborn Woman Marries the Slave of Another, or a Freeborn Man the Female Slave of Another.

If any freeborn woman should marry, or commit adultery with the slave of another, even though he should belong to the king; as soon as this shall come to the knowledge of the judge, he shall order the parties to be separated immediately, that they may suffer the punishment they deserve, to wit: each one a hundred lashes. And if, after this, they should commit the offence a second time, the judge shall order them to be arrested and brought before him, and they shall each receive another hundred lashes. And if they should be guilty for the third time, they shall receive another hundred lashes, and the woman shall be delivered over into the power of her relatives. And if, at any time afterwards, her relatives should permit her to return to the slave, she shall become the slave of the master to whom the latter belongs. And whatever children shall be born of this union shall follow the condition of the father, and remain in slavery. The relatives of the woman, however, shall inherit her property, according to the rules of inheritance. But if the children who are born of this union shall prove, by a lawful witness, that for thirty years they have been free, they shall be exempt from servitude; provided that their parents, within the thirty years for which time the children have proved themselves to be free, should have rendered no service to their master, by reason of which their children might be subject to slavery. And we direct that this law shall also apply to freeborn men who marry the female slaves of the king, or those of any one else whomsoever.

FLAVIUS CHINTASVINTUS, KING.

IV. Where a Freedwoman, or a Freedman, Marries the Slave of Another.

If any woman who has been freed should unite herself with the slave of another, or should marry him; the master of the slave shall notify her three times, in the presence of three witnesses, to leave him, and if, after the third notification, she should be unwilling to do so, she shall become the slave of the master of him with whom she is living. But if she should not have been notified before any children are born, then she shall remain free. It is the rule that the blood relations of a slave shall belong to his master, because those cannot be free who are born in this condition. This law likewise shall apply to men who have been set free, who unite with the slaves of others. But if any woman who has been set free should marry the slave of another, after the permission of the master has been granted, through any contract or agreement with the latter, then such contract shall be valid.

V. Where any one gives in Marriage his Slave, of Either Sex, to the Slave of Another.

Whoever gives his female slave, as a wife, to the slave of another, without the knowledge of the master of the latter, and this should be established by certain proof, the said master shall have the wife of the slave, along with all of her children, as his own slaves. And he who marries the female slave of another to his own slave, we ordain shall also be subject to this law.

VI. Where a Woman contracts a Second Marriage in the Absence of Her Husband.

No woman, in the absence of her husband, shall have liberty to marry another man until she has learned, by certain evidence, that her husband is dead; and he, also, who wishes to marry her must make diligent inquiry for that purpose. But if they should neglect to do this, and should be unlawfully married, and afterwards the former husband should return, they shall both be delivered up into his power, to be disposed of at his will, and he shall have the right to sell them or do whatever he pleases with them.

FLAVIUS CHINTASVINTUS, KING.

VII. Where a Master Marries one of his Slaves to a Freewoman, declaring him to be a Freeman.

The acts of wicked men must be resisted, lest unbridled depravity prevail. Many persons, induced by avarice, are accustomed to wickedly deceive freeborn women and girls by inducing them to accept their slaves as husbands, representing them to be freeborn; in order that any children they have, may afterwards be reduced to slavery. Therefore, that this fraud may be abolished, we decree by the present law, that persons guilty of such deception shall be branded with infamy; and those slaves who are found to have been represented as freemen by the aforesaid evil-minded persons, shall be, along with their children, forever free; just as if their masters had publicly liberated them; and the women or girls who married said slaves shall have, as their own, all the property which was either received by, or promised to, them at the time of their marriage; if they can establish by any suitable proof, that their husbands were given to them under the representation that they were free. But if any girl or woman, as aforesaid, or her parents, should not be able to prove this; the master shall possess said girl or woman, along with her children, as slaves, and shall be entitled to all their property. And this law shall also apply to those female servants who are known to have married freemen under similar circumstances of fraud, as well as to persons who have been set free, and who are proved to have married the slaves of others.

ANCIENT LAW.

VIII. Where a Freewoman Marries without the Consent of her Parents.

If any freeborn girl should marry a freeman before the latter has consulted her parents, and if he then should obtain consent to have her as his wife, he shall pay the legal dowry to her parents; but if he can not furnish that sum, the girl shall be again placed under their control. If she should have been voluntarily married without the consent and knowledge of her parents, and they should then be unwilling to receive her, she shall not inherit along with her brothers, for the reason that she married without the permission of her parents. If her parents should give her any of their property, she shall have full liberty to dispose of it at her pleasure.

TITLE III. CONCERNING THE RAPE OF VIRGINS, OR WIDOWS.

ANCIENT LAW.

I. Where a Freeman carries off a Freewoman by Force, he shall not be permitted to Marry her, if she was a Virgin.

If any freeman should carry off a virgin or widow by violence, and she should be rescued before she has lost her chastity, he who carried her off shall lose half of his property, which shall be given to her. But should such not be the case, and the crime should have been fully committed, under no circumstances shall a marriage contract be entered into with him; but he shall be surrendered, with all his possessions, to the injured party; and shall, in addition, receive two hundred lashes in public; and, after having been deprived of his liberty, he shall be delivered up to the parents of her whom he violated, or to the virgin or widow herself, to forever serve as a slave, to the end that there may be no possibility of a future marriage between them. And if it should be proved that she has received anything from the property of the ravisher, on account of her injury, she shall lose it, and it shall be given to her parents, by whose agency this matter should be prosecuted. But if a man who has legitimate children by a former wife should be convicted of this crime, he alone shall be given up into the power of her whom he carried off; and his children shall have the right to inherit his property.[1]

FLAVIUS RECESVINTUS, KING.

II. Where Parents remove their Daughter from the Power of a Ravisher.

If the parents of the woman or girl who has been carried off should rescue her, the ravisher shall be given up to them, and, under no condition whatever, shall she be permitted to marry him; and should they presume to marry, both shall be put to death. If, however, they should take refuge with the bishop, or should claim the privilege of sanctuary, their

[1] The crime of rape was considered by the Visigothic legislator in the original and broader acceptation of the term, and not according to the more limited significance attaching to it at the present day. It included, therefore, the offences of abduction and kidnapping; all survivals of practices observed by mankind in their natural condition; one of whose customs, marriage by capture, still prevails among certain barbarous nations. By the Visigoths, as by the Romans, rape, theft, and some other crimes, were classed as private wrongs, to be expiated by the infliction of personal vengeance. For this reason, the ravisher was delivered up to the tender mercies of the relatives of the victim; or, reduced to servitude, he was compelled to serve the latter for life.—[ED.

lives shall be granted them; but they shall be separated and delivered over as slaves to the parents of the woman.

III. Where the Parents of a Girl, who has been Betrothed, consent that she should be Carried Away by Another.

If parents should connive at their daughter being carried away, after she has been betrothed to another, they shall be compelled to pay the latter four times the amount of the dowry agreed upon; and the ravisher shall be delivered up as a slave, absolutely, under the law, to the man who was betrothed to the girl.

ANCIENT LAW.

IV. Where Brothers, either during the Life of their Father, or after his Death, consent that any one should Carry Away their Sister by Force.

If, during the life of their father, any brothers should consent to, or connive at, the carrying off of their sister, they shall receive the penalty to which ravishers are liable, excepting that of death. But if, after the death of their father, they should give up their sister to a ravisher, or permit her to be carried off by him; for the reason that they have disposed of her in marriage to a person of vile character, or against her own will, when they should have protected her honor, they shall lose the half of their property, which shall be given to their sister, and, in addition, they shall each receive fifty lashes in public: so that others, admonished by this, may take warning. All accessories, who were present, shall receive the punishment prescribed by another law. And the ravisher, inexcusable by a former law, shall lose both his property and his rank.

ANCIENT LAW.

V. Where any one Carries away by Violence a Woman who was Betrothed to Another.

If any one should carry off a woman betrothed to another, we hereby decree that half of the property of the ravisher sha l be given to the girl, and the other half to her betrothed. But if he should have little or no property, he shall be given up, with all his possessions, to those above mentioned; so that the ravisher having been sold as a slave, they may have an equal share in the price paid for him. The ravisher himself, if the crime shall have been consummated, shall be punished.

ANCIENT LAW.

VI. Where a Ravisher is Killed.

If any ravisher should be killed, it shall not be considered criminal homicide, because the act was committed in the defence of chastity.

FLAVIUS CHINTASVINTUS, KING.

VII. Within what Time it is Lawful to Prosecute a Ravisher; and Whether any Marriage Contract can be entered into with Him by the Girl or her Parents.

The ravisher of a virgin or a widow can only be prosecuted within thirty years after the commission of the crime. If a marriage contract should be entered into by him with the parents of the girl, or with the girl herself, or with the widow, said contract shall not be illegal. After thirty years have elapsed, as aforesaid, all prosecutions shall be barred.[1]

---

[1] The Statute of Limitations could be pleaded in few crimes, under the Visigothic Code, and especially was this true where the defendant had been guilty of what we would call a felony. The reason for its adoption in this instance is obscure, and this law may have been enacted for some special purpose, or to fit some particular case; retroactive legislation being common under the Visigothic Monarchy. In all other laws published under this Title, marriage between the parties is not only absolutely prohibited, but every precaution is taken to make it impossible. As the former decrees and enactments are not stated to have been abrogated by the promulgation of the above-mentioned law, its application and enforcement would seem to have been difficult, to say the least. Such conflicting legislation was, however, not unusual under the polity of the Visigoths.—[ED.

FLAVIUS RECESVINTUS, KING.

VIII. Where a Slave carries off a Freewoman by Force.

It is the province of equity to make laws concerning the future, where doubt exists in the present. Where slaves, with the knowledge, or under the order of their master, carry off any woman by force, the master shall be required by the judge to give the satisfaction required by law. And if slaves should perpetrate such crimes against the will of their master they shall be arrested by the judge, and, after having been scalped, shall receive three hundred lashes with the scourge. Any slave who has violated a freeborn woman shall undergo the extreme penalty of the law.

FLAVIUS CHINTASVINTUS, KING.

IX. Where a Slave carries off a Freedwoman by Force.

If a slave should be convicted of having carried off a woman who has been freed, and if the said slave is of good character, and the woman also, his master shall pay a hundred *solidi* on his behalf. Should he be unwilling to do this, he must surrender the slave, without delay, so that it may not be possible for him to marry the woman. If, however, they should be married at any time, and children should be born to them, the master shall have both the slave and his children, as slaves. But if a slave should be known to be coarse and degraded, and should be convicted of having carried off a freedwoman of good character, his master shall pay to the aforesaid woman as much as the slave is worth, and the latter shall receive a hundred lashes with the scourge, shall be scalped, and shall forever remain in servitude in the power of his master.

FLAVIUS CHINTASVINTUS, KING.

X. Where a Slave carries off the Female Slave of Another by Force.

If a slave should carry off the female slave of another by force, he shall receive two hundred lashes, and have his head shaved; and, if the master of the female slave desires it, he shall be separated from her.

XI. Concerning those who Deceive Girls, or the Wives of Others, or Widows; and Concerning those who Compel by Force, and without the Royal Command, any Freeborn Girl or Widow to take a Husband.

Everything that pollutes the honor and dignity of human life must be restrained by law. Therefore those who solicit wives to commit adultery, or deceive the daughters of others; or widows; or women who are betrothed; whether they use, as their agents, persons who have been freed, or who are born free, or slaves of either sex; as soon as their crime shall be made apparent by positive testimony, they shall be arrested, along with their emissaries, by order of the judge; and shall be delivered up into the power of him, whose wife, daughter, or betrothed relative, they are convicted of having solicited, to be disposed of at his pleasure; as he is the person whom the conjugal condition, or the relationship by blood, designates as the legal avenger of such a crime. Any person who shall, by force, compel a freeborn girl or widow, without the royal order, to take a husband, shall be compelled to pay five pounds of gold to him to whom the injury was done; and the marriage shall be declared void, unless the woman shall consent to it of her own free will.

THE GLORIOUS FLAVIUS RECESVINTUS, KING.

XII. Concerning Freemen and Slaves who are Proved to have been Implicated in the Crime of Rape.

Any one who is known to have assisted, or to have been present, at the carrying off of any woman by force, if he is a freeman, shall pay a fine of six ounces of gold, and shall publicly receive fifty lashes with the scourge. If he is a slave, and acted without the consent of his master, he shall receive a hundred lashes. But if he should commit this crime with the consent of his master, the latter must give such satisfaction in his stead as has already been stated.

TITLE IV. CONCERNING ADULTERY.

ANCIENT LAW.

I. Where a Woman Commits Adultery with, or without, the Connivance of her Husband.

If any one should have intercourse with the wife of another by force, and the party who committed the crime should have legitimate children by a former marriage; he himself, without his property, shall be delivered up to the husband of the woman. But if he should have no legitimate children to whom his property can legally descend, he shall be surrendered, with all his possessions, into the power of the husband, to be disposed of at his pleasure. And if the woman should have consented to the act, both of them shall be delivered up to the husband.

ANCIENT LAW.

II. Where a Girl or a Woman who has been Betrothed is found Guilty of Adultery.

If a marriage contract has been entered into between an intended husband and the parents of an intended wife; or with the woman herself, if she has the right to make the contract; the dowry being duly given, and an agreement made in writing, before witnesses, according to custom, and as is prescribed by law; and, afterwards the girl or the woman is convicted of having committed adultery, or of having betrothed herself to another man, or of having married; she, along with her unlawful husband, or adulterer, or betrothed to whom she has given herself contrary to her solemn agreement, shall be delivered up as slaves, with all their property, to the person to whom she was first betrothed; in case the adulterer, or violator of the law, should have no children by a former marriage, or the woman herself should not have any.

But if it should be proved that they have legitimate children, then all their possessions shall belong to those children. But the man and the woman who have committed adultery, or have betrothed themselves, or have married, shall both be delivered up as slaves into the power of him to whom the aforesaid woman bound herself by her marriage contract.

ANCIENT LAW.

III. Concerning the Adultery of a Wife.

If the wife of any one should commit adultery, and not be caught in the act, her husband may accuse her before a judge by the introduction of competent evidence. And if the adultery of the woman should be plainly manifest, both adulterer and adulteress, according to the provisions of a former law, shall be given up to the husband, to be disposed of in any way he may select.

ANCIENT LAW.

IV. Where an Adulterer, along with an Adulteress, is Killed.

If the husband, or the man who was betrothed to the woman, should kill the adulterer along with the adulteress, it shall not be considered criminal homicide.

FLAVIUS RECESVINTUS, KING.

V. Where her Father, or her Relatives, Kill a Girl who has been Guilty of Adultery in their House.

If a father should kill his daughter, while she is in the act of committing adultery in his own house, he shall be liable to no penalty or reproach. But if he should wish to spare her life, he shall have full power to dispose of her and the adulterer, according to his will. Likewise, her brothers or her uncles, after the death of her father, shall have the same power.

ANCIENT LAW.

VI. It is not Lawful for Slaves to put Persons to Death who are taken in Adultery.

While parents have the undoubted right to kill adulterers caught in their houses, slaves have no such authority. But if slaves should discover them, they may keep them in honorable custody, until they can be delivered over to the master of the house, or to the judge; and, after having been found guilty by reliable evidence, the legal penalty shall be inflicted upon them.

ANCIENT LAW.

VII. Where a Girl, or a Widow, goes to the House of Another, in order to commit Adultery, and the Man should wish to Marry Her.

If a freeborn girl, or a widow, should go to the house of another for the purpose of committing adultery, and the man who is implicated should wish to marry her, and her parents, if she has any, should acquiesce; he shall give to the parents of the girl as large a sum as they may demand, or as much as shall be agreed upon between him and the woman herself. But the woman shall not share with her brothers in the inheritance of her parents, unless the latter desire it.

ANCIENT LAW.

VIII. Where a Freeborn Woman commits Adultery with Any One.

If any freeborn woman should be detected in having voluntarily committed adultery with any man, and if, afterwards, he should wish to marry her, he shall be permitted to do so. But if he should be unwilling, she shall be considered guilty of having voluntarily committed a crime.

ANCIENT LAW.

IX. Where a Freeborn Woman commits Adultery with the Husband of Another.

If any freeborn woman should commit adultery with the husband of another, and should be convicted of it by conclusive evidence, she shall be surrendered to the wife of the husband with whom she was guilty, that the revenge of the woman injured may be fully satisfied.[1]

ANCIENT LAW.

X. Slaves of Both Sexes may be Tortured to reveal the Adultery of their Masters.

In order to prove the commission of adultery by either a master or a mistress, their slaves of both sexes may be put to the torture, in order that the truth may be the more certainly discovered and established, beyond question.

---

[1] No one can doubt that, under such conditions, it was "fully satisfied." This is another instance where the punishment of a personal injury was regarded, not as an offence against the community, and a breach of good morals, but as a case demanding private retribution, as is specifically stated in the law itself.

The distinctions between the crimes of rape, adultery and fornication, as now established, are not clearly set forth in the Visigothic Code. Intercourse with a widow is designated adultery. The rape of a woman of any condition, is frequently called adultery with violence. The excessively harsh penalties prescribed for such offences, and which, as a rule, were only limited by the caprice or compassion of the party injured, are a relic of the customs of the Northern barbarians, with whom female chastity was as much the rule as, on the other hand, it was the exception among the warmer-blooded nations of Southern Europe. Most of the laws relating to crimes against women are termed "ancient," showing their derivation from a remote antiquity, or Roman origin.—[ED.

ANCIENT LAW.

XI. Whether it shall be Lawful to set a Slave at Liberty, in order to Conceal the Crime of Adultery.

If any one, for the sake of concealing the truth, and for fear a slave may be tortured in order to prove an act of adultery, should liberate that slave, his act shall be void.

XII. Concerning the Property of Husbands or Wives who have committed Adultery.

We have already decreed, by a former law, that an adulterous wife, as well as the adulterer, shall be delivered up to her husband. And, because doubt concerning the disposition of their property may sometimes arise in the minds of the judges, therefore we consider it necessary to especially provide, that if the adultery of the wife should be manifest upon evidence introduced by her husband, and if neither adulteress nor adulterer should have legitimate children by a former marriage, the entire inheritance of both of them, along with their persons, shall be delivered up into the power of the husband of the woman. But if the adulterer should have legitimate children by a former marriage, his property shall belong entirely to them, and only his person shall be surrendered to the husband of the adulteress. But if the adulterous wife should be known to have legitimate children, either by a former, or later marriage, the portion belonging to the children of the former marriage shall be set apart and delivered to them; but the husband shall have the portion which would otherwise belong to her children born after she had been convicted of adultery, and he may bequeath it, after his death, to those children. And, after the adulterous wife has been brought back into the power of her husband it shall not be lawful for any marital relations to exist between them. If, in violation of this, such relations should thereafter exist, he himself shall have none of her property, and all of it shall be given to her legitimate children; or, if there are no children, to her other heirs. A similar decree is hereby made concerning persons who have been betrothed.

FLAVIUS CHINTASVINTUS, KING.

XIII. Concerning those Persons who have a Right to bring Accusations of Adultery, and what Proof of the Crime should be Made.

If the law does not punish the perpetrators of crime, their audacity will have no bounds. For this reason, and because certain wives who hate their husbands abandon themselves to adultery, and so affect the minds of their husbands, either by the administration of drugs, or by the devices of witchcraft, that they are unable to publicly accuse their wives or to leave them, on account of the affection they bear them; therefore, in such cases it is hereby decreed, that if the adulteress or her husband have any legitimate sons who are of age, it shall be lawful for them to act in the place of the husband, and to prove the fact of adultery in court. But if there are no sons, or they have not the proper age or experience to conduct this matter lawfully; in order that there may be no delay in the punishment of adultery; or for fear that the adulteress may kill her husband; or her children or relatives may, for this reason, be deprived of her property; it is hereby decreed that the relations of the husband, shall have the power, under such circumstances, of accusing the said adulteress. And if, after accepting this trust, the adultery of the woman should be plainly proved in court, then both parties who have been convicted of this crime shall be at once given up, with all their property, to serve as slaves those who, according to the provisions of the law, have proved this accusation.

We make, however, an exception in favor of such as have manifested signs of repentance, and seem to be worthy of pity; and we hereby decree that they shall receive the punishment of the scourge. And if the sons of the adulteress were not of sufficient age, at the time the crime was committed, to appear in court, the relatives of the husband, after the death of the latter, if there are no sons, shall be entitled to the property of the woman. If the sons should be unwilling, or not of a sufficient age or experience to prosecute the adulteress; then the nearest relative of the husband, who produced evidence of the crime, shall have the fifth part of the property of the adulteress for his pains, and the other four-fifths shall belong to the sons aforesaid. If there should be any lukewarmness on the part of the relatives, or negligence on the part of the sons, or if the parties should be corrupted by gifts; the conduct of such matters shall not be committed to persons of this character; and should the cause come to the knowledge of the king, he shall determine, according to his mercy, either by whom the case must be prosecuted, or how much of the property of the woman the prosecutor shall have as a fee for his trouble. But because it is difficult to prove the adultery of a woman by the evidence of persons who are free, as generally this crime is perpetrated in secret; henceforth, whenever the evidence of a freeborn person is not available to prove adultery, it shall be lawful for the person aforesaid, to whom it is granted by the present law to bring an accusation of this kind, to put the slaves of both parties to the torture, that the crime may be proved in court.

ANCIENT LAW.

XIV. Where a Freedman, or a Slave, has been Convicted of having committed Adultery, with Violence, upon a Freeborn Virgin, or Widow.

If any one should compel a virgin or widow, who is freeborn, to commit adultery or fornication; if he should be freeborn, he shall be scourged with a hundred lashes, and be given forever to serve as a slave her whom he has injured. A slave convicted of such a crime shall be burned. And a freeman who has been proved to be guilty of a crime of this kind, shall never be permitted to marry her whom he has violated. But if the woman herself, after she has received the man as a slave, should marry him, she shall then undergo the penalty of her base action, and shall, along with all her property, be delivered over to her own heirs, to forever serve as a slave.

ANCIENT LAW.

XV. Where a Freeman, or a Slave without the Knowledge of his Master, commits Adultery with the Female Slave of Another.

If any one should be convicted of having committed adultery with a female slave outside the house of her master, the latter shall have the power of punishing only the female slave. Where either a freeman or a slave is convicted of the commission of such a crime with a female slave in the house of her master; if he should be freeborn, and the slave of good reputation and superior rank, he shall receive a hundred lashes, without any imputation of infamy. If the slave is of inferior rank, she shall receive fifty lashes; and a male slave, guilty of such an offence with the female slave of another, shall receive a hundred and fifty lashes.

ANCIENT LAW.

XVI. Where a Female Slave is proved to have committed Adultery with Another by Force.

If any one should violate the person of a female slave, and should be seized in the house of her master; or if he should be convicted of having committed the crime anywhere else; if a slave, he shall receive two hundred lashes; if a freeman, fifty; and the latter shall be compelled to pay, in addition, thirty *solidi* to the master of the female slave. But if the master should have ordered the slave to commit the act, the latter shall undergo the penalty and scourging prescribed by a former law.

ANCIENT LAW.

XVII. Concerning Freeborn Women, or Female Slaves, of Bad Character; and Where Judges Refuse to Investigate or Punish their Crimes.

If any freeborn girl or woman should publicly practise fornication, be known as a harlot, and be shamelessly given to soliciting men; after having been arrested by the governor of the city, she shall receive in public two hundred lashes, and shall be sent away, under the condition that she shall not, afterwards, be guilty of similar conduct, or ever again enter the city. And if she should ever return, she shall be sentenced by the governor to receive three hundred lashes more, and shall be given as a slave to some pauper, and never be permitted to go freely about the city again. And if she should admit that she has pursued her evil life with the knowledge of her father and mother, and thus should seem to have acquired her degradation through association with her parents, and her father and mother should be convicted of having had such guilty knowledge; each of them shall receive a hundred lashes.

If a female slave should be convicted of leading such a life, she shall be arrested by order of the judge; shall receive three hundred lashes in public; and, having had her head shaved, shall be returned to her master, with the understanding that he will cause her to be removed to such a distance from the city, or will sell her in such a locality, that she shall be unable to return. But if he should be unwilling to send her away, or to sell her, and she should return, he shall receive fifty lashes in public; and the said female slave shall be given to some pauper whom the king, judge, or governor may select, with the admonition that she be not again permitted to enter the city. If she should declare that she had acted with the consent of her master, gaining money for him through her vicious practices, and he should be publicly convicted of this, he shall receive the same number of lashes as she would otherwise have received.

And, in like manner, we decree that all others should be dealt with, who either in villages or towns, have been arrested for similar crimes. If any judge should be unwilling to investigate such offences, or prosecute, or correct them, he shall receive a hundred lashes by order of the governor of the city, and shall pay thirty *solidi* to him whom the king shall designate.

FLAVIUS RECESVINTUS, KING.

XVIII. Concerning the Impurity of Priests and other Ministers of Religion.

As sacred authority demands purity of life, so it should also be required of its ministers; and it is our duty to put an end to all unlawful conduct, and attempt to act in compliance with the Divine commandments. Therefore, if it should be established by undoubted evidence, that any priest, deacon, or sub-deacon, has married or committed fornication or adultery with a widow doing penance, a virgin, a wife, or any other woman; as soon as the fact shall come to the knowledge of the bishop, or the judge, he shall put an end to such a connection at once.

When the offender has been brought back under the power of his ecclesiastical superior, he shall be placed in confinement, and compelled to do penance according to the holy canons of the Church; and if the bishop, through indulgence, should neglect to place him under restraint as aforesaid, he shall pay two pounds of gold to the royal treasury, and shall no longer be permitted to delay the punishment of the offender. Where the bishop is unwilling to act, he shall either call a council, or bring the matter to the attention of the king.

Such women as are implicated in the aforesaid enormities, shall be given a hundred lashes by order of the judge; and all access to them shall be prohibited; and the law, as established by the canons of the Church concerning this offence, shall be enforced by the bishops. In avenging such crimes, we do not grant the right to accuse or punish to every one indiscriminately, unless the proof should be overwhelming, or the guilt of the parties fully established; as we disclaim all intention of opposing the precepts of the Holy Fathers, or of violating, in any way, their ancient and sacred privileges.[1]

---

[1] The extraordinary leniency shown by this law to ecclesiastical culprits, as compared with laymen guilty of the same offence, openly displays the bias of the legislative power. There was one rule for the priest, and another, and a very different one, for his parishioners. It will be noted, also, that no provision is made for the punishment of the higher clergy; while it was notorious that the bishops and metropolitans were the greatest of all offenders, where women were concerned. As they framed the laws which governed the people, and were presumed to receive their inspiration from heaven, they naturally came to regard themselves as above their own decrees, and not liable to their penalties and restrictions. The dissolute character of the priesthood in those times, and long subsequently, is well known to every student of history. The indulgence with which the bishop was accustomed to regard the failings of his subordinates is disclosed by the fine imposed upon him for neglect to discipline the former. No mercy is shown to the women involved, and, what is unusual, no distinction is made where the latter belong to different castes, or stations in society. It is probable that this law, so far as the punishment of the clergy was concerned, "was more honor'd in the breach than the observance."—[ED.

TITLE V. CONCERNING INCEST, APOSTASY AND PEDERASTY.

I. *Concerning Incestuous and Adulterous Marriages in General.*

II. *Concerning Incestuous and Adulterous Marriages and Debauchery, either with Holy Virgins, or with Widows and other Women while doing Penance.*

III. *Concerning Men and Women who Illegally Assume the Tonsure and Dress of Religious Orders.*

IV. *Concerning the Restraint of Fraud Peculiar to Widows.*

V. *Concerning Pederasty*

VI. *Concerning Sodomy, and the Manner in which the Law should be Enforced.*

VII. *Concerning Adultery committed with the Concubine of a Father, or a Brother.*

FLAVIUS CHINTASVINTUS, KING.

I. Concerning Incestuous and Adulterous Marriages in General.

No one shall marry, or maintain incestuous relations with, any woman belonging to the family of his father, or his mother; or of his grandfather, or his grandmother; or with the betrothed of his brother, or the widow of any of his relatives. Therefore, it shall not be lawful to defile the blood of such as are related even to the sixth degree, either by marriage or otherwise; those persons only being excepted, who have been married with the permission of the king, before the making of this law, and the said persons shall, in no way, be affected by its provisions. This law shall also apply to women. If any person should violate it, the judge shall immediately order them to be separated, and shall cause them to be placed in monasteries, according to their sex, there to perform perpetual penance. The disposition of the property of these offenders has been provided for by another law

FLAVIUS RECESVINTUS, KING.

II. Concerning Incestuous and Adulterous Marriages and Debauchery, either with Holy Virgins, or with Widows and other Women while doing Penance.

It is our royal duty to promulgate laws to be enforced throughout all the provinces of our kingdom, to the end that crime may be prevented in the future, and that justice may put an end to the deeds of the wicked. Many persons, in defiance of the admonitions of the Divine Law, and in opposition to the honorable duties of life, are accustomed, either by violence, or with consent, to contract marriage with virgins who have been devoted in the service of God, and have taken the vow of chastity with the benediction of the priest, and according to the canons of the Church; or with other women nearly related to themselves; and, in this way, have polluted with vice that chastity which was dedicated to God, or which should have been respected on account of the ties of consanguinity. Such conduct, whether it relates to men or women, is both abhorrent to good morals, and a reproach to the True Faith. Therefore, in the name of God and the Holy Catholic Church, we decree that, hereafter, as is also provided by the ecclesiastical canons, no one, either by force or consent, shall take as a wife, any virgin devoted to God, or any widow who has assumed the habit of any order; or any one who is performing penance; or any near relative of their own; or any one with whom his connection might be branded with infamy; because that cannot be a true marriage, which from good becomes evil, and which, under a false name, is nothing more than incest and fornication. And if any other persons in our kingdom should attempt to commit a crime of this kind, they shall be separated, and condemned to perpetual exile, at the instance of the judge or priest, even if no one should accuse them; nor shall any time which may have elapsed, be pleaded in their defence.

The property of such persons which has been seized for the crime, shall belong to the children of a former marriage; and if there should be no such children, to those born of this marriage; and the latter shall not be liable to reproach on this account, for those who are born out of wedlock are purified by the ceremony of baptism. But if there should be no children whatever, the inheritance shall descend to those to whom the provisions of former laws have given legitimate succession. The same regulation shall apply to persons in orders, whom the Canon Law forbids to marry.

Those women are excepted from this decree who have been forced into marriage, and have not subsequently given their consent thereto. Any judge, or priest, who is aware that such an offence has been committed, and neglects to punish it, shall be compelled to pay five pounds of gold to the royal treasury; and, in case he should not be able or willing to inflict such punishment, he shall bring the matter before the king, in order that he may impose the penalty which is not in the power of the magistrate or priest to inflict.

FLAVIUS CHINTASVINTUS, KING.

III. Concerning Men and Women who Illegally Assume the Tonsure and Dress of Religious Orders.

We should eradicate the reproach of apostasy, in order that we may enjoy the favor of God. For if we think it is an evidence of piety to punish sins of less importance, to a much greater extent should we visit with severe censure any crime committed against the Divine Power. Therefore, we decree by this law, which shall remain perpetually in force hereafter; that whoever adopts the dress of a religious order, and assumes the honorable mark of the tonsure, either for the purpose of performing penance, or through the pious wishes of parents, and without any suspicion of fraud; or through their own will and devotion to the Church; and afterwards, apostatizing, resumes intercourse with the laity; shall, at the instance of any one, be brought again by force under the control of the religious order to which they belong; and, branded with infamy, shall be forever confined in monasteries, and subjected to the severest penance. In cases of this kind, indulgence shall only be shown to those who have been influenced by the deceit of others, or such as have returned to the order of their own accord; provided that among such persons a man has not taken another wife, or a woman another husband. And those also shall be exempt from the operation of this law, who assumed their vows when they neither knew what they were doing, nor remembered what they had done. The property of persons practising such deception shall belong to their sons and their relatives, as follows: if the man is married and has children, and should have received any gift from his wife, it shall be transferred to her, and, after her death, shall descend to their children. But if she should be dead, or they should have no children, the lawful heirs of the offender shall have the property. But whatever, at any time, the husband received through his wife, shall belong to her nearest heirs.

This law shall also apply to women; for instance, where any virgin or widow, as a penitent lays aside the clothing of the laity, and afterwards resumes it; or marries; she shall undergo the same penalty and loss of property as has been decreed concerning men, to wit: the children and heirs of such a woman shall have her property. The relatives of a husband, however, shall be entitled to any gift previously presented by him to his wife. And, since women are more frequently involved in the fraud of apostasy, we hereby decree that whatever should be given by a man to his betrothed, or to his wife, before or after the nuptials, by way of dowry, shall belong, not to the heirs of the wife, but to the heirs of him who gave the dowry. Persons guilty of such offences shall not have the right to accuse any one, or to testify, or to transact any business whatever in court; because those cannot be trusted in secular matters, who have been proved guilty of sacrilege in affairs relating to our Holy Religion.

FLAVIUS EGICA, KING.

IV. Concerning the Restraint of Fraud Peculiar to Widows.

Certain widows are accustomed to shrewdly mingle fraud with devotion, and, by the union of religious and secular garments, give themselves an opportunity for transgression at their will. Thus, during the time of their mourning, they put on a religious dress; and, afterwards, for purposes of deception, put on other garments under the religious habit; and for this reason, to those who see them, appear other than what they are. Wherefore, that an end may be put to fraud of this kind, we decree, by this law, that hereafter, when any widow wishes to excuse herself for practising this deception, that within she wears one kind of dress, and outside another; that portion which is visible, and which she has assumed for purposes of duplicity, shall be considered as designating her as a member of a religious order; and thus, not what she has adopted for the commission of sin, but what the eyes of every one perceive, is to be accepted as the sign of her religious profession. Any widow who, hereafter, attempts to excuse herself in this way, shall not only be subject to the penalties of the law, but shall also undergo the punishment prescribed by the canons of the Church, and shall not escape the justice of the king.

FLAVIUS CHINTASVINTUS, KING.

V. Concerning Pederasty.

That crime must not be unpunished which, in the violation of morality, has always been considered most execrable; we therefore decree, in cases of pederasty, where their guilt has been proved after proper investigation by the judge, that both parties shall be emasculated without delay, and be delivered up to the bishop of the diocese where the deed was committed, to be placed in solitary confinement in a prison; so that, against their will, they may expiate the crime which they are convicted of having voluntarily perpetrated.

If, however, any one should have been forced to commit this horrible offence, and is proved to have done so unwillingly, he shall then not be liable to punishment, if the person who discovered the crime should be present as a witness; but he who engaged in it voluntarily shall undergo the full penalty. The children, or legitimate heirs of married men who have been found guilty of this crime, shall have their property; and it shall be lawful for their wives, having received back their dowries, and retaining all their possessions, to afterwards marry whomsoever they will.

FLAVIUS EGICA, KING.

VI. Concerning Sodomy, and the Manner in which the Law should be Enforced.

The doctrine of the orthodox faith requires us to place our censure upon vicious practices, and to restrain those who are addicted to carnal offences. For we counsel well for the benefit of our people and our country, when we take measures to utterly extirpate the crimes of wicked men, and put an end to the evil deeds of vice. For this reason we shall attempt to abolish the horrible crime of sodomy, which is as contrary to Divine precept as it is to chastity. And although the authority of the Holy Scriptures, and the censure of earthly laws, alike, prohibit offences of this kind, it is nevertheless necessary to condemn them by a new decree; lest if timely correction be deferred, still greater vices may arise. Therefore, we establish by this law, that if any man whosoever, of any age, or race, whether he belongs to the clergy, or to the laity, should be convicted, by competent evidence, of the commission of the crime of sodomy, he shall, by order of the king, or of any judge, not only suffer emasculation, but also the penalty prescribed by ecclesiastical decree for such offences, and promulgated in the third year of our reign.

FLAVIUS CHINTASVINTUS, KING.

VII. Concerning Adultery committed with the Concubine of a Father, or a Brother.

It was decreed by a former law, what should be done in cases where incest was committed by persons related by blood. And because it is not of less importance that the bed of the father or brother be not polluted, we command, in addition, that no blood relative of theirs shall ever commit adultery with either the concubine of his father or his brother, nor with any one whom he knew his father or his brother had ever sustained intimate relations with, whether she be a free-woman or a slave; nor shall the father commit such adultery with the concubine of his son. And if any one should knowingly commit such an offence, his heirs, should he have no legitimate children, shall obtain his property; and he himself shall be subjected to penance, and shall undergo the punishment of perpetual exile.

TITLE VI. — CONCERNING DIVORCE, AND THE SEPARATION OF PERSONS WHO HAVE BEEN BETROTHED.

I. *Where a Woman, justly or unjustly, is Separated from her Husband.*

II. *There shall be No Divorce between Married Persons.*

III. *There shall be No Separation between Persons who are Betrothed.*

I. Where a Woman, justly or unjustly, is Separated from her Husband.

No one can legally marry a freewoman who has been repudiated by her husband, unless he knows that they have been divorced, either by written evidence, or in the presence of witnesses. And if any one should act otherwise, as soon as the governor of the city, or his deputy, or the judge of the district, shall become aware of the fact, where the parties are noble, and the judge is unable to imprison or separate them; he must straightway bring the affair to our attention, that they may receive the punishment which they deserve. But if they are persons of inferior rank, the judge shall immediately cause them to be separated. And the woman who, without the consent of her former husband, has married again, as well as the man who ventured to take her as a wife, shall be delivered up absolutely to her former husband, to be dealt with according to his pleasure. If, however, the case between the former husband and his wife has not yet been decided; or if her former husband has married another woman; or, indeed, if he has left his wife unjustly; he shall lose the dowry which he gave her, and it shall absolutely belong to her, nor shall he be entitled to receive any of her property. If he should have sold, or fraudulently disposed of, any of the property of his wife, the judge shall compel him to make restitution. Where the woman, through fear of her husband, or deceived by any of his representations, should have made any written agreement concerning her property for his benefit, her agreement shall be null and void, and all the property which it disposed of shall be restored to her.

FLAVIUS CHINTASVINTUS, KING.

II. There shall be No Divorce between Married Persons.

If the violation of the wife of another is a crime, how much more is she to be condemned who voluntarily commits this sin. For the reason that there are many reckless men who, either through ambition or desire, or induced by some fraud, and despising their own wives, seek those of others, we therefore decree by this law, which is to be perpetually observed; that no man, except for the manifest cause of fornication, shall at any time, leave his wife, nor shall he divorce himself from her, either in the presence of a witness, or by any instrument in writing, or under any pretext whatever. Where her husband is able to prove her guilty of adultery, the crime having been established by sufficient evidence, she shall be given up to him by the judge to be disposed of as he pleases; in accordance with the provisions of a former law. If, however, she should manifest a desire to enter a religious order, the priest shall ascertain the wishes of both of them, so that, afterwards, neither will be able to offer any excuse for their conduct, in case either should marry again. But if, under any other circumstances, a man, rejecting his wife, should fraudulently obtain from her a document in writing, relating to a separation, such document shall have no validity whatever, and the wife shall be entitled to recover the sum she received as a dowry; and if the unprincipled husband should have any property, it shall be given to their children. But if there should be no children by this marriage, or by a former one of the husband, the wife shall receive his entire property, in addition to her dowry, as aforesaid; and if she should be dead, her sons shall have the right to bring the matter before the court; so that, the crime being proved, the man may undergo the sentence of the law. All the children either by this marriage or by a preceding one of the husband, shall, as we have said, share equally in the property. But if the parties should have no children; and there should be none living of the first marriage of the husband; and it should appear that the woman has children by a previous marriage of her own; it shall be lawful for the latter to share in their mother's rights in this property; and, on their application, under the present law, they may obtain the entire possessions of the man who has been condemned. Where there are no children of the aforesaid persons, husband and wife, her nearest relatives shall be entitled to the inheritance of her property, providing they should have instituted proceedings leading to the conviction of the husband. Where a husband, for the sake of divorce, or for security to himself, extorts any instrument in writing from his wife, or, without doing this, having abandoned his wife, should marry another; he shall receive two hundred lashes in public, and shall be scalped, as a mark of degradation; or he may be condemned to perpetual exile, or be given as a slave to any one whom the king may select. Any woman who, knowing at the time, or having discovered subsequently, that her husband has another wife living, shall make no objection to this; shall, at once, be given up to the former wife of her husband; so that, with the exception of depriving her of life, she may have the privilege of disposing of her as she pleases. And if, even after the death of the first wife, this crime should be proved by her children, or, if there should be no children, by such heirs as have the right to prosecute; the guilty woman shall be given into their power, to be disposed of in the same manner as the injured wife would have had a right to dispose of her, the infliction of death alone being excepted. And, for the reason that women are accustomed very frequently to cause scandal by leaving their own husbands, on account of their attachment to kings and judges; therefore, we decree that if any woman either by the aid of the king, or through inducements held out to her by any one else, should separate from her husband, or consent to marry another man; she shall be surrendered, with all her property, into the hands of her lawful husband, and shall be liable to the same penalty imposed upon the husband under similar circumstances, as hereinbefore stated, and her property shall be disposed of in a similar manner.

Likewise, this same rule shall apply to men, where one shall presume to marry the wife or the betrothed of another; the following cases being excepted: where the husband of the woman should have been found guilty of pederasty; or should have surrendered his wife to another man against her will; or should have permitted this to be done; and, for the reason that such villiany ought always to be condemned by Christians, that man shall never be permitted to marry another woman, if he should desire to do so. Where the spurious marriage has actually taken place, the husband must be delivered up as a slave to some one, according to due process of law; and if the woman should be unwilling to longer live with her legal husband, she must afterwards live a chaste life; nor shall she be permitted to marry again until her aforesaid husband is dead.

FLAVIUS RECESVINTUS, KING.

III. There shall be No Separation between Persons who are Betrothed.

We have elsewhere prescribed the same punishment for transgressions committed by persons of equal rank. Therefore, the provisions of a former law relating to the persons as well as property, of men and women who have been betrothed, shall be, and is, hereby confirmed; and if any person after the dowry has been given, or the marriage contract has been legally drawn up, in violation of his, or her, solemn obligations, should marry any one else, without the consent of all parties; he, or she, shall be liable to all the penalties of a former law; and if it should appear that on account of sickness, rather than through fraud, such person is desirous of entering some religious order, he or she shall be permitted to do so, subject to the regulations of the above-mentioned former law.

BOOK IV.

CONCERNING NATURAL LINEAGE.

TITLE I. CONCERNING THE DEGREES OF RELATIONSHIP.

I. The Nature of the First Degree.

In the first rank of the first degree are included the father and the mother; in the second rank, the son and the daughter; but no other persons.

II. The Affinity of the Second Degree.

In the second degree and the first rank, are included the grandfather and the grandmother; in the second, the grandson and the granddaughter; in the collateral line, the brother and the sister, which persons have a twofold origin, for the father and the mother are derived from both the grandfather and grandmother; the grandson and granddaughter, from both son and daughter; the brother and sister, from both father and mother. And likewise, the persons in the following degrees, in whatever relationship they stand to each other, are, in the same manner, of twofold origin. Persons in the second degree are thus said to be of double derivation, because there are two grandparents, paternal and maternal; and two kinds of grandchildren, descended either from the son or from the daughter. The brother of the father, or the brother of the mother, who are called respectively the paternal or maternal uncles, belong to the collateral line, and they, in like manner, are of double origin.

ANCIENT LAW.

III. The Relationship of the Third Degree.

The third degree includes, first the great-grandfather and the great-grandmother; second, the great-grandson and the great-granddaughter; in the collateral line, the son and the daughter of the brother and the sister; the paternal uncle and the paternal aunt, that is to say, the brother and the sister of the father; and the maternal uncle and the maternal aunt, that is to say, the brother and sister of the mother.

ANCIENT LAW.

IV. The Consanguinity of the Fourth Degree.

In the fourth degree come first the great-great-grandfather and the great-great-grandmother, and then the son and daughter of a great-grandchild; in the collateral line, the grandson and granddaughter of the brother and the sister; then the cousins of both sexes, the sons and daughters of the paternal uncle, and the children of the maternal uncle and aunt; then other cousins, the children of the father's sister; and also cousins who are born of two sisters; and besides, the great-uncle and the great-aunt by the father's side; then the great-uncle and great-aunt by the mother's side. There is no necessity of explaining this any further than is here stated.

ANCIENT LAW.

V. The Origin of the Fifth Degree.

The fifth degree includes, in the first place, the great-great-great-grandfather and the great-great-great-grandmother; secondly, the great-great-great-grandson and the great-great-great-granddaughter, and, in the collateral line, the great-grandsons and great-granddaughters of brothers and sisters; male and female cousins by the father's side, the sons and daughters of cousins by the father's side, and the children of great-uncles and aunts on both father's and mother's side. Next come the brothers and sisters of the paternal great-grandfather and the brothers and sisters of the maternal great-grandfather. The above-mentioned degrees of relationship we cannot define by other means, or in other words, than those in which they are here set forth.

ANCIENT LAW.

VI. The Limits of the Sixth Degree.

To the sixth degree belong, first, the great-great-great-great-grandfather and the great-great-great-great-grandmother; then the great-great-great-great-grandson and the great-great-great-great-granddaughter; next, in the collateral line, the son and the daughter of a great-grandchild of the sister; the sons of a father's brother and the sons of a father's sister; cousins on both sides of the house; paternal and maternal great-aunts, and the grandsons and granddaughters of paternal great-uncles and maternal great-aunts. To whom are added, in the collateral line, the children of the great-uncles and the great-aunts of both father and mother; that is to say, of the brother and the sister of the paternal great-great-grandfather, and of the brother and sister of the maternal great-great-grandmother. No better explanation of this matter can be given than we have written above.

VII. The Persons in the Seventh Degree who are not Mentioned by the Laws.

In the seventh degree those who are related in the direct line are not specifically designated by name; but the collateral line embraces the sons and daughters of great-grandchildren of brothers or sisters, and the sons and daughters of their cousins of both sexes. There exist, then, seven degrees of relationship, and no more, because, according to the nature of things, names could not be found for others, nor more heirs be begotten in the space of an ordinary lifetime.

TITLE II. CONCERNING THE LAWS OF INHERITANCE.

I. Brothers and Sisters shall Share Equally in the Inheritance of their Parents.

If the father or mother should die intestate, the sisters shall have the property equally with their brothers.

II. The Children shall Come First in the Order of Succession.

If a man should die intestate, his children shall stand first in the order of succession; if there are no children, the inheritance shall descend to the grandchildren; if there are no grandchildren, then the great-grandchildren shall have a right to it; and if the decedent should leave neither children nor grandchildren, nor father nor mother, then his grandfather or grandmother, should either be living, may claim the inheritance of his estate.

ANCIENT LAW.

III. Where there are no Heirs in the Direct Line, Collateral Heirs shall Inherit the Property.

When any of the above-named persons of the first or second degree, in the direct line of succession, are not living, then collateral heirs shall be sought for to inherit the property of the man who died intestate. And such persons as are only distantly related can claim nothing while nearer heirs are still living.

IV. Who shall Succeed to the Property of Those who have left no Written Wills, or have made no Disposition of their Possessions in the Presence of Witnesses.

In the case of those who die, and make no disposition of their property either by gift or by will, or do not declare their intentions in the presence of witnesses; their next of kin shall inherit from them.

V. Concerning Inheritance by Brothers and Sisters, and by such of these as are not descended from the same Parents.

Where a man leaves only brothers and sisters, they shall inherit his property, share and share alike, provided they are all children of the same father and mother. But if some should be descended from a different father or mother from the others, the inheritance shall go to the brothers and sisters having the same father and mother as the decedent. Such children as are born of different parents, but of the same mother, shall inherit the property of the mother, share and share alike. Those also who are descended from different mothers, but the same father, shall share in a like manner.

VI. Where he who Dies leaves Grandfathers or Grandmothers.

If any one should leave a paternal grandfather and grandmother, his entire property shall descend to them. So also if he should leave a paternal grandfather and maternal grandmother, they shall inherit his estate equally; and the same disposition of it shall be made, if he should leave both a paternal and a maternal grandmother. This equitable division of his estate shall apply only to such portions of it as he has acquired by his own efforts; and whatever he may have inherited from his ancestors, or his parents, shall descend to the heirs of the latter in the direct line of succession.

VII. Where he who Dies leaves Aunts.

Where the decedent dies intestate, and leaves only a paternal uncle and aunt, and a maternal uncle and aunt, they shall inherit the property in equal parts.

ANCIENT LAW.

VIII. Where he who Dies leaves Nephews.

Where the decedent does not leave any brothers or sisters, but does leave nephews and nieces; if one of them should be the son of one brother, and the others the children of another brother or sister, the inheritance shall be divided among them, share and share alike.

IX. A Woman shall be entitled to a Share in an Entire Inheritance.

A woman shall inherit, equally with her brothers, the property of their father or mother; of their grandparents, on the paternal and the maternal side, as well as of their brothers and sisters; and also any property which may be left by a paternal uncle, or a cousin, or a nephew, or a niece. For it is only just that those who are nearly related by blood, should enjoy the benefit of hereditary succession.

X. As a Woman has a Right to a Share of an Entire Inheritance, so he who is next in Succession shall Inherit the Remainder of the Property.

Women shall share all property left by relatives on the maternal side, with those in the same degree of relationship, whether they be uncles, aunts, or cousins. For those should have the inheritance who are the most nearly related to the deceased.

ANCIENT LAW.

XI. Concerning the Inheritance of Husband and Wife, respectively.

Husband and wife shall inherit from each other, respectively, when they leave no relatives nearer than the seventh degree.

XII. Concerning the Inheritance of Property from Clerks and Monks.

The church to which they are attached shall inherit the property of all clerks, monks, and other persons in orders, who have left no heirs under the seventh degree, and who have made no disposition of their estate.

XIII. After the Death of their Mother, Children shall remain under the Control of their Father; and What Disposition he shall make of their Property.

If the mother should die, the children shall remain under the control of the father. And, if she should die while her husband is still living and he should not marry again, he shall have charge of the children born of the marriage, and may retain possession of their property, with the understanding that he is not to sell, damage, or dispose of it in any way, but shall preserve it intact for the benefit of his children. But, in common with his children, he shall enjoy the income from said property, and shall be entitled to reserve from it all their necessary expenses. If, however, the father should marry again, he shall not relinquish the care of the children, because it is not just that his authority over them having been abandoned, they should be placed under the guardianship of another; but he shall still retain control over them and their property, as hereinbefore mentioned. But he must at once draw up an inventory of their property in his own hand, in the presence of a judge, or of the heirs of his deceased wife; and he must also bind himself by a written obligation, that those relatives who are legally entitled to it shall have the guardianship of the children in the case of his death; in order that none of the property of the latter may be lost, but may be protected by him, in every way, from injury or diminution in value. If the father, after having married a second time, should refuse to act as guardian of his children, then the judge shall appoint the nearest relative of the mother to take charge of them as guardian. And if either his son or daughter should marry, they shall at once receive their portion of their mother's estate; excepting the third part, which he may reserve for himself, as authorized by law.

The father, as soon as a son or daughter has reached the age of twenty years, shall give to them half of what they are entitled to from their mother's estate, provided that they should not have already married. The remaining half the father shall reserve for himself during his lifetime, and, after his death, it shall descend to his children. This same regulation shall apply also to grandchildren. When the father has alienated any of the aforesaid property, or has retained it beyond the time prescribed by law, everything belonging to his children by right of inheritance from their mother, shall be given to them, at once, by way of complete restitution.

ANCIENT LAW.

XIV. Where a Mother remains a Widow, she shall have an Equal Portion of the Inheritance with her Children; and How a Mother ought to Dispose of the Property of her Children.

A mother, during her lifetime, or so long as she remains a widow, shall share equally with her children in the income derived from the estate of her deceased husband. But she cannot give away, or sell, or bestow upon any of her children her share of the aforesaid property. And if the children should become aware that their mother, either through negligence, or through hatred of them, was about to dispose of any of said property, they may, at once, make application to the governor of the city, or to the judge, in order that the latter may warn their mother not to alienate such property, and only to use the income of it. She, however, shall have the right to give to her children any or all of said income, and she can unquestionably dispose of any profits derived from the same. And if it should be proved that she has alienated any of her portion, full restitution must be made therefor after her death.

After the death of the mother, whatever she received from her husband shall be equally distributed among the children, because they must not be defrauded of their paternal inheritance. If the mother should marry again, from that very day the children can claim as their own that portion of their father's property which their mother received at his death.[1]

---

[1] The right of dower, established by the Visigothic Code, is Roman in origin. It was derived from the bestowal of the dowry, "*res uxorica*," which was an almost indispensable part of every marriage contract, and with which it is sometimes now confounded. While, under the Roman law, the dowry was given by the intended wife or her relations to the intended bridegroom, or to some member of his family, with the Visigoths it came from the bridegroom, and represented, in fact, the purchase money paid for the bride; a survival of the ancient barbarian custom of marriage by purchase, just as the wedding-ring is symbolical of the presumed subordination of the wife to her husband, a ceremony whose purpose, as well as significance, have both long since been forgotten.

Both the rights of dower and curtesy, as defined by the legal polity of the Visigoths, it will be seen, are practically the same as they now

XV. No Wife can lay Claim to what her Husband has Gained by the Labor of her Slaves.

If the husband should acquire any property through the labor of his wife's slaves, or in any foreign enterprise, his wife shall have no right to such property, either during his lifetime, or after his death for a husband who has control of his wife, as stated in the law of the Holy Scriptures, shall also have full authority over her slaves; and everything which he has gained by the services of the latter, or by those of his own slaves, in any undertaking, shall belong to him absolutely. And if the said slaves, while they are engaged with their master in any expedition or enterprise, should commit any wrong, or do any injury, he who brought them with him shall be responsible for their conduct, and shall make restitution, should they be found guilty. It has thus very properly been determined that, as their master profits by their labors, he should also be responsible for any damage they may cause

THE GLORIOUS FLAVIUS RECESVINTUS, KING.

XVI. Concerning such Property as the Husband and Wife together have Accumulated during their Married Life.

When persons of equal rank marry one another, and, while living together, either increase or waste their property, where one is more wealthy than the other; they shall share in common the gains and losses, in proportion to the amount which each one holds. If the value of their possessions is the same, neither has a right to assume superiority over the

---

exist under the laws of England, and of those of many of the States of the Union. Considering the lapse of time, the differences of race and religion, the wide divergence of political systems, and the antagonistic character of many of the social usages observed during epochs separated by thirteen centuries, this fact is very remarkable. Whilc the wife had a right to the use of half of the deceased husband's property during her lifetime, he had a right to the use of only one third of hers, as he has today. The favor generally shown to the wife in the stipulations of the marriage contract, are largely the result of the independence enjoyed by the sex under Teutonic and Scandinavian customs.—[ED.

other. For, it is not unusual, where such property is equal in amount, for one party, in some way, to take advantage of the other. And if it should be evident that the possessions of one exceed those of the other in value, as above stated, there shall be an apportionment of it made, showing what either shall have the right to claim after the death of the other, and what either shall have a right to dispose of to his or her children, or to heirs, or in any other way that may be desired. This provision shall apply to, and be observed in, all cases relating to the estates of both husbands and wives. The distribution and possession of other property concerning which an agreement in writing has been entered into by both parties, shall be held and enjoyed by them according to the terms of that written agreement. If the husband should acquire any property, either from strangers, or during any public expedition, or by the donation of the king, or of a patron, or of any of his friends, his children or his heirs shall have a right to claim it, and shall have absolute power to dispose of it as they wish. The same rule shall apply to women who have received gifts from any source.

XVII. In what way a Child may Inherit Property.

Ambiguity frequently produces error where a reasonable explanation is not given to elucidate a fact that is doubtful. Many persons deny that a child dead in infancy can have, at any time, a right to inherit from its parents, and we desire now to put an end to such disputes. For the origin of nature is such, that he who is born uses the senses of sight and touch before anything else. Who, therefore, can inherit any earthly possessions who died almost before he was sensible to light? And in what way can he be the possessor of property for whose control he was not destined, and who has scarcely had the use of the elements of which he was formed? And he who has hardly been blessed by the light of heaven; how can the unexpected inheritance of the world enrich him when suddenly removed by death? With what reason can he claim the rights of the living, who is more nearly associated with death than with life, and who thus quickly dying in the midst of light, has fallen back into darkness? Therefore, that the inheritance of an infant may belong to its nearest relatives, and the fact that he was living be clearly proved; and as the child had a right to eternal life, so also that it may have a right to terrestrial life; we hereby decree that no child of either sex shall inherit, unless it has been proved that it lived for the space of ten days after its birth, and shall have received the holy sacrament of baptism, so that the father or mother of the child who shall be entitled to its inheritance, may, before its death, prepare it for its entrance into heaven; and that while still living, it shall obtain the possessions of the earth with their transitory benefits. And thus, while heavenly possessions are provided for it, it shall also be permitted to acquire those of the earth; and although while dead, it cannot benefit by the things of earth, it can, at least, enjoy those of heaven.

FLAVIUS CHINTASVINTUS, KING.

XVIII. How the Parents of a Child can Inherit from Him.

Where the father is dead, and the son or daughter should have lived ten days or longer, should have been baptized, and then should die; whatever either would have inherited from the estate of his or her father, may be claimed by his or her mother. And, in like manner, if the mother should die, the father shall not be entitled to the share of the deceased child, unless he be able to prove that that child has lived ten days, or longer, and has been baptized. And if neither father nor mother in whom these rights are vested, should leave any children, the entire inheritance shall be divided among the other descendants; but they shall not have the power to give to each grandchild more than the third part of the aforesaid property. And if they should wish to give any of it to the Church, or to freedmen, or to any one else, they shall have the right to dispose of only the fifth part of it in this manner, as prescribed by a former law. But where neither children nor grandchildren, nor great-grandchildren should be living, they shall have the right to make such disposition of their property as they desire.

If said parents should die intestate, then such other of their relatives as are next of kin shall be entitled to the aforesaid property. Thus, if after the death of a child, the father should inherit its estate, and should die intestate, the inheritance shall belong to those heirs who are entitled to it by law. In like manner, if the mother should inherit the estate of her deceased child, and should die intestate, all interest in that estate shall belong to her nearest heirs; on this condition, that the grandchildren of the son or daughter who died while their father and mother were living, shall inherit such a portion of the estate of their grandfather or grandmother as their own parents would have inherited had they been living. But if a son having a wife and children should die during the life of his father, before his father has given him all that he was entitled to from his estate, and his sons should also die during the life of their grandfather, the daughter-in-law shall receive only so much as the father had formerly set aside for her husband. Nor can the widow claim any more than this from her father-in-law or any of his relatives. But if the son had been living with the father, and had not yet received anything from him; the son's widow shall then only be entitled to what she obtained as a dowry at the time of her marriage. Where the son, in obedience to his father's wishes, permitted the latter to retain what he was entitled to from his mother's estate, and should bequeath it at his death to his wife, or to any one else; such bequest for the benefit of the wife or of others, if made in writing, shall be valid: provided his mother did not have other sons by the same husband. If, however, other sons should be living, the provisions of the former law must be carried out

FLAVIUS CHINTASVINTUS, KING.

XIX. Concerning Posthumous Children.

We fulfil the injunctions of the Divine Law when we provide for those who are yet unborn. Therefore, when a man cut off by death, leaves his wife pregnant, we decree that the child who is born afterwards shall share equally with those who are already born. But if he should leave no issue, and should bequeath his property to any person, the latter shall only be entitled to receive the fourth part of it. The three remaining parts shall descend, without question, to the posthumous child. Where a husband and wife before they have children, enter into a written agreement, mutually bestowing their property upon one another, and, afterwards, should have children; such a disposition of property, if their children are living, shall be void; and the children may take and hold the entire property of their parents, with the exception of the fifth part, which the parents shall have the right to dispose of otherwise. But if one of them, that is to say, either the husband or wife, before the marriage was consummated, should be proved to have made for the benefit of the other a written agreement disposing of property, it shall remain in full force; and such donation cannot, in any way, be overthrown by children subsequently born of their marriage.

THE GLORIOUS FLAVIUS CHINTASVINTUS, KING.

XX. He who leaves no Children, has full Power to Dispose of his Property as he Pleases.

Every freeborn man and woman, whether belonging to the nobility, or of inferior rank, who has no children, grandchildren, or great-grandchildren, has the unquestionable right to dispose of his or her estate at will; nor can any arrangement that either may make, be set aside by any relatives of theirs belonging either to the direct or to the collateral line. For those belonging to degrees of relationship other than the above, in the direct line, cannot, in the order of nature, receive the inheritance. Such relatives can, however, inherit from the intestate in accordance with the law which defines their rights.

TITLE III. CONCERNING WARDS AND THEIR GUARDIANS.

FLAVIUS CHINTASVINTUS, KING.

I. What a Minor Is.

It is a part of the practice of the duties prescribed by law, to so care for the rights of minors that they shall suffer no loss of their inheritance. Up to this time, little children left by a father have been called minors, for the reason that the mother has not less responsibility and care, on their account, than when both parents were living; and therefore we now decree, that henceforth any children left by father or mother, and who have not yet attained the age of fifteen years, shall be designated minors.

FLAVIUS CHINTASVINTUS, KING.

II. From what date Time is to be Computed in Bringing Lawsuits relating to Minors.

Where a question arises concerning the time within which an action at law can be maintained for the recovery of property in which minors are interested, we decree that an estimate must be made of the period which has elapsed since the parents have lost possession of said property; that is to say, it must be determined whether the entire number of years from that date, when added to those of the minor shall amount to fifty; and, if the number should be greater than that, the minor shall not be entitled to recover. And, moreover, if the parents of the minor in their lifetime, shall have neglected to assert their rights for the space of thirty years, the said minor shall not be permitted to prosecute such a claim as their representative.[1]

III. How the Guardianship of Wards shall be Entered upon; what Portion of their Property they shall Receive, and what Portion shall be Given to their Guardians.

After the death of the father, the mother shall have the guardianship of the minor children, if she should wish it, provided she remains a widow; and she shall make an inventory of the property to which the children are entitled, by means of which their rights to their inheritance may be established. But if the mother should marry again, any one of the sons who has attained his majority, that is, who has reached the age of twenty years, may assume the guardianship of his younger brothers; and shall see that their property is not alienated, or dissipated through neglect, by themselves, or by any one else. But, in case he himself should use it up, or sell it, or give it away, or permit it to be lost through his own negligence: as soon as his brothers shall have become of age, he shall be compelled to make restitution out of his own share, of whatever was wasted by him. He shall, however, be allowed the tenth part of the income for the purpose of living, to the end that he may not burden with extravagant expenses what should be reserved for the minor heirs. Where he spends his own money, or uses his own property for the necessaries and business of all, and this fact is brought to the attention of the judge, he shall be reimbursed for his expenditures out of the entire estate left by his father. If any of the brothers should not be of lawful age, or of proper character to undertake the guardianship of orphans, a paternal uncle or a cousin may assume this duty; and if neither the paternal

[1] There is some ambiguity in this and in the preceding chapter, growing out of the use of the term *pupillus* in the text; it denoting indiscriminately, minor, ward, and orphan. The provisions would apply with equal propriety to any or all of these, but it is most probable that minors alone were intended to be designated.—[ED.

uncle nor his son should be found worthy, then a guardian shall be selected by the other relatives in the presence of the judge.

Where neither the mother, nor any one else, assumes the guardianship, an inventory of all the property which the father left shall be drawn up and signed by her and by witnesses, from the number of three to five, and shall be placed in the keeping of any bishop or priest whom the relatives may select, to be delivered to the children when they have attained their majority.

It is also hereby provided that if any suits are brought against minors, their guardian, should he desire it, has a right to defend such actions. If, however, he should neglect to do so, a judgment shall be rendered by the court in favor of the plaintiff, without prejudice to the rights of the minors to have the matter reviewed, when they shall become of lawful age. If the party who made the claim should lose his case when the minor has reached his majority, he shall be compelled to restore to the minor, or to his relatives, or to any one who may have a right to it, whatever property he obtained under the judgment aforesaid, along with any income it may have produced, and any profits which may have accrued from its possession; and he shall be compelled to pay ten *solidi* in addition, because he has prosecuted a claim which was not valid in law. Where a guardian desires to defend any action brought against his ward in court he shall have full authority to do so; but if the rights of the ward should be affected, or his property impaired or lost through his neglect, the guardian shall afterwards be compelled to make restitution.

THE GLORIOUS FLAVIUS RECESVINTUS, KING.

IV. Guardians shall have no Right to Exact from Wards in their Charge any Instruments in Writing whatever.

As minors are unable to care for themselves or their property, it has been wisely provided by the laws that they should be subjected to the authority of guardians, and that their business should be transacted for them for a stated number of years. For the reason, however, that certain guardians, by means of either persuasion or threats, defraud those whose interests it is their duty to carefully protect, and compel them to enter into agreements that they will not demand an accounting of their property, or exact bonds or other written instruments from their wards, by means of which they seek to prevent inquiry into their actions: therefore, that our solicitude for the rights of such wards may the better appear in all matters where such rights are involved, we hereby decree that the following law must be strictly observed, to wit: that in the case of such wards, even when they have passed the age of fourteen years, where the guardian or guardians who had charge of their persons and property shall be found to have caused the execution of any bond or written instrument of any description, which enures to the benefit of said guardians or any person designated by them, then such bond or instrument shall be void, and of no force whatever in law.

When the time shall come that he who has been under guardianship shall have the right to assume the management of his own affairs, the guardian shall give a complete account of the care of his ward's property, in the presence of a priest or a judge, and shall receive from his former ward a full discharge from all obligations; so that, all restraint being removed, the said ward may come into full possession of his property, and have the right to dispose of it at his pleasure. But if it should happen that, while the guardianship is in force, the ward should be attacked by a dangerous illness, and should wish to dispose of his property by will, he can do so, provided he has completed his tenth year, according to the provisions of a former law.

If the guardian, while living or dying, should give any of the property belonging to his ward to his own children, or to any persons whomsoever, and no account of the same was made to the wards, according to the terms of the inventory which was made at the time the guardianship was accepted, and proof of this should be legally established, those who received said property from the guardian shall make full restitution to the wards. All wards shall have the benefit of this legal remedy, except where, by the lapse of time, and having passed the age of fifteen years, their rights shall be extinguished by law.

TITLE IV.—CONCERNING FOUNDLINGS.

I. *Where Anyone Casts Away, or Abandons, a Freeborn Child, he shall Serve as its Slave.*

II. *Where a Male or Female Slave shall be proved to have Cast Away a Child, with, or without the Knowledge of his or her Master*

III. *What Compensation for Support anyone shall Receive for the Bringing up of a Child committed to his Care by its Parents.*

I. Where Anyone Casts Away, or Abandons, a Freeborn Child, he shall Serve as its Slave.

If anyone, induced by compassion, should rescue, and care for a child, of either sex, who has been abandoned, and such child, after having been brought up, should be acknowledged by its parents; where the latter are freeborn persons, they shall either give a slave, or the price of one, as compensation for the service performed. If they should neglect to do this, compensation shall be made by order of the judge of the district; and the parents who have been guilty of such wickedness shall be condemned to perpetual exile. Where he who casts away the child has not sufficient property to redeem it, he shall serve as its slave; and he whom the pity of others has preserved, shall enjoy complete freedom. It shall be lawful for the judge both to prosecute and impose sentence for this crime whenever committed.

II. Where any Male or Female Slave shall be Proved to have Cast Away a Child, with or without the Knowledge of his or her Master.

If a slave, of either sex, in order to defraud his or her master, should expose and abandon their own child, without the knowledge of said master, and anyone should bring it up, the latter shall be entitled to receive the third part of its value; but, under such circumstances, the master must swear or prove that he was ignorant that his slave had abandoned the child. If, however, it should be shown that the master was aware of the fact, the child shall become the slave of him who reared it.

III. What Compensation for Support anyone shall Receive for the Bringing up of a Child committed to his Care by its Parents.

If anyone should accept from its parents a little child to be reared, he shall receive as compensation one *solidus* every year, until the child has reached the age of ten; but he shall be entitled to no further compensation after it has completed its tenth year, because after that time the services of the child should be sufficient to pay for its support. And if he who seeks to take the child again should be unwilling to pay this sum, it shall be held in slavery by him who reared it.

TITLE V. CONCERNING SUCH PROPERTY AS IS VESTED BY THE LAWS OF NATURE.

I. Concerning the Disinheriting of Children; and What Disposition Parents should make of their Property.

As soon as we have ascertained that any unlawful acts have been committed, it behooves us to prevent, by legal measures, similar occurrences in the future. For many persons living reckless lives, squander their property upon strangers, either on account of riotous living, or through the unwise counsel of others, and, as a result of this, leave their inoffensive children or grandchildern weak and penniless; for those cannot be of any benefit whatever to the community upon whom the duty of labor has not been enjoined by the example and virtues of their parents. And, in order that, under such circumstances, the rights of the community may not be sacrificed, or children or grandchildren be deprived of the benefits of that natural affection which should be bestowed upon them, the law, by which a father or mother, or grandfather or grandmother, have the right to give their property to a stranger, should they wish to do so, or a woman to dispose of her dowry in any way that she pleases, is hereby abrogated; and we decree that the following more equitable law shall be observed by all, to wit: that neither parents nor grandparents shall have the absolute right to dispose of all their property, nor that children nor grandchildren shall, through an unjust will, be deprived of the inheritance of their parents and grandparents; therefore, any father or mother, grandfather or grandmother, who wish to bestow any of their property upon their children or grandchildren, must observe the following rule, viz: that in the bestowal of said gifts upon their children or grandchildren they do not exceed the third part of their property; nor shall it be lawful for them to transfer any of their property to any stranger, unless they should not have any legitimate children or grandchildren living.

The following, however, we decree shall be observed, as being in accordance with the dictates of reason: that if the father or mother, grandfather or grandmother, should decide to bequeath, by any instrument in writing, any portion of the third part of their property, as aforesaid, to their children or grandchildren, in compliance with the laws governing inheritances, all such proceedings shall be forever inviolable; and whatever bequest concerning said property may be made, shall have full and uncontrovertible validity. Nor shall it be lawful for the child or grandchild who has received any of the said third part of the estate from their parents, to claim anything more, unless they should prove to be entitled to it by some former bequest of their parents or grandparents.

If those having children or grandchildren, should wish to bestow anything upon the Church, or upon freedmen, or upon anyone else, they shall have the right to dispose of the fifth part of what remains, after the said third part has been reserved. The authority of such persons to dispose of the said fifth part is indubitable; but, in such cases, either the third part of the property which is to be bequeathed to the children, or the fifth part which is to be otherwise disposed of, as aforesaid, must be separated from the remaining property, and a proper estimate made of the same. But whatever anyone has received through the generosity of the king, shall, under no circumstances, be included in the estimate of either the third or the fifth parts of the estate aforesaid; for, according to another law, whatever anyone has acquired through the royal bounty shall be absolutely at his disposal.

It has been already provided that children and grandchildren cannot be disinherited by their parents for any trifling offence. The grandfather and grandmother, as well as the father and mother, shall have the right to chastise and restrain their children and grandchildren, as long as they remain members of the family. And if a son or daughter, grandson or granddaughter, should attempt to inflict any serious injury upon their parents or grandparents; that is to say, if he or she should give any of them a blow with the fist; or a kick; or strike them with a stone, or with a scourge, or with a whip; or should insolently seize any of them by the foot, or by the hair, or even by the hand; or be guilty of any shameless assault upon them; or should publicly accuse them of crime; then, any child or grandchild convicted of such an offence, shall receive fifty lashes with the scourge, in the presence of the judge, and shall forfeit all claim to the inheritance of its grandparents or parents, should the latter so desire. But if, repenting of its conduct, it should implore the pardon of those whom it has offended; and, through the love of its parents, it should be again received into favor, and designated as an heir; it shall not be deprived of its inheritance, or be accounted infamous, on account of the punishment which it has received.

FLAVIUS CHINTASVINTUS, KING.

II. What Part of her Dowry a Woman has a Right to Bequeath.

For the reason that many women to whom the privilege was granted of disposing of their dowries as they pleased, have been found to have bestowed them upon persons with whom they were living illegally, to the injury of their children or grandchildren; therefore, we declare it to be both necessary and proper that those for the rearing of whom the marriage was celebrated, should receive some benefit from said property. In pursuance whereof we decree that, if any woman has children or grandchildren, and should wish to bestow a gift upon the Church, or upon freedmen, or upon any other person or persons; she shall not have the right to dispose of more than the fourth part of her dowry in this manner. Three fourths of it shall be left, without question, to her children or grandchildren, whether there be one, or many of them. On the other hand, a wife shall have full power to dispose of her entire dowry, in any way she pleases, when she leaves no legitimate children or grandchildren. Nevertheless, it shall not be lawful for any woman who has married two husbands, or more, to give the dowry she has received from one husband, to the children or grandchildren of another; but the children and grandchildren born in a certain line of descent shall, after the death of their mother, have the entire dowry given by their father or grandfather.

FLAVIUS CHINTASVINTUS, KING.

III. What Property Parents should Bestow upon their Children, at the Time of their Marriage.

Wherever wrong is done by parents to the interests of their children it must be remedied by law. Therefore, because the duplicity of parents sometimes prompts them to deprive their children of what they have given them at the time of their marriage, we hereby declare such acts to be void; and decree that the following law shall hereafter be observed forever, to wit: that if any property should be transferred to any person, either by writing, or in the presence of witnesses, at the time of his or her marriage, excepting such as is usually given in the way of ornaments or clothes, as a marriage gift, whether said property consists of slaves, lands, vineyards, buildings, clothing, or jewels, presented by the parents to the children, either at the time of the marriage, or after it, the said children shall have full power to dispose of such property as they wish, with this exception: that, after the death of their parents, the inheritance shall belong to the children exclusive of what said parents have previously given to them according to law, and an equal distribution of said inheritance shall be made among the heirs; so that a son or daughter shall have full power to dispose of what they received from their parents at the time of their marriage, according to the provisions aforesaid.

After the death of the parents, an inventory shall be made, and the property which was donated at the time of the marriage shall be appraised, and the other heirs shall receive an equivalent in value to the amount of said property; and all shall then share equally in the remainder of the estate of the parents.

FLAVIUS CHINTASVINTUS, KING.

IV. Concerning Children Born of Different Parents; and What Distinctions Parents may Make in the Disposition of their Estates.

If a man marries several wives, and has children by all of them, and any of his sons or daughters should die intestate, his or her brothers or sisters shall be entitled to the estate, provided the decedent left neither children nor grandchildren; and said heirs shall have a right to claim it after proving that they are descended from the same father and mother. Where there are children by one father and by different mothers, those only who are descended from the same father have a right to an equal division of the property belonging to him. With regard to those who are sprung from one mother and different fathers, we prescribe the following regulations, to wit: that if a woman should have children by different husbands, only those brothers and sisters who are the children of the same father and mother shall have a right to the inheritance, descending either in the paternal or maternal line from such as have died intestate, or without offspring or descendants. As it has been established by a former law that the grandchildren shall not be deprived of the third part of the estate of their grandparents, it shall be lawful for the grandsons and granddaughters who have lost either of their parents, to share equally with their paternal or maternal uncles in the estates of their grandfathers and grandmothers; that provision only of said law remaining valid, by which it was decreed that parents and grandparents may bestow their property upon their children and grandchildren, or may give away what they please to a stranger.[1]

[1] As the law of primogeniture, so popular with mediæval and modern nations, was not recognized by the Roman jurisprudence, so it was

V. Concerning such Property as Children may have Acquired during the Lives of their Parents.

Any son who, while his father and mother are living, acquires any property, either through the favor of the king, or through the generosity of his patron, shall be entitled to absolute control of the same, and shall have the right to sell, or give it away to any one he chooses, as has already been provided by our laws; nor can his father or mother claim any of said property while the son is living. Where, on the other hand, a son obtains property, not through royal generosity, but by his own labor, or during some public expedition; should he be living with his father at the time, the latter shall be entitled to the third part of said property, and the other two-thirds shall belong to the son.

---

also rejected by the Visigothic legislator. The testamentary distribution of estates under the Code was governed by far more equitable principles than obtain, even in our time, among many peoples who have enjoyed, for centuries, the experience and advantages of a highly developed civilization. While the testator was, for the most part, unhampered in the final disposition of his property, he could not disinherit any of his children without just cause, and that cause was required to be specifically stated in his will. Where children or grandchildren shared equally in the estate of their parents or grandparents, all cause for family dissensions on account of favoritism or undue influence, was absolutely removed. As it was provided by law that the estate of the decedent must descend in the direct line, to the exclusion of stepchildren, another source of dissatisfaction and temptation to fraudulent interference with the rights of the next of kin was permanently disposed of.

The interests of all heirs were jealously guarded. Even the dowry of the wife, peculiarly her own property, as it represented the purchase price paid for her by her husband, could not be alienated, to the prejudice of her children. The dutiful conduct of the latter was insured by the law which declared all their rights in the estates of their parents to be forfeited, in case they were guilty of gross insult or violence toward the former. In the case of wards and minors, there is probably no body of laws which protects with more solicitude the interests and property of such helpless beings, than do the provisions of the Visigothic Code.—[ED.

BOOK V.

CONCERNING BUSINESS TRANSACTIONS.

TITLE I. ECCLESIASTICAL AFFAIRS.

THE GLORIOUS FLAVIUS RECESVINTUS, KING.

I. Concerning Donations to the Church.

If we are compelled to do justice to the merits of those who serve us, how much greater reason is there that we should care for the property set apart for the redemption of our souls and the worship of God, and preserve it intact by the authority of the law. Wherefore, we decree that all property which has been given, either by kings, or by any other believers whomsoever, to houses devoted to Divine worship, shall eternally and irrevocably belong to said churches.[1]

---

[1] This decree, promulgated about 660, is one of the first of the statutory declarations recognizing the principle of mortmain. The Codes of both Theodosius and Justinian contained similiar, but far less sweeping provisions relating to the acquisition of property by the Church; but these were concerned, for the most part, with bequests.

II. Concerning the Preservation and Restoration of Property Belonging to the Church.

We are of the opinion that it vitally concerns the interests of our kingdom, to provide by our laws that the temporal rights of the church shall be protected. Therefore, we hereby decree, that, as soon as a bishop has been consecrated, he shall straightway proceed to make an inventory of the property of his church in the presence of five freeborn witnesses; and to this inventory the said witnesses shall affix their signatures. After the death of a bishop, and as soon as his successor has been consecrated, the latter shall require a second inventory of the church property to be made; and if it should appear that said property had, in any way, been diminished, then the heirs of said bishop, or those to whom his estate was bequeathed by will, shall make up the deficiency. If a bishop should sell any of the property of the church, his successor shall lay claim to that property, along with all its rents and profits, and restore it to the church, after having returned the price paid for it to the purchaser, and no reproach shall attach to such proceedings. And we hereby decree that this law shall be observed in every respect by priests and deacons, as well as by bishops.

ANCIENT LAW.

III. Concerning Sales and Gifts of Church Property.

If a priest or bishop, or any other member of the clergy, should sell or give away any of the property belonging to the church, without the consent of the other ecclesiastics, we declare that such a transaction shall not be valid, unless said sale or donation should have been made in accordance with the holy canons

---

From the nature of the case, however, in the organization and perpetuation of ecclesiastical societies, custom and necessity must early have rendered real property inalienable by bodies which never die; and which are encouraged to add to their wealth by every expedient, honorable and dishonorable, but are prohibited by tradition, policy, and legal enactment from conveying their possessions to the laity.—[ED

IV. Concerning Church Property in Charge of Those Devoted to the Service of the Church.

Where heirs of a bishop or of other ecclesiastics, who have placed their sons in the service of the church, obtain lands or any other property through the generosity of the clergy, and then return to the laity, or abandon the service of the church whose lands or other property they hold, they shall at once forfeit all such possessions. And this provision must also be observed by all the clergy holding ecclesiastical property, even though they have held it for a long time; for the reason that the canons have so decreed. The widows of priests or of other ecclesiastics, who have devoted their sons to the service of the church, solely through gratitute to the latter, shall not be deprived of any property possessed by the fathers, which was originally derived from the church.[1]

FLAVIUS EGICA, KING.

V. Concerning the Repairs of Churches, and Divers Other Matters.

The different regulations established in former times by the Holy Fathers concerning ecclesiastical affairs shall be still observed, so far as they are consistent with the interests of the church. As antiquity, which has been the cause of the destruction of many lofty buildings, has not spared the houses of God; it is eminently proper that such of the latter as are in danger of destruction should be repaired. As a result of this necessity it has been made a source of reproach to our organization, that the greed of certain priests has

[1] Priests and deacons, under the Visigothic ecclesiastical system, which, it must not be forgotten, was at all times practically independent of papal authority, were permitted to marry; as were their Arian predecessors. Such a union, however, was subject to certain restrictions. It could only be entered into once; the bride had to be a virgin; and where the husband was raised to a higher dignity in the Church he was compelled to, at once, repudiate his wife. The marriage itself was an impediment to promotion, as priests without families were much more sure to rise in their profession than those who had contracted marital obligations.—[ED.

caused their parishes to be oppressed by repeated forced contributions; and that many churches have been impoverished under pretence of repairs. Consequently it has been decreed and confirmed by our Council that the third part of the ecclesiastical revenues, which the ancient canons have set apart for that purpose, shall be used for the repairs of churches, whenever required. And when churches are to be repaired, it is better to learn this fact from the worshippers themselves, and the repairs should then be made under the personal care and direction of the bishop. For, although according to the provisions of the ancient canons, every bishop has the right to reserve for himself the third part of the revenues of his diocese, if he should desire to do so; so, also, he had no right to exact from the parish churches, by means of arbitrary proceedings, the remaining two-thirds of the said revenues; nor was he at liberty to give away any of such property to anyone by way of compensation for services performed. We deem it necessary to decree that a single priest shall never have charge of more than one church at a time; nor hold any other office; nor by ecclesiastical authority act as guardian; nor, in any way, have charge of the property of wards; and any congregation which possesses ten pieces of property is entitled to a priest, but such as have less than ten shall be united with other churches. And if any bishop should disregard this our regulation, and should hereafter venture to disobey it, he shall expiate his offence by two months' excommunication.[4]

[4] The holding of a plurality of livings by a single ecclesiastic, an abuse which, in after times, assumed such gigantic proportions under papal rule, especially in England, where, by reason of the hardships it produced, it promoted in no small degree the progress of the Reformation, was scarcely known to the Arian, or Catholic clergy of Spain. The enjoyment of the revenues of one, or a greater number of benefices by a layman, no matter how wealthy or powerful the latter might be—a custom elsewhere so prevalent—was not provided for by the sacerdotal legislature of the Visigoths in their Code of laws; for the reason, no doubt, that such a thing was deemed too improbable for serious consideration.—[ED.

THE GLORIOUS FLAVIUS WAMBA, KING.

VI. Concerning the Arbitrary Conduct of Bishops.

God, the just Judge, who loves right eternally, does not wish that justice should be subject to time, but rather that time should be governed by the principles of equity. God himself is the personification of justice, and to him should be given whatever is bestowed by the faithful upon the church through motives of devotion; for God, as mediator accepts the vows of every true and sincere worshipper. And vows should never be renounced which are known to have proceeded from, and been confirmed by, a sense of justice; and, therefore, he commits a fraud upon God who unjustly takes from him his property. He also violates the rules of justice who corruptly interferes with the vows of others. While, as has been said, God is justice, what madness is it for anyone to remove from God's possession any property under the claim of prescription, alleging that he has held it for thirty years? For many rash bishops, prompted by avarice, are in the habit of bestowing upon their cathedral churches, or upon various individuals, or paying out as wages for labor performed, the donations that have been given to their dioceses by the faithful, and, in this way, they not only break the vows of the donors, but are also guilty of sacrilege, in that they thereby defraud the Church of God; for it has been long established that to defraud the church is sacrilege. And when they are urged to make restitution, they decline to do so, because their predecessors acted in the same manner; or refuse to make amends, because they claim to have held the property in question for thirty years. Thus they attempt to maintain their cupidity and rapacity by right of prescription; and instead of at once making reparation for their fault, they attempt to confirm and legalize it by the operation of time. He must be considered a person of great impiety who asserts such a claim, and acknowledges that, for thirty years, he has done injury to God, and refuses to make amends for the injury after that period has elapsed.

Therefore, since these most iniquitous abuses are defended under a pretence of justice, and as we are not concerned with the past, but with the future, we shall now proceed to make regulations applicable to the time of our own reign. For the reason that, hereafter, all temptation to avarice may be removed, we hereby decree that it shall not be lawful for a bishop to appropriate any property belonging to the churches of his diocese; or, if any has already been appropriated, to allege that he is entitled to the same on account of his possession for thirty years; but, whenever the facts have been established, he must make restitution at once. As, in order that a long period may pass without a claim being made, the nobility sometimes are guilty of such oppression of ministers of the church that the latter do not dare to assert their rights against such eminent persons, concerning property which has been appropriated by the latter, and lest the voice of the despoiled church remain forever silent, we decree that hereafter, it shall be lawful, where this offence has been admitted by the parties or detected by anyone, in any place, that the claim shall be instituted with all possible speed in the following manner, to wit: that the heirs of the founders of the church shall act as prosecutors, if they are present; but, if they should not be present, and even if they should be, but are unwilling to act, then the governor of the province, or the governor of the city, or the deputy of either of them, or anyone else who has legal cognizance of the matter, shall have the right to act as accuser and prosecutor.

Where any bishops who, in past times, have committed the offences hereinbefore mentioned, and have been in adverse possession of church property for thirty years, and declare that they hold said property by the right of prescription; such persons we leave to the justice of God, for we decline to pass judgment upon them. But whoever, up to the time when this law is promulgated, shall not have had possession of such property for the space of thirty years, shall be compelled to restore it intact to the church, but no penalty shall be required of them. And where any bishop, who from the day of the adoption of this law, should appropriate anything given by the faithful to the churches of God, and should use such property for his own benefit, or for that of his cathedral church, or should bestow any of it upon any person whomsoever, his act shall not be confirmed by any lapse of time; and, according to the above-mentioned decree, whenever he shall have been convicted of the commission of such acts by anybody, he shall be compelled to restore the property which he took, along with lawful amends out of his own possessions, to that church which has been defrauded. If he should not have the means to make full restitution out of his own property, on account of his abuse of authority, he shall undergo the penalty of excommunication prescribed by the canon of the eleventh Council of Toledo; that is to say, if the property that was appropriated was worth ten *solidi*, he shall purge himself of guilt by twenty days of penance. If the value of the property appropriated should be greater or less, the proportion of days to be passed in penance shall always be doubled; and he also shall undergo a similar penalty who retains possession of any property taken from a diocesan church, which has been appropriated by his predecessor.

Any judge who neglects to carry out the provisions of this law, or delays the proceedings without just cause, or does not notify the king that he may take cognizance of the affair, shall be liable to the same penalty as the bishop who committed the offence, and shall pay said penalty out of his own property to the church whose cause he neglected to decide. This law not only applies to property which has been bestowed upon minor and diocesan churches, but to that in which all assemblies included under the general name of churches are concerned; that is to say, monasteries and convents of men and women.

We also think it proper to add the following provisions to this law: that all bishops who ordain priests and rectors in the churches of their dioceses shall give them instructions concerning the rights of the churches to which they are ordained; that is to say, if any bishop should have in his keeping any document defining the rights of any church in his diocese, he shall show it to the rector of that church, so that the latter may be familiar with the rights of said church, as well as with the documents conferring the same, and not be ordained in ignorance of them, and, what is worse, through the wickedness and duplicity of the bishop, the will of the benefactor of the church be not publicly known. It is also decreed that priests and rectors shall not only have the opportunity to inspect such documents, but shall also be entitled to copies of the same, confirmed under the hand of the bishop, to enable them to direct the affairs of the church committed to their care without any uncertainty, and to enforce the rights to which it is justly entitled. Given and confirmed in the name of God, at Toledo, on the tenth day of the Kalends of January, in the fourth year of our reign.

THE GLORIOUS FLAVIUS WAMBA, KING.

VII. Emancipated Slaves of the Church, who are still Bound to Render it Service, shall not be Permitted to Marry Persons who are Freeborn.

Great confusion of lineage results where inequality of rank causes degradation of offspring; for what is derived from the root is inevitably found in the fruit of anything. For how indeed can he bear a title of honor, whose parents are bound by the obligation of servitude? We refer to this matter because many of the slaves of the church are set free, but nevertheless do not enjoy absolute liberty; for the reason that they are still bound to serve the church from which they deduce their origin; and who, contrary to natural laws, contract marriages with freeborn women, and seek to have freeborn children who, in fact, are not so; and thus what ought to enure to the public good, becomes in fact a burden to it, both in respect to person and property; as whatever children are born from such an infamous marriage, following the position inferior in rank, from birth become the property of the church, along with all their possessions. Wherefore, that such insolent conduct may be put an end to hereafter, we decree by this law, that if a slave of any church, while it is still entitled to his services, should be freed, and accept his liberty from the priest, he shall not be permitted to marry a freeborn woman. Those, however, who have been freed in the regular manner, and are absolutely exempt from all service to the church by the Canon Law, shall have the right to marry freeborn women, and shall be entitled to claim all honor and respectability for their offspring.

But if any of those set free, who are still under the dominion of the church, should venture hereafter to marry any free-woman; as soon as the judge shall be apprised of the fact, both parties shall be scourged three times, as has been provided in a former law concerning freemen and slaves, and the judge shall cause them to be immediately separated; and where they are unwilling to be separated, each shall remain in the condition in which he or she was previously, and any children born of them shall become slaves to the king.

Whatever property has been bestowed by any free person upon any freedman, together with such property as a child of either sex sprung from them can acquire, possess, or waste, shall belong entirely to the heirs of said free person at his death; and, if such heirs should be lacking, it shall become the lawful possession of the king, to be disposed of absolutely at his pleasure. This law shall not only apply to men, but also to women; that is to say, where either a freedman or a freedwoman owing services to the church should be so bold as to marry a freeborn person.

The following exception shall be observed in the execution of this law, to wit: whoever shall be born of such parents within thirty years of its promulgation, shall not follow the condition of that parent who is bound to give service to the church, but shall be free, along with all the property inherited from his or her parents, both noble and plebeian. Given and confirmed at Toledo, on the twelfth Kalends of January and the fourth year of our reign.

TITLE II CONCERNING DONATIONS IN GENERAL.

ANCIENT LAW.

I. A Donation Extorted by Violence is Void.

A gift extorted by force and fear has no validity whatever.

II. Concerning Royal Donations.

Donations conferred by royalty upon any person whomsoever, shall belong absolutely to him to whom they are given; so that he who is thus honored by the royal munificence shall have the power to dispose of any property derived from such a source in any way that he chooses. If he who received such gifts should die intestate, the donations aforesaid shall belong to the legal heirs in regular succession, according to law, and the royal favor can in no way be infringed upon; because it is not fitting that the will of the prince should be interfered with, where the recipient of royal bounty has not been guilty of crime.

III. Concerning Property Given to a Husband or a Wife by the King.

We especially decree that a wife shall be entitled to no part of any property presented by the king to her husband, unless the latter should bestow a portion of it upon her by way of dowry. And, likewise, should the gift be made to a wife, her husband shall have no right to any of it; nor can he lay claim to it after her death, unless his wife should give or bequeath it to him.

ANCIENT LAW.

IV. Concerning Property, in Addition to the Dowry, given to a Wife by her Husband.

If a wife should, at any time, in addition to her dowry, accept from her husband property acquired by him as a gift, or by profligate conduct, or the proceeds of claims collected by him, she shall have the absolute disposal of said property until the day of her death, according to the terms of the will of her husband, even though there be children born of that marriage. She shall have the power to expend or use the income of such property, just as the testator has designated by will; and, during her lifetime, she shall enjoy unhampered possession of all such property, the income of which shall be used for her expenses. But if the testator should not make any special disposition of said income, his children shall have the right to said property after his death; and, upon no occasion, shall his wife be allowed to alienate any part of it, excepting the income. Where there are no children by said marriage, the wife shall have full control of all property given her by her husband, according to the terms of his will. But if she should die intestate, the said property shall revert to her husband if he is living, and if he should not be living, it shall belong to his heirs. And we decree that the same rule shall apply to husbands who, at any time, have received gifts of property from their wives.

ANCIENT LAW.

V. Concerning Property given to a Husband by his Wife; and Where a Wife has been Convicted of Adultery.

If a husband should give any property to his wife, and she, after his death, should remain chaste, or should marry another husband, she shall have the power of disposing of the property given her by her first husband according to the terms of his will, if she should have no children. If she should die intestate and without children, the property shall revert to her husband if he is living, and if not, it shall belong to his heirs. But if she should have been convicted of adultery, or other meretricious conduct, she shall lose any property which she obtained from her husband, and it shall belong to his heirs, or to his legitimate children.

FLAVIUS CHINTASVINTUS, KING.

VI. Concerning Property Donated Verbally, or Conveyed by Instruments in Writing.

Any property given away in the presence of witnesses can under no circumstances be reclaimed by the donor. And even if it should happen that what is given is situated elsewhere, the donation cannot, for that reason, be revoked, provided it is made in writing; because it is evident that the gift is absolute, when the instrument conveying it is in the name of, and for the benefit of him who receives it. It, however, must be noted, that if the donor should say that he neither delivered such an instrument nor directed it to be delivered, but that it was taken from him; then the party to whom the property was given may prove by witnesses that it was transferred to him, or directed to be so transferred by the donor, or placed under his control by the will of the testator; and, when he shall have produced such testimony, the gift shall be deemed valid. Where he neglects to introduce competent testimony, he who executed the instrument shall make oath that he neither delivered it, nor directed it to be delivered, nor that he voluntarily executed it; and the instrument shall then be returned to him by whom it was claimed, and shall remain invalid, if the latter so desires. But it is proper to add, that if anyone should execute an instrument disposing of any property for the benefit of any one whomsoever, and, in his lifetime, should not deliver it to him for whose benefit it was made, and it should be found after the death of the former; he for whose benefit the donor has made disposition of said property, shall have the right to claim it, along with all the property therein described; for it is evidently just that a document which the donor, while living, preserved, and which never appeared to be altered in any way, should have full force in law. If, however, the donor while living did not relinquish possession of either the instrument or the property, but kept them, and made other dispositions in his will, the latter shall be valid; because a will always takes precedence in law of documents previously executed, but not delivered. If he to whom the property was given should die before receiving it it shall belong to the donor or to his heirs. And where the gift should be made under this condition, to wit, that the donor should have possession of it during his lifetime, and that, after his death, it should go to him for whom he intended it, he shall have the privilege of changing his mind when he wishes, even though he should have suffered no injury; because the case is similar to that of the execution of a will. But if he who is deceived by a fraudulent gift, and with the expectation of profiting by an empty promise, shall expend anything for the benefit of the donor, he shall be entitled to receive from the donor himself, or from his heirs, compensation in damages for any loss he may have sustained on that account. And if anyone should choose to give away any property he has received, either by ordinary gift or by the authority of any written document, the party to whom he gives it shall have the same right to it as the original donor. If he who received the gift should die during the life of the donor, he shall have the right to dispose of said gift at his pleasure; and should he die intestate, the gift shall not revert to the donor, but shall descend to the heirs of him who received it.

VII. Concerning Gifts Bestowed upon One Another by Husband and Wife.

If a husband should give any property to his wife, he must describe it in a written instrument and affix his signature or seal thereto. And, in order that his gift may be valid, it is necessary that two or three freeborn witnesses should attest the document. This law shall also apply to a wife who wishes to confer any gift upon her husband, provided the gift was not extorted by the husband through violence; to the end that the provisions of the law relating to the disposition of property may be, in every respect, preserved.

TITLE III. CONCERNING THE GIFTS OF PATRONS.

I. Where Anyone who has been Placed under the Control of Another, or of the Son of that Person, Deserts either his Patron, or the Children of the Latter.

Where anyone, having a client under his protection, gives him arms or anything else, such gifts shall be the absolute property of the client. If the latter should desire to select another patron, he shall have full authority to do so, for one cannot restrain a freeborn man because he happens to be under his control; but, in such a case, everyth ng to which the patron is entitled shall be given to him. The same rule shall apply to the children of a patron as well as to those of him who was under his protection; and the former shall have a right to any donations that have been given to the latter. Where a client abandons his patron without the latter's consent, he shall be required to restore to him any property which the patron may have given to the parents of the client. And if anyone who has been placed under the protection of another, should acquire any property while he is under such control, half of said property shall belong to the patron or his children, and the other half shall remain in the possession of him who earned it. Where a client leaves a daughter and no sons, in such case we decree, that the daughter shall remain under the protection of the patron. If the patron should provide a husband for her, of equal rank, and anything should be given to her father or her mother, it shall belong to her by right of inheritance. But if, contrary to the will of her patron, she should select for herself a husband of inferior rank, whatever has been given to her father by the patron or by his relatives, shall be restored to said patron or to his heirs.[1]

---

[1] The institution of patron and *libertus*, or client, adopted by the Visigoths almost without alteration, dates back to the primitive ages of Rome. The regulation was recognized by the Law of the Twelve Tables, and was modified by various enactments during the eras of the Republic and the Empire. Its survival, during all the vicissitudes attending the Roman domination, attests its peculiar adaptability to the national character, and to the political and social organization of the people who established it. It presents a greater analogy to the Highland clan than to any other modern institution, although marked and radical differences exist between the two; the strongest resemblance being in the devoted allegiance due to both the *patronus* and the chieftain. By the ordinary act of manumission the slave became a *libertus* or freedman; a term of much more limited significance than it has at present. The former master then became the protector and guardian of his freedman; and, in return for this protection, the latter was bound to perform certain duties, which he could not evade without the reproach of ingratitude, and the certainty of punishment. One of these obligations was that of military service, which differed from those subsequently required by the law of the Feudal System, only in that it was not especially rendered as a condition for the tenure of a fee. The relation of patron and client, which, under the Romans, could only be dissolved between individuals by death, or by the loss of his freedom by the client for misconduct or insolence, was not so strictly observed among the Visigoths Under their system, the freedman had a right to transfer his allegiance to another patron; an act which caused the forfeiture to his former master, of at least half his property. Not only individuals, but churches, and municipal bodies, could exercise patronal rights. While the term client was generally applied by both nations to a manumitted slave, it had in fact, a much broader meaning; and denoted any person who voluntarily placed himself under the care or supervision of another of superior rank or power. This institution had more influence in preserving and perpetuating the distinctions of caste—that most pernicious and fatal of evils which cause the disintegration of nations and overthrow of governments—than any other arbitrary and oppressive regulation of ancient times.

ANCIENT LAW.

II. Concerning Arms given to Bailiffs who have been Appointed for the Defence of Anyone, and the Acquisitions of said Bailiffs.

Arms given to bailiffs for purposes of defence, can under no circumstances be reclaimed by the donor, but whatever property a bailiff acquired, while in office, shall remain in the possession of his patron.[1]

III. Concerning Property Acquired through the Appointment of a Patron, or which has been Donated by Him.

As has been hereinbefore stated, if anyone, while under the protection of another, should acquire any property while living with him, and should prove unfaithful to his patron, or wish to abandon him; the patron shall be entitled to half the property so acquired, and the other half shall belong to him by whose exertions it was obtained, and whatever the patron has given him he shall be entitled to keep.

ANCIENT LAW.

IV. Concerning Property Accepted and Acquired through the Office of Patron.

As has been stated elsewhere, if anyone should abandon his patron and claim the protection of another, and he to whom he applies should give him land, the patron whom he has deserted is entitled to any land, and to whatever else he himself may have given him.

---

[1] Among the clients owing services to a patron, were the *buccelarii*, who derived their appellation from the *buccela*, or ration, furnished them. They may be designated "bailiffs," as their duties resembled, in many respects, those of the Spanish *alguazil*. They formed part of the armed retinue of the patron, accompanied him to war, and guarded his property in times of revolution and disorder.—[ED.

TITLE IV. CONCERNING EXCHANGES AND SALES.

ANCIENT LAW.

I. What Constitutes a Valid Exchange, and what a Valid Purchase

An exchange, if not made under fear or force, shall have the same validity as a purchase.

ANCIENT LAW.

II. If the Vendor is not a Person of Good Character, he must give a Surety.

If the vendor is not a person of highly respectable character, he shall give a freeborn bondsman as surety to the purchaser, and the sale shall then be valid.

ANCIENT LAW.

III. Any Sale made under Compulsion shall be Void.

Any sale evidenced by an instrument in writing shall be perfectly valid. If there should be no written evidence of it, and it should be proved that the price was paid in the presence of witnesses, the purchase shall be legal. A sale shall be void in case it was extorted by violence or fear.

ANCIENT LAW.

IV. In Case the Price should not be Paid, after Earnest Money has been Given.

He who receives earnest money for the sale of anything, can be forced to fulfil his contract. But if the purchaser, either through sickness or unavoidable necessity, cannot be present upon the designated day, he may appoint any one he chooses to pay the price at the time agreed upon. But where he himself is not present, or does not appoint any one to act for him, he shall only be entitled to receive the earnest money which he gave, and the contract shall be cancelled.

ANCIENT LAW.

V. Where only Part of the Price is Paid.

If only a part of the price is paid, and the balance should not be forthcoming, the sale shall not be invalid on this account. But if the purchaser should not pay the balance of the price at the time appointed, he shall pay interest on what he owes; unless it should be agreed upon by both parties that the property in question shall be returned to the vendor.

FLAVIUS RECESVINTUS, KING.

VI. Where Fraud is Committed in Stating the Price of whatever is Sold.

If, in the sale of property, a smaller price is paid than was agreed upon, and the purchaser should, fraudulently, and against the will of the vendor, declare that he has paid a higher price than he should have done, he shall be compelled to pay to the vendor double the amount of which the latter has been defrauded.

ANCIENT LAW.

VII. Where Anyone says that he Sold his Property for Less than it was Worth.

This rule must be observed in all sales where any property consisting of lands, slaves, or any species of animals, is disposed of, to wit: that no one shall attack the validity of the transaction by declaring that he sold the property for less than it was worth.

ANCIENT LAW.

VIII. Concerning Those who Sell, or Give Away, the Property of Others.

Whenever a dispute arises concerning the ownership of property which has been sold or given away: that is to say, if it should be established that anyone has sold or given away what belonged to another, no blame shall attach to the purchaser. But he who has been so bold as to sell or give away the property of another, shall be forced to pay double its value to the owner thereof, shall return the price which he has received to the purchaser, and shall undergo the penalty prescribed by the bill of sale. Whatever the purchaser, or he who received the gift, shall have added to the value of the property which was bought, shall be estimated by the judges of the district; and full satisfaction of the same shall be made, either by the vendor or the donor of said property, to him by whose efforts its value has been increased. The same rule shall apply to every description of property, including slaves and animals.

ANCIENT LAW.

IX. It shall not be Lawful to Sell, or Give Away, Property whose Ownership is in Dispute.

It shall not be lawful to give, or sell, or in any way transfer possession of, any property whose ownership is in dispute: that is to say, which any one else claims, or of which he has a reasonable hope of recovery.

ANCIENT LAW.

X Where a Freeman Allows Himself to be Sold.

Any freeman who permits himself to be sold, and shares the price with the vendor, and, afterwards, desiring to cheat the purchaser, publishes the fact for the sake of reclaiming his liberty, shall not be heard, but shall remain in slavery;

for it is dishonorable that a freeman should voluntarily subject himself to servitude. But if he who sold himself, or permitted himself to be sold, should have sufficient property to redeem himself; or, if his parents should choose to give the price of his redemption to him who owns him; then the entire amount for which he was sold shall be returned to the purchaser, and the person who was the object of the sale shall regain his freedom.

ANCIENT LAW.

XI. Concerning Free Men and Free Women Sold by Slaves or Freemen.

If anyone should dare to sell or give away a freeborn person, the judge shall at once cause the offender to be arrested. And in order that the said freeborn person may be restored to his proper rank, the judge shall require the vendor of such person to pay a hundred *solidi* of gold; and if he should not have sufficient property to pay this sum, he shall receive a hundred lashes in public, and shall be delivered over as a slave to him whom he had the audacity to sell, or give away. If a slave should treat a freeborn person in this manner, after being arrested he shall receive two hundred lashes in public, by order of the judge, and having been scalped he shall be condemned to perpetual servitude. This rule shall apply also to donations and sales of freeborn women.

ANCIENT LAW.

XII. It shall be Illegal for Parents to Sell their Children, or, by any Contract whatsoever, to Place Them in the Power of Others.

It shall not be lawful for parents to sell, give away, or pledge their children. And no one who purchases or receives a child under such circumstances, shall have any legal right to it whatever, but, on the other hand, he shall lose the price, or the amount advanced as a loan, which he paid to the parents of said child.[1]

FLAVIUS CHINTASVINTUS, KING.

XIII. Concerning Sales by Slaves.

The property of another cannot be sold contrary to the will of him who is entitled to legal ownership of the same. Therefore, for the reason that an ancient law declared all sales by slaves invalid, which were made at the expense of their masters, we have determined to promulgate a more equitable decree, in order to bring the laws of the country within the bounds of justice; for it is better to amend the acts of those who have fallen into error, than to err in like manner. Wherefore, if any one, hereafter, should knowingly receive from any slave of either sex, who belongs to another person, a house, or land, or a vineyard, or any personal property, upon any terms whatsoever, the sale, gift, or pledge, made by such a person shall be invalid, and the delivery of the property shall not be required. Where the sale is attended with expense to the purchaser, the property shall be returned

---

[1] The irresponsible, and more than despotic authority vested by the Roman laws in the father over the son, was thoroughly repugnant to the Visigothic conception of justice and freedom, which had been transmitted through many generations of barbarian ancestors. The Roman father not only possessed the power of life and death over his children, but had the undisputed right to sell them into slavery. The parental and filial relation was hedged about with such restrictions that it was almost impossible to sever it during life. By the law of the Twelve Tables a son could not be free, unless he had been sold as a slave and manumitted, three times. His reduction to a condition of servitude carried with it many civil disabilities which could never be removed. The independence of a son of his father's control rendered his inheritance of the parental estate impossible. These oppressive regulations were either greatly modified, or entirely abrogated, by the more equitable policy of Visigothic legislation. In the case of female children also, under the latter system, principles more consonant with ideas of justice prevailed. The emancipation of the sex from arbitrary restraint also made great progress, when it is remembered that a woman, no matter what her age or position, was always considered by the Romans to be in a condition of tutelage.—[ED.

intact to the master of the slave, and the purchaser shall lose the price he paid for it; for it is but just that he should sustain loss who attempted to appropriate the property of another for his own advantage. But if the aforesaid slave should sell any animals, or any personal property, or any ornaments of any kind, which belong to himself, or which he had received from his master to be disposed of, such transaction shall be forever valid; and if the master of any servant who has made such a sale should wish to rescind the sale, and should declare that the property which was sold did not belong to the slave, but was his own, the sale shall not be rescinded, unless he who proposes to do so shall establish, either by the testimony of legitimate witnesses, or by his own oath, that the property which he seeks to recover did not belong to the slave, but to himself, and has been disposed of without his permission. This law shall apply only to chattels of trifling value, for the authority of the master is necessary in order to confirm a contract relating to the sale of property of great value and importance.

ANCIENT LAW.

XIV. Where a Slave, who has been Sold, Accuses his Former Master of Crime.

If anyone should sell a slave, and the latter should accuse his former master of crime, he who sold him may recover said slave from the purchaser by returning the price for which he was sold, in order that he may avenge upon him the crime of which he himself was accused. And we decree that the same law shall be observed concerning female slaves. No servant of either sex, whether sold, given, or exchanged, shall be tortured to obtain evidence against his or her former master, nor shall he or she be believed if they should accuse their former master of crime.

XV. A Master may Claim the Property of a Slave whom he has Sold.

If any one should sell a slave, and not know what property he possessed, he shall have power to make full inquiry, and to claim as his own, whatever property belonging to said slave that he can find.

ANCIENT LAW.

XVI. Whether a Slave may be Redeemed with his own Private Property.

If a slave should be ransomed with his own money, and his master should be ignorant of his possession of the same, he shall not be entitled to his freedom; because the ransom that he paid was not his own, but the property of his master.

ANCIENT LAW.

XVII. No One, against his Will, shall be Compelled to Sell his Slaves.

Laws frequently arise from legal disputes in court, and when evidence of fraud exists, it becomes necessary to promulgate new decrees to restrain acts dictated by shrewdness and duplicity. Many slaves of both sexes, influenced by the suggestions of others, are in the habit of taking refuge in churches, and there complaining of the injustice and oppression of their masters; in order that, through the intercession of priests, and the aid of religion, they may compel their masters to sell them. In this manner frequently an injury is inflicted upon the master; as when a priest, or any one else, representing himself as a purchaser, buys the slave, while in fact he is acting for another party; and, by this collusion, it sometimes happens that the slave is sold to an enemy without his master's knowledge, and thus, some one, under such circumstances, may obtain possession of the slave who could not have purchased him openly. We declare that, henceforth, the following shall be the law, viz: that no one, against his will, shall sell his slave; but the priest or custodian of the church, as provided by other laws, shall at once deliver the slave to his master, providing the latter pardons him for the fault he has committed; for it is highly improper that the slave should maintain his obstinacy and rebellion by taking refuge in a place where the doctrines of restraint and punishment are preached.

If any one should deceive a master in the manner aforesaid, he himself shall forfeit a sum equal to the price which was paid by him while acting as the agent of another; and, whether the master became aware of the fraud at the time of the transaction, or afterwards, he shall be entitled to recover the slave upon application to the court. He who acted fraudulently as the agent of another in the sale, shall be forced to give another slave of equal value to the master whom he deceived, in order that the wickedness of such a dishonorable transaction may be suitably punished.

THE GLORIOUS FLAVIUS CHINTASVINTUS, KING.

XVIII. Where a Slave, on Account of a Crime He has Committed, is Transferred to the Possession of Another.

We must not omit to provide, by legal enactment, for the settlement of questions frequently involved in dispute. For this reason, if a slave who has been guilty of crime should be transferred, either by gift, sale, or exchange, to another master, his former master shall either cause him to be delivered up to justice to be punished for said crime, or shall render full satisfaction to the party who has been injured. In case he who bought said slave is unwilling to answer for him, or to render satisfaction for his crime, he must return him to his former master, on receipt of the price which he paid; and his former master must answer to the person making the complaint, for the offence committed by his slave while under his control.

FLAVIUS CHINTASVINTUS, KING.

XIX. Concerning Property Belonging to Private Persons, and to the Court, which may not be Alienated.

If the care of private property must not be neglected, how much more important is it to guard the interests of the public, whose possessions should always be preserved, or increased. For this reason, persons attached to the court, or private persons who are under obligations to furnish horses to the king, or who exercise any duties in connection with the royal treasury, shall have no right to sell, give, or exchange, any property in their possession. But if it should happen that any of them, either willingly, or impelled by necessity, should transfer all of his property, either by sale, donation, or exchange; both he who disposed of, and he who received it, shall have an inventory of the same drawn up, in which all of said property shall be specifically described; but he who has received only half of the said property, or a certain portion of the same, in slaves, lands, vineyards, and houses, shall be accountable for only the price of the portion which has been thus disposed of. And if any one purchasing property of any kind from such persons, should not, as aforesaid, within a year, render an account of the transaction in writing, showing the source from which said property was derived; as soon as information of this shall come to the king, or the governor, or the judge, the former possessor shall lose the price he received, as well as the property which was disposed of; but the king shall have the power to either restore said property to him who transferred it, or to bestow it upon any one else, should he desire to do so. It shall, however, be lawful for persons attached to the court, as well as for private persons, to sell, give, or exchange, property among themselves, provided he who receives said property shall not refuse to account for it publicly; but no plebeian shall have the right to sell his land. And if any one, after the adoption of this law, should purchase vineyards, lands, houses, or slaves from men employed in the public service, he shall inevitably lose the price paid for said property.

ANCIENT LAW

XX. Where Anyone Sells, or Gives Away Property, whose Possession should first have been Transferred by Judicial Decree.

If anyone should sell or give to any person any property which is in litigation, before the claim of his adversary to said property shall have been judicially determined, or should permit any one to make use of said property, so that the possessor may be deprived of its control, without an order of court, he in whose possession the property formerly was shall have it at once restored to him by the judge, and the adverse party shall not be permitted to claim it again, even if his title to the same is found to be good. And he who gave such property, or permitted it to be made use of, as aforesaid, for the reason that he can allege no just excuse for such conduct, sha l be forced to give something of equal value to said property, or to the price paid for it, to his adversary; because he appropriated something before his title to it was legally established.

XXI. Of Slaves Captured and Sold by the Enemy.

If any slaves, residents of our kingdom, should be taken by an enemy, and said slaves should be recovered by our subjects, every one who recaptures a slave shall have one-third of what is estimated to be his just value, and shall restore him to his master; but if said slave was sold by the enemy to him, he shall make oath as to the price which he paid for him, and shall receive from the master said amount, together with a sum equal to any increased value which may have accrued since the capture of said slave, and the latter shall be at once restored to his master.

XXII. For what Price this Book shall be Bought.

In order that any extortion on the part of a vendor and any unnecessary expenditure by a purchaser, may alike be prevented, it is decreed by the present law, that it shall not be legal for a vendor to sell a copy of this book for more than four hundred *solidi*, or for the purchaser to give more than that sum. And if any one should presume either to give, or to receive, an amount greater than that above mentioned, he shall receive a hundred lashes by order of the judge.[1]

---

[1] This affords curious and instructive information as to the cost of books in the seventh century. The silver *solidus* is meant, as, where any coin referred to is of gold, the fact is always stated in the *Forum Judicum*. As the *solidus* was nominally worth $4.00 of our money, but in reality $44.00, taking into consideration the difference of values at that and the present time, it will be seen that the price fixed by law, of a copy of the Visigothic Code, was $17,600.00. This appears incredible, but it must be borne in mind that all books were in manuscript; that few persons were qualified to write them; and, as ignorance was almost universal, the demand for literature was extremely limited. The preparation of a literary work was then a formidable and expensive undertaking. Most of the books of that age, and, indeed, for centuries subsequently, were of a religious character, such as missals, fabulous chronicles of the Church, and spurious and imaginary biographies of saints. Making the sale of a collection of laws at a price above a certain sum a penal offence, punishable with the scourge, is an example of crime unique among the *mala prohibita*.—[ED.

TITLE V. CONCERNING PROPERTY COMMITTED TO THE CHARGE OF, OR LOANED TO, ANOTHER

ANCIENT LAW.

I. Concerning Animals Hired to Another.

If anyone should take in charge a horse, or an ox, or an animal of any kind, in consideration of a certain sum of money, and the animal should die, he shall give something equal to its value; whether the sum agreed upon was for the mere keeping of the animal, or for the use of it. But if he who had charge of said animal, should receive no compensation, and should prove that the animal was dead, he shall be entitled to nothing, and nothing shall be required of him, for this reason; as he who had charge of the said animal has established by oath that its death was not due to his guilt or negligence, no liability shall attach to him for the same. The same rule shall apply to property which has been loaned.

ANCIENT LAW.

II. Concerning Animals Loaned for the Purpose of Labor.

Where anyone rents or hires to another a beast of burden, horse, or any other animal, and it should die of disease while under the control of him who received it, the latter shall make oath that said animal did not die either through his fault or neglect, and he shall escape all liability. But if the death of said animal should have been caused by want of exercise, or by overloading, or by too much work, or by abuse, an animal of equal value shall be given to the owner. But if said animal should cause any injury or damage to anyone, he who had charge of it at the time shall be liable for the same.

ANCIENT LAW.

III. Concerning Things which have been Loaned, and afterwards Destroyed by Fire, or Lost by Theft.

If any gold, silver, ornaments, or money, which have been entrusted to anyone either for safe keeping, or to be sold, should be lost, or consumed by fire, along with his own property, in the house of him who had charge of them, and the latter should produce witnesses, and give a written statement specifying the property which has been lost, and should swear that nothing has been saved, he shall incur no liability, except for the gold and silver, which cannot be burned. And if any person, while the house was burning, under pretext of affording assistance, should appropriate any property, the owner shall make diligent inquiry, and, if detected, the culprit shall pay four times the value of the article stolen; and if any of the property which has been loaned should be found, it shall be restored at once to the owner. Where it is proved that the article in question had been stolen, a reasonable time shall be granted for the pursuit and arrest of the thief; and if he should be caught, he shall be forced to restore to the original owner the property of the latter, and whatever else may be obtained from the thief shall belong to him to whom the stolen property was entrusted. But if the thief should not be arrested within the appointed time, a sum equal to half the value of the property loaned or hired, shall be paid to the owner by him who had charge of the same, so that the loss may be equally borne by both. If, subsequently, the owner of the property should find it in the possession of him to whom it was entrusted, and who had declared that it had been lost or stolen, when, in fact, it had been fraudulently concealed by him, he shall undergo the penalty for theft as prescribed by law.

ANCIENT LAW.

IV. Concerning Lost Money, and the Interest on the Same.

If anyone should receive a sum of money and bind himself in writing to pay interest on the same, and the money should be lost through no guilt or negligence of the debtor, the creditor shall be entitled to the principal alone, and cannot collect interest. But if the money was lost through his own fraud or crime, the borrower shall pay both principal and interest; and where the latter has gained any profit from the use of said money, and it should afterwards be lost, if the profit should be as great as the principal the borrower shall be liable for both principal and interest.

ANCIENT LAW.

V. Concerning Property Committed to the Charge of Another, and Lost by Accident at Sea.

Where anyone entrusted with the property of another loses it, either by fire, shipwreck, or some other accident, but at the same time saves all his own property from destruction, he shall be compelled to render full satisfaction for what was in his charge, and shall not be suffered to set up any defence. But if he is known to have saved any portion of his own property, he must return to him whose goods he had charge of, a sum in proportion to the property lost or saved, which a court shall decide to be equitable. If he should lose all his own possessions, and save the property which was entrusted to his care, the same rule shall apply; and he shall receive such a part of what he has saved as a judge, after due consideration, shall decide him to be entitled to For in such cases it is not just that he alone who has exposed himself to great danger should sustain loss, and, while he was attempting to save articles of inferior value belonging to another, should lose all his own possessions.

ANCIENT LAW.

VI. Concerning Property Entrusted to a Slave without his Master's Knowledge.

If any property entrusted to a slave for safe keeping, without the knowledge of his master, should be lost, no responsibility therefor shall attach to either the master or the slave. For the fault is his who entrusted his property to the slave of another, the master being ignorant of the fact. If the property aforesaid should be an animal, and it should be lost through the fraud of shepherds, the master shall be compelled to pay for it. The same rule shall apply to property entrusted to another, which has been consumed or wasted through the fraud or malice of those to whose charge it was committed.

ANCIENT LAW.

VII. Where a Slave Fraudulently Demands Property Entrusted by his Master to Another.

If a master desiring to borrow, or to hire any property, should send his slave for the same, and the latter should abscond with said property, the master shall be compelled to make restitution. But if the slave should falsely represent that his master had sent him, and the property should be given him to be taken to his master, and he should either destroy or lose said property, and absconding, cannot be found, the master shall make oath that he had not sent the slave upon such an errand, and that he did not know that he had gone; and, under such circumstances, he shall incur no liability. The master, as well as the person who entrusted the slave with the property, shall exert themselves to the utmost to find him. We hereby decree that this same rule shall apply to all property entrusted to anyone without compensation.

ANCIENT LAW.

VIII. Concerning Legal Interest.

Where anyone loans money at interest, he shall not have a right to demand more than three *siliquæ* per annum, for every *solidus;* the debtor shall pay one *solidus*, as annual interest, for every eight *solidi*, and the creditor may claim from the debtor the principal and the aforesaid interest. If the creditor, by a written agreement, should extort from the necessities of the debtor a sum, as interest, in excess of the above amount, the contract, being contrary to law, shall be invalid. But if any one should thus violate the law, and should receive the sum which was agreed upon in writing, the usurious interest shall not be returned.[1]

ANCIENT LAW.

IX. What shall be Paid for the Use of Fruits of the Soil.

Whoever shall lease to another the dry and moist fruits of the earth, that is to say, wine and oil, or any other kind of provisions, shall not be entitled to receive for the use of the same more than the third part; that is to say, he shall pay a *modius* as rent for every two others which he receives. This law we direct shall apply to the fruits of the earth alone, as we have already published decrees concerning the loaning of money.

---

[1] Twelve and a half per cent was the ordinary rate; but, in some instances, it was much higher. The law against usury was habitually violated by the Jews, who extorted enormous rates of interest both from individuals and from the Crown.—[ED.

ANCIENT LAW.

X. Who are Entitled to Wills, or Instruments in Writing, which have been Entrusted to the Keeping of Anyone.

A will which has been entrusted to the keeping of anyone, after its attestation by witnesses, as is provided by law, shall be delivered to the heir who has the largest interest in the inheritance. But if it should be given to anyone else, or should be delivered to an enemy, he who delivered it shall pay a double fine to the person he wished to defraud. Where anyone is entrusted with a document in which parties have a joint interest, that is to say, wills, decrees, agreements, donations, or other legal instruments of this kind, and should give them to one person in the absence of another who is equally interested therein, he who surrendered such documents must recover them, and restore them without delay, to all those who have a common interest in their preservation.

TITLE VI. CONCERNING PLEDGES AND DEBTS.

FLAVIUS RECESVINTUS, KING.

I. Where Articles are not Pledged.

All persons shall not have the right to pledge property; and if any freeborn person should seize a pledge belonging to another, and which he has refused to accept as such, he shall be compelled to pay double its value. A slave, however, shall be required to restore only the pledge, and shall receive a hundred lashes.

ANCIENT LAW.

II. Where Pledges are Deposited and afterwards Stolen.

Where anyone deposits a pledge with another, as security for a debt, and it should be stolen, he who deposited it shall bear the loss.

ANCIENT LAW.

III. Where Articles are Pledged as Security for Debts.

If a pledge is deposited as security for a debt, and the debt be evidenced by an instrument in writing, and he who deposited the pledge should not pay the debt at the appointed time, the pledge shall be kept safely for its owner for the space of ten days, or it shall be carried to him, if he is at hand, and he shall be notified to make payment. But if the debtor should, through negligence, fail to come on the appointed day, or should put off the payment of the debt, additional interest may be collected. But if the ten days have elapsed, as has been hereinbefore stated, and the debtor should not discharge his obligation, the creditor may bring the article pledged before the judge, or the governor of the city, and shall have the right to collect, after the seizure of said pledge, whatever amount may be deemed equitable, in the opinion of the judge or in that of three respectable persons. The creditor can afterwards reserve whatever is due him from the proceeds of the sale of the property pledged, and the owner of the same shall be entitled to the remainder.

FLAVIUS RECESVINTUS, KING.

IV. Where a Pledge is not Restored when the Debt is Paid.

If anyone who has loaned money upon a pledge and, after the debt has been paid at the time appointed, should delay the restoration of the property pledged to its owner; or should sell the same before the time appointed by law, as aforesaid; or should appropriate it for his own use; or should bestow it upon another; or should maliciously refuse to surrender it; he shall be compelled to restore the pledge intact to its owner, and to pay him, in addition, half its estimated value.[1]

---

[1] All the laws relating to bailments, included under this and the preceding Title, are of ancient origin; that is, borrowed, almost without change, from the Roman jurisprudence. The responsibility of the bailee for property entrusted to him, is determined by the same principles which experience and a sense of equity, in all ages, have demonstrated to be just and expedient, and which form the basis of similar contracts at the present day. The requirement of ordinary or extraordinary diligence and care was then, as now, dependent upon the question whether one or both parties derived benefit from the bailment. In case of gross negligence or fraud, the bailor was entitled to an animal or article of equal value to the one lost or destroyed; just as he can now, under similar circumstances, recover damages in a suit at law. The forfeiture of half the value of the property loaned, when it was stolen, and negligence was not established, or even alleged, is a novel regulation, and one especially calculated to render the bailee more careful and alert. The custom of pawning property as security for money loaned is, no doubt, as ancient as any business transaction, and is the *pignori acceptum* of the Roman, and Civil and Common Law authorities. The question of negligence does not

FLAVIUS CHINTASVINTUS, KING.

V. Where a Person is Liable for many Debts, or has Committed many Crimes.

Where an individual has been guilty of offences against many persons, or owes debts to different creditors, he who first establishes his claim either in writing, or by oral testimony, or by the acknowledgment of the party himself, and has thereby shown that he is liable to him for damages, or is indebted to him for money loaned, shall have the preference; and said person shall be required to satisfy the claim, regardless of its priority in time; or shall be sentenced by the judge for the offence he has committed against the law. Where several parties to whom he is indebted, should proceed against him at one and the same time, he shall satisfy his obligations to such persons according to the value of their claims; or, should he prove insolvent, he shall serve all of them as a slave. But in the settlement of the claims, it must be taken into consideration by the judge, that the largest creditor is entitled to the greater portion of the property, and that the remainder should be divided among the other creditors as the judge himself may determine. If the debtor should not have property sufficient to discharge his obligations, as soon as this fact has been established the debtor shall be given up by the judge to his creditors, to serve them, for all time, as a slave.

FLAVIUS CHINTASVINTUS, KING.

VI. In what way the Debt of a Person who is Dead, or any Injury he has Committed, shall be Inquired Into.

If the guilt of any person has not been established during his lifetime, it is undoubtedly monstrous to accuse him of

---

seem to have been considered where a pledge was stolen; for, in this case, the entire loss was sustained by the bailor, and not half of it, as when the article was merely loaned by way of accommodation, and no remuneration for its use was expected.—[ED.

crime after his death. Where anyone, hereafter attempts to commit such acts, in order to defraud the heir of a person who is dead, he shall be restrained by the following law, to wit: that if any person shall accuse one who is dead of having been guilty of violence toward himself, or of having fraudulently deprived him of his property, or of having destroyed it, or of having owed him money, or of having perpetrated any unlawful act, as provided for in a former law, no credit shall attach to his assertions, unless he shall be able to indubitably establish their truth by competent written or oral evidence. And if he should be able to prove his allegations, and the deceased person concerned should have left no children, but should have bequeathed his property to freedmen, or to other persons, the said persons shall be forced, under the instructions of the judge, to pay, in proportion to the property they have received, the amount due the creditor of the deceased. And if the latter should have left children, and they should have possession of his property, they shall be required to settle all claims which the creditor has proved to be due him from their father. If the aforesaid debtor should have died without making any disposition of his estate, his nearest relatives, or those who claim, or are in possession of, said estate, shall be liable for his pecuniary obligations. But if he who is said to have been liable for any such claims, should die without leaving any property, his children and his relatives shall be free from all liability and reproach. Where the deceased leaves some assets, but not enough to satisfy all the claims against him, and his sons or relatives, or those who are in possession of his estate, should be unwilling to satisfy the said claims in full out of their own property, they must immediately deliver to the creditor all the property which has been left by the deceased.

TITLE VII. CONCERNING THE LIBERATION OF SLAVES, AND FREEDMEN.

XVII. *Neither Freedmen, nor their Descendants, shall either Marry, or act Insolently towards, the Family of their Patron.*

XVIII. *Freedmen who have Entered any Religious Order, shall not be Returned to the Service of their Masters.*

XIX. *In what manner Royal Freedmen and their Descendants shall Defend the King, while Serving in the Army; and with whom Those in the Public Service shall March.*

XX. *Concerning Freedmen who are Guilty of Transgressions.*

ANCIENT LAW.

I. Where Slaves are Liberated, either by Instruments in Writing, or in the Presence of Witnesses.

If anyone at the point of death, should liberate his slaves either by an instrument in writing, or in the presence of witnesses; his will shall be valid, provided it be proved within six months by from three to five credible witnesses. And if said testator should give anything to said freedmen, and the fact should be proved by either written or oral evidence, said freedmen shall be entitled to said property.

II. Where a Slave Belonging to One, or to Several Persons, is set at Liberty.

If anyone should liberate the slave of another, or one belonging to several persons, with intent to defraud the master or masters, of said slave, his act shall be void in law; and whoever sets free the slave of another, shall be compelled to give one to his master in his place. But if the master should consent to his emancipation, he shall be entitled to two slaves in his stead; and the liberated slave shall enjoy complete freedom; and this law, we decree, shall apply also to female slaves. If anyone wishes to grant unconditional freedom to any slave whom he owns in common with another, and such an act should take place in the presence of a priest or deacon, said ecclesiastic must prevent it; because the liberation of any slave made under such circumstances is illegal. Where a party desires to confer freedom upon a slave, he must first make terms with the other owners, and obtain the absolute proprietorship of said slave, by means of money, or by gift of their interest in him; and then, if he should wish to set him free in the presence of a priest or a deacon, the act of manumission shall be valid. But if anyone should confer absolute freedom upon a slave owned in common, in the presence of a priest or deacon, without the consent of the other owner, or owners, he shall lose his share of said slave, and his associates shall be entitled to the same. If, however, he should wish to dispose of his share of said slave he shall have the right to do so.

ANCIENT LAW.

III. Concerning Those who Declare that they are Free.

If a slave should declare that he is free, the judge shall give him protection, and afford him time to produce evidence, either written or oral, establishing the fact of his freedom. But only such time shall be granted that the service he owes to his master will not be lost, or his own rights suffer injury.

ANCIENT LAW.

IV. Whether he who is enjoying Liberty can be Returned to Slavery.

Where any person in the enjoyment of liberty is claimed by another as a slave, he shall not be immediately delivered into the possession of the claimant, and the judge must determine previously whether said claimant shall give security not to treat said person with injustice or cruelty.

V. Whether he who is Sought to be Returned to Slavery, can be Deprived of any of his Property.

If anyone should deprive a freeman or one who has been set free, of any property, and, afterwards, should wish to claim him as a slave, he must restore what he deprived him of, before prosecuting his claim.

FLAVIUS CHINTASVINTUS, KING.

VI. Whether he who has been Declared to be Free by his Master, in Court, can be again Reduced to Slavery on the Demand of said Master.

If anyone, in court should declare by his testimony that a person was free, and, afterwards, should wish to claim him as a slave, he shall give the person whom he attempted to oppress another slave, by way of reparation, and he whom he endeavored to injure shall remain free.

ANCIENT LAW.

VII Where Anyone, Influenced by Fear, Asserts that he is a Slave.

Anyone who, influenced by fear, declares himself to be a slave, shall not be restrained of his liberty, but shall be brought into court, and should he prove that he is free, shall be dismissed by the judge; but if it should be shown that he is a slave, he shall straightway be returned to his master.

ANCIENT LAW.

VIII. Where a Freeman is Claimed as a Slave; or where a Slave Declares Himself to be Free.

If anyone wishes to claim a freeman as his slave, he must show what right he has to his possession and service; and if the slave should assert that he himself is free, he must, in like manner, establish the existence of his freedom. The judge must take the testimony of persons of highly respectable character, and there must be more than one witness on each side. But if the judge, having been corrupted by a bribe, should unjustly oppress an innocent person, he, as well as the claimant, shall immediately be compelled to pay the penalty prescribed by law in the case of those who render unjust decrees.

ANCIENT LAW.

IX. For what Reasons Freedom, once Given, shall be Revoked.

If anyone should liberate a male or female slave, and it should be proved that this has been done in the presence of two or three witnesses; that is to say, if he should deliver the instrument granting freedom to said slave publicly, in the presence of legitimate witnesses, and should specify in said instrument that the slave himself should be free from the time said instrument was executed, without conditions, and with no reservations, whatever, in favor of himself; he shall have no power to revoke said act of manumission, unless the liberated slave should be insolent to him, or do him some injury, or accuse him of some crime; and for the commission of such offences, his freedom may be revoked. But if the master shall say he liberated the slave under certain conditions, or with some reservation of his authority over him, and these facts do not fully appear from the terms of the written instrument, the witnesses who were present shall testify concerning the terms of the instrument aforesaid, and, afterwards, judgment shall be rendered according to what the terms of said instrument are found to be.

ANCIENT LAW.

X. Where a Freedman Inflicts Injury upon him who Gave him his Freedom.

If a freedman should wrong his former master in any way; or should strike him with his fist, or with any weapon; or should pursue him with false accusations, whereby he may be in danger of his life; the said master shall have power to reduce said freedman to slavery, provided he proves the commission of said offences in court.

ANCIENT LAW.

XI. A Freedman shall not be Permitted to give Testimony against his Former Master, or against the Children of the Latter.

It shall be unlawful for a child, or other heir, to revoke the manumission of a slave liberated by his father; for the act of a parent must always be religiously respected by his children; nor shall a freedman, or any of his descendants, be permitted to testify against the children of him to whom they are indebted for their freedom; and if they should offer any testimony of this kind, they shall not be heard by the court, but shall be reduced to their former servitude. But in other matters they shall have a right to assert their claims against the children or grandchildren of their patron, so far as is consistent with the principles of justice.

FLAVIUS RECESVINTUS, KING.

XII. Freedmen shall not be Permitted to Testify in Court.

Neither freedmen nor freedwomen shall be permitted to testify in any cause, except where the testimony of freeborn persons is not available, as is allowed in the case of slaves; because we deem it improper that by the evidence of freedmen injury should be done to those who are freeborn. Persons, however, who are descended from freedmen, shall be fully competent to testify.

ANCIENT LAW.

XIII. Concerning the Disposition of the Property of a Person who has been set Free, should he Die without Leaving Legitimate Children.

Where a liberated slave dies without leaving any legitimate children, and his patron should have given him anything after he had been set free; or even if he should have forsaken his service, and attached himself to another; all his property shall revert to his former master, or to the heirs of the latter. And if said freedman should remain on the estates of his patron, and should acquire any property by the fruits of his labor, half of said property shall belong to the patron, and the freedman shall have a right to dispose of the other half at his pleasure. If he should place himself under the protection of another patron, and, while in his service, he should acquire any property, the master who liberated him shall be entitled to half of it, and the other half shall descend to the nearest relatives of the freedman, whether they be slaves or free; or he shall have the right to bestow said half of said property upon anyone he may select; but whatever he received from his former master shall belong to the latter.

The same rule shall apply in the case of female slaves who have been liberated, and we add the following provision, as being conformable to justice, to wit: that no freedman or freedwoman who has received his or her liberty from either master or mistress, shall abandon the latter while they are living. And should they venture to do so, they shall lose the property which they have received, and shall be forcibly returned to the service of their master or mistress.

FLAVIUS CHINTASVINTUS, KING.

XIV. Concerning the Conditions Imposed by a Master, where Slaves are Liberated by an Instrument in Writing.

When anyone confers liberty upon a slave by an instrument in writing, and specifies therein that it shall not be lawful for him to dispose of his own property; and afterwards the person who has been set free sells it, or gives it away, his act shall be absolutely void; and his patron, or the children of the latter, shall be entitled to all of said property. But if no such condition was made, the freedman shall have a right to do what he pleases with his own possessions; and should he die intestate, and leaving no legitimate children, even though his master has inserted no other condition in the instrument conferring liberty upon him, his patron or the children of the latter, shall be entitled to his entire estate.

FLAVIUS CHINTASVINTUS, KING.

XV. Concerning the Liberation of Slaves belonging to the Crown.

If no ambiguity should arise in the determination of legal questions, we should not be under the necessity of making laws for future generations. For the reason that, under the pretence of liberty fraudulently asserted by slaves, the public service is often injuriously affected, and without any prejudice to the well-deserving, but as a warning to those who act rashly, we hereby decree, that, should freedom be granted hereafter to a slave of the Crown, the act shall be invalid, unless confirmed by the royal signature.

ANCIENT LAW.

XVI. Concerning the Property of Slaves belonging to the Crown, who have been Liberated.

We do not permit freedom to be given to slaves of our court without our consent, and if this should be done, the act shall be void, and only that freedom shall be legal which is bestowed under our direction. And, in like manner, it shall be unlawful for the slaves of our court to sell their own slaves or lands to freemen; for they shall have the right to make such sales only to other royal slaves; and if they should wish to give their lands or slaves to the Church or to the poor, such gift or disposition by will, shall be void. We, however, grant the following concession to them for the sake of piety: that they shall have a right to bestow a certain portion of their property upon the Church, or the poor, for the benefit of their souls; and if they have no possessions excepting lands and slaves, we grant them authority to dispose of said lands and slaves, but only to others of our slaves, as has been hereinbefore mentioned, and no freeman shall be permitted to purchase said property; but they shall have the right to give the proceeds of said sales of lands and slaves to the Church, or the poor, for the benefit of their own souls, as hereinbefore stated.

THE GLORIOUS RECESVINTUS, KING.

XVII. Neither Freedmen, nor their Descendants, shall either Marry into, or act Insolently towards, the Family of their Patron.

We occasionally see excessive arrogance displayed by slaves, and are compelled, at the same time, to pity the degradation of their masters. For some slaves, after they have obtained freedom, or the descendants of such slaves, aspire to marry into the family of their masters; or do some wrong to the children or grandchildren of the latter. And as an inferior rank is ennobled by the gift of freedom, so, in like manner, an illustrious race is disgraced by marriage with an inferior caste. Thus a distinguished family is degraded by such a connection, through the acts of those very persons who, by its means, have enjoyed the blessings of liberty. Therefore, that the splendor of natural lineage may not be deprived of its dignity; and the slave, remembering his former condition, may not aspire to privileges to which he is not entitled, and which cannot be granted him: it is hereby decreed that if any freedman, or the descendants of said freedman, belonging to the class of manumitted slaves, or anyone connected with them by affinity or blood, however distantly related, should attempt to contract marriage with any of the family of his former master, or with any of his descendants; or should bring any action at law against them, except for just and legal cause, either on his own behalf, or on behalf of others; or should inflict any injury upon them; or should cause them any vexation or annoyance; or should oppose them as members of an opposite political faction; he shall be at once delivered up as a slave to those against whom he committed these offences. And, indeed, it is impious that when a condition of slavery has been abolished, the dignity of freedom should be degraded; and that, while the slave is exalted, the master is abased, and the children of the latter suffer injury, because the slave has power to inflict it.

FLAVIUS RECESVINTUS, KING.

XVIII. Freedmen who have Entered any Religious Order, shall not be Returned to the Service of their Masters.

Any freedman who has been honored by presentation to the Church by his master, or whom the condition of his emancipation, or his membership in a religious order, has devoted to the service of the Church, can under no circumstances whatever, be returned to the control of his former master, or of his heirs. For whatever is known to belong to God can never be again subjected to the dominion of man.

THE GLORIOUS FLAVIUS EGICA, KING.

XIX. In what manner Royal Freedmen and their Descendants shall Defend the King, while Serving in the Army; and with whom Those in the Public Service shall March.

We attempt to rule the country subject to our crown by the adoption of just laws, when, for the public good, we provide defenders who may protect it against enemies. And while there is no lack of defenders of the throne, it is not improper that the numbers of the same should, for the purpose of repelling foreign foes, be increased by the addition of such slaves as have received their freedom through the royal favor. Wherefore, because it is necessary that such persons should afford their assistance to those to whom they are indebted for their liberty, we especially decree by this law, that all such freedmen and their descendants shall, in time of war, be included among the guards of the king; and the latter shall assign them their places in the ranks, and prescribe the duties they shall perform. And if any freedman should, in time of war, remain at home; and should not, in obedience to the royal order, join the army with the rest; he shall be delivered up as a slave to the person from whom he received his liberty. Those only shall be exempt from this penalty, who, by order of the king, or the governor, have been charged with the performance of some other duty; or who were prevented from joining the army by sickness, or by some other unavoidable necessity.

FLAVIUS EGICA, KING.

XX. Concerning Freedmen who are Guilty of Transgressions.

We have often heard of freedmen who, after the restraints of servitude have been removed, desert those who set them free, and assert that they are the equals of their masters, or of their descendants. Wherefore, we now, with all due deliberation, publish the following decree, to wit: that if any person, of either sex, who has been set free, or any of their children, should be guilty of any subtlety or deceit, or fraudulent conduct towards their former masters, or towards their children, grandchildren, or any descendants of the latter, or should show them any disrespect, at any time, they shall be immediately returned to slavery. And the children of persons guilty as aforesaid, shall be delivered up to perpetual servitude, according to the provisions of a former law.

BOOK VI.

CONCERNING CRIMES AND TORTURES.

TITLE I. CONCERNING THE ACCUSERS OF CRIMINALS.

ANCIENT LAW.

I. A Slave, Accused of a Crime, may be Demanded of his Master by the Officials of the District.

Where a slave is charged with a crime, the judge shall first notify the master, superintendent, or agent, who has control of the accused, and order him to produce the slave in court; and should he refuse to do so, the governor of the city, or the judge may compel him to produce said slave. If the master, or he who has charge of his affairs, cannot be found, the slave shall be arrested and tried by the judge.

THE GLORIOUS FLAVIUS CHINTASVINTUS, KING.

II. For what Offences, and in what Manner, Freeborn Persons shall be put to the Torture.

If moderation is displayed in the treatment of crimes, the wickedness of criminals can never be restained. Therefore, if anyone should, in behalf of the king or the people, bring an accusation of homicide or adultery against a person equal to him in rank, or in palatine dignity, he who thus seeks the blood of another shall first have an opportunity to prove what he alleges. And if he cannot prove it in the presence of the king, or those appointed by the royal authority, an accusation shall be drawn up in writing, and signed by three witnesses; and the accused person may then be put to the question.

If the latter, after undergoing the torture, should prove to be innocent, the accuser shall at once be delivered up to him as a slave, to be disposed of at his will, except that he shall not be deprived of life. But if he should be willing to make a compromise with his accuser, he may accept from the latter as large a sum as may compensate him for the sufferings he has endured. The judge shall take the precaution to compel the accuser to specifically describe the alleged offence, in writing; and after he has done so, and presented it privately to the judge, the torture shall proceed; and if the confession of him who is subjected to the torture should correspond with the terms of the accusation, his guilt shall be considered to be established. But if the accusation should allege one thing, and the confession of the person tortured the opposite, the accuser must undergo the penalty hereinbefore provided; because persons often accuse themselves of crime while being tortured. But if the accuser, before he has secretly given the written accusation to the judge as aforesaid, should, either in his own proper person, or by anyone else, inform the party of what he is accused, then it shall not be lawful for the judge to subject the latter to torture, because the alleged offence has become publicly known. This rule shall also apply to all other freeborn persons. But if the accusation should not be that of a capital crime, but merely of theft, or of some minor breach of the law, nobles, or persons of superior rank, such as the officials of our palace, shall, upon such an accusation, under no circumstances, be put to the question; and if proof of the alleged offence is wanting, he who is accused must declare his innocence under oath.

All persons of inferior rank, and freeborn persons, when accused of theft, homicide, or any other crime, shall not be tortured upon such an accusation, unless the property involved is worth more than fifty *solidi*. But if the property is of less value than fifty *solidi*, and the accused is convicted upon legal testimony, he shall be compelled to make restitution, as prescribed by other laws; or if he should not be convicted, after purging himself by oath he shall receive the satisfaction granted by the law for those who have suffered from an improper demand for torture.

We hereby especially provide that a lowborn person shall not presume to accuse a noble or one of higher rank than himself; but if such a person should accuse another of crime, and proof of the same should be wanting, the person accused shall at once purge himself of all guilt by oath, and swear that he never took, nor has in his possession, the property on account of which he was prosecuted; and oath having been made, as aforesaid, he who brought the false accusation shall undergo the penalty for the same, as prescribed by a former law. But whether the person subjected to the torture is a noble, one of inferior rank, or a freeman, he must be tortured in the presence of the judge, or of certain respectable men appointed by him; and in such a way as not to lose his life, or the use of any of his limbs; and because the torture must be applied for the space of three days, if, as the result of accident, or through the malice of the judge, or the treachery of anyone else, he who is subjected to it should die; or if the judge, having been corrupted by the bribes of the adversary of the accused, should not prohibit the infliction of such torments as are liable to produce death; the judge himself shall be delivered up to the nearest relatives of the accused person, that, on account of his injustice, he may undergo at their hands the same sufferings which he unlawfully inflicted upon the accused.

If, however, he should declare himself under oath to be innocent, and witnesses who were present should swear that death did not result from any malice, treachery, or corruption of which he was guilty, but only as a result of the torture itself; for the reason that the said judge did not use his discretion to prevent excessive cruelty, he shall be compelled to pay fifty *solidi* to the heirs of the deceased; and if he should not have sufficient property to pay said sum, he shall be delivered up as a slave to the nearest heirs of the former. The accuser shall be surrendered to the nearest relatives of the deceased, and shall suffer the penalty of death, which he suffered who perished through his accusation.[1]

ANCIENT LAW.

III. For what Offences, and in what manner, Slaves, of Either Sex, shall be put to the Torture, on account of the Crimes of their Masters.

No slave, of either sex, shall be tortured in order to obtain evidence of crime against either his or her master or mistress, unless for adultery; or for some offence against the Crown, or against their country; or for counterfeiting, homicide, or witchcraft. And if slaves tortured for such reasons should be proved to be cognizant of the crimes of their masters,

---

[1] The savage *Lex Talionis* of the Mosaic Code, which demanded "an eye for an eye and a tooth for a tooth," was permitted by the Visigothic jurisprudence, as is disclosed by this and other chapters. In most instances it was authorized where, on account of the poverty of the culprit, a pecuniary compensation was not forthcoming. Notwithstanding the abuse to which it was inevitably liable, there is certainly a measure of stern and retributive justice in the provision consigning a false accuser to the vengeance of the family of his deceased victim; as well as in the case of a wicked and corrupt judge, who maliciously permitted an innocent man to be tortured to death. The *Lex Talionis* was not unknown to the Romans, and is referred to in the Twelve Tables; but, in after times, their ideas of the proper functions of judicial tribunals, in the infliction of penalties, were too correct to countenance either its acceptance or enforcement.—[ED.

and to have concealed them, they shall be punished along with their masters in such way as the king may direct. But if they should voluntarily confess the truth before being put to the question, it will be sufficient if they undergo the torture in order to confirm their testimony, and they shall not suffer the penalty of death. But any slave of either sex, who, after being put to the torture for a capital crime, should also implicate his or her master, and the commission of said crime can be proved by competent evidence, they shall be subject to the same punishment as their master.

FLAVIUS CHINTASVINTUS, KING.

IV. For what Offences, and in what manner, a Slave, or a Freedman, shall be Tortured.

Where a slave is accused of any crime, the accuser must, before the torture is inflicted, bind himself to give to the master in his stead, another slave of equal value, if the innocence of the slave should be established. But if the accused slave should be found innocent, and should die, or be disabled from the effects of the torture, the accuser must at once give to the master two other slaves, each equal in value to the one killed or disabled. The one who was injured shall be free, and remain under the protection of his master; and the judge who neglected to use moderation in the infliction of torture, and thus violated the law, shall give to the master another slave equal in value to the one who perished by torture.

In order that all doubt may be removed concerning the value of slaves in dispute, no statement of artificial or fraudulent value of the same shall be accepted; but information of their age and usefulness shall be obtained by personal examination of the slaves themselves; and if he who was disabled was skilled in any trade, and he who injured him when he was innocent possesses no slave proficient in the same trade, he shall be forced to give to the master a slave skilled in some other trade; but if he should not have such a skilled artisan, and he whose slave was injured by the torture should not be willing to accept another in his stead, then the accuser shall pay to the master the value of the slave that was injured, according to a reasonable estimate made by the judge, or by men of respectability and established character. It must, however, be observed, that no one shall presume to subject any freeborn person or slave to torture, unless he shall make oath in the presence of a judge, or his representative, the master of the slave or his agent being also present, that through no artifice, fraud, or malice, he is inflicting torture upon an innocent person. And if, after having been put to the question he should die, and his accuser should not have the means to make the reparation required by law, he himself shall be reduced to slavery, for the reason that he was the cause of the death of an innocent man. And if anyone, through treachery, should attempt to subject the slave of another to torture, and the master of said slave should prove that he was innocent of crime, the accuser shall be compelled to give to the master of the accused slave another of equal value, and to reimburse said master for any reasonable expense that he has incurred in defence of his slave, until, in the opinion of the judge, full satisfaction has been rendered by the unjust accuser to the master of the innocent slave.

In case a slave is found guilty of a minor offence, the master, if he chooses to do so, shall have a right to compound the same; but every thief shall be scourged according to the degree of his guilt. Where a master is not willing to give satisfaction for graver offences, he must immediately surrender the slave to justice. Any freeborn person who desires to subject a respectable freedman to the torture, in the case of a capital crime, or of offences of less gravity, shall not be permitted to do so, unless the value of the property involved in the accusation amounts to at least two hundred and fifty *solidi*. But if said freeborn person should be of inferior rank, and a boar, he may be tortured, if the value of the property amounts to a hundred *solidi*.

Where he who is put to the question should, through want of proper care, be disabled, then the judge who did not exercise moderation in the infliction of torture, shall pay two hundred *solidi* to him who suffered by his negligence; and he who caused him to be tortured unjustly, shall be compelled to pay him three hundred *solidi;* and if he should die while undergoing torture, the judge, as well as the accuser, shall each pay to the nearest relatives of the deceased the sums of money aforesaid. And, in like manner, in the case of freedmen of still lower rank, should anyone of them undergo mutilation or death, through want of caution on the part of those employing the torture, half of the sum hereinbefore mentioned as applying to respectable freedmen shall be paid to him who was tortured, should he be still living, or, if he is dead, to his heirs.[1]

---

[1] Ignorance, inhumanity, and contemptuous disregard of the principles underlying the law of evidence, have, in all ages, impelled semi-barbarians and churchmen to the employment of torture. The absolute unreliability of such a means of eliciting truth, one would naturally suppose would cause it to be rejected by nations in the enjoyment of advanced educational facilities and occupying a high rank in the scale of civilization. Such, however, was far from being the case. An inheritance of the atrocities of the Inquisition, it was still used in France and Spain during the eighteenth century. In Scotland, which was subject to the Civil Law, it was not forbidden until the time of Queen Anne. Although prohibited by Magna Charta, and absolutely unknown to the Common Law of England, torture was, nevertheless, frequently employed as late as the reign of Charles I. A form of it, the *peine forte et dure*, applied where a prisoner accused of felony stood mute, was authorized by the Statute I, 3, Edward I. During the reign of the tyrannical Henry VIII, the question was in high favor with that monarch and his legal advisers, and the public tormentor, while his profession carried with it the highest possible degree of execration and infamy, was the object of both fear and adulation among the rabble. Such famous lawyers as Sir Edward Coke and Sir Francis Bacon, were earnest advocates of the efficacy of the rack in extorting evidence from recalcitrant witnesses and suspected traitors. In none of the above mentioned instances, were any restraints imposed upon the zeal or malevolence of those entrusted with the application of this relic of barbarian procedure. Under the judicial system of the Visigoths, however, the abuse of torture, or even negligence in its employment, was severely punished; and sometimes, as may be seen from the above, retribution was exacted by the no less iniquitous *Lex Talionis*. Pecuniary compensation for damages sustained through malice, or neglect of proper care, or where an innocent person was put to the torture, while an inadequate return for the wrong inflicted, was not, under similar circumstances, sanctioned by the customs and practice of more cultured nations, nine centuries subsequently. As a

THE GLORIOUS FLAVIUS CHINTASVINTUS, KING.

V. In what way an Accusation shall be Brought to the Notice of the King.

If any person should bring a false accusation against another before the king, and should allege that he has plotted against the throne, the people, or his country, or that he was committing, or had committed some act to their prejudice; or had been guilty of some fraudulent act against the authority of the Crown, or of those exercising judicial functions; or had executed, or published any forged document; or had coined any spurious money; or had been guilty of giving poison, or of practising witchcraft; or of committing adultery with the wife of another; he who brings accusation of these and similar crimes, the punishment of which involves the loss of life and property, where he can establish the truth of his charges, shall, in no way, be subject to censure. But if his assertions should prove to be false, and it should be evident that he had only made them through hatred, and in order that he whom he attempted to accuse might suffer death, or bodily injury, or the loss of his property; he shall be delivered over into the power of him he accused, that he may himself suffer the penalty which he endeavored to inflict upon an innocent person.

---

slave was a chattel, he possessed no civil rights, and his master, for this reason, had the privilege to compound his offence, if it were not of too serious a character. The fixing of a prescribed limit, in the value of the property involved, for less than which the question could not be employed, is derived from the arbitrary tariff of fines imposed for the loss of limbs, and other personal injuries, which has always been in use among semi-civilized races. Distinction in point of rank and social position was sedulously observed by the Visigoths in the case of the infliction of torture, as well as in the imposition of penalties for violating the laws and in all subjection to civil disabilities. The worse than useless character of this mode of examination was never considered by mediæval authorities, although it was ably set forth many centuries previously by Cicero, in the following terse and vigorous language: "*Regit quæsitor, flectit libido, corrumpit spes, infirmat metus, ut in tot rerum angustiis nihil veritati loci relinquatur.*"—[ED.

Where anyone states that he is in the possession of any fact which should be brought to the notice of the king, and should be, at the time, in the place where the court was sojourning, he shall straightway reveal all that he knows, or shall communicate it to the ears of the king through the agency of some reliable person. If, however, at the time, the king should be at a distance, and the said party should believe that information in his possession relating to the accusation of another, ought to be sent to the king by the hands of a messenger, he must draw up a letter, and in it set forth plainly what he wishes to say concerning the alleged guilt of the accused; and he must do this in the presence of him whom he has selected to convey the information to the king. And, in order that he may not be able to deny the aforesaid communication, three witnesses, known to be men of respectable character, must, in the presence of one another, affix their seals or signatures to said letter.

FLAVIUS CHINTASVINTUS KING.

VI. How Kings should Practice the Duties of Mercy.

Whenever a supplication is made to us on behalf of those who have been implicated in any crime against our majesty, we willingly give attention to such appeals, and exercise the prerogative of mercy when it is consistent with our power. We must, however, refuse to interfere when a crime of this kind has been committed against the nation and our country Yet, if a prince should desire to be merciful to persons of such wicked character, he shall have the right to do so, with the approval of the ecclesiastics and the principal officers of the court.

VII. He Alone shall be Considered Guilty who Committed the Crime.

Punishment for all crimes shall be visited upon the authors of the same; and a father shall suffer no penalty on account of his son; nor a son on account of his father; nor a wife on account of her husband; nor a husband on account of his wife; nor a brother on account of his brother; nor one neighbor on account of another; nor any person on account of a relative; but he alone shall be adjudged to be guilty who is responsible for the offence, and the crime shall die with him who committed it. Neither successors nor heirs shall, under any circumstances, be placed in jeopardy on account of the acts of their parents.

TITLE II. CONCERNING MALEFACTORS AND THEIR ADVISERS, AND POISONERS.

FLAVIUS CHINTASVINTUS, KING.

I. Where a Freeborn Man Consults with a Soothsayer Concerning the Health, or the Death of Another.

Whoever plots the death of the king or any of his subjects, and, with a view to the execution of such a crime, consults diviners, augurs, or soothsayers; should he be freeborn, he shall be scourged, and be condemned to perpetual slavery in the public service, after the confiscation of all his property, or he shall be delivered up as a slave to anyone whom the king may select; and those who have given him advice shall undergo the same penalty. And if any children should be implicated in the crime of their parents, they shall be punished in like manner. But if said children should be innocent, they shall not be degraded in rank, and shall enjoy full and undisturbed possession of all the property which their parents have lost. Slaves who are implicated in such offences shall be tortured in various ways, sold, and transported beyond sea; as the vengeance of the law does not excuse those who have voluntarily participated in such infamous proceedings.

FLAVIUS CHINTASVINTUS, KING.

II. Concerning Poisoners.

Different kinds of crimes should be punished in different ways; and, in the first place, freemen or slaves who are guilty of preparing, or administering poison shall be punished in like manner; as for instance, if they should give poisoned drink to anyone and he should die in consequence; in such a case those who are guilty shall be put continuously to the torture, and be punished by the most ignominious of deaths. But if he who drank the poison should escape with his life, the party who administered it shall be given up into his power, to be disposed of absolutely as he may desire.

FLAVIUS CHINTASVINTUS, KING.

III. Concerning Malefactors and their Advisers.

Enchanters, and invokers of tempests, who, by their incantations, bring hail-storms upon vineyards and fields of grain; or those who disturb the minds of men by the invocation of demons, or celebrate nocturnal sacrifices to devils, summoning them to their presence by infamous rites; all such persons detected, or found guilty of such offences by any judge, agent, or superintendent of the locality where these acts were committed, shall be publicly scourged with two hundred lashes; shall be scalped; and shall be dragged by force through ten villages of the neighborhood, as a warning to others. And the judge, lest, hereafter, the aforesaid persons may again indulge in such practices, shall place them in confinement, and see that they are provided with clothing and food, to deprive them of an opportunity of inflicting further injury; or he may lay the matter before the king, to be disposed of at his royal pleasure. Those who are convicted of having given advice to such persons, shall each receive two hundred lashes in the assembly of the people, in order that all who have aided in the commission of such a crime may not go unpunished.

FLAVIUS CHINTASVINTUS, KING.

IV. Concerning Those who are Guilty of Acts of Witchcraft, or any Injury towards Men, Animals, or any kind of Property whatsoever.

We decree, by the present law, that if any freeman or slave, of either sex, should attempt to employ, or should employ, witchcraft, charms, or incantations of any kind with intent to strike dumb, maim, or kill, either men or animals; or injure anything movable; or should practice said arts to the detriment of crops, vineyards, or trees; he shall suffer in person and property the same damage he endeavored to inflict upon others.[1]

---

[1] This would have been readily accepted as law under James I, a thousand years subsequently; and, no doubt, would have been indorsed as sound by Cotton Mather, whose sanguinary executions for witchcraft took place nearly eleven centuries after the death of the Visigothic king, Chintasvintus. The penalties for sorcery set forth in the *Forum Judicum*, were far less harsh than those prescribed by the Anglo-Saxon jurisprudence. The punishment of death was not permitted by the former, except where life had been lost through the effect of incantations or charms; a rare occurrence, as may well be surmised; and torture by fire is not even referred to, still less tolerated. In this instance, as in many others, the more lenient policy of the barbarian appears in striking contrast to the fierce and blind intolerance and cruelty of nations in the possession of superior culture and intelligence, and living in a far more progressive age.—[ED.

TITLE III. CONCERNING ABORTION.

ANCIENT LAW.

I. Concerning Those who Administer Drugs for the Production of Abortion.

If anyone should administer a potion to a pregnant woman to produce abortion, and the child should die in consequence, the woman who took such a potion, if she is a slave, shall receive two hundred lashes, and if she is freeborn, she shall lose her rank, and shall be given as a slave to whomever we may select.

ANCIENT LAW.

II. Where a Freeborn Man Causes a Freeborn Woman to Abort.

If anyone should cause a freeborn woman to abort by a blow, or by any other means, and she should die from the injury, he shall be punished for homicide. But if only an abortion should be produced in consequence, and the woman should be in no wise injured; where a freeman is known to have committed this act upon a freewoman, and the child should be fully formed, he shall pay two hundred *solidi;* otherwise, he shall pay a hundred *solidi*, by way of satisfaction.

ANCIENT LAW.

III. Where a Freeborn Woman Causes another Freeborn Woman to Abort.

Where a freeborn woman, either by violence or by any other means, causes another freeborn woman to abort, whether, or not, she should be seriously injured as a result of said act, she shall undergo the same penalty provided in the cases of freeborn men.

ANCIENT LAW.

IV. Where a Freeborn Man Produces Abortion upon a Slave.

Where a freeborn man produces abortion upon a female slave, he shall be compelled to pay twenty *solidi* to the master of the slave.

ANCIENT LAW.

V. Where a Slave Produces Abortion upon a Freeborn Woman.

Where a slave produces abortion upon a freeborn woman, he shall receive two hundred lashes in public, and shall be delivered up as a slave to said woman.

ANCIENT LAW.

VI. Where a Slave Produces Abortion upon a Female Slave.

Where a male slave produces abortion upon a female slave, he shall be compelled to pay ten *solidi* to her master, and, in addition, shall receive two hundred lashes.

FLAVIUS CHINTASVINTUS, KING.

VII. Concerning Those who Kill their Children before, or after, they are Born.

No depravity is greater than that which characterizes those who, unmindful of their parental duties, wilfully deprive their children of life; and, as this crime is said to be increasing throughout the provinces of our kingdom and as men as well as women are said to be guilty of it; therefore, by way of correcting such license, we hereby decree that if either a freewoman or a slave should kill her child before, or after its birth; or should take any potion for the purpose of producing abortion; or should use any other means of putting an end to the life of her child; the judge of the province or district, as soon as he is advised of the fact, shall at once condemn the author of the crime to execution in public; or, should he desire to spare her life, he shall at once cause her eyesight to be completely destroyed; and if it should be proved that her husband either ordered, or permitted the commission of this crime, he shall suffer the same penalty.[1]

[1] While abortion, as is well known, was not a crime at Common Law, and, under statutory regulations, was for a long time not considered punishable until the period of quickening; it was, however, recognized as a serious offence by the Romans, whose legislation on the subject was copied by the Visigoths. The wide variation of the penalties prescribed was, as is usual, largely dependent upon the social standing of the culprit; excepting in the provisions of the seventh chapter, where the innate cruelty of barbarian retribution is disclosed by one of the most frightful of punishments.—[ED.

TITLE IV. CONCERNING INJURIES, WOUNDS, AND MUTILATIONS INFLICTED UPON MEN.

I. Concerning the Injury of Freemen and Slaves.

Where one freeborn person strikes another any kind of a blow upon the head, he shall pay five *solidi* for a bruise, ten *solidi* if the skin be broken, twenty *solidi* for a wound extending to the bone, and a hundred *solidi* where a bone is broken. If a freeborn man should commit any of the above named acts upon the slave of another, he shall pay half of the above named penalties, according to the degree of his offence. If one slave should strike another, as above stated, he shall pay a third part of the above penalties, proportionate to his offence, and shall receive fifty lashes. If a slave, however, should wound a freeborn person, he shall pay the largest sum hereinbefore mentioned, which is exacted from freeborn persons for assaults upon slaves, and shall receive seventy lashes. If the master should not be willing to give satisfaction for the acts of his slave, he must surrender him on account of his crime.

II. Concerning Insolent Persons and their Acts.

If anyone with a drawn sword, or armed with any kind of weapon, should insolently enter the house of another, with the design of killing the master of the same, and should be himself killed, no one shall be held responsible for his death; but if he who entered said house should kill anyone, he shall be put to death at once. But if he should not commit any crime, he must at once give satisfaction, according to law, for any injury resulting from his act. And if he who entered the house of another by violence, should steal anything there, he shall be compelled to pay elevenfold the value of what he carried away. And if he should not have the means to pay the amount due, he shall be given up to serve as a slave; and if no damage should result from his violent entrance into the house, and he should not steal anything therefrom; for the mere fact of his forcible entry, he shall be compelled to pay ten *solidi* and shall receive a hundred lashes in public; and if he should not be possessed of said sum, he shall receive two hundred lashes. If any other freeborn persons, who were not under his orders or subject to him, or under his protection, should enter with him into the house; all of them, as giving consent to a high-handed and illegal act, shall undergo similar condemnation and penalties. If they should not have the property wherewith to render satisfaction, each one of them shall receive a hundred and fifty lashes; but they shall not lose the right to testify in court. But if they were under the protection, or in the service of the aggressor, and it is proved that he ordered them to commit the act of violence, or that they participated in it with him, the patron alone shall be held liable for all damage committed, as well as for the penalty; for they were not guilty who only carried out the orders of their superior. If a slave should commit such an act of violence without the knowledge of his master, he shall receive two hundred lashes, and shall be compelled to restore whatever he carried away. If, however, the slave acted with the knowledge of his master, the latter must give satisfaction for his act, as has been hereinbefore provided in the cases of freeborn persons.

FLAVIUS CHINTASVINTUS, KING.

III. Concerning the Law of Retaliation, and the Amount to be Paid in Lieu of the Enforcement of said Law.

The bloody rashness of some persons must be legally revenged by even the most severe penalties; for when anyone fears that he will suffer for what he has done, he is liable to abstain from the commission of crime. Therefore, if any freeborn person should dare to shave the head of another; or should mark, or scar him by violence inflicted either upon his face, or upon any other part of his body, by the use of a scourge, a whip, or any weapon; or, by maliciously dragging him upon the ground, should soil or defile him; or should maim him in any part of his limbs; or should restrain him of his liberty, by placing him in jail, or in any other place of confinement; or should order him to be imprisoned by others; or to be kept in custody and sold as a slave; having been apprehended by the judge, the same person shall receive by way of retaliation, whatever he inflicted, or attempted to inflict, upon another. And if he who suffered from his violence, or endured insult through his agency, should desire to receive pecuniary compensation from the culprit, he shall be entitled to recover such a sum as he may estimate will compensate him for the injuries he has sustained. We forbid, however, retaliation to be made for a blow with the fist or with the foot, or for any stroke upon the head; lest, when the retaliation is inflicted, a greater or more dangerous injury may result.

Where an aggressor commits such acts without causing any injury to the limbs, for a slap, he shall receive ten lashes; for a blow with the fist, or a kick, he shall receive twenty lashes; for a stroke on the head, if the blood should not flow, thirty lashes. And if he by whom the injury was produced, or who is said to have instigated it, where the act was not deliberately committed, but was the result of a sudden quarrel, should prove that it was caused by the fault of another, and against his own will, and, in the affray, an eye should have been lost, he shall pay a hundred *solidi* as a penalty. But if it should appear that the party injured can still see with the damaged eye, he may accept a pound of gold from the aggressor, by way of compensation. Where anyone is struck on the nose, and it should be entirely destroyed, the culprit shall pay a hundred *solidi.* If the blow upon the nose should be of such a character as to lay open the nostrils, the judge shall impose a penalty according to the deformity produced; and we decree that the same rule shall apply to injuries done to the lips and to the ears. A hundred *solidi* shall be paid for any injury to the loins. Whoever cuts off the hand of another entirely, or injures it with a blow so that the party cannot make use of it, shall pay a hundred *solidi* by way of reparation for such injury. Fifty *solidi* shall be paid for the loss of the thumb; for that of the forefinger, forty *solidi;* for that of the middle finger, thirty; for that of the fourth, twenty; for that of the fifth finger, ten *solidi.* Similar sums also shall be exacted for injuries inflicted upon the feet. For every tooth lost by violence, twelve *solidi* shall be paid. Whoever breaks the leg of another, and the latter thereby is rendered lame, shall pay him a pound of gold; and all the provisions above stated in regard to such injuries, shall apply where the rights of freemen are involved. But if a slave should commit any of the unlawful acts hereinbefore specified, or should he only shave the head of a freeman, he shall be delivered up into the power of the latter to be dealt with according to his pleasure. If, on the other hand, a freeborn person should shave the head of a slave belonging to another, or should give orders to shave the head of a peasant, he shall pay his master ten *solidi.* Where the slave is of superior rank, the offender shall not only be forced to pay the aforesaid sum of ten *solidi* to his master, but shall also receive a hundred lashes. If he has maimed the slave in any part of his body, or has ordered another to mutilate him, he shall receive two hundred lashes; and shall be compelled to give to the master of said slave, another of equal value to the one he has injured, by way of satisfaction. And if any freedman should commit any of the crimes hereinbefore specified against any freeman; for the reason that he was of inferior rank, not only shall the violence he committed be visited also upon him, but he shall, in addition, receive a hundred lashes with the scourge. And if a person born free should injure a freedman in any of the ways hereinbefore mentioned, he shall pay the third part of the amount for which freeborn persons are liable. If one slave should mutilate another without the knowledge of his master, or should shave his head, he shall undergo the same injury which he has inflicted, and shall receive a hundred lashes in public. If a slave, without the knowledge of his master, should seize and confine a freeborn person, he shall receive two hundred lashes in public. But where a slave commits any of these acts, with the consent of his master, the master only shall undergo the penalty, and pay the damages which are prescribed by this law in the case of freeborn persons. Where a freeborn person imprisons the slave of another who is innocent, he shall pay three *solidi* to his master. If one slave should imprison another, without the consent of the latter's master, he shall receive a hundred lashes. Where the slave committed the act, with the knowledge of his master, the master of said slave shall be compelled to pay three *solidi*. If any freeborn man shall detain the innocent slave of another in custody, day or night, or should cause him to be detained by another, he shall pay to the master of the said slave, for every day that he is thus restrained of his liberty, three *solidi*, and for every night an equal sum; and if the innocent slave is proved to have been thus imprisoned by the said freeman for several days, the latter shall be compelled to pay to the master the same sum of three *solidi* for every single day and night during which said slave was imprisoned. Any freeman who shall strike the slave of another with a whip, or scourge, or any kind of weapon, in such a way as to cause the blood to flow, or a bruise to appear, shall pay to the master of the slave one *solidus* for every blow inflicted; or, if serious injury should result, by which he who was struck was either killed or maimed, the offender shall pay for such an act, whatever sum the court, in its judgment, shall deem proper. Where one slave commits an assault upon another slave, the judge shall determine, according to the nature of the injury, the amount of the sum to be paid by the slave, or his master; which sum shall be equal to half that paid by a freeman under similar circumstances, and the slave shall receive a hundred lashes, in addition, for his insolence. All the provisions of this law shall apply to the cases of men as well as to those of women, in order that the questions left to the discretion of the judge by this and other laws, may be quickly decided.

If a judge, influenced by friendship, or corrupted by a bribe, should not dispose of a case in an equitable manner, or should neglect to at once impose a penalty, he shall be deprived of his judicial power for the future, and shall be compelled by the bishop, or the governor, to render satisfaction out of his own property, to an amount which said bishop or governor shall determine, to him to whom he refused to do justice; in order that he, who voluntarily refused to redress the wrongs of another, may be forced to undergo the loss of his own possessions.

ANCIENT LAW.

IV. Where a Person Deprives a Traveller of his Liberty, against the Will of the Latter, and with Intent to do him Injury.

If anyone, while on a journey, should be unlawfully restrained of his liberty by another, and no indebtedness should exist between them, he who has been so restrained shall be entitled to five *solidi* for the injury he has undergone; and if the offender should not have such a sum, he shall receive fifty lashes. But if one party should be indebted to another, and should refuse to pay the debt, the creditor may, without inflicting any injury upon him, bring him before the judge of the district, and the latter shall make such an order as he thinks to be just. Where a slave commits such an act, without the order of his master, he shall receive a hundred lashes. But if he should have done this under the direction of his master, said master shall be liable for the payment of the sum hereinbefore mentioned.

FLAVIUS CHINTASVINTUS, KING.

V. He who Violates the Law by Inflicting Injury upon Another, shall undergo the same Punishment which he Himself Inflicted.

It is no less a fault to be ignorant of the laws than, knowing them, to commit crimes. Wherefore, whoever, up to this time, or hereafter, has perpetrated, or shall perpetrate, any act forbidden by law, and shall either declare that he was ignorant of the law, or shall plot to carry out any act that shall enure to the injury or danger of anyone, alleging, at the same time, that such act is not prohibited by law, and that for this reason he cannot be held liable for its commission, and should such person be convicted, he shall at once undergo the same dangers, ignominy, tortures, suffering, or pecuniary loss, which he inflicted, or attempted to inflict, upon another; shall receive, in addition, a hundred lashes in public, and shall be scalped, as a mark of perpetual infamy.[1]

FLAVIUS CHINTASVINTUS, KING.

VI. He shall not be Considered Guilty who Struck Another, when the Latter was about to Strike Him.

It is no crime to resist another, where the violence of the attacking party is manifest. Whoever, therefore, should recklessly attempt to strike, or should strike, another with a whip, or sword, or with any weapon whatsoever, and the offender should then be so wounded by the party whom he attacks that he dies, such death shall not be considered homicide, nor shall he be liable to any reproach who struck the fatal blow; because it is more proper for a living person

---

[1] It is probable, from the extreme cruelty of the penalty imposed for professing ignorance of the laws of the land, that this defence had been frequently set up by criminals, and that it had, in not a few instances, been pleaded with success. There is not, in the entire Code, a sentence exceeding this in severity, as the crime itself is supposed to have been sufficiently expiated by the infliction of the *Lex Talionis*.—[ED.

to defend himself against an angry man, than to be revenged after his own death. And whoever, in anger, draws a sword against anyone, even though he should not strike him, shall be forced, on account of his insolence, to give ten *solidi* to him whom he thus threatened.

FLAVIUS RECESVINTUS, KING.

VII. Where a Slave Insults a Freeborn Person.

No slave, however respectable he may be, shall act insolently, arrogantly, or seditiously, towards a person of noble and illustrious lineage; and, should one be guilty of such conduct, he shall be sentenced by the judge to receive forty lashes with the scourge. A slave of inferior position shall be punished with fifty lashes with the scourge. Where a person of exalted rank first provokes the slave of another, and is insulted in consequence, he must attribute it to his own bad behavior; since, as he was forgetful of honor and patience, he only received what he deserved.

ANCIENT LAW.

VIII. Where One Freeborn Person Strikes Another.

If one freeborn person should inflict a wound upon another, and the wounded person should die at once, the attacking party shall be punished for homicide; and if he who was wounded should not die immediately, the aggressor must either be confined in prison, or released on bail. Should the person who was wounded escape with his life, he who injured him must pay him twenty *solidi*, on account of the attack alone; and, if he should not have that sum, he shall receive two hundred lashes in public, and, in addition to this, he shall be compelled to pay such damages, for the wound he inflicted, as may be assessed by the judges.

ANCIENT LAW.

IX. Where the Slave of Another is Mutilated by a Freeborn Person.

If any freeman should voluntarily mutilate the slave of another, he shall be compelled to give at once to his master, another slave of equal value; and he shall retain the one that was injured, to be cared for at his expense until he is cured. And if he should afterwards recover, the person who inflicted the wound shall pay such an amount in damages as may seem just to the court. And should he, afterwards, be restored to his master, safe and sound, said master shall receive him again as his slave. The aggressor, on account of the boldness of his act, inasmuch as he did not commit murder, but only ventured to wound the slave of another, shall pay ten *solidi* to his master.

X. Where a Slave Strikes a Freeborn Person.

If a slave, without the order of his master, should strike a freeborn person, and the latter should die at once, from the effect of the blow, the slave shall be punished for homicide; but if the wounded person should not die immediately, the slave shall be imprisoned; and if he who was wounded should recover, his assailant shall receive two hundred lashes. The master, if he should wish to do so, may pay, in satisfaction of the injury, whatever sum may be assessed by the court; and, if he should refuse to do this, the slave shall be given to the party injured, in satisfaction for his crime.

XI. Where One Slave Mutilates Another Slave.

Where one slave inflicts mutilation upon another, he shall receive a hundred lashes, in addition to the pecuniary satisfaction due for the wound; and if, as a result of said wound, the other should be partially disabled, the judge shall estimate how much his value has been diminished in consequence. If his master should refuse to accept the sum thus estimated, as satisfaction, he shall be entitled to receive the price of the slave who was injured, or one of equal value, from him whose slave committed the attack; and said master shall retain the mutilated slave as his own. We decree that this law shall also apply to female slaves.

TITLE V. CONCERNING HOMICIDE.

FLAVIUS RECESVINTUS, KING.

I. Where One Kills Another without Knowing it.

Whoever kills another ignorantly and unintentionally, if he has cherished no animosity against him, is not guilty of murder according to the Word of God; for it is not just that he should suffer the penalty of homicide who committed the act against his will.

FLAVIUS CHINTASVINTUS, KING.

II. Where One Kills Another without Seeing Him.

If one man should kill another, either standing, coming, or passing by, not being aware of his presence at the time, where no cause of enmity had previously existed between them, and he who committed the homicide shall declare that he did it involuntarily, and shall be able to prove this in court, he shall depart in safety.

FLAVIUS RECESVINTUS, KING.

III. Where One, being Pushed, Kills Another.

If anyone, either by accident, or by being pushed in any way, or by rushing headlong upon another, should kill him, he shall not be liable to the penalties of homicide. But if one man should push another, and, impelled by that push, the latter should kill a third party, and he who gave the push did so without malice, he shall pay a fine of a pound of gold, because he neglected to avoid the commission of an injury.

THE GLORIOUS FLAVIUS RECESVINTUS, KING.

IV. Where One, Seeking to Strike Another, Kills a Third Person.

Whenever, in a quarrel, anyone, while endeavoring to strike his adversary, unwillingly kills a third person, a legal investigation must be made to determine who originated the quarrel; and if it should be found that he was guilty who was first struck at, then he who strired up the strife, although he escaped the blow, yet, because it is apparent that he was the cause of the homicide, shall pay a fine of a hundred golden *solidi*. He who struck the blow shall pay fifty *solidi* to the nearest relatives of the person who was killed. Thus both pay a penalty; one, because he intentionally gave an opportunity for the commission of homicide; the other, because he unintentionally committed said homicide.

FLAVIUS RECESVINTUS, KING.

V. Where One is Killed while Interfering in a Quarrel.

If any freeman should interfere in a quarrel for the purpose of making peace, and should be killed in consequence, and he who struck him shall be able to prove, either by his own oath, or by the testimony of respectable witnesses, that the act was not committed intentionally, because the party who struck the fatal blow did not wish to commit assault or homicide upon the person who was killed, he shall pay a pound of gold to the relatives of the person who lost his life; and, in like manner, if any wound was inflicted under similar circumstances, the person who inflicted it shall pay a third part of the aforesaid sum; for the reason that the death of him who interfered for the purpose of making peace should not be unavenged.

FLAVIUS RECESVINTUS, KING.

VI. Where One, Intending to Inflict a Slight Injury, Kills Another.

Where anyone, attempting to commit an injury, gives a kick, or a blow with the fist, or commits any other violent act, and death should result, the guilty party shall be punished for homicide.

VII. Where One, in Sport, or Recklessly, Kills Another.

Whoever incautiously, or recklessly, or in sport, or in a crowd, unintentionally, by a fatal blow, strikes or kills anyone; because no malicious intention or desire to injure existed, shall incur no infamy for having committed an assault or homicide, even though he should be convicted by oath, or by the testimony of witnesses; nor shall he be liable to punishment by death, because he did not kill the person intentionally. But, for the reason that he struck the fatal blow without due caution, and did not attempt to avoid an accident, he shall pay a pound of gold to the nearest relatives of the deceased, and shall receive fifty lashes with the scourge.

FLAVIUS RECESVINTUS, KING.

VIII. Where One Kills Another through Immoderate Punishment.

If it should happen that a scholar, or any person under the patronage, or in the service of another, while undergoing moderate corporeal punishment, inflicted by his teacher, patron, or master, should die as a result of the same; and that he who inflicted the punishment entertained neither hatred or malice toward him whom he killed; he shall neither be rendered infamous, nor punished on account of the homicide; for the reason that it is said in the Holy Word of God that he shall be unhappy, who does not inflict punishment.

FLAVIUS RECESVINTUS, KING.

IX. Where a Freeman Kills a Slave by Accident.

If a freeman should kill a slave not intentionally, but by accident, he shall be compelled to pay to the master of the slave one-half of the amount which has been provided by way of reparation in the case of freeborn persons, under similar circumstances

FLAVIUS RECESVINTUS, KING.

X. Where a Slave Kills a Freeman by Accident.

If a slave should kill a freeborn person not intentionally, but accidentally, he shall pay the same sum which a former law has provided in the case of other freeborn persons. But if the master should be unwilling to pay said sum for his slave, the latter must, at once, be given up to justice.

ANCIENT LAW.

XI. Where One Man Intentionally Kills Another.

Every man who kills another intentionally, and not by accident, is liable to punishment for homicide.

FLAVIUS CHINTASVINTUS, KING.

XII. No Master shall Kill his Slave without Good Reason; and Where One Freeman Kills Another.

If anyone who is guilty of crime, or of giving wicked counsel to another, cannot escape punishment, how much more liable is he who deliberately and maliciously commits homicide? For this reason, as very frequently, through the excesses of cruel masters, slaves are deprived of their lives, without having committed any crime; it is proper that this license should be entirely abolished by means of the following law, which shall be hereafter observed by all, to wit: that no master or mistress shall deprive either their own slaves, or the slaves of others, of life, without an order of court. But if such a slave should acknowledge his guilt of a crime for which he is liable to punishment by death, his master or his accuser shall straightway communicate the fact to the judge of the district where the deed was committed; or to the governor of the city, or the governor of the province; and if, after an investigation, it is evident that the crime has been committed, the culprit shall receive, either from the judge or from his own master, the punishment of death, which he deserves.

If the judge should be unwilling to order him to be executed he shall commit his sentence of death to writing, and the master shall then have the power to either kill him, or to spare his life. If a slave, of either sex, while resisting his or her master, should strike him with a sword, stone, or with any weapon; or should attempt to strike him; and the master in his own defence, should immediately kill the slave, he shall not be punished for homicide, if it is evident that he defended himself; that is to say, if he can establish by the testimony, or the oaths of other slaves who were present, and by his own oath, that he was acting in his own defence. Where any person, through malice, either acting himself or through the agency of another, kills his own slave, he shall be deprived of the right to testify in court thereafter, as a mark of infamy; and, in order that such rashness may be prevented, he shall be exiled as long as he lives, and be forced to do penance, and his property shall be given to those whom the law has designated as his nearest heirs. Anyone who shall deliberately or intentionally kill, or order to be killed, a slave, of either sex, belonging to another, shall be compelled to give two slaves of equal value, to the master of the one who was killed; and the homicide, according to the provision hereinbefore stated, shall be sentenced to perpetual exile. And if either a master or a mistress, influenced by a sense of injury, or by anger, while inflicting punishment upon a slave of either sex, whether their own, or belonging to another, should kill such slave by a blow; and should be able to prove, either by witnesses, or by his or her own oath, that he or she involuntarily committed said homicide; such person shall not be amenable to punishment under this law. Where any male or female slave admits that he or she has, at the instigation, and with the consent of their master, killed a fellow slave or any other person, and, having been put to the torture, should accuse their master of having planned the crime for his own benefit; said slaves shall be publicly scourged with a hundred lashes, and shall be scalped as a token of infamy. If, however, the master should swear that he has not ordered, or influenced said slave, in any way, he shall not be considered guilty under this law; and the slave who committed the homicide shall be delivered up into the power of the master of the slave who was killed, to be disposed of at his pleasure; for any slave who kills another slave must be surrendered to the master of the latter.

Where a freeborn person has been convicted of having killed anyone by treachery, and for the purpose of robbery, while the latter was either on a journey or at home, he shall be at once punished for homicide; and as anyone who by counsel, or by order, instigates another to commit murder, is to be regarded as more infamous than he who perpetrated the deed, it is hereby especially provided that, except in the case of slaves, as hereinbefore set forth, if either a master or a mistress should order a freeborn person, of either sex, to be killed by a slave, and, after a severe, public investigation by torture, confession of the crime is made by said slaves, implicating their master or mistress, their testimony concerning the latter shall not be received, unless they are able to confirm it by the evidence of reputable witnesses. The master who is thus accused, must, at once, in the presence of the court, purge himself of all guilt by oath. Those who confess that they committed the homicide, shall either be punished for the crime, or shall be surrendered to the parents or the relatives of him who was killed, that they may do with them whatever they desire. Where the master is unable to make oath, as aforesaid, the male or female servant who has perpetrated such an infamous act, shall receive two hundred lashes, and shall be scalped as a mark of infamy. The master, by whose order such wickedness has been committed, shall suffer the punishment of death.

If several freeborn persons, by common agreement, should plan the perpetration of a homicide, he who struck the blow, or actually committed the deed, shall be put to death. The others, however, who are convicted of having plotted the crime, although they did not take an active part in its perpetration, shall nevertheless, on account of their wicked counsel, each receive two hundred lashes in public, and undergo the ignominy of being scalped. And, in addition, each shall be compelled to pay fifty *solidi* to the nearest relatives of the deceased, and should any of them not be possessed of such a sum, he shall be delivered over to them to be their slave forever.[1]

---

[1] The various degrees of homicide, as set forth in the preceding chapters, were clearly understood if not specifically designated, by the Visigothic legislator. Chapter XI, which describes the crime corresponding to murder in the first degree, is the only one of undoubted Roman origin; all the others being the acts of Councils, or the edicts of kings. In the first and second chapters, the circumstances which characterize excusable homicide are stated; and in the third, fourth, fifth, sixth, and seventh, the conditions attending the crime of manslaughter are explicitly defined. The vital question of intent, or the existence or non-existence of malice prepense, is referred to repeatedly, both in a positive and negative manner, whenever homicide is described. The humane protection afforded the slave from the cruelty of his master, as provided for by Chapter XII, suggests what frightful abuses must have previously resulted from the unrestrained

FLAVIUS RECESVINTUS, KING.

XIII. No One shall Deprive a Male or Female Slave of a Limb.

By a former law we have restrained masters, actuated by unbridled rage, from putting their slaves to death. Now that they may not deform man, who was made in God's own image, while in the act of practising cruelty upon those who are subject to them, we must forbid corporeal mutilation. For which reason, we decree that if any master or mistress, without a preliminary investigation in court, should openly and wickedly, deprive their slave of his nose, lip, tongue, ear,

---

exercise of magisterial tyranny. The guilt of the accessory-before-the-fact was not considered as great as that of the principal; as the penalty to which the former was liable, while being severe, as well as in the highest degree ignominious, fell short of the infliction of death. The horror with which a parricide has always been regarded, was likewise felt by the Visigoths, as is disclosed by his summary execution by the same means that he employed to take the life of his victim; a form of the *Lex Talionis* which was only made use of in the case of crimes of peculiar atrocity. The blinding to which a murderer was subjected, who had claimed the right of asylum, was far from being an exhibition of clemency, and certainly entailed greater suffering than the extreme penalty otherwise prescribed by the law. Homicide was justifiable, as has been seen, when committed in self-defence against an attacking party; in certain cases of trespass *vi et armis*, and where a father killed his adulterous daughter in his own home, or a husband caught an adulterer with his wife, *in flagrante delicto*. In the latter instances the offender was especially exonerated from all blame, on account of the provocation; and, therefore, could not be held for manslaughter, as he now can be, under the statutes of the majority of our States. Justification could also be pleaded where a criminal was killed while committing highway robbery, larceny, or burglary; the latter (*furtum nocturnum*) being a much more comprehensive term than ours, and including all kinds of nocturnal depredations. The employment of that popular American fiction, the "unwritten law," by means of which so many homicides have been acquitted, and which appeals so strongly to the primitive sense of retributive justice which still dominates humanity, was thus openly endorsed by the Visigothic Code. Insanity, as a defence for homicide, was utterly unknown to the legal systems of antiquity; and it is only under the highly artificial conditions of modern civilization that this theory has attained such an extraordinary, and often pernicious, development.—[ED.

or foot; or should tear out his eye; or should mutilate any other part of his body; or should order anyone else to perpetrate any of these acts; he or she shall be sentenced by the bishop in whose territory they live, or where the deed is proved to have been committed, to three years of exile, with penance.

Where such persons have children, who are not implicated with them in their crime, the latter shall take charge of all their property, and care for it; and shall restore it, with an account of their management of the same, when their parents return from exile. If, however, they have no legitimate children, the judge shall give said property into the keeping of other relatives; who, in like manner, upon return of the exiles, must restore to them said property, with an account of their management of the same. But should there be no such relative, the judge himself shall take charge of the property and preserve it, and, in like manner, give an account of it, when the parties return from exile.

THE GLORIOUS FLAVIUS RECESVINTUS, KING.

XIV. Any Person may bring an Accusation of Homicide.

If no one should be willing to accuse another of homicide, the judge, as soon as he learns that the crime has been committed, shall have the power to apprehend the guilty party, that he may receive the sentence he deserves; for the punishment of the crime may be unduly deferred, either on account of the absence of the accuser, or because some collusion exists between him and the murderer. A wife shall have the right to inquire into the death of her husband, or into any injury he has suffered at the hands of another; and a husband has, likewise, the same privilege in the case of a wife, and may demand that the crime be avenged by law. If either husband or wife should die while they had the intention of prosecuting a criminal, and, in consequence thereof, said prosecution should be left incomplete, their children or relatives, who stand next in the line of hereditary succession, shall have full power to accuse the offender, or the homicide, and to carry on the prosecution just as parents can do. The children or aforesaid relatives, shall not be entitled to the property of the offender or homicide, unless he should have previously undergone the punishment prescribed by law for his crime. If the judge, after having been notified, should refuse to avenge the crime, and, by reason of his delay or neglect, the matter should finally be brought to the attention of the king, the judge shall be compelled to give half of the legal composition for the homicide; that is to say, two hundred and fifty *solidi*, as a penalty for his disregard of his judicial duties. No one shall have a right to claim the property of anyone who is punished for a crime, before the sentence prescribed by law for said crime has been pronounced by the court.

FLAVIUS CHINTASVINTUS, KING.

XV. Both Relatives and Strangers have a Right to Accuse a Person of Homicide.

As it is proper that those who are guilty of other crimes should receive the penalties which they deserve, it must be regarded as infamous that homicides, whom it is but right should be treated with greater severity, should escape without punishment. Therefore, that no one who has committed a homicide may escape, or think that, by making excuses, he can avoid the consequences of his crime; the right of prosecution is hereby given, in the first place, to the relatives of the deceased; and if said relatives should be either lukewarm, or dilatory in inquiring into the death of their relative, then other relatives, as well as strangers, shall have the right to prosecute the offender. Any person who fraudulently attempts to defend or excuse a homicide, shall be compelled to pay to the accuser, double the amount which he has corruptly received. For no one guilty of homicide can ever feel secure, so long as he knows that everyone has the right to prosecute him.

FLAVIUS CHINTASVINTUS, KING.

XVI. Where a Homicide Takes Refuge in a Church.

We are not unmindful that, heretofore, many laws have been enacted, and penalties to be inflicted upon the guilty prescribed according to the nature of the crime, whether it be homicide or some other offence. Yet, because the authors of these wicked deeds who are as ready to commit them as they are cunning in seeking opportunities to escape punishment, and, as they, for the most part, betake themselves for protection to the churches of God, while, at the same time, they do not fear to commit crimes in violation of the Divine precepts; for the reason that wickedness of this kind should never go unpunished, because it destroys life, and frequently impels the minds of men to the commission of worse offences, we promulgate the following decree, to be observed through all time, to wit: That, as the law directs that every homicide or malefactor shall be punished, so, whoever, according to his own impulse, or evil disposition, commits such a crime, shall never be released from liability to the law, by any excuse or influence; but in case he should take refuge at the Holy Altar, a pursuer shall not presume to remove him from it without the consent of the priest. The priest having been consulted, however, and oath made that the party sought is a criminal, and liable to be publicly condemned to death; the priest himself shall drive him from the altar, and eject him from the choir; so that he who is pursuing him may arrest him.

He who has thus been driven from the church shall not, however, be liable to the penalty of death; but the sight of his eyes shall be entirely destroyed; or he may be delivered up into the power of the parents or relatives of him whom he killed; and the latter shall have the right to dispose of him at their pleasure, excepting they shall not put him to death; as a warning to prevent the intentions of depraved men from being carried into effect, when they know what punishments are prepared for them; and that he whom a wicked impulse often drives to the commission of an unlawful act, may, through terror, abstain from evil.

FLAVIUS CHINTASVINTUS, KING.

XVII. Concerning Parricides, and the Disposition of their Property

As no homicide intentionally committed is left unpunished by our laws, and as he who kills a blood-relation is more deserving of death than an ordinary murderer; we therefore promulgate the following edict, to be hereafter observed through all ages: That whoever shall be guilty of parricide; that is to say, whoever shall purposely, or actuated by the impulses of a depraved mind, kill his father, his mother, his brother, his sister, or anyone else nearly related to him, shall be immediately arrested by the judge, and put to death in the same manner as that by which he deprived his victim of life. Where the party guilty of the crime of parricide has no children, all his or her property shall belong to the nearest heirs of the person killed. If he or she should have children by another marriage, half of said property shall belong to the heirs of the person killed, and half to the children of the parricide, provided they were not implicated in the crime of the father or mother; but, if they were implicated in said crime, all of said property shall belong to the children of the deceased But if neither the parricide nor his victim should have left any children, then the parents of the person who was killed, or his nearest relatives, or such persons as have taken upon themselves the duty of avenging his death, shall have the undoubted right to claim for themselves the entire property of said parricide.

ANCIENT LAW.

XVIII. Concerning Those who Kill Others Related to Them by Blood.

If a father should kill his son; or a son his father; or a husband his wife; or a wife her husband; or a mother her daughter; or a daughter her mother; or a brother his brother; or a sister her sister; or a son-in-law his father-in-law; or a father-in-law his son-in-law; or a daughter-in-law her mother-in-law; or a mother-in-law her daughter-in-law; or if any of said persons should kill anyone else related to them by blood or lineage, they shall be condemned to death. And, if on account of his crime, the homicide should flee to a church, or take refuge at the Holy Altar, he shall be delivered up into the power of the parents or relatives of him whom he killed; and they shall have full authority to dispose of him, according to their pleasure, except to deprive him of life. And we decree that all his property shall go to the heirs of the person kil'ed, as hereinbefore provided; or be forfeited to the Crown, should the person killed leave no near heirs; for a homicide, if liberated, has no right to the enjoyment of his property, even should he escape the penalty of death.

XIX. Where One Blood Relative is Accidentally Killed by Another.

If a father should kill his son; or a son his father; or a mother her daughter; or a brother his brother; or any person one nearly related to him; and he who commits such an act should be impelled by injury, or should be acting in self-defence, and it can be proven in open court, by respectable witnesses, who are worthy of credit, that the parricide was committed in self-defence; the party accused shall be in no danger of his life, and shall be discharged, without loss of property or subjection to torture; such discrimination being used as is proper in all cases of homicide.

FLAVIUS RECESVINTUS, KING.

XX. Where One Slave Kills Another by Accident.

If one slave should be convicted of having accidentally killed another, his master shall pay to the master of the slave who was killed, by way of compensation, one half the sum required by law, under similar circumstances, where death ensues as the result of an accident. If the master should refuse to give satisfaction as aforesaid, he must surrender the slave to the master of the one who was killed.

ANCIENT LAW.

XXI. Concerning Those who Destroy their Souls by Perjury.

If anyone, on account of oppression of any kind, should knowingly conceal the truth or should perjure himself; as soon as the fact shall come to the knowledge of the judge, he shall be arrested; shall receive a hundred lashes; shall be branded as an infamous witness; and shall never again be permitted to testify in court. And, as has been provided by a former law relating to perjury, a fourth part of his property shall be given, by order of the judge, to him whom he attempted to defraud.

BOOK VII.

CONCERNING THEFT AND FRAUD.

TITLE I. CONCERNING INFORMERS OF THEFT.

I. Concerning Informers and Persons who give Information of Theft.

A judge shall not inflict torture upon any person accused of crime, before he who brings the accusation (if he is unwilling to produce the informer in court), enters into an obligation in writing, confirmed by the signatures of three witnesses, that if the accused is proved to be innocent by competent evidence, he himself will suffer the penalty which he attempted to inflict upon another. After the innocence of the accused has been established, the accuser shall be placed in custody by the judge, until he brings the informer into court, that the truth may be ascertained; and, should he not produce said informer, he shall, without delay, give his name, so that, when brought before the judge, he may prove what he has alleged. If, however, the judge is unable to elicit the truth, on account of the intervention of some powerful person, or the patronage of a noble, or through fear of the royal power, he must attempt to bring the matter to the attention of the king, if he be near at hand; but, if he is at a distance, he must lay his information before the bishop, or the governor of the province; in order that the superior authority of these officials may cause the matter to be properly investigated. Where the judge neglects to give such notice, the complainant shall be indemnified, at the expense of the said judge, for the entire property lost or stolen, by order of the king or of the bishop. If the informer cannot prove what he alleged, he alone shall be liable to make amends for the consequences of his act. If the property stolen is of great value, and a freeborn person is implicated, he shall return ninefold the value of the property, by way of reparation, and shall be rendered infamous; and, if the culprit is a slave, he shall pay sixfold the value of the property, and shall receive in addition, a hundred lashes. Where said freeman has not sufficient property to render satisfaction as aforesaid, he shall be surrendered as a slave to him whom he attempted to render infamous by a false accusation, and to him whom he attempted to deceive. If a slave should not have the property wherewith to render satisfaction, as aforesaid, or, if his master should be unwilling to pay the sum required in his behalf, he shall at once surrender the slave in satisfaction of his crime.

II. A Slave, Acting as Informer, must not be Believed, unless the Testimony of his Master is also Given.

If a slave, without the knowledge of his master, should give information of a theft, his statement shall not be believed, unless his master should testify that he was trustworthy, and should thereby establish his honor and credibility.

ANCIENT LAW.

III. Where the Informer Knew of the Commission of the Theft.

If the informer should be proved to have had knowledge of the theft, he shall incur no penalty, and shall not be subject to payment of damages; but he cannot demand any reward for the information he furnishes, because it is sufficient compensation for him to be permitted to depart in safety. Where the property stolen was divided between him and the thief, he shall only be required to restore to the owner what he received and kept for himself.

ANCIENT LAW.

IV. Concerning the Compensation of an Informer.

Where anyone gives information concerning a thief, even if he should not personally have been aware that the theft was committed, he shall not receive any more for the information he furnishes than the stolen property was worth; and then only after full satisfaction has been made to the owner. If the circumstances should be such, that the execution of the thief was necessary, and no property belonging to him could be found; or if he was a slave, and his master claimed his property as his own, and therefore no compensation was available for him who was robbed; in such cases the third part of the property recovered shall be set aside as a reward for the information, and the informer shall not be permitted to demand more than that amount.

ANCIENT LAW.

V. Where an Innocent Person is Accused of Crime by an Informer.

When anyone is accused of crime, that is to say, of poisoning, witchcraft, theft, or any other unlawful act, his accuser must go before the governor of the city, or the judge who has jurisdiction in the district, in order that the case may be investigated according to aw; and as soon as the commission of the crime has been established, the governor or the judge shall cause the culprit to be arrested; and if he should not be convicted of a capital offence, the accuser shall be compelled to give him pecuniary satisfaction; and where the latter has not the means to do so, he shall be delivered up to him as a slave. Where the accused person is proved to be innocent, he shall be discharged; and the accuser shall pay both the penalty and the damages for which the accused would have been liable, had he been convicted. Neither the governor nor the judge shall presume to apply torture, unless in public; lest there may be some collusion, so that an innocent man may suffer unjustly. But he shall not undergo the penalty for the crime until its commission has been proved in court by competent testimony; or, as has been provided for by other laws, before the accuser has bound himself to substantiate the charge; and then, and then only, torture may be applied in the presence of the judges.

TITLE II. CONCERNING THIEVES AND STOLEN PROPERTY.

I. He who is Searching for Stolen Property must Describe it.

Whoever makes a demand for any stolen property, must privately describe to the judge what he seeks, and show, by manifest proof, what he has lost; as the truth may not be established, where sufficient evidence is not introduced.

ANCIENT LAW.

II. Where a Slave Commits a Theft Before, or After, he has Received his Freedom.

If a slave should be guilty of theft, and should be afterwards set free by his master, the master shall not be liable for any loss on account of any acts previously committed by said slave; but the slave himself shall suffer the penalties prescribed by the law against the perpetrators of crime. Where he commits a theft after he has received his freedom, he shall be compelled to make the same reparation as he would have done while a slave, and shall receive a hundred lashes. If said offence should not be of such a character as to render him liable to be returned to slavery, he shall remain in the full enjoyment of his freedom.

ANCIENT LAW.

III. Where a Slave, who has Become the Property of Another Master, Commits an Unlawful Act.

If a slave who has passed under the control of another master, should steal anything from his former owner, or should inflict any injury upon anyone, the judge shall determine whether he committed the crime; and if he is convicted, his last master, should he desire, may render satisfaction for the acts committed by said slave. But if he should refuse to do so, the slave must be surrendered to be punished according to the nature of his offence.

IV. Where a Freeman Commits a Theft in Company with the Slave of Another Person.

Where a freeman is implicated with the slave of another person in the commission of any crime, whether they steal, or appropriate any property, or are guilty of any other unlawful act; each shall be liable for half the pecuniary compensation required by a former law, and both shall be scourged together in public. And if the master should not be willing to render full satisfaction for the act of said slave, the latter must be surrendered in lieu thereof. But if they have committed a capital crime, the slave and the freeman shall, at the same time, be condemned to death.

ANCIENT LAW.

V. Where a Master Commits a Theft in Company with his Slave.

If a master should commit a theft in company with his slave, we hereby decree that the master, and not the slave, shall make full pecuniary reparation for the same; and the master shall receive a hundred lashes in public, as prescribed by law. The slave, however, shall go free, because he obeyed the commands of his master.

ANCIENT LAW.

VI. Where a Slave, Belonging to Another Person, is Instigated by Anyone to the Commission of Unlawful Acts.

If anyone should instigate the slave of another person to commit a theft, or any other unlawful act; or should persuade him to do anything contrary to his own interest, which may also be the occasion of loss to his master, in order that, by his evil and iniquitous influence, he may fraudulently obtain possession of said slave for himself; and, after proper investigation by the judge, the fraud is detected, the said master shall not lose his slave, or be liable to any penalty; but he, by whose artifice and persuasion, the slave was induced to commit the crime, in order that he might obtain possession of him as aforesaid, shall be forced to pay to the master of the slave sevenfold the value of the property stolen, or the legal damages prescribed for his act. The slave shall receive a hundred lashes in public; for the reason that, despising his master, he plotted against him, and, after the infliction of said punishment, he shall be restored to his master.

ANCIENT LAW.

VII. Concerning those who Knowingly Associate with Thieves.

Not only he who actually commits a theft, but also any person who was aware of it at the time, or knowingly received the stolen goods, shall be considered a thief, and liable to the penalty prescribed for the crime.

FLAVIUS RECESVINTUS, KING.

VIII. Where Anyone, Ignorantly, Buys Stolen Property of a Thief.

It shall not be lawful for a freeman to buy any property from a person unknown to him, unless he can produce a reliable person as a witness, and thereby be able to allege the excuse of ignorance. If he should do otherwise, he shall be compelled by the judge to produce, within a reasonable time, the person of whom he bought said property; and if he cannot find him, he must prove his innocence, either by oath or by witnesses, and show that he did not know that the vendor was a thief; and he must restore the property which he purchased to the owner, after having received from the latter an amount equal to half the price paid for said property; and both shall promise, under oath, that they will make diligent search for the thief. If, however, the latter cannot be found, the purchaser shall only be compelled to restore to the owner the property which he bought. In case the owner of said property should know the thief, and should be unwilling to expose him, he shall lose the property absolutely, and the purchaser shall possess it in peace. This law shall also apply to slaves.

ANCIENT LAW.

IX. Where Anyone, Knowingly, Buys Stolen Property of a Thief.

If anyone should, knowingly, purchase stolen property of a thief, he must at once declare from whom he bought it, and afterwards must make restitution, just as the thief should do. If he should not be able to find the latter, he shall be compelled to pay double the amount required from thieves, because it is evident that he who purchases stolen property is on the same legal footing as a thief. Where a slave commits such an act, he shall pay half the amount required of free-born persons, or his master shall surrender him in satisfaction of his crime.

ANCIENT LAW.

X. Concerning Money, and Other Property, Stolen from the King.

If anyone should steal, or appropriate to his own use, money or other property belonging to the public treasury, he shall restore ninefold its value.[1]

ANCIENT LAW.

XI. Concerning the Stealing of Bells from Cattle.

If anyone should steal a bell from a mare or an ox, he shall pay one *solidus;* from a cow, two *tremisæ;* from a ram or other cattle, one *tremisa*

---

[1] It is rather remarkable that the theft of royal property should only have been punished by the imposition of a fine equal to that prescribed where a private individual was robbed. It is evident that, under a strict construction of this law, no other penalty could be inflicted.—[ED.

XII. Concerning the Theft of Mill Machinery.

If anyone should steal any of the parts of a mill, he shall return what was stolen; shall also pay the fine provided by law as punishment for other thefts; and shall receive, in addition, a hundred lashes.

FLAVIUS CHINTASVINTUS, KING.

XIII. Concerning the Punishment of a Thief.

A freeman who steals the property of another, shall pay to the owner nine times the value, and a slave six times the value, of the property stolen; and each shall receive a hundred lashes with the scourge. If the freeman has not sufficient pecuniary resources to pay said fine; or if the master should refuse to render satisfaction for the act of his slave; he who was guilty of the theft shall become forever the slave of the owner of the stolen property.

ANCIENT LAW.

XIV. A Thief, when Taken, shall be Brought Before the Judge; and Where a Freeman Commits a Theft in Company with a Slave, Both shall Undergo the Same Penalty.

When a thief is arrested, he shall be brought into court, and, if freeborn, shall pay nine times the value of the stolen property, and shall receive a hundred lashes publicly, in the presence of the judge. If, however, he should not have the means wherewith to make restitution, he shall forfeit his liberty, and become the slave of him whom he robbed. A slave shall make restitution sixfold for the property stolen; shall receive a hundred lashes in the presence of the judge; and shall be kept in custody until his master is notified to immediately give satisfaction for his act; and, should he not do so, he must, at once, surrender the criminal to the party who suffered the loss.

It is also provided by this law, that if a slave and a freeman, or several slaves and several freemen, should, while together, steal any animal, or any other article of property, they shall make but one compensation for the same; that is to say, freemen shall pay half of its ninefold value, and slaves half of its sixfold value; but they all shall receive the same number of lashes as hereinbefore provided. The aforesaid provision shall also be observed in the cases of slaves and freemen, where property of great value was stolen, and they shall be scourged before the judge as hereinbefore stated.

ANCIENT LAW.

XV. Where a Thief, Defending Himself with a Sword, is Killed.

If a thief should be killed in the daytime, while defending himself with a sword, no responsibility shall attach to anyone on account of his death.

ANCIENT LAW.

XVI. Where a Thief is Killed at Night, while he is Being Taken.

If a thief should be surprised at night, and should be killed while he is attempting to remove stolen property, his death shall under no circumstances be punished.

ANCIENT LAW.

XVII. Concerning Property Injured or Destroyed; and the Reparation to be Made for what has been Damaged or Stolen.

Where anyone damages property or clothing belonging to another, or does any injury to a traveller while on a journey, or deprives him of anything by stealth, he shall immediately give satisfaction according to law; but shall not be compelled to pay the full value of the baggage of the traveller, but only an amount equal to what he damaged, or stole from him.

ANCIENT LAW.

XVIII. Concerning Property Rescued from Shipwreck.

Where property has been saved from conflagration, ruin, or shipwreck, and any of it is abstracted or concealed by any person; he shall be compelled to pay fourfold the value of the same.

ANCIENT LAW.

XIX. Concerning the Property and the Heirs of Thieves.

Where anyone obtains the property of a dead thief, either by will or inheritance, he shall not be liable to any penalty, because the crime died with the perpetrator; but he shall be liable to satisfaction in damages, for the reason that the thief would have been so liable, had he lived. If the damages incurred amount to more than the inheritance, he must surrender the latter in its entirety.

ANCIENT LAW.

XX. Concerning Those who Rescue Thieves and Other Criminals after their Capture.

If anyone should rescue a thief or any other criminal who is in custody, or permit him to escape; if he is a person of rank, he shall receive a hundred lashes in the presence of the judge for his insolence, and shall be compelled to produce in court the party whom he set free. If another person who has no claim against a thief, should arrest him, he shall receive for his services a fourth part of the sum due from the thief in satisfaction of his crime. Where the latter cannot afterwards be found, he who liberated him shall be liable to the punishment prescribed for theft; and shall be compelled to pay, out of his own property, a sum equal to that which the thief would have been compelled to pay, had he been convicted. If, however, he is a person of inferior rank, and should produce the thief in court, he shall receive for his insolence a hundred lashes. Where he is not able to find the thief, he shall be liable to both the penalty and damages for theft, to the same extent as the thief himself would have been liable after conviction.

If anyone should release a person accused of another crime than theft, he shall received a hundred lashes in like manner; and if he cannot find or produce the party he liberated, he shall at once suffer the same punishment to which the law declares the accused would have been liable, had he been found guilty. If a slave should commit this offence, without his master's knowledge, he shall receive two hundred lashes for his insolence, and shall be compelled to produce the person whom he released. If he should not produce him, then his master, should he wish to do so, may pay for him the sum demanded as compensation for the crime; but if he should be unwilling to pay said sum as provided by law, he must surrender the slave in satisfaction for damages, or to be punished.

ANCIENT LAW.

XXI. Where a Slave Steals from his Master, or from a Fellow-Slave.

If a slave should steal anything from his master or from his fellow-slave, what shall be done with him lies entirely in the discretion of his master; and the judge has no right to interfere in the matter, unless the master should wish him to do so.[1]

ANCIENT LAW.

XXII. Within what Time, after his Arrest, a Thief must be Brought Before the Judge.

When anyone arrests a thief, or any other criminal, he must straightway conduct him before the judge; and he must not keep him in his house longer than one day, or one night. If anyone should violate this provision, he shall be forced to pay five *solidi* to the judge for his insolence. If a slave should do this, without the knowledge of his master, he shall receive a hundred lashes, but if he should do it with the

---

[1] This chapter, a survival of the irresponsible authority exercised by the Roman *dominus*, is the only one in the Code where the fate of a slave, guilty of crime, is specifically and absolutely left to the will of his master. It is possible that, on account of the facility afforded for the commission of such offences, the possession of extraordinary power was supposed to be required, as a safeguard.—[ED.

master's consent, all liability for damages shall be incurred by the latter. If the slave is of superior rank, his master shall be compelled to pay a fine of ten *solidi*, half of which sum shall belong to the judge, and the other half shall be given to him who is known to have suffered the injury.

FLAVIUS RECESVINTUS, KING.

XXIII. Where Anyone Secretly Kills an Animal Belonging to Another.

If anyone should, secretly or at night, kill a horse, an ox, or any other kind of animal belonging to another, he shall be compelled to pay ninefold the value of the same. If it is not possible to convict him, he shall purge himself of guilt publicly, by oath. Where a slave commits such an offence, under the direction of his master, and this is proved by competent evidence; the master of the slave shall be compelled to make restitution ninefold, as a thief would have done. If a slave should not be convicted by testimony, he shall be tortured; and after it has been established that he committed the crime, he shall either pay sixfold the value of the animal killed, or shall be transferred to the service of him whom he injured. If, however, he should prove to be innocent, the complainant shall render satisfaction to the master of the slave, as provided by other laws.

TITLE III. CONCERNING APPROPRIATORS AND KIDNAPPERS OF SLAVES.

THE GLORIOUS FLAVIUS RECESVINTUS, KING.

I. Where Anyone Seizes the Slave of Another.

If any freeborn person should seize and appropriate a slave belonging to another, he shall be compelled to give to the master another slave, of equal value, by way of restitution. If a slave should commit this offence, he must return the slave whom he has seized to the master of the same, and he shall then receive a hundred lashes. If the slave that was seized cannot be produced in court, the master must give another slave, of equal value, to him who sustained the loss; to be kept by him until the slave who was carried off is restored, when the other slave, who was surrendered in his place, shall be returned to his own master.

FLAVIUS RECESVINTUS, KING.

II. Where a Freeman is Convicted of Having Stolen the Male or Female Slave of Another.

If a freeman should kidnap the male or female slave of another, he shall be compelled to give, by way of reparation, four slaves of the same sex to the master or mistress of said slave, and shall receive a hundred lashes in public; and if he should not have the property wherewith to make restitution, he himself shall be reduced to slavery.

ANCIENT LAW.

III. Concerning Kidnapped Children of Freeborn Persons.

If anyone should kidnap the son or daughter of a freeborn person, of either sex; or should lure them from home, and cause them to be taken into other provinces of our kingdom, or into any foreign country; he who is guilty of such an atrocious crime, shall be delivered up to the father or mother of the child; or to its brothers, if there are any; or to its nearest relatives; to be killed or sold into slavery. Should they wish to do so, they may exact from the kidnapper, the legal compensation for homicide; that is to say, three hundred *solidi:* because for a child to be sold by its parents, or to be kidnapped, is as serious a crime as the commission of homicide. If, however, the kidnapper should recover the child from the foreign country where it has been sent, and bring it again to its native land, he shall pay a hundred and fifty *solidi:* that is to say, half of the composition for homicide; and should he not be possessed of said amount, he shall be condemned to servitude.

ANCIENT LAW.

IV. Where One Slave Kidnaps Another Belonging to a Person not his Master.

If one slave should steal another, who is the property of another master, without the knowledge of his own master, he shall receive a hundred and fifty lashes in the presence of the judge, and the kidnapped slave shall be restored to his master. And he whose slave was stolen shall not be entitled to demand a reward from the master of the kidnapper for the capture of the kidnapped slave. If, however, the slave who was kidnapped should not be found, the master of the kidnapper shall be compelled by the judge to give another slave of equal value, or the kidnapper himself, up to him whose slave was stolen; to serve until such time as his own slave shall be restored to him, when the other slave shall be returned to his master.

ANCIENT LAW.

V. Where a Slave, at the Command of his Master, Kidnaps a Freeborn Person.

If a slave, by order of his master, should kidnap a freeborn person, the master shall be liable for such satisfaction in damages as has been elsewhere provided in the case of free-born persons, and shall receive a hundred lashes in public; but the slave himself shall incur no penalty, having acted under the command of his master.

VI. Where a Slave, without the Knowledge of his Master, Kidnaps a Freeborn Person.

If a slave, without the knowledge of his master, should kidnap a freeborn person, he shall be delivered up, without delay, to the parents of said person, to be disposed of absolutely at their pleasure. If, however, the kidnapped person should be brought back, and the master should desire to give satisfaction for the act of his slave; he shall pay a pound of gold, as compensation for the injury inflicted upon said freeborn person.[1]

---

[1]The enforcement of the *Lex Talionis* in case of the kidnapping of a freeborn person indicates the abhorrence with which the crime, ever regarded by all nations as one of the most atrocious in the calendar, was viewed by the Visigoths. As slaves were valuable articles of property, the legislation of the Code was principally directed against those who stole them. The kidnapping of women, having been already provided for under the title of Rape, is, for that reason, not referred to here.—[ED.

TITLE IV. CONCERNING THE CUSTODY AND SENTENCE OF CONDEMNED PERSONS.

I. *Where a Judge is Asked to Punish Crime, and is afterwards Treated with Contempt.*

II. *The Governor of the City shall Aid the Judge in the Arrest of Persons Accused of Crime.*

III. *Where a Person Breaks out of Prison, or Influences the Jailer for that Purpose.*

IV. *Concerning the Compensation which may be Received from those in Custody.*

V. *Where a Judge who is Lenient to Offenders against the Law, Releases a Criminal.*

VI. *Concerning the Punishment of a Judge who Improperly Discharges a Criminal.*

VII. *A Person Guilty of Crime shall Receive the Sentence of the Law not Secretly, but in Public.*

THE GLORIOUS FLAVIUS RECESVINTUS, KING.

I. Where a Judge is Asked to Punish Crime, and is afterwards Treated with Contempt.

If anyone should accuse another of theft, before a judge, and should afterwards be guilty of contempt of court, by accepting anything from the thief by way of compensation, without the judge's knowledge, he shall be compelled to pay five *solidi* to the judge, on account of his insolence. Where a slave, without the knowledge of his master, is guilty of this offence, he shall receive a hundred lashes, and his master shall incur no liability whatever, on account of his act. But if he should do this with the consent of his master, the latter shall be compelled to pay the sum hereinbefore mentioned.

ANCIENT LAW.

II. The Governor of the City shall Aid the Judge in the Arrest of Persons Accused of Crime.

Whenever a Goth, or anyone else, is accused of crime, the judge must use every effort to arrest him. If, however, the judge himself is not sufficiently powerful to apprehend and imprison him, he may apply to the governor of the city for assistance, to effect what his authority of itself is not sufficient to accomplish. The aforesaid governor must immediately employ all his power to that end, in order that a person guilty of crime may not defy the law.

ANCIENT LAW.

III. Where a Person Breaks out of Prison, or Influences the Jailer for that Purpose.

If anyone should break out of prison, or should use undue influence upon the turnkey, or upon the jailer himself, or upon any keeper who has charge of prisoners, by means of which any prisoner should be unlawfully released, without the order of the judge; he shall suffer the same punishment which the escaped or liberated prisoner himself would have suffered.

ANCIENT LAW.

IV. Concerning the Compensation which may be Received from those in Custody.

Where a judge has charge of persons who have been arrested, or where officers have arrested them, or have received them for safe keeping; none of them shall be entitled to exact anything from said prisoners, on account of their keeping, or of their discharge, in case such prisoners should prove to be innocent. But where they are proved to be guilty, said officers shall not be forbidden to demand from each prisoner, one *tremisa.* If the party arrested should be released, upon giving the pecuniary compensation required by law, the judge himself shall pay over said sum to those who are entitled to the same, except the tenth part of it, which he himself shall have a right to retain for his trouble. If anyone should accept a larger amount than we have stated, he must restore it, twofold, to him from whom he exacted it.

ANCIENT LAW.

V. Where a Judge who is Lenient to Offenders against the Law, Releases a Criminal.

Where a judge, corrupted by a bribe of any description whatever, puts an innocent man to death, he himself shall be punished in like manner. If he should discharge a person who has committed a capital crime, he shall pay sevenfold the amount which he received for his release, to him who was injured by the criminal; and, stripped of judicial power, and rendered infamous, he shall be compelled by the judge who succeeds him, to produce in court the party whom he released; so that the latter, when convicted, may undergo the punishment which he deserved.

THE GLORIOUS FLAVIUS RECESVINTUS, KING.

VI. Concerning the Punishment of a Judge who Improperly Discharges a Criminal.

A judge shall not spare a criminal, on account of the patronage or friendship of any person. If, in his leniency and partiality, he should not vindicate the innocent, or should discharge the guilty, he shall not be put to death, or undergo any mutilation of body; but shall only pay the sum required by law in satisfaction for homicide, or of any other crime which may be involved.

ANCIENT LAW.

VII. A Person Guilty of Crime shall Receive the Sentence of the Law not Secretly, but in Public.

When a judge inflicts the death penalty upon a criminal, he shall execute the sentence of the law not in secret and retired places, but publicly, in the sight of all.

TITLE V. CONCERNING FORGERS OF DOCUMENTS.

I. Concerning those who Forge Royal Orders and Mandates.

Whoever shall change, impair the force of, omit something from, or interpolate anything into, any part of our royal decrees or mandates; or shall alter the date of the same; or shall make or attach a forged seal to any of them; if said person is of high rank, he shall forfeit half of all his property, and it shall be confiscated for the benefit of the royal treasury; if, however, he is a person of inferior station, he shall lose the hand with which he committed the crime. Where the judges, or other authorities before whom the hearing was to be had, or for whom the order of the king was intended, die; then either the bishop of the diocese, or any other bishop, or the judges of the territory adjacent to that affected by the order, shall have full authority to act in their stead; to promulgate the decree; and to make such disposition of the matter as, in their judgment, shall appear to be legal and just.

FLAVIUS CHINTASVINTUS, KING.

II. Concerning those who Forge Documents, or Attempt to Forge Them.

Whoever forges a document; or publishes it; or knowingly makes an addition to it; or produces it in court; or anyone who suppresses, abstracts, mutilates, impairs the force of, or changes, a genuine document; and whoever engraves, makes, or attaches a false seal, and is found guilty of such infamous crimes, shall, with all his abettors, lose the fourth part of their property, if they are persons of noble rank. If any person should steal, or deface a document belonging to another, and should afterwards confess, in the presence of the judge, that he had stolen or defaced said document, and this confession should be corroborated by witnesses, said testimony shall have the same force in law as the destroyed or defaced document would have, if it still existed in its integrity. But if the contents of the document cannot be shown with certainty, he who drew it up shall be permitted to prove by his own oath, or by a witness, what said document contained; and the testimony so given shall establish the contents of said document.

When the property of those who have been condemned is not sufficient to pay the fine prescribed by law, they, with such possessions as they have, shall be delivered up, as slaves, to those whom they have defrauded. He who sustained the injury or loss, shall receive, by order of the king or the judge, three quarters of the fourth part of the property hereinbefore mentioned; and the fourth part of the same shall be reserved for the king, to be disposed of at his royal pleasure. Persons of inferior rank, or of infamous character, who have been convicted of these offences, must sign a confession as hereinbefore provided; and shall forever be the slaves of those who suffered by their fraudulent acts. In addition to the above penalties, culprits of inferior, as well as of superior rank, shall receive a hundred lashes with the scourge. If a slave commits such an offence, and it should appear that he was influenced by other persons, all parties implicated in the crime, and who are proved to have either stolen, concealed, or mutilated, the document in question, shall become slaves forever to those who were injured by their unlawful acts. But if it should appear that said acts were committed under the orders of a master, he shall be responsible for all damages sustained. We also decree that this same rule shall apply to all who, for the sake of gain, either suppress or mutilate any documents belonging to others, with the view to inflicting upon them either loss or injury. Such persons also shall be considered forgers, and shall suffer the penalty hereinbefore provided, according to their rank.

Where nothing which is set forth in this chapter appears to have been done; that is to say, if no one is convicted of having mutilated, torn, forged, or concealed, a document belonging to another, or of having committed any other offence described by this law, but that the person accused has merely lost said document through negligence, accident, or want of care; or where he declares that it has been stolen from him; if a witness who subscribed said document be still living, his testimony, taken in court, will be amply sufficient to establish its validity. Where it appears that the witness who subscribed said document is dead, and other lawful and intelligent witnesses can be found, who will testify that they saw said document, and are thoroughly acquainted with its contents; then he who lost the document in question, may prove by the testimony of said witnesses, by a public investigation in court, the former existence and the contents of said document, and thereby establish its validity.

ANCIENT LAW.

III. Concerning those who Forge, or Serve, False Orders in the Name of the King, or a Judge.

He who ignorantly publishes an edict issued in the name of the king or a judge, shall not incur the guilt of forgery; but he must at once disclose who gave him the said edict. If he should be unwilling to name the person, or to admit that he received the edict from him, he himself shall then be punished for forgery, according to his rank; as is hereinbefore provided in the cases of those who make or utter forged documents. But if both the parties should be aware that the forgery had been committed, both shall be considered forgers.

ANCIENT LAW.

IV. Concerning those who Falsify a Will against the Consent of a Party while Living, or Disclose the Contents of the Same.

Whoever shall forge the will, or any document containing an order, or any instructions, of a person still living, or shall disclose the contents of the same contrary to the wishes of said party, shall be deemed guilty of forgery.

ANCIENT LAW.

V. Concerning those who Attempt to Forge or Conceal the Will of a Person Already Deceased.

Whoever shall conceal the will of a deceased person, or shall insert any forged matter therein, shall lose whatever property he would have been entitled to, through the bequest of the testator in said will, and said property shall belong to those whom he attempted to defraud; and he shall, besides, bear the infamy attaching to the crime of forgery. Even if he should have little or nothing to gain from such an act, he shall nevertheless be condemned as a forger.

ANCIENT LAW.

VI. Where Anyone Assumes a Fictitious Name, or Adopts a False Lineage, or Relationship.

Whoever assumes a false name; or changes his lineage; or claims a fictitious parentage; or is guilty of any other imposture; shall be considered a forger

FLAVIUS CHINTASVINTUS, KING.

VII. Concerning Documents Fraudulently Dated, Prior to their Execution.

The cunning of certain persons often requires the enactment of new laws, as soon as the employment of new and wicked forms of fraud, contrived for the deception of others, becomes publicly known. Henceforth, for the reason that many persons, with the intent to deceive their creditors, enter into false obligations in writing, which allege their indebtedness to others; we hereby promulgate the following law, which is to be perpetually valid, to wit: Wherever anyone who is indebted to another, should fraudulently draw up any writing in which he asserts that he is indebted to a third party, and, thereby anyone should be deceived; and, by means of said fraudulent document, he should contrive to nullify the claim of a party to whom he is justly indebted; or if it should happen that anyone should craftily, and fraudulently deceive another to the above mentioned end, not in writing but verbally; the party guilty of such offences shall be publicly branded as infamous, shall be liable in damages to him whom he has defrauded, and shall also be punished as provided in the law concerning forgery. He, also, shall be liable to similar damages and penalty, who has been convicted of having stated that he was indebted to another, by means of a fraudulent paper, executed subsequently to the one evidencing his indebtedness to his genuine creditor. He who shall be convicted of having made such a fraudulent document, as well as he for whose benefit it is alleged to have been executed; where the latter is known to be cognizant of the fraud; shall be liable to the damages and penalty hereinbefore provided; and the fraudulent document, having been declared void, the validity of the other, although it was apparently subsequently executed, shall be firmly established.

FLAVIUS RECESVINTUS, KING.

VIII. Concerning Later Documents Fraudulently Executed.

It is but just that he who is recognized as the heir of a deceased person, should discharge the debts of the latter. For the reason, therefore, that fraud ought, under no circumstances, to be excused, we hereby decree that the following law shall be forever observed, to wit: That whoever gives to any person, by any instrument in writing, any property whatever, no matter where said property may be situated, and he who gave such property shall not be the owner thereof; or if he was the owner, what he has given, he has already pledged to another by a former written document, or has conveyed it to anyone else under some contract; and he should subsequently dispose of said property, which was either not his own, or had been previously pledged to another, as aforesaid; as soon as the commission of said fraudulent act shall become known; he who is guilty, should he still be living, shall be liable for the amount mentioned in said instrument executed by him, and shall suffer whatever penalty it prescribes. But if the fraud should not become known until after his death, either his heirs shall be compelled to execute, for the benefit of the complainant, whatever the maker of said fraudulent instrument promised therein; or if the amount promised, or the penalty set forth in said forged paper, shall be greater in amount than the property left by said person, and his heirs should be unwilling to make satisfactory amends for the act of their ancestor; they shall be forced to surrender, at once, their entire inheritance to the complainant. Where there are no heirs, the entire property of the deceased shall, by the provisions of the present law, be given up by those to whom it was left by the deceased, or by those who have possession of the same.

This rule shall also apply in cases where it is found that he for whose benefit the prior instrument was drawn up, is implicated in the fraud; so that he who actually drew up the paper, as well as he who knew that this was done, shall both be liable for the satisfaction of the obligation, and to the imposition of the penalty set forth in the instrument subsequently executed; and both shall likewise undergo, in person and in property, the penalties provided by a former law in the case of those who are guilty of forgery.

ANCIENT LAW.

IX. Concerning those who Falsely Write, or Publish, Decrees and Edicts of the King.

The unlawful and wicked conduct of certain persons renders it necessary that laws should be enacted for the restraint of future generations; so that those over whom reproof has no influence, may be amenable to legal censure and coercion. And, for the reason that it is well known that many not only write out royal orders themselves, but also promulgate them, and publish documents confirmed by the signatures of notaries, whereby many things have been introduced into the laws of our kingdom, and many provisions have been written, or attempted to be added, which have not received the sanction of our authority; nor are suitable to our people, not having been dictated by the principles of justice or truth; and, in consequence, our subjects have been greatly vexed by injuries, spoliation, and other annoyances; we therefore promulgate the following edict: that, now and hereafter, no notary whosoever, no matter to what rank or race he may belong, (with the exception of the public notaries, or those attached to the royal service and their sons, and such as have received special commissions from the king, or any orders or appointments issued by the royal authority) shall write or publish any spurious document, purporting to have been issued by the king, or shall attempt to offer any such document to any notary, to be confirmed by his signature; but only the public notaries, and our own notaries, and those of our successors, and such as have been especially appointed by us, shall have authority to write or publish any royal order or edict. Whoever shall be found guilty of violating this law, whether he be freeman or slave, shall receive two hundred lashes, by order of the king or the judge; shall be scalped as a mark of infamy; and have, in addition, the thumb of his right hand cut off; as punishment for having attempted to commit unlawful acts which were contrary to the dignity of the throne.[1]

---

[1] The mildness of the sentence imposed for the crime described in this chapter, which seems to include the capital offences of treason and *lèse-majesté*, as well as the lesser one of forgery, is most extraordinary and inexplicable. Although "the divinity that doth hedge a king" was not fully recognized or appreciated by the Visigoths of the seventh century, whose monarch was the creature of an ecclesiastical council, and not infrequently deduced his origin from any but a princely house, it is still inconceivable that these offences being particularly directed against the regal dignity, should have been regarded as personal and of trifling moment, for it can be readily conjectured what serious trouble and embarrassment a spurious edict, purporting to emanate from the throne, might cause.

The "notaries" herein referred to were secretaries, shorthand writers or amanuenses.

This law is of Roman origin, and the amputation of a finger or a hand, while not unusual under that system, was a more prominent feature of Greek penal legislation, from which the Romans, at the time of the adoption of the Law of the Twelve Tables, borrowed many of their punishments.—[ED.

TITLE VI. CONCERNING COUNTERFEITERS OF METALS.

I. Concerning the Torture of Slaves, in Order to Convict their Masters of Counterfeiting Money; and the Reward of Witnesses who have given Information of the Same.

We do not forbid that slaves should be tortured, in order to convict their master or mistress of counterfeiting; as, by this means, the truth may be the more easily ascertained. If a slave belonging to another person should give information of such a crime, and it should prove to be true, he shall be given his freedom, if his master consents, and the latter shall receive his value from the public treasury; and if he does not consent, the slave shall receive three ounces of gold from the public treasury. Where the informer is a freeman, he shall be entitled to six ounces of gold, on account of the service which he has rendered.

FLAVIUS CHINTASVINTUS, KING

II. Concerning those who Debase Solidi, or Other Coins.

Where anyone debases, pares, or files, *solidi*, he shall be arrested, as soon as the judge is apprized of the fact; and, if he is a slave, his right hand shall be cut off. If he should be arrested a second time, for the same offence, he shall be brought before the king, to be disposed of at the royal pleasure. Where the judge hesitates to discharge his duty in a case of this kind, he shall forfeit the fourth part of his property, which shall be confiscated for the benefit of the treasury. If the offender is a freeman, he shall forfeit half of his property to the treasury; if he is of inferior rank, he shall lose his freedom, and shall be given up as a slave to whomever the king may select. Whoever shall engrave or make counterfeit money, no matter who he may be, shall undergo a similar sentence and penalty.

ANCIENT LAW.

III. Concerning those who Debase Gold by a Mixture of Other Metals.

Whoever receives gold to be made into ornaments and debases the same, by the mixture of brass, silver, or any other metal of inferior value, shall be deemed guilty of theft.

IV. Where Artificers of Metals are found to have Abstracted a Portion of what was Entrusted to Them.

Goldsmiths, silversmiths, and all other workers in metals, who abstract anything from what has been entrusted or delivered to them, shall be deemed guilty of theft.

V. No One shall Refuse to Accept a Golden Solidus of Legal Weight.

No one shall dare to refuse to accept a golden *solidus* of legal weight, provided it is genuine; nor demand other money in exchange for the same, unless it should be of short weight. Whoever shall act contrary to this law, and refuse to accept a golden *solidus* of legal weight, or shall demand a premium, in exchange for the same, as aforesaid; shall be compelled by the judge to pay three *solidi* to him from whom he refused to accept the coin. This law shall also apply to *tremisæ*.

BOOK VIII

CONCERNING ACTS OF VIOLENCE AND INJURIES.

TITLE I. CONCERNING ATTACKS, AND PLUNDER OF PROPERTY.

THE GLORIOUS FLAVIUS RECESVINTUS, KING.

I. The Patron, or the Master, shall Alone be Held Guilty, if, by his Orders, a Freeman or a Slave should Commit any Unlawful Act.

We hereby establish as a general principle of law, that whenever a freeborn person, a freedman, or a slave, is known to have committed any unlawful act by the order of his patron or his master, said patron or master shall be held liable for all satisfaction and composition for the same; for he who obeys the orders of his superior, cannot be considered guilty, because it is evident that he did not commit the act by his own will, but under the command of one possessing authority over him.

II. Where a Party in Possession is Expelled by Force.

Whoever forcibly deprives another of property in his possession, before the ownership of said property shall have been determined by a decision of the court; shall ose his case, even though he have the better claim. He who was the victim of the violence, shall receive the property in the same condition as it was when taken from him, and shall be entitled to undisturbed enjoyment of the same. If, however, any person should forcibly seize property which he could not obtain by a decree of court, he shall not only lose his case, but shall give to the injured party property of equal value to that of which he deprived him.

ANCIENT LAW.

III. Where Many Persons Unite in Causing Bloodshed.

Whoever collects a mob for the purpose of committing bloodshed, and makes an attack upon another, whereby he sustains bodily injury; or incites or orders others to commit such acts; as soon as the judge shall be informed of the same, he shall, at once, cause the guilty party to be arrested. And in order that he may be rendered publicly infamous, he shall receive fifty lashes in the presence of the judge, and shall be compelled to name all who were with him, or participated in his offence; and if his said associates should not be under his patronage, every freeman among them shall receive fifty lashes. If, however, slaves are participants in the crime, and belong to another master, they shall each receive two hundred lashes publicly, and in the presence of the judge, as a warning to others.

FLAVIUS CHINTASVINTUS, KING.

IV. Where a Person is Shut up by Violence, Inside his own House, or within his Gate.

Whoever forcibly confines the owner of a house inside his dwelling, or within the courtyard of the same, and prevents him from having free egress, or orders others to do so, shall, as a penalty for his insolence, pay to the owner of said house thirty *solidi*, and, in addition to this, shall receive a hundred lashes. All other persons who aided and abetted him in his unlawful act, and are not under his protection, where they are freeborn, shall each pay fifteen *solidi* to those who suffered the injury; and shall, for the insolence of which they are guilty, each receive a hundred lashes. Any slaves who are guilty of this offence, and did not act under the order of their master or mistress, shall each receive two hundred lashes. If, however, the owner of a house should be boldly and violently prevented from entering the same, in such a manner that he is, for the time, entirely deprived of control over his house, his family, and his other property, which is a far more serious offence, the author of such an infamous crime shall be liable for all damages incurred, and shall also receive a hundred lashes. Any freemen who are participants in a deed of this kind, if they are not under the patronage of the principal actor in it, shall each receive a hundred lashes, and be compelled to pay three hundred *solidi* to those who have suffered the injury. If, however, any slaves, without the knowledge of their masters, should have voluntarily committed such a crime, they shall undergo the penalty prescribed for slaves under such circumstances, as hereinbefore stated; and no responsibility for their acts shall attach to their masters. They also shall be liable to the same penalty, who, on their own responsibility, and without an order of the king or a judge, forcibly seize a house belonging to another; or presume to represent said property as their own; or affix their seals to the same.

FLAVIUS CHINTASVINTUS, KING.

V. Property, while in the Possession of Another, shall not be Seized, Except Under Legal Process.

No governor, deputy, steward, superintendent, agent, or attorney, or any freeborn person or slave, shall daringly presume to seize any property in the possession of another; or claim it, in the name of the king, or of his superior or master, before a judicial decree has been rendered establishing the ownership of said property. And if, without waiting for a trial, such a person should seize said property while in the possession of another, or which is known to belong to some one else; everything that he seized or removed, whether it consists of real estate or personal property, he shall restore twofold to him whose rights have been invaded; and he shall be compelled to give to the complainant, the profits accruing each year, while said property was in his possession; and which he shall solemnly declare under oath that he has collected. If a slave should commit such an act without the consent of his master, he shall, in addition to the abovementioned penalty, receive two hundred lashes in public. Where the owner is not satisfied with double the amount of the value involved, as reparation, he must restore the property which was taken, as well as the profits of the same, to him who seized or removed it; and the latter, under direction of the judge, must surrender the slave by way of compensation for the illegal act. Under all circumstances, however, a careful investigation must be made, lest the slave may have committed the act through some artifice or fraud of him who owned the stolen property; and if this is found to be the case, the master who thus instigated, or permitted wrong to be done, shall restore to the owner sevenfold the value of the property which the slave abstracted; and the master shall retain undisturbed possession of his slave.

ANCIENT LAW.

VI. Where a Person is Guilty of Asking Others to Commit Depredations.

If any person should instigate others to plunder, and, in consequence, they should destroy anything, or steal any property, or animals; they shall be compelled to restore elevenfold the value of the property so stolen or destroyed, to him who was robbed. Any freemen who were present at the time of the commission of the crime, shall each be compelled to pay five *solidi;* and, if they should not have that sum, they shall each receive fifty lashes. Any slaves who commit such an act, without the consent of their masters, shall each receive a hundred and fifty lashes, and be compelled to restore the stolen property intact.

VII. A House shall not be Entered in the Absence of the Master, or while he is on a Public Expedition.

No one shall molest the house of a person who is absent, or while he is on a public expedition. Moreover, if anyone should seize property which he could have obtained by a decree of court, while the other party to the suit was absent, he shall restore said property twofold. If, however, he should seize anything which he could not legally obtain, he shall restore threefold the value of the same. Where anyone, before he departs on a public service, is summoned by the judge to the hearing of a case, he must answer in his own proper person; or he may authorize an agent in writing, and in the presence of the judge, to act for him in the matter. But if he should neither give such authority, nor answer in court, and, having absented himself, should thus abandon his case; the judge, after a proper investigation, shall order the property claimed by his adversary to be delivered to him.

The absent party, however, shall have the right to reopen the case on his return.

FLAVIUS RECESVINTUS, KING.

VIII. Where the Slaves of a Person who is Absent on a Public Expedition Commit Unlawful Acts.

If the slave of any person who is absent upon the public service should be implicated, or detected in the commission of any crime, or other unlawful act, he shall be apprehended by order of the judge, and be punished by law, according to the nature of his offence; but if said offence should be of such a character, that the absent master would be liable therefor, or that the slave should be surrendered to another, the culprit shall be kept in custody by the judge until the return of his master, so that the latter may render satisfaction for his acts, should he wish to do so, or, should he be unwilling, that he may surrender the slave. Where a slave is unjustly put to death or subjected to torture, the said master, upon his return, shall have a good cause of action against the judge.

ANCIENT LAW.

IX. Concerning Those who, while on a Public Expedition, Commit Robbery or Other Depredations.

Those who commit robbery while in the army, shall make fourfold restitution. If they should not have the property wherewith to do so, they shall restore the article stolen, and receive fifty lashes. Should a slave, however, commit this offence, against the will of his master, he shall restore the stolen property, and receive two hundred lashes. All governors of provinces, judges and stewards, shall, without delay, require the enforcement of this law, as we are unwilling that our kingdom should be ravaged by depredators.

ANCIENT LAW.

X. He in whose Possession Stolen Property has been Found, shall be Compelled to Name his Associates in the Crime.

Whenever any evidence of crime, or any stolen property shall be found in the possession of any one, the latter shall, at once, be compelled to name his accomplices; and if he should refuse to do so, he shall be held liable for all damages incurred. If he is a person of superior rank, he shall either give a valid explanation of his illegal act, or shall restore, elevenfold, the value of the property stolen or destroyed; and shall receive a hundred lashes in public. If any part of the proceeds of a robbery should be found in the hands of a slave he shall receive two hundred lashes in public and shall be compelled to give up his accomplices.

XI. Concerning Those who are Guilty of Giving Directions to Others for Purposes of Robbery.

Any freeman, or slave, who shall give information concerning anything, in order that it may be stolen, or that the property of any person should be destroyed, or that he may be robbed of his flocks, or beasts of burden; as soon as the guilty party shall have been convicted by competent evidence, he shall receive a hundred lashes, because he gave information by means of which a crime was committed.

ANCIENT LAW.

XII. Concerning Those who Rob, or Inflict Annoyance upon Anyone, while he is on a Journey, or at Work in the Country.

Anyone who removes any property by violence, or robs another, while the latter is upon a journey, or occupied in farm labor, shall, after a judicial investigation, restore fourfold the value of the property stolen, or appropriated; and if he should cause any bloodshed, or personal injury, he shall render complete legal satisfaction for the same. If a slave should commit such an offence, without the knowledge of his master, he shall receive a hundred lashes; and his master shall be liable for the compensation due for his act. If his master should be unwilling to pay the sum required, he shall at once surrender the slave.[1]

ANCIENT LAW.

XIII. Whether a Person Caught in the Act of Robbery may be Killed.

Where anyone takes the property of another by force, and is wounded, or killed in the act, he who inflicted the injury shall incur no legal responsibility for the same.

---

[1] The penalty above described for an offence of such gravity as highway robbery, seems to be grossly inadequate. It is, however, a peculiarity of the Visigothic Code that, for many breaches of the law which we class as misdemeanors, it authorizes punishments generally inflicted for the commission of felony, and *vice versa*. Perhaps the courts construed the expression "complete legal satisfaction," to mean the sentence usually imposed for theft. There can be little doubt that the obscurity of the language which often characterizes the edicts of the *Forum Judicum*, would, under a less strict and impartial judicial system, have offered many opportunities for the escape of an offender from the legal consequences of his crime.—[ED.

TITLE II. CONCERNING ARSON AND INCENDIARIES.

I. Concerning those who set Fire to Houses, either Within or Without a City.

Whoever sets fire to the house of another in a city, shall be arrested by order of the judge, and condemned to be burned alive; and shall pay out of his own property the loss incurred by the owner of the house, as well as the price of the house itself, should the latter be consumed. He whose house was burned shall swear to the amount of property therein, in the presence of as many witnesses as the court may direct, and shall not demand the value of more than he was possessed of, nor shall he put an excessive estimate upon the value of his house; and if, after he has made oath, he should be convicted of any fraud, he shall be compelled to pay twice the amount of the sum exacted as legal compensation, to whomever the same is due. But if the fire kindled in the house aforesaid should spread through the neighborhood, the property of the incendiary shall be equitably distributed in proportion to the damage incurred by those who lost their house, or their chattels. If, after satisfaction has been made to him whose house was set on fire, it should be found that he still had some property remaining, he must then swear, in the presence of witnesses, that he did not demand a greater sum than he had lost. And if, after having made such an oath, it should be found that he has perjured himself, he shall be compelled to pay double the amount prescribed by law, to him whom he attempted to defraud. Whoever sets fire to a house outside a city, shall pay for all property burned in said house, and shall also, at once, pay the value of the house to the owner; but he whose house has been burned must declare, under oath and in the presence of witnesses, that he does not demand a greater sum than he has lost. And if, after having been sworn, it should appear that he did exact a greater sum, he shall be compelled to pay double the amount to him who sustained the injury.

If any houses adjoining the one which was set on fire should be consumed, and any property of the incendiary should remain, out of which the owners of said houses can be partially or wholly indemnified, they shall be entitled to their share. They, also, must make oath, in the presence of witnesses, that they do not claim an amount in excess of their losses; and if it is found that they have perjured themselves, or have demanded an excessive sum, they shall pay double the amount thus exacted, to him who was the victim of the fraud, and the incendiary shall receive a hundred lashes. Anyone having been convicted of such an offence, who does not possess the property wherewith to make restitution, shall be reduced to slavery.

Where a slave is convicted of incendiarism inside or outside a city, and his master should wish to liberate him from the punishment of so heinous a crime, he shall, without delay, render full pecuniary satisfaction for the same, and the slave shall receive two hundred lashes in public. He whose house was burned, shall be compelled to swear that he does not claim a larger sum than the property was worth. If the master should be unwilling to render satisfaction for the act of his slave as aforesaid, the slave shall be surrendered to be punished, and shall be beheaded.

II. Where Forests are set on Fire.

Anyone who burns a grove belonging to another, or any pine or fig tree, or any other tree, of any description whatever, shall be arrested by order of the judge; shall receive a hundred lashes; and shall render pecuniary satisfaction for the injury done; the amount of which shall be determined by the estimate of competent appraisers. If a slave should commit this offence, without the knowledge of his master, he shall receive a hundred and fifty lashes. Where the master is unwilling to render satisfaction for the act of his slave, he shall surrender him, in full amends for the same, even if the loss occasioned by said slave should amount to double or triple his value.

ANCIENT LAW.

III. Where a Conflagration Results from the Smouldering Campfire of a Traveller.

Whoever, while encamped during a journey, kindles a fire, either on account of the cold, or for the purpose of cooking food, must use care lest the fire spread, and that it may not break out in thorns, or dry forage, by which it is easily fed; and if it should be rekindled, he must extinguish it. If, however, the fire should extend, and any crop, threshing floor, vineyard, house, or orchard, should be consumed thereby, he who neglected to extinguish the fire which he kindled shall be compelled to pay the full value of all the property consumed.

TITLE III. CONCERNING INJURIES TO TREES, GARDENS, OR GROWING CROPS OF ANY DESCRIPTION.

ANCIENT LAW.

I. Concerning the Compensation for Cutting Down Trees.

Where anyone, without the knowledge of the owner, cuts down a tree belonging to another; if it is a fruit tree, he shall pay three *solidi;* if it is an olive, five *solidi;* if it is an oak of large size, two *solidi;* if it is an oak of small size, one *solidus;* and for a tree of any other species of considerable size, he shall pay two *solidi.* For such trees, although they do not bear fruit, are useful for many purposes. And this compensation shall be made if the trees should be only cut down; for if they should be cut down and carried away, either similar trees must be given in their stead, or double the above named sums must be paid.

ANCIENT LAW.

II. Where Anyone Destroys the Garden of Another.

Where anyone destroys the garden of another, he shall, at once, be compelled by the judge to pay to the owner a sum equal to the amount of damage which he has caused. If a slave should be guilty of this offence, he shall, in addition to the payment of said damages, receive a hundred lashes.

ANCIENT LAW.

III. Where Injury, or Homicide, Results from the Cutting Down of a Tree.

If anyone should cut down a tree, and any injury should result; or if the tree, in falling, should kill anyone; he who cut it down shall be responsible for the same. If, however a number of men should be in the neighborhood of said tree, and the party should previously notify them that the tree was about to fall; and if, after he gave such notice, anyone should be injured or killed by the falling branches, he who cut down the tree shall incur no liability whatever. But if the fall of the tree should cripple or injure any person who is old, or weak, or asleep, or unable to take care of himself; or any cattle of any description; the guilty party shall give to the master for every quadruped, one of equal value; and where a man is killed, he shall be deemed guilty of homicide. In case any person should be mutilated or crippled, he who caused the damage, shall be compelled to render satisfaction as prescribed by law; and if anyone should forcibly cut down a tree belonging to another, he shall at once render full compensation therefor. If the owner of a tree should have refused to permit it to be cut down, and any person should be killed while he was cutting it, no responsibility shall attach to anyone on account of his death.

ANCIENT LAW.

IV. Where a Tree is Partially Cut Down, or is Injured by Fire.

Where a tree has been partly cut down, or has been burned anywhere by fire, and, in the absence of him who, without malicious intent, cut it, or began to burn it, the tree should fall, said party shall in no way be responsible for any damage caused by said tree in its fall.

ANCIENT LAW.

V. Concerning the Cutting Down, Tearing Up, or Burning of Vines; and the Seizure of Growing Crops.

Whoever burns, cuts down, or tears up by the roots a vineyard belonging to another, or lays waste the same, shall be compelled to give two vineyards of equal value to the master thereof, and the owner of the vineyard which was destroyed shall still retain possession of it. If anyone forcibly seizes the fruit of a vineyard, he shall restore twofold the value of said fruit, and shall also make twofold restitution of whatever he has destroyed; and the value of the same shall be ascertained by the oath of those who were collected there at the time of the vintage. A slave who commits such an offence without the order of his master, shall receive ten lashes for every vine torn up or destroyed, and shall make restitution of all the fruit he has taken; or, if his master should wish to render satisfaction for his act, he shall pay a *solidus* for every six vines destroyed. But if great injury should have been done, and his master should be unwilling to render satisfaction for it, he shall surrender said slave without delay.

ANCIENT LAW.

VI. Where Fences are Cut Down, or Burned.

If anyone should cut down a fence anywhere, or should burn the fence of another; if he is a person of rank, he shall both repair said fence, and make reparation in damages. Where, however, any loss of crops has resulted to the owner from the destruction of said fence, said person shall not only pay the damages, as estimated by appraisers, but shall pay ten *solidi* in addition. Where said enclosure was an orchard with or without fruit, or a meadow, he shall be compelled to pay five *solidi*. Where the enclosure was a field where there were no fruit trees, the offender shall only be required to repair the fence. If a person of inferior rank should commit such an act, he shall pay the appraised value of the fruit or grain destroyed; shall repair the fence; and shall receive fifty lashes in public. Where the guilty party is a slave and acts without the knowledge of his master, he shall pay all damages incurred, repair the fence, and receive a hundred lashes. If the destruction of the fence was caused by accident, he shall only repair the same; for the reason that an act involuntarily committed is no crime.

ANCIENT LAW.

VII. Where Fence Posts are Cut.

Whoever cuts down the posts of a fence, or the tree trunks of a hedge belonging to another, or burns the same (even though the land enclosed by said fence or hedge contains no fruit or crops of any kind) shall be compelled to pay fourfold the value of the property destroyed. Where, however, there are fruits or crops of any kind within said enclosures, the guilty party shall be forced to pay one *tremisa* for every post or tree trunk cut down, or burned; and if any damage should result to said fruit or crops, he shall be liable for the same. We hereby decree that this rule shall also apply to the case of gardens.

ANCIENT LAW.

VIII. Where Anyone is Caught with a Vehicle, in a Wood Belonging to Another.

If any person should find another in his forest with a vehicle for the purpose of carrying away material for barrel-hoops, or any other kind of wood, without permission, the trespasser shall lose both oxen and vehicle, and the owner shall also be entitled to whatever the thief or trespasser has with him.

ANCIENT LAW.

IX. Concerning the Unreasonable Enclosure of Orchards, Vineyards, and Pastures.

If the owner of a vineyard, meadow, or pasture-field, should surround it with ditches, for the purpose of causing annoyance, and in such a manner that it cannot be crossed, unless through a vineyard or growing crop; anyone who passes through the latter shall not be responsible for any damages resulting therefrom. Where anyone surrounds open fields with ditches, travellers may disregard them, nor shall anyone presume to drive them out of said fields.

ANCIENT LAW.

X. Where Animals are Voluntarily Loosed in Fields where there are Crops, or in Vineyards.

Anyone who shall, intentionally, drive beasts of burden, oxen, or any kind of cattle into a vineyard, or field of growing grain, belonging to another, shall be compelled to pay all damages, after they have been appraised. If he is a person of high rank he shall pay a *solidus* for every horse, or ox, and for every head of other cattle, a *tremisa*, to him who has sustained the injury. If he is a person of inferior rank, he shall pay for the property destroyed and one half its value, in addition; and shall receive forty lashes in public. If a slave should commit such an act, without the authority of his master, either he, or his master, must pay all damages incurred, and the slave shall receive sixty lashes.

ANCIENT LAW.

XI. Where Animals Damage Growing Crops.

Where animals belonging to any person injure the vineyard or growing grain of another, the owner of said animals shall give to the person whose property was damaged, as much of another vineyard or field, with its fruit or crop, as is equal in value to that destroyed by said animals. If the owner of said animals should not have a field or vineyard with which to make restitution, he shall give as much fruit or grain as shall be estimated to be equal in value to the land in question.

ANCIENT LAW.

XII. Where an Enclosed Field is Ruined by Flocks.

If anyone turns cattle into an enclosed meadow, at such a time that the grass will not grow afterwards, so that it can be cut, and he who committed this act should be a slave, he shall receive forty lashes with the scourge, and shall give to the owner of said meadow, hay equal in amount to that which was destroyed. If he is a person of inferior rank, he shall pay one *tremisa* for every two head of cattle, and make restitution for the hay; if he is a person of superior rank, he shall pay one *solidus* for every two head of cattle, and shall make restitution for the hay, according to its value, as aforesaid.

ANCIENT LAW.

XIII. Where Fruits of any Kind are Destroyed by Animals.

If anyone should find a horse, or any cattle belonging to another in his vineyard, field of grain, meadow, or garden, he must not drive them out in anger, lest they be injured thereby; but, having driven them home, he must shut them up, and notify the owner; that the amount of damage caused by said cattle may be appraised by themselves, or by their neighbors. Both parties must visit the field in question; and, after they have examined it, that part of the pasture, vineyard, meadow, or crop, which was injured shall be measured, and they must then wait until the fruit is gathered, or the crop harvested, in order that the damage may be estimated by its comparison with that portion of the field which was uninjured; and the fruit shall be gathered, or the grain harvested, in the presence of witnesses, both from that portion which was damaged, and that which was intact; and whatever deficiency shall appear in the portion invaded by the cattle, must be made up by the owner of said cattle. The cattle, after the field shall have been measured, as aforesaid, shall be returned to their owner, as is provided by law. If any of them should be injured, on account of the unbridled anger of him who drives them out, the latter shall only pay their full value to their owner, and shall be entitled to retain all that he has mutilated or killed; provided, however, that he has previously paid for them. Where any cattle, while being driven out, are injured by accident, and not by design; or should be killed, or should fall upon posts, or stakes; the party driving them shall only be liable for one half the damages sustained, as has been provided by other laws.

ANCIENT LAW.

XIV. Where, while Anyone is Driving Cattle out of Cultivated Fields, Another Person Rescues them, or Takes Possession of them afterwards, Secretly or by Force.

Where anyone rescues cattle by force from any person driving them out of his own vineyard or field of grain; if he is a person of high rank, he shall pay five *solidi*, and be responsible for double the damage sustained, after appraisement of the same; if, however, he should be a person of inferior station, and should not have the means wherewith to make restitution, he shall receive fifty lashes, and shall be compelled to pay double the amount of damages. If a slave should be guilty of this offence, he shall receive a hundred lashes in the presence of the judge; and no reproach or responsibility whatever shall attach to his master. Where any person removes cattle from a house, or out of an enclosure, or seizes them by force, he shall pay eight *solidi* to the party injured, and shall also be liable to double damages. If a slave should do this he shall receive a hundred lashes, and his master shall fle in no way responsible.

XV. Concerning Animals Found in Vineyards, Fields of Grain, or Meadows.

Anyone who finds, and takes up beasts of burden, or cattle of any kind, in his vineyard, field of grain, meadow, or garden, shall, on that day or the following, give notice thereof to the owner of said cattle. If the owner should refuse to come, or send for them, the amount of damage shall be appraised by the neighbors, and full satisfaction of the same shall be required by the judge from said owner. If he who took up the cattle should prove or swear that the damage was committed by said animals, and the owner of the cattle should not come to receive them, or should not be present at the appraisement of the damage; he who took them up shall only give them water and keep them shut up for three days; and the owner, who neglected to be present at the appraisement, shall have no claim against the party retaining said cattle for the space of three days. When the three days are elapsed, he may let the animals go, and turn them loose, if their owner should still refuse to come for them; and, on account of the evident contempt of the latter, he shall be compelled to pay double the amount of the damages appraised. But if the owner of said cattle should come to him whose property was injured, and ask him to have the amount of the damages appraised, and to deliver up the cattle to him, and the former desiring to kill said cattle, should not acquiesce; if it should be proved that he has done this, he shall pay for every head of large cattle one *solidus*, and for every head of small ones, one *tremisa*. This law shall also apply to those who, before three days have elapsed, did not give notice that the cattle were shut up. If a slave should commit this offence, without the consent of his master, he shall receive a hundred lashes, and his master shall incur no responsibility whatever on account of his act.

ANCIENT LAW.

XVI. Where Animals Depart from Fields of Growing Grain Before they are Driven Out.

If any beasts of burden, or cattle, should depart from orchards or fields of grain, before they are driven from the same, it shall not be lawful to take them up, because it is not known whether they caused the damage or not. But if the owner, or any neighbor, should drive them out, said owner shall be liable for any injury they may have caused.

ANCIENT LAW.

XVII. Where Anyone Mutilates an Animal found in a Field of Grain.

If anyone should cut off the lips, tail, ears, or any other member of any cattle, or other animals, which he has found in his orchard, vineyard, or field of growing grain, or should kill them, or should inflict upon them any other injury, they shall become the property of the party who thus kills or mutilates them, and he shall at once give to the owner others of equal value.

TITLE IV. CONCERNING INJURIES TO ANIMALS, AND OTHER PROPERTY.

ANCIENT LAW.

I. Where a Horse, or any other Animal, which has been Tied Up, is Removed, or Injured, in any way, Without the Consent of the Owner.

If any person should free a horse, or any other animal belonging to another, from its halter, or from its hobbles, without the knowledge of the owner, he shall pay him a *solidus*. If said horse, or other animal, should die, in consequence, said person shall give its owner another of equal value. If he should use said animal to travel, or to work with elsewhere, without the knowledge of the owner, he shall be compelled to give him another of equal value; provided the owner should find him on that day, or on the following one. If said animal should not be found by the third day, the person who took it shall be deemed guilty of theft.

FLAVIUS RECESVINTUS, KING.

II. Where any Animal which has been Loaned, is Used against the Direction or Will of the Owner, or is Abused.

Anyone who, contrary to the wishes or understanding of the owner, abuses an animal which he has borrowed, by driving it too fast or too far, or by overloading it, shall pay a *solidus* for every ten miles traversed by said animal. If they should have gone less than ten miles, the distance, as well as the work, shall be estimated, and compensation shall be made accordingly. If said animal should be crippled, or killed, it shall belong to him who committed the injury, and he shall give one of equal value to the owner.

ANCIENT LAW.

III. Where the Mane or Tail of a Horse, or of any Other Animal, is cut off by Anyone.

Anyone who disfigures the mane of a horse belonging to another, or cuts off its tail, must at once give to the owner of the same another animal of equal value. Should any other animal be mutilated in this manner, the third part of a *solidus* must be paid for every one so mutilated.

ANCIENT LAW.

IV. Where Anyone Castrates an Animal Belonging to Another.

Whoever castrates any quadruped used for racing purposes, without the knowledge or consent of the owner; or castrates any animal which ought not to be castrated; shall be compelled to pay double the value of said animal to the owner of the same, who has been damaged on account of his malice.

ANCIENT LAW.

V. Where Anyone Produces an Abortion upon a Beast of Burden Belonging to Another

Whoever produces an abortion upon a mare, shall give to the owner of the same a foal, one year old, by way of compensation.

ANCIENT LAW.

VI. Where Anyone Produces an Abortion upon any kind of Animal Belonging to Another.

If anyone should produce an abortion upon a cow, he shall be compelled to give another, along with her calf, to the owner; and he himself shall be entitled to the animal injured. This law shall also apply to the cases of all other quadrupeds.

ANCIENT LAW.

VII. Where Animals of any kind Injure One Another.

Where beasts of burden, or any kind of cattle, injure others belonging to another person, the owner of those that caused the damage shall give to the owner of the former, others of equal value, and the injured ones shall become his own property.

ANCIENT LAW.

VIII. Where a Person Kills an Animal Belonging to Another, whether he has been Injured by said Animal, or Not.

Where any person, without provocation, is convicted of having killed or wounded an animal belonging to another; he shall be compelled to give one of the same value to the owner thereof, by way of reparation; if he is a slave, he shall receive fifty lashes in public; but if he is a freeman, he shall pay a fine of five *solidi*. Where, however, said animal was killed or mutilated, on account of some damage it had committed, said person shall be liable for the value of said animal, and for nothing more.

ANCIENT LAW.

IX. Where an Ox, Belonging to Another, is Used for Labor, without the Consent of its Owner.

Where anyone, without the knowledge of its owner, attaches his ox to a vehicle, for the purpose of hauling anything, or uses said ox for any other purpose, he shall give another, of the same value, to the owner thereof.

ANCIENT LAW.

X. Where Animals, of any kind, Belonging to Another, are Overworked in the Threshing of Grain.

Whoever works a horse, or any other animal, belonging to another, upon a threshing floor, shall pay a *solidus* for each animal so used. If said animal should die in consequence, he shall both pay the *solidus* aforesaid, and give another animal, of the same value, to the owner.

ANCIENT LAW.

XI. Where Cattle, which have done no Injury, are Shut Up.

Whoever confines any cattle in an enclosure, when no damage has been previously caused by them, if he is a slave, and has done this without his master's knowledge, he shall receive forty lashes; and if he is a freeman, he shall be compelled to pay one *tremisa*, for every two cattle, to the owner thereof. In case any of said cattle should be mutilated or killed, compensation for the same shall be made, as provided by a former law.

ANCIENT LAW.

XII. Where an Animal Causes Injury to Anyone.

Where any quadruped, while under the control of its owner, causes any damage, the owner shall either surrender said animal to the party who sustained the injury, or shall make such other amends as shall be ordered by the judge.

ANCIENT LAW.

XIII. Where an Animal is Injured, or Killed, by a Blow.

Where anyone strikes a beast of burden belonging to another, so that, by reason of the blow, said animal is either crippled or killed, he who struck the blow shall be compelled to give to the owner of said animal another of equal value, and shall be entitled to the animal that was injured. If said person should not have a beast of burden wherewith to make restitution, as aforesaid, he shall pay the appraised value of the animal to the owner thereof. A similar rule shall apply to horses and to all other animals.

ANCIENT LAW.

XIV. Where Cattle Belonging to Another, with or without the Knowledge of the Owner, are Mingled with the Herd or Flock of the Latter.

If any cattle belonging to one person should be mingled with those of another, and the owner of the latter should be aware of the fact; and said cattle should leave, of their own accord, without his knowledge; the owner of the strayed cattle shall take the oath of the other party, that they were not removed through any guilty design, or fraud on his part; and that he has not appropriated them for his own use, or transferred them to anyone; and, under such circumstances, he shall incur no liability. If, however, he should drive said cattle to his house, and should not inform the judge, or give public notice of the fact, within eight days, he shall pay double the value of said cattle, by way of satisfaction.

XV. Where Anything Intended to Frighten an Animal is Fastened to it, and it should be either Injured, or Killed, in Consequence.

Any person who should be known to have attached to a horse's tail, the head or bones of a dead animal, or anything else by which it might be frightened, and, in consequence, the horse, while running, should be injured, or killed; said person shall be compelled to immediately give to the owner a sound animal, on account of his transgression of the law. Where, however, the horse sustains no injury, the offender shall receive fifty lashes, and, if he be a slave, he shall receive a hundred lashes with the scourge.

ANCIENT LAW.

XVI. Where a Vicious Animal, while on the Premises of its Owner, Kills Anyone.

Where any person has in his possession an ox, a bull, or any other animal which is known to be vicious, said animal must at once be killed, lest it injure someone. If, after the owner has been informed by the neighbors of the vicious disposition of said animal, he should still retain possession of it, and defer killing it through fear, or for some other reason; and said animal should subsequently kill, cripple, or wound anyone, said owner shall give the satisfaction required by law in case of homicide; that is to say, the regular compensation provided in the cases of men and women, children and slaves, of both sexes. Thus, if said animal should kill a person of eminent rank, five hundred *solidi* shall be paid. In the case of freedmen, half of the above sum, that is to say, two hundred and fifty *solidi*, shall be given by way of satisfaction. If said animal should kill a slave belonging to another, the master of said slave shall receive, by way of reparation, from the owner of said animal, two slaves of equal value to the one that was killed. For a freeman of inferior rank twenty years of age, who has been killed, three hundred *solidi* shall be paid; and the same sum shall be required for the deaths of all persons up to the age of fifty; for all persons killed, who are from fifty to seventy-five years old, two hundred *solidi* shall be paid. A hundred *solidi* shall be sufficient for all who are over seventy-five years of age. For those who are aged fifteen, a hundred and fifty *solidi* shall be exacted, and for those of fourteen years, a hundred and forty *solidi;* for those of thirteen, a hundred and thirty *solidi;* for those of twelve, a hundred and twenty; for those of eleven, a hundred and ten; for those of ten, a hundred; for those of nine, eight, or seven years, ninety *solidi* shall be paid. For children of six, five, or four years, eighty *solidi;* for those of three or two years, seventy *solidi;* and for those of one year, sixty *solidi* shall be required. If said animal should kill the daughter or wife of any person, who is between the age of fifteen and forty years, two hundred and fifty *solidi* shall be paid; for those between the ages of forty and sixty, two hundred *solidi;* and for all beyond that age, a hundred *solidi* shall be paid. For any female of fifteen years or under, the owner of said animal shall be required to pay half the amount of compensation, according to the age of the victim, as has been provided in the case of boys.

ANCIENT LAW.

XVII. Where Anyone Rids himself of a Vicious Animal, or Still Retains it in his Possession.

Whoever has in his possession a vicious ox, or any other dangerous animal, must either kill or dispose of it, and notify his neighbors that he has done so. If he should not kill or dispose of it as aforesaid, but should keep it, he shall be liable for any damage caused by said animal while under his control.

ANCIENT LAW.

XVIII. Where Anyone Teases an Animal and is Injured by it, he Alone shall be Responsible for the Injury.

Whoever shall provoke a vicious ox, dog, or any other animal, to attack him, shall alone be responsible for any damage resulting to himself from the attack of said animal.

ANCIENT LAW.

XIX. Where a Dog that has been Irritated, whether the Provocation was Wanton or not, is Proved to have Injured, or Killed Anyone.

Where a dog bites another person not his owner, and said person is known to have been crippled or killed, in consequence thereof, no responsibility shall attach to the owner of the dog, unless it shall be proved that he caused said dog to make the attack. If, however, he should encourage his dog to seize a thief, or any other criminal, and the latter should be bitten while in flight, and should be crippled, or die from the effects of the bite, the owner of said dog shall incur no liability therefor. But if he should cause said dog to injure an innocent person, he must render satisfaction according to law, in the same manner as if he himself had inflicted the wound.

ANCIENT LAW.

XX. Concerning a Vicious Dog.

Where a vicious dog, belonging to anyone, kills sheep, or destroys other animals, and is caught, the owner of said dog must, as soon as he is notified, surrender it to him whose sheep were first injured, in order that he may kill it. If, however, he should be unwilling to kill the dog himself, or surrender him, as aforesaid, the owner of the dog shall be liable to double the value of any animals thereafter destroyed by him.

FLAVIUS CHINTASVINTUS, KING.

XXI. Concerning Injuries to Clothing.

Whoever, at any time, cuts the clothing of another, or tears it, or so soils it that the spots cannot be removed without injury to the garment, shall be responsible for said act, and shall give the owner a new garment of equal value.

Should he, however, not own such a garment, he shall be compelled to give to the owner the value of a new one, similar to that which he spoiled; and he shall be entitled to the one that was damaged. If the guilty person should be a slave, and his master should refuse to grant satisfaction for his act, he must at once surrender said slave to be punished according to the degree of the crime.

ANCIENT LAW.

XXII. Where a Trespasser Falls into a Trap set for Wild Animals.

Where a person sets traps for wild animals in his vineyard or field, and anyone, while attempting to commit a theft, should be caught in any of said traps, the party injured shall alone be to blame, for the reason that he was trespassing on the premises of another.

ANCIENT LAW.

XXIII. He who sets Snares or Traps for Wild Beasts, must Inform his Neighbors of the Places where said Snares are Set.

Where anyone, in order to catch wild beasts, digs pits in his fields or vineyards, or sets snares, or fixes bows and ballistas in retired or deserted places, remote from any highway, which are not often visited by man, and where cattle have not easy access, and an animal belonging to any person should be injured or killed by the contrivances placed for wild beasts, as aforesaid, the negligent hunter, through whose act the animal was killed, shall pay the value of the same to the owner, because he did not use a proper degree of care. Said hunter should previously give notice to all the neighbors; and if, after such notification, anyone is injured by the traps aforesaid, he who set them shall not be liable, because the party injured subjected himself to danger, in disregard of the warning he had received. If, however, anyone coming hoom a distance, and who had not been previously notified, sfruld ignorantly fall into any of said snares, and should be injured or killed thereby, he who set said snares or traps for wild beasts shall pay the third part of the compensation prescribed by law, for persons injured or killed; for the reason that men, while on a journey, should not, without their knowledge, be exposed to such dangers.

ANCIENT LAW.

XXIV. Concerning Injuries Resulting from the Obstruction of Highways.

Where a public highway is obstructed, no one shall be legally liable who breaks down a fence, or a wall, crossing or enclosing it. And he who encloses or obstructs a public highway, shall be conducted by order of the judge to the fence or wall traversing it, shall there receive a hundred lashes, and be compelled to remove said obstruction, and restore the highway to its former condition, even though there should be a growing crop upon the same. If, however, the act should have been committed by a person of great power and exalted rank, he shall be required to pay twenty *solidi*. Other persons guilty of such an offence shall each be compelled to pay ten *solidi*, and all sums, obtained in this manner, shall go to the benefit of the public treasury.

ANCIENT LAW.

XXV. Of the Space that is to be Preserved along Public Highways.

No one shall rashly violate our laws by enclosing a highway leading to any of our cities or provinces, but a full half *arepennis* shall be left on each side of the same; in order that sufficient space may be available for all travellers.[1] Any

---

[1] Between one twelfth and one fourteenth of an acre. The great Roman highways, portions of which are still in good preservation in some of the provinces of the Spanish Peninsula, and especially in Estremadura, were usually from eleven to fifteen feet wide; and, with the space required by the Visigothic laws to be left unenclosed for the

person of rank who violates this law, shall be fined fifteen *solidi*. Persons of inferior station shall be fined eight *solidi* for the benefit of the public treasury. Whoever has a field of grain, a vineyard, or a meadow, along a highway of this description, may enclose the same with a fence or hedge; and, should he be too poor to do so, he shall have the right to protect his field by a ditch.

ANCIENT LAW.

XXVI. Where the Animals of Persons, Traversing Fields that are not Enclosed, are Driven Away.

Whoever drives to his house, and shuts up, any horses, cattle, or other animals that are crossing open and vacant fields, which anyone had a right to enclose by ditches, shall be compelled to pay one *tremisa* for every two head of cattle so taken up by him. If, however, he should merely drive them out, so that they cannot be pastured, the damaged party shall be entitled to receive one *tremisa* for every four head of cattle excluded from said fields. If the act aforesaid should be committed by a slave, without the knowledge of his master, he shall receive a hundred lashes by order of the governor of the city, or of the judge; and his master shall incur no legal liability by reason of his act.

---

passage of cattle, were sometimes sixty to a hundred feet in their entire width.

The Visigothic surface measures were partly Roman, partly Gallic, and partly Gothic. The standard, the *Jugerum* .622 acre, was older than the Roman Republic; the *Arepennis*, equal to half a *Jugerum*, was used by the Gauls; and the *Aratrum*, or "ploughland," corresponded to an area of a hundred and twenty acres, approximately, and is of Northern derivation. The *Aratrum* was divided into "oxgates," or "oxlands," being as much arable soil as could be tilled by an ox, usually fifteen acres, but varying according to country and custom. For purposes of description, the latter term, evidently an importation of the Danes or Saxons, is frequently employed in the ancient English works on tenures; particularly where the latter were of the classes designated as "base," and "in gross"; as well as in conveyances and leases, where absolute accuracy of boundaries was either unnecessary or unattainable. The divisions of "ploughland" and "oxgate" were used much more recently in Scotland than in England.—[ED.

ANCIENT LAW.

XXVII. Animals Driven along the Highway Cannot be Excluded from Open Pastures.

All persons travelling through pasture lands which are not enclosed, have the right to deposit their baggage, and to pasture their beasts of burden, and their oxen therein. Such persons, however, shall not remain longer in one locality than the space of two days, unless they obtain the consent of the owner of the land to do so; nor shall they cut down valuable trees or oaks, to the roots, without permission of the owner of the same. They shall not be forbidden, however, to cut off such branches as may be necessary to feed their animals.

ANCIENT LAW.

XXVIII. He who has Land under Cultivation along the Bank of a River, has a Right to Enclose the Same.

Whoever cultivates land in a place traversed by a stream, where there is a ford through which cattle can pass, must enclose his crops with a fence. Should he fail to do this, and any damage should result through his neglect, he shall not be entitled to damages from any person, because it is not just that his own negligence should be the occasion of loss to another.

ANCIENT LAW.

XXIX. Concerning the Right to Enclose Streams.

No one shall, for his own private benefit, and against the interests of the community, obstruct any stream of importance; that is to say, one in which salmon and other sea-fish enter, or into which nets may be cast, or vessels may come for the purpose of commerce. He shall, however, not be forbidden to build a fence as far as the middle of the channel, where the water is deepest, provided he leaves half of the body of the stream free for the use of others.

Should anyone violate this law, the obstruction may be removed either by the governor of the city, or by a judge, without any further proceeding. If the party concerned is a person of high rank, he shall pay ten *solidi* to those whose rights were invaded, and if he is a person of inferior station, he shall pay them five *solidi*, and receive fifty lashes.

Where one person owns land on one side of a river, and another on the other side, they shall not be permitted to entirely obstruct the same, through each claiming that he has right to obstruct his half; but they shall not be prohibited from placing their fences as far as the middle of said stream, provided one fence be placed some distance above the other. If, however, there should be only one part of said stream where fences can be built, this shall be done in such a manner that nets may be cast there, and vessels may freely pass. If the governor of a city, or any other person, whosoever, should destroy the fence of anyone, contrary to this decree, he shall pay ten *solidi* to the owner of said fence. If the culprit should be a person of inferior rank, he shall be compelled to pay five *solidi* to the owner of the fence, and shall receive fifty lashes by order of the judge of the district, and if he should be a slave, he shall receive a hundred lashes.

XXX. Concerning Those who Damage Mills and Ponds.

If anyone should injure a mill by violence, he shall be compelled to repair the damage within twenty days; and, in addition, shall pay twenty *solidi*. If he should not make such repairs within the time aforesaid, he shall be compelled to pay twenty additional *solidi*, and shall receive a hundred lashes. The same law shall apply to injuries to mill ponds, and to all other artificial bodies of water. Where a slave commits this offence, he shall repair the damage, and receive a hundred lashes.

FLAVIUS RECESVINTUS, KING.

XXXI. Concerning Those who Steal Water from Streams Belonging to Others.

There are many districts where little or no rain falls, and where water is supplied by streams; and it has been found that wherever such streams fail, no crops can be raised. Henceforth, wherever there are any important streams, and anyone secretly, or maliciously takes water from the channels of others, he shall pay a *solidus* for every four hours that said water runs. Where said streams are of smaller size, he shall pay one *tremisa* for every four hours, as aforesaid. And for as many hours as the water is proved to have flowed upon the lands of others, for an equal number of hours the supply of water shall be restored to the owner. If a slave should commit such an act of his own accord, where water is taken from large streams he shall receive a hundred lashes, and where it is taken from small streams, fifty lashes.

TITLE V. CONCERNING THE PASTURAGE OF HOGS, AND CONCERNING STRAYS.

I. *Where Hogs are Pastured on Acorns, Either without Authority, or under Contract.*

II. *Where Hogs are Fed on Acorns on Land Belonging to Several Persons.*

III. *Where Hogs Turned on Land to be Fed on Acorns, under Contract, are Taken away by Stealth, Before the Tenth Part of Said Hogs are Delivered.*

IV. *Where Hogs are Found Wandering in Woodland.*

V. *Where a Drove of Animals, of any Kind, Enter upon the Pasture-land of Another Person.*

VI. *Public Notice shall be given of Strays by him who Finds them.*

VII. *Whoever Finds any Strays shall take Proper Care of the Same.*

VIII. *No Stray Animal shall be Either Sheared, Branded or Appropriated by Anyone.*

I. Where Hogs are Pastured on Acorns, Either without Authority, or under Contract.

Whoever finds any hogs in his woodland, at the time acorns are ripe, must take something by way of pledge from the swineherd; and give notice to the master, or parents of the owner, that should they so desire, he will permit said hogs to run in his woodland, until the customary time to pay one tenth of said hogs, as compensation, has elapsed; and when said tenth has been delivered, he shall restore the pledge which he took from the swineherd. If, however, the owner should be unwilling to allow said hogs to run in his woodland, and he should find them there a second time, he shall have a right to kill one of them as a protection to his property, even when they are but few in number. Where there are many of said hogs, he shall have the right to kill two of them, and he shall incur no liability for said act; and if he should find said hogs there for the third time, he must notify the owner thereof, that he can still leave his hogs upon his premises, if he will agree to give the tenth of said hogs by way of compensation, according to custom. If, however, the owner of the hogs should be unwilling to make such a contract, and the owner of the woodland should find them upon his premises for the third time, as aforesaid, he shall be entitled to retain one tenth of their entire number. If anyone, under such a contract, should leave his hogs in the woodland of another, and said hogs should feed until winter upon the lands of a third party, he who entered into the contract shall nevertheless be required to surrender his tenth of the same. If, after winter has set in, he who brought the hogs to the woodland, should be unwilling to keep them there, he shall be compelled to give to the owner of the woodland one twentieth of the number according to custom.

II. Where Hogs are Fed on Acorns on Land Belonging to Several Persons.

Where a dispute arises between persons holding oak forests in common, for the reason that one has more hogs there than the other, he who has the smaller number shall have a right to have the land so divided that each one may keep his hogs upon his own portion, in such a way that an equal number may be placed upon the same sized tract of land; and, afterwards, the tenths due for pasture shall be set apart in the same proportion as the divisions of the land.

ANCIENT LAW.

III. Where Hogs Turned on Land to be Fed on Acorns, under Contract, are Taken away by Stealth, Before the Tenth Part of said Hogs are Delivered.

Where anyone puts his hogs under contract, in the woodland of another, and secret y removes them, before the customary tenth has been paid, he shall be considered a thief, and shall not only pay the tenth which is due from him, but shall also be liable for the compensation provided by law for the crime of theft. If the offender should be a slave, and should have acted without the knowledge of his master, he shall receive a hundred lashes; and his master shall be liable for no damages, but must deliver the tenth which is due. If, however, the slave should have done this under the orders of his master, the latter must give pecuniary satisfaction, as in the case of theft.

ANCIENT LAW.

IV. Where Hogs are Found Wandering in Woodland.

Where anyone finds hogs straying in his woods, he must either notify his neighbors, or shut up said hogs. If the owner of the hogs should not make his appearance, he who took them up shall be entitled to keep one, and shall notify the nearest judge that he has stray hogs in his possession. Then, if the owner of the same should not be found, he may keep them as his own, and exact the tenth part of their number, in compensation for pasturage, as is customary; and when the master does come, he shall be entitled to a reasonable compensation for keeping said hogs, which compensation shall be fixed by the judge, and shall depend upon the time they were under the care of the person who took them up.

V. Where a Drove of Animals, of any Kind, Enter upon the Pasture-land of Another Person.

Where a flock of sheep, or a drove of cattle enter upon the pasture-lands of another, the same rule shall be observed as has been determined in the case of hogs. But travellers or strangers shall incur no responsibility, for the reason that it is well determined that they have the right to use pastures which are not enclosed. He who encloses his own part of a pasture, and uses that of another, in the absence of the master thereof, must not do so without the consent of the owner of the same.

THE GLORIOUS FLAVIUS RECESVINTUS, KING.

VI. Public Notice shall be given of Strays by him who Finds them.

It shall be lawful to take up horses, or any other animals, that have strayed; but he who does so, must immediately give notice of the fact to the bishop, the governor, the judge, the other authorities of the district, or to a public assembly of the neighbors. If said party should not give such notice, he shall incur the penalty of theft. A similar rule shall apply to other property taken up under the same circumstances.

ANCIENT LAW.

VII. Whoever Finds any Strays shall take Proper Care of the Same.

Whoever finds animals wandering without a keeper, must take them up, so that they will not sustain any injury; and, while they are in his charge, must care for them, as though they were his own. Where the owner of a horse, or any other animal, finds him safe and sound, he shall pay for each of said animals, four *siliquæ*, to him who has cared for it, and, in addition, as much as the latter has expended for the sustenance of the same. If, however, the person who took up said animal should injure it, he shall be compelled to give two others, of the same kind, to the owner thereof.

VIII. No Stray Animal shall be Either Sheared, Branded or Appropriated by Anyone.

No one shall clip or sell a stray horse which he has taken up, nor shall he place any mark or brand upon any oxen, or cattle, of any description whatever. If anyone should sell, or give away, a stray animal, he shall be held as a thief under the law. Whoever shears a stray animal, shall be compelled to pay three *solidi*, and he shall be liable to the same penalty, who places a mark, or brand of any kind, upon such an animal.[1]

[1] The reader cannot have failed to remark the striking analogy existing between the laws of the *Forum Judicum* relating to strays, and our own statutory enactments on the same subject. Indeed, aside from some of the penalties imposed, and the amount of compensation allowed, the regulations are, in many instances, almost identical. Unlike a great part of the Visigothic legislation, where trespass, and other violations of the law of real property are involved, few of the provisions concerning strays are derived from Roman sources. Most of them are unquestionably survivals of the ancient legal traditions of the wandering Gothic tribes, the great bulk of whose wealth consisted of flocks and herds of sheep and cattle.—[ED.

TITLE VI. CONCERNING BEES, AND THE DAMAGE THEY CAUSE.

I. Where a Person Finds Bees on his Property.

Where anyone finds bees on his premises, whether in his grove, or in the rocks, or in the trees, or in any place whatsoever, he must make three marks, or characters, in testimony of possession, for the reason that where only one mark is made, it often gives occasion for fraud. If another person should make a mark of his own in the same place, or should erase any which have already been made, he shall pay double the value of the bees to him whom he defrauded, and shall also receive twenty lashes.

II. Where Bees Cause any Damage.

Should anyone build an apiary in a town or village, and any damage should result to others thereby, he must straightway be notified to move it elsewhere, that the bees may not inflict further injury upon men or animals in that locality; and if, after such notice, the owner should neglect to move said apiary, and any quadruped should be injured by the bees, the owner of the latter shall give two animals for every one that is killed, and one for each that is crippled, to the owner thereof; and shall be entitled to keep said injured animals; and shall be compelled to pay five *solidi* for neglecting to heed the warning of the judge.

FLAVIUS RECESVINTUS, KING.

III. Concerning the Theft of Bees.

Any freeman who enters an apiary for the purpose of theft, and is caught there, even though he should take nothing, for the mere fact that he has been arrested in such a place, shall pay three *solidi*, and receive fifty lashes. If, however, he should have taken anything, he shall be compelled to pay ninefold its value, and shall receive the number of lashes aforesaid. If a slave should enter an apiary, without stealing anything, he shall receive a hundred lashes; and if he should steal anything, he shall be compelled to restore sixfold the value of the same; and if his master is unwilling to render satisfaction for his act, he must deliver said slave to him who suffered the loss.

BOOK IX.

CONCERNING FUGITIVES AND REFUGEES.

TITLE I. CONCERNING FUGITIVES, AND THOSE WHO CONCEAL, AND ASSIST THEM IN THEIR FLIGHT.

I. *Where a Freeman or a Slave is Found to have Concealed a Fugitive.*

II. *Where a Fugitive is Released from his Chains by any Person.*

III. *Within what Time a Fugitive Slave that has been Found, shall be Produced Before the Judge.*

IV. *Where Anyone, Ignorantly, Receives a Fugitive Slave, and Cares for Him.*

V. *Where Anyone Persuades the Slave of Another to Flee, or Shows him Hospitality.*

VI. *Where a Man, Unknown to be a Slave, is Received by Another, and Remains with him Several Days.*

VII. *Where a Slave, Knowingly, Directs a Fugitive Slave in his Flight.*

VIII. *Concerning the Reception of Fugitive Slaves; and Whether a Master or a Slave may Receive a Fugitive Slave Belonging to Another.*

IX. *Where a Fugitive Slave Comes to the House of any Person, Notice of the Fact must be Given to the Neighbors and Authorities of the District.*

X. *Where a Slave that has been Sold into a Foreign Country, Returns as a Fugitive, and is Sold a Second Time, he shall be Entitled to his Freedom.*

XI. *Where a Fugitive Slave Takes Refuge with Another Person, an Investigation must be Made, to Ascertain whether he was not Sent by his Master, in Order that the Latter might Receive Compensation from the Person who Received said Slave.*

I. Where a Freeman or a Slave is Found to have Concealed a Fugitive.

Where a freeman conceals a fugitive slave, he shall be compelled to give up said slave to his master, along with another slave of equal value. If a slave, without his master's knowledge, should conceal another slave who is a fugitive, both shall receive a hundred lashes; and the master shall be in no respect responsible for damages.

II. Where a Fugitive is Released from his Chains, by any Person.

If anyone should set free the slave of another, while the latter is fettered with irons, or bound in any way, he shall give to the master of the slave ten *solidi*, on account of his interference. In case he should not have the property wherewith to pay said amount, he shall receive a hundred lashes by order of the judge, and shall, at once, restore the slave to his master. Where said slave cannot be found, he shall be compelled to give another of equal value to the master; or, if he should not have the means to render satisfaction, he shall himself be delivered up as a slave to him whose own slave he released. Where a slave committed this offence without the knowledge of his master, he shall receive a hundred lashes in the presence of the judge; and if the slave who was set free cannot be found, he who liberated him shall be delivered up to the master of the one who was reeased. But whenever the fugitive slave shall be found, he shall be restored to his master, and the one who was surrendered in his place shall be returned to his master. If, however, one slave should release another with the knowledge of his master, said master must make such compensation as has been hereinbefore provided in the case of freeborn persons.

III. Within what Time a Fugitive Slave that has been Found, shall be Produced Before the Judge.

Where a fugitive slave takes refuge with any person, the latter must straightway bring him before a judge. Should he not produce him as aforesaid, and the slave should remain with him until the eighth night, and then go elsewhere, the person who sheltered him shall be compelled to give two slaves of equal value to his master. If, however, he should be found to have concealed the slave who took refuge with him, he must restore him and give another slave to the master, without delay; because he neglected to give notice to the latter within the legally appointed time.

IV. Where Anyone, Ignorantly, Receives a Fugitive Slave, and Cares for Him.

Where any person ignorantly receives a fugitive slave, and treats him with hospitality, and he should not remain in his house longer than one day or one night, he shall make oath before the master who is searching for said fugitive, that he did not know that he was a fugitive slave; and, if he can prove, without doubt, that he did not conceal him, he shall incur no liability whatever. If, however, said slave should remain in his house for the space of two, three, or four days, for any reason whatever, the said person must show where he was, or by whom he was sheltered, afterwards; and he must either find the fugitive within six months, or prove with whom the slave took refuge after he left his house. If he should not be able to find said slave, he must purge himself by oath of all complicity in his flight, as well as of all knowledge with whom the slave took refuge subsequently; and he shall either restore the fugitive, or give another slave of the same value to his master. If the fugitive should be afterwards found, the slave given in his place shall be returned to his former master, and the latter shall incur no liability whatever.

V. Where Anyone Persuades the Slave of Another to Flee, or Shows him Hospitality.

If anyone, knowing him to be a fugitive, should persuade the slave of another to escape, or anyone should entertain or disguise said slave, and the latter is found, the party aforesaid shall be compelled to give two others of equal value to his master. Should said fugitive not be found, said party must give three slaves of equal value to his master. The same rule shall also apply to the case of female fugitives.

VI. Where a Man, Unknown to be a Slave, is Received by Another, and Remains with him Several Days.

If a stranger, who is a fugitive, should remain, for the space of five or seven days, upon the premises of any person, he who received or entertained him, must give notice of the fact, before the eighth day, to the judge, or governor of the nearest town or province, as has been provided by the law recently promulgated, concerning fugitive slaves; in order that said fugitive may be examined by the authorities, and it be ascertained who he is, and why he has come to that locality. In this way, every provision of the law relating to the treatment of fugitive slaves which we have recently published, shall be complied with in every respect. The greatest diligence must be employed throughout all the provinces of our kingdom, to the end that the appearance of a fugitive, as aforesaid, may become publicly known upon the day of his arrival, or the day afterwards. Where, however, the person who entertains a fugitive slave does not give notice within eight days, and permits him to remain in his house, he shall restore the fugitive to his master, and give the latter another slave, as a penalty for not having given the notice required by law. If, however, the fugitive should escape, he who entertained him must find him; and, if he cannot do so, he shall be compelled to give two slaves of the same value to his master.

VII. Where a Slave, Knowingly, Directs a Fugitive Slave in his Flight.

Where one slave knowingly assists another in his flight, he shall receive a hundred lashes, whether the fugitive is found, or not; and the master of the delinquent shall be in no way responsible for his act.

VIII. Concerning the Reception of Fugitive Slaves; and Whether a Master or a Slave may Receive a Fugitive Slave Belonging to Another.

If a fugitive slave should take refuge at the house of any person, and, being unknown to said person, should receive assistance from him, and then straightway continue his journey, no liability of any kind shall attach to him who entertained, as it were, a passing traveller, after said person has sworn that he whom he assisted was unknown to him. But where a fugitive remains, for two or three days, in the house of said person, the latter must cause him to be produced, as was provided by a former law, before the eighth day, before the authorities of the district; that is to say, before the judge, deputy, or governor, along with a competent witness. A thorough investigation shall then be made by the judge, or other magistrate, to ascertain whether said fugitive is a slave; and, should he be such, when he escaped from his master, as well as when and where he took refuge with the party who produced him. Said examination shall be committed to writing, and signed by the judge, or other official, who conducted the investigation.

If the fugitive should declare that he is a slave, he shall be delivered up to the party who produced him, and the latter, within eight days, must return him to his master. Where the latter lives at a distance from the place the slave was taken, the number of days during which the fugitive remained under the control of him who received him, shall be computed, and twenty miles shall be set down for each day; and when said person shall restore the fugitive to his master, either in his own person, or by an agent, he shall be entitled to receive the compensation allowed by law in such cases; that is to say, one *tremisa* for every thirty miles traversed by said fugitive slave. If, however, on account of the great distance, it should be a hardship for the party who received the slave to restore him to his master, he must deliver him, in the presence of witnesses, either to the steward in control of any property of the master in the neighborhood, or to a magistrate of the district; and, having received from him the compensation hereinbefore specified, he shall be free from all liability whatever. If, however, the fugitive, when brought before the judge, and interrogated by him, should refuse to disclose whose slave he is, he who produced him must leave him in the custody of the judge. The judge shall keep said fugitive in strict confinement, and shall bring him before the king, in council, within the time, and according to the manner, hereinbefore prescribed, in order that further inquiry may be had, in a place where general publicity may secure the identification of the fugitive. The preceding law having thus been established, whoever, hereafter, does not obey the same, and produce a fugitive before the judge, whether he is known to be a slave, or not, and where he is a slave, does not restore him to his master, shall be compelled to restore him, and give another slave, by way of satisfaction. If the fugitive should die, the master shall be entitled to receive two slaves, of equal value, from him who sheltered him. The judge shall also be liable to a similar penalty, should he neglect to execute the law as hereinbefore provided. If a slave, without the consent of his master, should shelter another who is a fugitive, he shall receive a hundred lashes in the presence of the judge; and the fugitive shall be returned to his master, upon the demand of the latter. If, however, the fugitive, who was sheltered by a slave, should not be found, the master of him who sheltered the fugitive shall be compelled to give in his stead another slave, of the same value, to the owner of the same. If the master should be unwilling to render satisfaction for the act of his slave, he must deliver up the offender by way of amends.

IX. Where a Fugitive Slave Comes to the House of any Person, Notice of the Fact must be Given to the Neighbors and Authorities of the District.

Where a fugitive slave takes refuge in the house of any person, the latter must give notice to the authorities of the district; and should he desire to keep said fugitive in custody, in his house, it shall be lawful for him to do so. When the master of said slave comes after him, he shall be restored to him, and he who sheltered said slave shall incur no liability. But if, in the meantime, the said fugitive slave should betake himself elsewhere, he who gave notice to the authorities shall make oath, in their presence, that he did not persuade said fugitive to escape, or assist him in his flight, and that he is ignorant of his present whereabouts; and, after having done this, he shall be in no way responsible.

X. Where a Slave that has been sold into a Foreign Country, Returns as a Fugitive, and is Sold a Second Time, he shall be Entitled to his Freedom.

Where a master sells his slave, and he is taken into a foreign country, and afterwards returns, and his master sells him a second time, the master shall be forced by the judge to redeem said slave from the purchaser; and the latter shall then be liberated, and subjected to no further annoyance. He who, actuated by avarice, thus placed a slave, returning from a foreign country, in bondage a second time, shall be compelled to give to the purchaser another slave of the same value, in addition to the price which was paid. The former master of the returned slave shall not sell him, or have any right to his services; but said slave shall be forever entitled to the full enjoyment of his freedom.

ANCIENT LAW.

XI. Where a Fugitive Slave Takes Refuge with Another Person, an Investigation must be Made, to Ascertain whether he was not Sent by his Master, in Order that the Latter might Receive Compensation from the Person who Received said Slave.

A fugitive slave shall be compelled to disclose the name of his master, and shall be thoroughly examined by the judge, in order to ascertain whether his master did not cause him to take refuge with another person for the sake of illegal gain. And if it should be established that his master was guilty of fraud, whereby he desired to implicate another in the crime of having knowingly concealed his slave, he shall be liable for such damages as are imposed upon those who wilfully conceal slaves. For it is but just that he who is guilty of such malignant treachery should pay the penalty which he attempted to impose upon another.

ANCIENT LAW.

XII. Where a Slave, Falsely Declaring that he is Free, Serves Another for Hire.

Where a fugitive slave asserts that he is freeborn, and remains with anyone, for hire, in a place where he is unknown, he shall be produced and examined before the judge, as has been provided by a former law. And if the investigation should disclose that he is merely a laborer, and not a fugitive slave; and if, afterwards, this should be found to be false, and his master should appear; he who ignorantly employed him, not knowing that he was a fugitive, shall in no wise be held responsible. The master, however, shall receive the compensation due to the slave, according to the contract made by the latter. If the slave should escape from his master a second time, and should take refuge with him who formerly employed him, he must at once deliver him up to the judge, or restore him to his master; and if he should not do so, he shall be liable to the penalty imposed upon those who shelter fugitive slaves.

XIII. Where a Fugitive Slave is Found in the House of any Person.

Where a fugitive is found in the house of a person of rank, or of anyone else, whether he declares that he is free or not, he shall, without delay, be delivered up to whoever claims him. He in whose house said slave was found shall require security that he shall be brought into court, and that he shall not be tortured, in any way, before his case is decided, until he himself establishes the fact of his freedom, or he who claims him proves that he is a fugitive slave. Where the claimant is unwilling to do this, the fugitive shall remain in charge of him who found him, until it is ascertained what disposition the judge shall make of him.

FLAVIUS RECESVINTUS, KING.

XIV. Concerning the Reward for Arresting a Fugitive Slave.

Whoever arrests a fugitive slave, shall be entitled to one *tremisa* for every thirty miles, or less, which said slave has traversed in his flight, and a *solidus* for every hundred miles, as a reward for the capture; and the number of *solidi* paid shall increase with the number of miles traversed. He who finds a fugitive slave, must deliver him, at once, with all the property which is in his possession, to his master. If, however, a fugitive slave should escape from his captor, the latter must swear before the master that the fugitive did not gain his liberty through any design or fraud on his part, and he shall then incur no liability therefor. But if, after having made oath as aforesaid, he should be proved to have accepted anything from said fugitive, or to have committed any fraud, whereby the latter might take refuge elsewhere, and said fugitive should be afterwards found, said party shall be required to give another slave, of the same value, to his master; but if the fugitive should not be found, he shall be compelled to give him two slaves in his stead.

XV. Where a Fugitive Slave Falsely Declares that he is Freeborn.

Where a fugitive slave comes among persons to whom he is unknown, and asserting that he is freeborn, afterwards marries a freeborn woman, and said woman, or her parents, or relatives, should be convinced of the fact that he is a slave, and the judge should have investigated the matter, in behalf of the woman, and the master of said slave should add his testimony; no reproach shall attach to said woman, nor shall she be liable for any damages, but she shall continue to be free, and any children she may have had by said slave, shall follow the condition of their mother. She shall not be separated from said slave should she desire to remain with him, provided his master gives his consent.

FLAVIUS CHINTASVINTUS, KING.

XVI. Where a Fugitive Slave, Declaring that he is Freeborn, Marries a Freeborn Woman.

For the reason that fugitive slaves falsely declaring themselves to be freemen, frequently contract marriages with freeborn women, we now decree by the following law, that where a slave, having escaped from his master, by any means whatever, takes refuge with anyone, whether he declares that he is free or not, and, under such circumstances, marries a freeborn woman, the issue of said fraudulent union shall invariably follow the condition of the father; and when the master of the slave appears, he shall have a right to claim as his own, not only said fugitive, but also his children, and such property as they may be possessed of. A similar rule shall apply to female slaves who, escaping from their masters, presume to contract marriages with freeborn men.[1]

---

[1] This law was evidently intended to repeal the preceding one, although this is not specifically stated. Its enactment, as is set forth in the preamble, was demanded by the constantly increasing number of marriages between freeborn persons and slaves. The degradation attending such unions does not seem to have been regarded by the masses with the same prejudice that actuated the law-making power, whose interest it was to rigidly maintain the barriers of caste.—[ED.

FLAVIUS CHINTASVINTUS, KING.

XVII. Concerning Property Acquired by Fugitive Slaves.

If a fugitive slave should acquire any property through his labor and skill, when his master appears, the latter shall have the right to the whole of it. But where his master finds him in possession of property stolen from another, he can advance no claim to it, but must restore said property to him who lost it. If, however, said fugitive slave should have caused any damage, or committed any crime, he who concealed him must render satisfaction for the same.

FLAVIUS CHINTASVINTUS, KING.

XVIII. Concerning Those who Refuse to Restore Fugitive Slaves to their Masters.

For the reason that many persons are prone to controversy, and frequently pervert the meaning of the laws; and because it was declared by an ancient law that whenever a master comes upon his slave he may take him; and for the reason that said persons frequently refuse to surrender a fugitive slave, and, under such circumstances, cause delay, that they may have the benefit of the services of said slave for a time; and also, as said delay is entirely useless, and it is unjust that a master, for the sake of a vile slave, should be compelled to remain, for an indefinite period, two or three hundred miles from home; and because such proceedings are rather the result of artifice than of truth; we hereby decree that henceforth, whenever anyone refuses to surrender a fugitive slave to his master, or to the agent of the latter, or rescues him after he has been arrested, he shall be compelled to restore said fugitive to his master, along with four other slaves of equal value; or, if said fugitive should die, he shall be compelled to give his master five slaves of equal value; and if the fugitive should afterwards be found by said person, or by his former master, he shall belong to the latter, and one of those who was given in his stead shall be returned to the donor of the same. And if a slave, without the knowledge of his master, should commit any of the offences hereinbefore described, and his master is willing, he must give two slaves, of equal value, by way of compensation, to the owner of the fugitive; but should he be unwilling to do so, the slave shall be delivered to the owner of the fugitive to be his property forever. The same rule shall apply in the case of female slaves.

ANCIENT LAW.

XIX. Where a Freeman, or a Slave, Undertakes the Concealment of Robbers.

Any freeman or slave who knowingly conceals robbers, shall be compelled to produce them, and shall receive two hundred lashes with the scourge; and should he not produce them, he shall be liable for the penalty for their crime.

XX. A Judge must Surrender a Fugitive Slave, with all the Property Found in his Possession, to his Master.

Whatever property a judge finds in the possession of a criminal or a fugitive slave, in the absence of him who has a right to claim said criminal or slave, must be delivered to the governor of the city, and kept by him, to be restored to the owner when he arrives.

EGICA, KING.

XXI. Concerning Fugitive Slaves, and those who Shelter Them.

It has been plainly set forth in former laws, by what means and investigations the secret escape of fugitive slaves may be repressed. But as, under various legal pretexts of judges, or through the fraud of those who shelter them, their flight is concealed, and the enforcement of the laws becomes difficult, and with the increasing number of fugitives, the facilities for their concealment become greater, to such an extent has this evil grown that there is scarcely a town, castle, village, or hamlet, where a number of fugitive slaves are not known to be in hiding.

Leaving the provisions of a former law relating to fugitive slaves in full force, we now decree that hereafter, whoever shelters a fugitive slave belonging to another, shall immediately subject him to a judicial examination, even though he should assert that he is freeborn, in order that it may be ascertained whether he is a freeman or a slave, and should he prove to be a slave, that he may be returned to his master. If, however, said person should not produce said fugitive in court, or restore him to his master, whether he proves to be either a slave or a freeman, said person shall receive a hundred and fifty lashes by order of the judge. In case he should be freeborn, he shall receive a hundred and fifty lashes, and shall pay in addition a pound of gold to the master of the fugitive slave, and should he not have the means to pay said sum, he shall receive two hundred lashes. All other residents of that neighborhood, whether they be natives, or foreigners, freemen or slaves, whether they belong to the clergy or are in the service of the Crown, shall be liable to similar penalties, if they do not give notice of said fugitive, or drive him from the possession of him who concealed him, when they are aware of the presence of said slave.

And we also provide that the following shall be strictly observed, to wit: that whenever any fugitive slaves come into any locality, all the inhabitants shall assemble, and shall make a thorough examination of said fugitive slaves, either by the application of torture, or by any other severe method; in order to ascertain whose slaves they are, when they escaped from their masters, and when they arrived in that vicinity; and to this end they must use every means possible, in order that said slaves may be delivered up, or sent to their masters, as provided by a former law. If, however, said persons should not comply with this provision, and should neither make inquiry concerning said fugitive slaves, nor endeavor to restore them to their masters, nor subject them to judicial examination, as aforesaid, but said slaves should subsequently be found in the place where they had first taken refuge, all the inhabitants of that neighborhood, both men and women, of whatever race, family, rank, or dignity to which they may belong, shall each receive two hundred lashes in public, by order of the judges. And if the *tiuphadi* or deputies, or all invested with judicial power, or officials of the treasury, or attorneys, or priests, or any employees of the royal service, should, in any way, connive at the concealment of said fugitive slaves, or should neglect to execute the sentence of this law upon all persons subject to their jurisdiction, they shall be arrested by the bishop, or the governor of the province, and shall publicly receive two hundred lashes. If any bishop having jurisdiction of such a cause either influenced by friendship, or corrupted by a bribe, or through lukewarmness, should not carry out the sentence of the law upon those who are guilty, he shall bind himself before God, and in the presence of the governor, or his deputy, that, by way of penance, for thirty days he will not touch wine or food, excepting each day at vespers, and then only a morsel of barley bread and a cup of water, for the sustenance of his body; and this bitter penalty he must endure for the reason that he refused to carry out the provisions of the law. We hereby admonish all judges and governors to execute the sentence aforesaid; and, should they neglect to perform their executive and judicial duties, they shall each forfeit three pounds of gold to the royal treasury.

Any person who, within the limits of Spain, desires to purchase any slave from a party unknown to him, must not conclude said purchase until inquiries have been made to determine whether said stranger is selling a slave of his own, or one belonging to some other person. Said inquiries shall take place in the presence of the judge, or of persons of respectability who are present where said slave is offered for sale; and the vendor of the slave shall make his statements under oath. The slave who is offered for sale shall himself be subjected to a severe examination; and, should it be ascertained that he is not the property of the person who offered him for sale, but that he belongs to another, then the judge shall order him to be restored to his master. The judge shall retain in custody the party who attempted to sell the slave of another, as well as the slave in question, until the arrival of the master, when the judicial examination shall be completed, and the satisfaction required by law shall be made.

Given and confirmed at Cordova, in the sixteenth year of our happy reign.[1]

---

[1] The great value of slaves, as articles of personal property, and the manifest sympathy of the people with them, seem to have prompted the enactment of this law, by which the inhabitants of an entire district were to be turned into a corps of detectives for the capture of fugitives; and the severest penalties were denounced against all, irrespective of age, sex, social standing, or rank, for non-compliance with its provisions. The statement that no community, large or small, was without a number of fugitive slaves, who, sure of the assistance of their neighbors, scarcely took the trouble to conceal themselves, indicates that human servitude was not popular with the majority of the people of the Iberian Peninsula. It would appear, also, that the magistrates, whose executive delinquencies rendered them liable to the same punishment as the offenders themselves, were frequently loth to execute the law. The marked consideration always shown the clergy by their legislative brethren, is again disclosed by the amusing inequality of penalties prescribed for the neglect of official duties. There is a great and painful difference between the limitation to one meal a day, for a month (a privation, it is hardly necessary to add, which might be readily evaded) and two hundred lashes, laid on vigorously with a scourge. This law gives us a curious insight into life in those times, and one that could have been derived from no other source; and it is especially instructive in the information it affords concerning the feelings entertained by all, except the comparatively few members of the privileged classes, towards those in the servile condition.—[ED

TITLE II. CONCERNING THOSE WHO REFUSE TO GO TO WAR, AND DESERTERS.

I. Where an Officer of the Army, Corrupted by a Bribe, Permits a Soldier to Depart, or does not Compel him to Leave his Home.

Where the commander of a force of a thousand men, corrupted by a bribe, permits a soldier to return to his home, he shall pay ninefold the amount which he received, to the governor of the city in whose territory he was at the time. If, however, without receiving any bribe, he should permit a soldier, who is well, to depart as aforesaid, or should not compel him to leave his home and join the army, he shall pay thirty *solidi;* a commander of five hundred men shall pay fifteen *solidi;* a centurion, ten *solidi;* and a decurion, five *solidi;* and the said sums shall be divided among the soldiers, by hundreds, where said sums were paid.[1]

II. Where Conscription Officers Appropriate the Property of those they call to Arms.

If the conscription officers of the army, when they summon the Goths to arms, should take anything from any person, or should presume to seize, against his will, any of his property, in his presence, or while he is absent, and this fact should be established in court, the offender shall be forced to restore said property elevenfold, and shall receive a hundred lashes in the presence of his assembled command.

ANCIENT LAW.

III. Where an Officer of the Army Abandons the War, and Returns Home, or Permits Others to do so.

Where a centurion deserts, in the face of the enemy, and returns home, he shall be beheaded. If, however, he should

[1] The military organization of the Visigoths bore a striking resemblance to those of modern armies, and coincided, in only a few unimportant particulars, with that of the Roman legion. Division by means of the decimal system, popular among all semi-barbarian races on account of its simplicity, and the facility of arrangement it affords, was universally employed. The commander-in-chief, styled in the Code, *præpositus hostis*, was usually a *dux*, or duke; the lieutenant-general a *comes*, or count. The commander of a thousand men, corresponding to our colonel, was denominated *tiuphadus;* next in rank came the *quingentarius*, who had charge of a battalion of five hundred; then the centurion, and the decurion, in command of a company of a hundred, and a squad of ten men, respectively. The conscription officers were called *compulsores exercitus*, and the quartermasters or commissaries, *annonarii.*

This military gradation was also maintained in civil life, in time of peace. The *dux* was the governor of the province in which he lived; the *comes*, the governor of the chief city of his district; the *tiuphadus* was responsible for the behavior of the thousand men, and their families, over whom he exercised control. All these, with several other civil functionaries, had the privilege of holding court, and were invested by the law with the title of judge: "*judicis nomine censeantur ex lege.*" See Code II, 1–25.—[ED.

seek sanctuary at the altar, or with the bishop, he sha l pay three hundred *solidi* to the governor of the city, and shall not be liable to the penalty of death. The governor of the city shall then notify the king of the occurrence, and the above mentioned *solidi* shall be divided among the soldiers under the command of said centurion. The latter shall not thereafter be entitled to the command of a hundred men, under any circumstances; but he may be appointed to the command of ten. Where a centurion, without the consent of the general, or of any of his superior officers, and induced by a bribe, or persuaded by the entreaty of any of his soldiers, permits said soldiers to return home, or releases them from service in the army, he shall be compelled to pay to the governor of the city where he was at the time, ninefold the amount he corruptly received; and, as has been hereinbefore stated, said governor shall, at once, give notice to the king; in order that the fine paid to said officer may, under our direction, be divided among the soldiers of his command. But if a centurion, without receiving any bribe, should permit a soldier to return home, he shall pay to the governor of the city ten *solidi*, as above mentioned.

ANCIENT LAW.

IV. Where an Officer of the Army, Deserting the Service, Returns Home, or Compels Others to do so.

If a decurion should leave his command and return to his home, or should refuse to leave his home and join the army, while he is in good health, he shall pay ten *solidi* to the governor of the city. And if he should permit anyone else to leave the army, he shall pay five *solidi* to the governor of the city; and said governor shall inform us of the fact, that, under our direction, said sum may be divided among the members of the command of said decurion. If a soldier, without the permission of any of his officers, should desert the army, and return home, or should refuse to leave his home in order to be enrolled in the forces of the king, he shall pay ten *solidi*, and shall be publicly scourged in the market-place.

ANCIENT LAW.

V. Where a Conscription Officer Receives a Bribe to Permit Soldiers who are not Ill, to Remain at Home.

Where any conscription officer accepts anything from any person, to release him from military service, he shall be compelled to pay to the governor of the city, ninefold the amount which he accepted; and where he neglects to enroll a person in the army, who was in good health at the time, even though he accepted no bribe from him, he shall be compelled to pay five *solidi* to the governor of the city. The commander of a thousand men shall make diligent inquiry by his centurions, and the centurions by their decurions, and if it should be ascertained that anyone was released from the service, either through bribery, or entreaty, or, remaining at home, refused to join the army, the *tiuphadus* shall then notify the lieutenant-general who, in his turn, must write to the governor in whose jurisdiction the offence was committed, in order that the latter may enforce the law provided in such cases; and said governor, as soon as they are collected, shall deliver all sums received as penalties to the officers entitled to receive the same. And if said governor should receive said penalties and appropriate them, or not surrender the same, he shall restore ninefold the amount which he received; and if, through the bribery or entreaty of anyone, he should delay to pay over any of said sums, he shall be compelled, out of his own property, to pay double the amount, to those among whom they should have been divided. If, after the collection of said penalties, he should not notify the king, in order that the latter may provide for their proper distribution, and should not surrender them, he shall be compelled to pay elevenfold the amount, by way of reparation.

ANCIENT LAW.

VI. Concerning those who Appropriate Army Rations, or are Guilty of Fraud in the Distribution of the Same.

We deem it advisable that, in every province and castle, some one shall be appointed as a collector of provisions, for the use of the army; and said collector, whether he be the governor of a city, or not, shall at once deliver all provisions collected by him in his district, to those who are entitled to receive the same. If it should happen, however, that the governor of the city, or the collector, should delay to deliver them, either because through his negligence, he has not taken possession of them, or because of his unwillingness to do so, the officers of the army may lodge a complaint against him on account of his refusal to deliver said provisions to those charged with their distribution. The general of the army shall then give notice to the king, and the days which have elapsed since said provisions should have been delivered shall be computed. Said governor of the city, or collector of provisions, shall then be compelled to pay from his own property, four times the value of said provisions, for each day lost by his neglect. We hereby decree that a similar rule shall apply to all officers of the army who are charged with such duties.

ANCIENT LAW.

VII. What Reward he who Rescues Slaves, or Property, from the Possession of the Enemy, shall be Entitled to.

Where any person makes a desperate attack upon the enemy, in order to rescue slaves, or money, or any other kind of property, and the owner of said property subsequently appears, and establishes his ownership of the same, two thirds of said property shall be restored to the owner, and he who recovered it shall be entitled to the other third for his services. In like manner, if any person should induce a slave to desert from the enemy, and should assist said slave, or offer him protection, and should afterwards restore him to his master, said person shall be entitled to receive a tenth part of the value of the slave, as a reward.

THE GLORIOUS FLAVIUS WAMBA, KING.

VIII. What Conduct shall be Pursued, when Public Scandal Arises within the Bounds of Spain.

Our solicitude for our subjects induces us, as we have already made laws to suppress litigation, to promulgate other regulations for the maintenance of protection and safety in the presence of war. For peace is the more easily preserved, and the common benefit more readily secured, where every one is compelled to perform his duty; and this may be best accomplished when omissions in former laws are remedied by the enactment of others hereafter. For this reason we desire to abolish such evil customs as are injurious to the interests of our country, through the neglect or ill conduct of our subjects. For, whenever an enemy invades the provinces of our kingdom, the urgent necessity of defence imposes itself upon those who inhabit the border, and, at such times, many of them, induced by hatred, or through treachery, disappear; so that, by this means, there is no mutual support in battle; and, under such circumstances, he who ought to give his service in the defence of his country, deserts his brethren; or, on the other hand, should he attack the enemy with too great audacity, while not properly supported, he runs imminent risk of being destroyed. We therefore decree that from this time henceforth, if any enemy should attack our country, all of our subjects, whether they be bishops or other members of the clergy, generals, or governors, as well as other officials of every rank who are in the public service, and whether, at the time, they are near the frontier invaded by the enemy, or within a hundred miles of the same, as soon as the necessity shall arise, and they shall be notified by their generals, governors, or any other officers; or whether information of said invasion shall come to their notice from any other quarter whatsoever; if they do not hasten to the defence of their country and of our people, and do not assist in such defence with all their valor and ability; or, upon any fraudulent pretext, or with any false excuse, attempt to escape their responsibility, so that their assistance may be lacking to their brethren in the protection of their country, and the enemy, by reason of their want of co-operation, should commit any injury in any province of our kingdom, or reduce any of its inhabitants to captivity; anyone who thus, through delay, fear, malice, or lukewarmness, fails to exert himself, with all his power, against our enemies for national defence, if he be a priest, or belong to any sacerdotal order, and does not have the means to satisfy the damages incurred by the invasion of said enemy, he shall be exiled to such place as the king may select. This sentence shall be imposed only upon bishops, priests, and deacons. All other members of the clergy shall undergo the sentence elsewhere prescribed for the laity.

And we hereby decree if the offender should be of noble rank, or of inferior station, that he shall forfeit his dignity and freedom, be reduced to slavery, and become the absolute property of whomever the king may select. For it is but just that he who neglects to defend the nobility of his race and maintain the integrity of his country, from whence he derives the dignity of his family, should receive this sentence; since he is both degenerate and useless, who openly refuses to defend the honor and possessions he derived from his ancestors. And, concerning the property of such transgressors, laity, and clergy, alike, who are inferior in rank, we decree as follows: that whoever, hereafter, commits such offences, shall render satisfaction for all damages done to our country, or to its people; and that, as a just punishment, those shall lose their dignity and honor, who, induced by malice or timidity, did not repel the attacking enemy, nor boldly showed themselves in the ranks of the national defenders.

Where any scandal arises within the limits of Spain, Gaul, Galicia, or in any other province of our kingdom, and said scandal affects, in any way, any of our subjects, or our government, or that of any of our successors, as soon as said scandal shall become public in the neighborhood, and anyone shall be especially notified of the same by any priest, clerk, general, governor, *tiuphadus*, deputy, or any other person, as elsewhere specified; and he does not straightway come to the defence of his king, his people, and his country, against whom said scandal has been circulated, and should not use all his efforts for the suppression of the same; if the party who is implicated in this infamous offence should be a bishop or any member of a clerical order, or a palatine or a noble of whatever rank, or a person of inferior station, he shall not only be sent into exile, but whatever property he is deprived of by judicial sentence, shall be given to the king.[1]

All persons, however, shall be exempt from the operations of this law, who are incapacitated by disease, or infirmity, from lending their aid to our faithful subjects as hereinbefore stated. Such persons as are prevented from actively exerting themselves as aforesaid, must, to the best of their ability, employ their power in aid of the bishops, clergy, and their brethren, and use their influence to the utmost in behalf of the royal dignity, and in the interest of their fellow citizens, and of their country; and, should they not do this, they shall be liable to the same penalties as actual transgressors. No person shall be liable to punishment, however, who can prove by a competent witness that he was prevented by illness, and was not able to afford assistance. We promulgate this law to abolish a vicious custom which has come down from former times, and deserves to be visited with severe legal censure, and to the end that unanimous concord may establish the peace of our people, and the defence of our country.

Given and confirmed on the Kalends of November, in the second year of our happy reign.

THE GLORIOUS FLAVIUS WAMBA, KING.

IX. Concerning Those who Fail to Enlist at the Appointed Time or Place, or Desert; and What Proportion of the Slaves Belonging to any Person shall Join the Army.

If those are designated lovers of their country who boldly throw themselves in the face of danger for its protection, should not such as refuse to defend it be classed as deserters? For as we believe that the former voluntarily desire to save their country, others who, when notified, do not exert them-

[1] While this is an early instance of the recognition of the offence of *scandalum magnatum*, subsequently regarded as a heinous crime against the Lord's anointed, and still, under the name of *lèse majesté*, punished with exemplary severity by many of the monarchs of Europe, it here assumes a broader significance than it did in later times, as it applies also to the people, and thus includes the torts of slander and libel.—[ED.

selves in its defence, and either delay to join the army, or, what is worse, after having been notified, choose to remain at home, or enter the ranks without arms or equipments; while some desirous of carrying on their work, conceal the great number of slaves they possess, and, for their own profit and safety, do not bring the twentieth part of the latter with them, desiring rather to preserve their crops than the bodies of their slaves, and, while they protect their property, leave themselves unprotected; thus showing greater diligence in the care of their possessions, than experience in arms, in order that, if they should prove victorious, they may have the more wealth to enjoy. Punishment must, therefore, be provided for such persons, since they disregard their duties to the state. Therefore, we order all subjects under our government to observe the following decree, to wit: that whenever the king shall issue an order for anyone to join the army, upon a certain day or date, or when he shall direct any of his generals or commanders to carry out any object for the public benefit, whoever receives such an order, or where he does not receive it in person, should be aware that it had been issued, or learns from any source, in what place the army is to assemble, shall make no delay, nor proffer any excuse whatever; but every such person shall present himself at the appointed place and time, as ordered by the king, general, commander, deputy, or any other official, invested with authority. Where anyone having thus been notified, or even if he has not been notified, but has received information, in any way, of the situation of the army, should be unwilling to march; or should neglect to present himself at the appointed time; if he is a person of high rank, that is to say, a general, governor, or any other officer of importance, he shall be deprived of all his property, and be driven into exile, by order of the king, and his confiscated possessions shall be at the absolute disposal of the latter. Where persons of inferior rank, as, for instance, commanders of a thousand men, recruiting officers, and all conscripts, delay to join the army, or neglect to report at the appointed time and place; or fail to march; or withdraw, under any fraudulent pretext, from military service; they shall not only each receive two hundred lashes, but shall also be scalped, and shall each forfeit a pound of gold to the king. And, should any of them not be possessed of the necessary amount, the king may then reduce said offender to perpetual slavery, and dispose of his property at his pleasure.

We decree, however, that those shall not be subject to punishment under this law, who have been freed from its operation by the royal order, or are exempt by being minors, or are incapacitated by age or sickness. If a person who is disabled by illness, should be able to prove, by a competent witness that, for this reason, he was unable to march with the army, he must devote such of his property as he can spare to the public benefit.

As we have already made provision concerning the general co-operation of all persons, we must now provide for money and supplies. Therefore, we hereby decree, that whenever anyone, whether he be general, count, or *gardingus*,[1] Goth, or Roman, freeman or manumitted slave, or any serf attached to the service of the Crown, joins the army, he shall bring the tenth of his slaves with him; and in order that said slaves may not come unarmed, but may be provided with the proper weapons, whoever brings them must furnish a part of them with suitable armor, and the greater portion must be provided with shields, two-edged swords, lances, bows and arrows, slings, and other arms, and he who brings them must parade them, armed in this manner, before the king, general, or commander-in-chief. Where anyone brings with him to the army less than the tenth part of his slaves, an estimate shall be made of the entire number of the latter, and whatever portion of the tenth part aforesaid is found lacking, shall be delivered to the king, to become his property, and be disposed of at his pleasure. And wherever anyone, who holds an office in

---

[1] The *gardingus* was the third in rank of the Visigothic nobility, coming after the *dux* and *comes*. Unlike either of them, however, he, as a rule, exercised no public employment; and being ordinarily a person of great wealth, and descended from a long line of ancestors, materially contributed, by the richness of his appointments, and the number of his retinue, to the pomp and splendor of the royal court.—[ED.

the palace, shall so conduct himself in the army, as not to use every effort in the service of his prince, or properly perform his military duties, along with his fellow soldiers; he shall be liable to the penalty of this law, except where his manifest weakness shall disclose the fact that he is incapacitated by illness. And if anyone, who has already joined the army, and ought to have followed a duke, or count, or patron, should delay, for any reason, and not appear on duty under his commander, or should not exhibit proper zeal for the public service, his rank shall not be taken into consideration, but he shall be liable to the penalty hereinbefore provided, concerning persons of inferior station.

The matters aforesaid having been settled and determined, it now remains to place restraints upon the avarice of those who are summoned to military service. Therefore, no governor of a province, governor of a city, commander of a thousand men, or anyone charged with the duty of governing the people, shall excuse any of our subjects from military duty, for the sake of a bribe, or for any other inducement whatever; or shall suffer orders, made on the march, to be contested, or the regulation concerning the providing of arms to be disregarded. Whoever is guilty of any of the offences aforesaid, and, for any cause, accepts a gift from any person, or exacts a contribution of any kind from a soldier or anyone else; if he is of high rank among the officers of the palace, shall pay fourfold the amount received, to him from whom he accepted it, and shall give a pound of gold to the king, on account of his presumption. Persons of inferior rank shall be deprived of their honor and dignity, shall be delivered up to the king, and be placed absolutely in his power, to be disposed of as he may direct.

TITLE III. CONCERNING THOSE WHO SEEK SANCTUARY IN A CHURCH.

I. No One, Claiming the Privilege of Sanctuary in a Church, shall be Taken from Thence by Force, Unless he Defends himself with Arms.

No one shall dare to remove, by force, any person who has sought sanctuary in a church unless said person should attempt to defend himself with arms.

II. Where a Person Seeks Sanctuary in a Church, and is Killed, while Defending himself with Arms.

Where anyone takes refuge at the door of a church, and does not lay down his arms, and is killed; the person who struck him shall be liable to no penalty or reproach therefor.

III. Concerning the Penalty for Removing a Man from a Church by Force.

Where anyone removes his slave or a debtor from a church, or the altar where he sought sanctuary, without the consent of a priest, or of some other ecclesiastic who has charge of sa d church; as soon as the fact has been brought to the notice of the judge, if he is a person of high rank, said offender shall be compelled to pay a hundred *solidi* to the church which sustained the injury. A person of inferior station shall pay thirty *solidi*, and if he should not have the means to do so, he shall be arrested by the judge, and receive a hundred lashes in public. The master shall then regain possession of his slave, and the debtor shall be surrendered to his creditor.

IV. A Debtor, or a Criminal, Cannot be Forcibly Removed from a Church, and must Pay such Debts, or Penalties, as are Due.

No one shall presume to seize a person who seeks sanctuary in a church, or at its doors; but he may petition a priest or a deacon to restore said person to him; and if a debtor or a criminal takes refuge there, and he should not be liable to the penalty of death, the ecclesiastic in charge of the church may interpose his good offices, and request that said party be pardoned or discharged. If a debtor should take refuge in a church, the church shall have no right to protect him, but the priest or deacon must surrender him, without delay, with the admonition that his creditor shall neither injure nor bind him who claimed the right of asylum; and the creditor must state, in the presence of said priest or deacon, within what time he shall expect the payment of the debt. Because the intervention of the church may be invoked for purposes of mercy, is no reason why persons should be deprived of their property. The laws relating to homicides and other malefactors are set forth under their respective titles.

BOOK X.

CONCERNING PARTITION, LIMITATION, AND BOUNDARIES.

TITLE I. CONCERNING PARTITION, AND LANDS CONVEYED BY CONTRACT.

I. A Partition Once Made, shall Remain Forever in Force.

A just partition once made, shall always remain in force, and, for no reason, shall it ever be altered thereafter.

II. No Partition made Between Brothers shall be Revoked, Even if it was not Made in Writing, but Only in the Presence of a Competent Witness.

We hereby decree that a partition made between brothers, even though it be not evidenced by an agreement in writing, shall remain in force, provided it can be proved by competent testimony; and, when this has been done, said partition shall have full validity in law.

III. Where a Partition is Made Among Many Persons by the Majority, and those Entitled to the Larger Share, it shall not be Changed by any Act of the Minority.

Where several heirs are interested in a partition of property, whatever is determined upon, as equitable, by a majority of the same, shall prevail, and shall not be interfered with thereafter by the minority.

FLAVIUS CHINTASVINTUS, KING.

IV. One Heir shall have the Right to Act for all the Others, either as Plaintiff or Defendant.

It was established by a former law that, where a cause is heard in court, one person shall not have the right to answer for another, unless the latter, who is equally interested, should be present, and should consent; and, for this reason, we consider it superfluous to make further provision in such matters, in cases where litigation arises, and each person must plead his own cause. However, lest through the artifice of an adversary, where a party interposes delay on behalf of one joined with him in the case, the term of thirty years may run against the complainant; after due deliberation, we hereby decree, that no excuse for delay shall be allowed in behalf of any party; and that any party to a suit may appear for all others joined with him, in the same manner as if he alone were interested. If, however, an heir should lose the suit either through corruption, or by his own negligence, the rights of none of his co-heirs shall be prejudiced thereby; and should any of them desire to reopen the case, they shall be permitted to do so. The law hereinbefore mentioned, which relates to this subject, is hereby abrogated; and we enjoin the observance of the present one upon all the people of our realm. And we hereby decree, that the same rule shall be observed where one of several parties interested in the prosecution of a claim thinks that a suit ought to be brought to collect it.

V. Where Anyone Violates a Contract Establishing a Partition, and Seizes a Portion of the Property.

Whoever violates the provisions of a partition made between heirs, and seizes any property belonging to a co-heir, shall forfeit as much of his own share as he attempted to take from the other.

VI. Where an Heir Plants a Vineyard, or Erects a House, on Land Belonging to his Co-Heirs.

Where anyone plants a vineyard, or builds a house, upon the land of any of his co-heirs, whether the owner of the same is ignorant of the fact, or consents to it, (even if he who planted said vineyard, or built said house, was ignorant of what part of said land belonged to his co-heirs), when he shall establish this, either by his own oath, or by the testimony of witnesses, he shall give to the owner upon whose premises he planted the vineyard, an equal quantity of land of the same value, and shall remain secure in the possession of the vineyard which he planted. If, however, he should plant said vineyard against the consent of the owner, he shall forfe't all right to the same. The same rule shall apply to buildings of every description. We also decree that if anyone should sell, give away, or exchange, land belonging to another; as soon as it shall be discovered that he had no title to the same, and if he who received said land should have built a house upon it, or should have planted a vineyard, olive-grove, garden, or orchard therein; or should have added anything to the value of said land by his labor; and the party to whom said land belongs should delay to claim it; or should be ignorant that it had been so disposed of; or should be unwilling to assert his rights to the same, in order to thereafter reap the benefit of the additional value it has acquired from the labor of another; when the said owner shall establish his title to said land in court, he shall receive another similar tract, double in value, from the party who made the illegal sale or transfer, and he who improved said land shall under no circumstances lose the fruits of his toil.

VII. Where one Person Plants a Vineyard on the Land of Another, to which he has no Title.

Whoever plants a vineyard upon the land of another, who is not his co-heir, without the permission of said owner either by force, or when said owner was ignorant of the fact, or absent (even if he should not have been forbidden to do so), shall lose the vineyard that he planted; for the reason that he ought to know that whoever appropriates the property of another should not profit twofold by his illegal act.

VIII. Concerning the Division of Lands Made Between Goths and Romans.

A division of arable lands or forests made between Goths and Romans, shall under no circumstances be interfered with, provided said division shall be proved to have been publicly made, and no Roman shall take, or claim for himself, any part of the two thirds of said land allotted to a Goth in said division; nor shall any Goth dare to seize, or claim for himself, any of the third part of said land allotted to a Roman, unless it should have been bestowed upon him by our generosity; and any division made between parents or neighbors shall not be disturbed by their posterity.

IX. Concerning Forests Still Undivided Among Goths and Romans.

In the case of forests which are still undivided, where any Goth or Roman has appropriated a portion of the same, and placed it under cultivation, we hereby decree that if any woodland of equal value belongs to the party bound under the law to make compensation, the person entitled to receive said compensation shall not refuse to accept the woodland aforesaid. If, however, the former should have no woodland of equal value, the tract which is under cultivation shall be divided between the two parties.

X. Whatever Acts a Slave may Perform, without the Order of his Master, shall be Void, except when Otherwise Provided by Law.

Wherever a slave makes a division of any property, or does any other act without the order of his master, except where authorized by law, we declare said act to be invalid, unless the master of said slave should be willing to sanction the same.

XI. Whoever Enters upon Land, under a Lease, must Comply with his Contract.

Whoever rents land under the terms of a legal contract, for a fixed annual rental, shall have possession of said premises, and must pay the rent at the end of each year, according to the terms of the lease; because no contract should be violated. Where the tenant neglects to pay the rent at the end of each year, the owner shall be entitled to the possession of his land; and he who did not comply with his contract shall, through his own fault, lose all the profit which might accrue to him under said contract.

XII. Where Lands are Leased, by a Written Contract, for a Term of Years.

Where the use of land is granted by an instrument in writing, for a certain term of years, he who received said land shall restore the same to the owner, at the expiration of said term, and shall do so without unnecessary delay, according to the conditions of the contract.

XIII. Where he who Rents Land under Contract, Cultivates a Greater Area than he has a Right to do, under the Conditions of the Same.

Whoever rents land under a lease, shall occupy as much of said land as the owner permits him to use, and no more. If, however, he should cultivate more land than he is entitled to under his contract, or should bring in others for that purpose, or his sons and grandsons, inmates of his house, should cultivate lands not included in his lease; or he should occupy any fields without the permission of the owner; or should, without authority, cut down any grove, for the purpose of having tillable land, or meadows, or to build fences out of the timber; he shall lose everything which he has appropriated without permission; and it shall rest in the discretion of the owner whether he shall increase the rent, or shall at once take possession of the land not included in the lease. And where only arable land is rented to any person and no woodland or pasture is included, no lessee shall have the right to use said woodland or pasture without the consent of the owner thereof.

XIV. Where a Dispute Arises Between Landlord and Tenant, Concerning Arable Lands, or Forests, which are Leased.

Where any dispute arises between the parties to a lease, concerning the quantity of land granted under said lease the lessor, if he is living, and if he is dead, his heirs, shall make oath that said lessor did not lease a larger tract of land than is designated by them. And after they have made oath as aforesaid, they shall attach their seals to the same in the presence of witnesses, to the end that no cause for dispute may arise thereafter. If, however, said parties should not be worthy of credit, or should be unwilling to make oath as aforesaid, or should have any doubt concerning the amount of land so leased, they shall not make oath and imperil their souls, but they shall divide each of the whole number of *aratra* received by themselves, as heirs of their parents, into fifty *arepennes:* so that every portion occupied or cultivated shall include said fifty *arepennes;* nor shall they presume to occupy any more than said portion measured and allotted to them, unless with the consent of the owner or owners of said land. Any tenant who occupies more than said quantity of land, shall pay double the amount of rent of the tract he illegally entered upon.

XV. Both Tenants must Pay the Rent for Land which has been Sublet.

Where a landlord receives a tenant on his land, and it afterward happens that the latter sublets a third of the same to another party, both shall be considered tenants of the landlord, and shall pay rent to him in proportion to the amount of land they occupy.

XVI. Where Goths have Appropriated any of the Third Part of Land Belonging to Romans, they shall Restore the Entire Amount to the Romans, under Order of Court.

Judges, governors, and other authorities, in all cases where Romans have been deprived of their lands, shall take them from those who occupy them, and restore them to the Romans, in order that the royal treasury may sustain no loss; provided, however, that the period of fifty years shall not have elapsed, so that, by limitation of time, the rights of the Romans to said lands may not have been lost.

FLAVIUS CHINTASVINTUS, KING.

XVII. Concerning the Partition of Property Among the Blood-Relatives of Slaves, and the Distribution of their Personal Estates.

It is the just province of the law to amend or repeal by new decrees, any former statutes which may be devoid of reason or equity; and the cause of abuses must first be determined, before laws can be enacted for their correction. As a son is born of both parents, why should he follow the condition of his mother, while he owes his being equally to his father. It is, therefore, but reasonable that we decree that where one slave has married a slave owned by another person, any issue of said marriage shall belong equally to the masters of both slaves. Where, however, there is but one son born to said parents, since he cannot serve both masters at once, he shall remain with his mother until his twelfth year, at which age he will be able to work. The master of the female slave shall then pay to the master of her husband one half of the value of the child, after said value shall have been appraised by men of respectability. A similar rule shall be observed in the cases of other children of slaves, where said children are not of even number. All personal property which said male and female slave has accumulated, while living under one roof, shall belong to both masters. And if said slaves should have accumulated any property on land belonging to a third person, or any building, or any real estate of any description, or any personal property that is not portable, the masters of said slaves shall have a right to the division of said property among themselves, in the same manner as if it had been acquired through relationship by blood. If one of the said masters should be opposed to the marriage of the slaves aforesaid, he may straightway separate them, under this condition: that, after said marriage shall have come to the knowledge of said masters, and they should not desire its continuance, they must dissolve it within a year. If, through their negligence, this reasonable time prescribed by law should have elapsed, whatever issue said slaves may have after that time, shall be equally divided between their masters; the sex, number, and ages of said children being taken into consideration. If more than a year should elapse without one or both of their masters being aware of said marriage, all issue of the same shall be divided between them, as aforesaid.

THE GLORIOUS FLAVIUS RECESVINTUS, KING.

XVIII. All Personal Property shall be Classed under One Title.

We often see wicked persons, for the purpose of contention, pervert the meaning of the law; and, in order to prevent such conduct, as far as possible, we desire to simplify matters whenever this can be done. Therefore, we decree that no difference shall exist in the classification of all kinds of personal property, whether said property be tangible, or merely held in trust by one for another; in order that the subtle distinctions which have arisen in the classification of said property may be abolished.

THE GLORIOUS FLAVIUS RECESVINTUS, KING.

XIX. Where a Contract is not Complied With, according to its Terms.

Whenever any person obtains possession of land, vineyards, or any other real estate, under a lease for the tenth part of its annual yield, or for any other payment, or consideration, whether said lease is in writing, or verbal, provided he who leases it does so under some contract for rent, the lessee shall, without demand or solicitation from the lessor, pay his rent regularly; nor shall the right of the landlord to said rent be affected, in any way, should he not do so. For wherever the provisions or covenants of a lease are not fulfilled, the right of the owner shall not be affected; because the controversy has not arisen through the act of the landlord, but through the fraud of the tenant. If the tenant should refuse to fulfil his contract, or to comply with any of its provisions, he shall pay double the amount to the landlord which he agreed to pay him under the terms of the lease. And if the tenant, alleging various pretexts, should not comply with his contract for such a time that the rights of the owner are lost by the limitation of the law, that is, for fifty years, he shall forfeit said property, with all the increase in value of the same resulting from his labors thereon.

TITLE II. CONCERNING THE LIMITATIONS OF FIFTY AND THIRTY YEARS.

I. After the Lapse of Fifty Years, Neither Goths nor Romans can Assert a Claim to Property.

Lands apportioned between Goths and Romans, which have not been claimed within fifty years, can under no circumstances be claimed afterwards.

II. No Fugitive Slave shall Again be Reduced to Servitude, after the Lapse of Fifty Years.

Fugitive slaves who have not been found within fifty years, shall not, after that time, be returned to servitude.

III. No Suit at Law shall be Brought Thirty Years After the Cause of Action has Arisen.

All suits at law, whether well founded or not, and also all criminal cases, which shall not have been brought or determined in thirty years; or any disputes relating to the ownership or possession of slaves, which have not been settled within that time, shall under no circumstances be prosecuted afterwards. Where any person attempts to bring a suit thirty years after the cause of action has arisen, he shall be barred by the limitation aforesaid, and shall be compelled to give a pound of gold to whomever the king may direct.

THE GLORIOUS FLAVIUS RECESVINTUS, KING.

IV. The Limitation of Thirty Years shall Run in all Cases, Excepting those where the Slaves of the Crown are Concerned.

Want of care and resolution in an owner often disturbs the rightful possession of property, and what vigilance was not exerted to preserve, illegal license appropriates. The passage of the aforesaid period of thirty years is seen to occur so constantly in human affairs, that now it does not seem to have originated in the institutions of man, but rather to have arisen, in the course of nature, from the affairs themselves; and for this reason, therefore, we hereby decree, for all time hereafter, that if any beneficiary of the king, or any employee of the Crown, except royal slaves, should have held any property belonging to anyone for the space of thirty years, he shall have the right to claim and retain said property for himself, forever; and the demand of no one shall avail against said limitation, after it shall have been legally established.

Royal slaves whose servile origin is publicly known, who are at large, and wandering from place to place, even though they should pay no taxes, and should lie concealed in hiding places, or remain under the protection of any person for the space of thirty years, as aforesaid, shall not thereby escape the restraints of slavery, but shall be restored to their original condition without regard to lapse of time. Those only shall be excepted from the operation of this law who have received their freedom from the king.

FLAVIUS CHINTASVINTUS, KING.

V. Concerning Claims made within Thirty Years.

Long continued possession frequently transfers the ownership of property from one person to another; for whatever anyone has held for thirty years without molestation, can never be lost through the claims of another. To the end, however, that the rights of claimant as well as those of possessor may be properly protected, we hereby decree that the following law shall be observed by all, to wit: that wherever any property has been held by any person for from twenty-five to thirty years, and another person should claim said property; and the possessor should be notified of said claim either by the judge or the claimant, and should fail to make restitution, or to answer within a reasonable time; or should interpose delay under any pretext; or should assert his claim while the possessor of said property is absent, that is to say, while he is in another province, or in the army; under such circumstances, the judge shall deliver said property into the possession of the claimant in the presence of three witnesses, in order that the limitation of time may not run against said claim. And if the judge should order the property in dispute to be delivered into the possession of the claimant by a bailiff, he shall issue a writ directed to said bailiff, signed by his own hand, and according to the form hereinafter specified; and if there should be other property than that claimed in the place where the latter is situated, in order that no dispute may arise, the doors or gates of the enclosure where said property is situated shall be sealed with the signet of the judge or of the bailiff, and shall remain sealed for eight days; and the claimant shall retain possession of it for only eight days; but he must not waste, spoil, or dispose of said property, in any way, but must care for the same to the best of his ability. After the expiration of that time he must leave the property intact, in the possession of him who originally held it, and no responsibility whatever shall attach to him who had possession of it for the eight days aforesaid. And he himself, or any of his family or descendants, shall have the right to assert their claim to said property, at any time within thirty years from the day when the claimant made the demand as aforesaid. And if said person should not be able to establish the justice of his claim, he shall render satisfaction to the owner of the property, as a person making an unjust demand for something to which he was not entitled. If he should damage said property, or dispose of it, in any way, while in his possession, he shall be compelled to restore fourfold its value; and neither he, nor any of his family or posterity, shall have a right to make any claim for said property at any time thereafter

We also hereby decree that if the property in dispute should consist of different articles, and should be situated in different places, an order issued by the judge relating to any one of said articles shall have the same force as if it related to all. The form of the order issued by the judge shall be as follows:—

ITEM.

WRIT OF INFORMATION. THE JUDGE TO THE BAILIFF.

We inform you that such-and-such a person claims property in the possession of so-and-so, and we hereby order you to place said property in the possession of said claimant, in the presence of two or three witnesses; to be left in his possession for the space of eight days only, according to the provisions of the law; and if you should find any property to which the seal of the owner thereof is not attached, you will attach your own seal thereto, to remain unbroken for the aforesaid term of eight days, in order to remove all cause of dispute or opportunity for fraud; and none of said property shall be removed by you.

FLAVIUS RECESVINTUS, KING.

VI. The Limitation of Thirty Years shall not Run while Persons are Exiled.

The more humanity is oppressed by misfortune, the more we should provide by our clemency for the evils with which it is afflicted. Wherefore, whenever any person of noble rank, or any freeman, or even a slave, is confined in prison, or sent into exile, by order of the king; and should afterwards be liberated, or pardoned, and return to his country, and anyone should have claimed any of his property during his absence; the time which he passed in confinement or exile shall not be counted as a part of the thirty or fifty year limitation barring a claim, or action at law; but the time during which he was imprisoned, or absent from the country, and unable to assert his rights, shall be excepted from the period of limitation aforesaid. In all other cases the laws which have already established periods of limitation relating to claims and actions at law, shall remain in force hereafter.

FLAVIUS EGICA, KING.

VII. Within what Time Slaves Belonging to the Crown can Again be Reduced to Slavery.

We hereby repeal the former law by which slaves belonging to the Crown could be reduced to their former condition of servitude, without consideration of the lapse of time, and, in the place thereof, issue the following decree, to wit: that whoever has had in his possession any slaves of the Crown for the space of thirty years, and said slaves have not been transferred to the possession of any other person during that time; or if any such slaves should wander from place to place, without paying any tax for the space of fifty years; said slaves shall under no circumstances be reclaimed by the Crown. But those persons under whose control such slaves were, for either the thirty or the fifty year period aforesaid, must make suitable compensation for their services to the royal treasury; to the end that one and the same law may prevail concerning the slaves of both prince and people.

TITLE III. CONCERNING BOUNDARIES AND LANDMARKS.

I. How Boundaries and Landmarks shall be Preserved.

We hereby decree that all ancient landmarks and boundaries shall stand as established in former times, and that they shall not be disturbed or removed.

II. Concerning the Destruction and Removal of Landmarks.

Whoever levels any landmarks for the purpose of travel, or dares to remove any established landmarks, for every landmark so fraudulently disturbed, if he is a freeman, he shall pay twenty *solidi;* and if he is a slave he shall receive fifty lashes, and shall restore said landmark. If any person while plowing land, or planting a vineyard, should involuntarily disturb a landmark, he shall restore the same in the presence of the neighbors, and shall not, thereafter, be liable to any damage or penalty for removing the same.

III What is to be Done when a Dispute Arises Concerning Boundaries.

Whenever a dispute arises concerning the boundaries of land, search shall be made for the old landmarks; that is to say, the mounds of earth, or squared stones, which, in ancient times, were made or placed in order to define the boundaries of lands; or for any stones which have been buried, and are carved to show that they were intended as landmarks. Should any of said landmarks be wanting, search must then be made for such trees as might have been marked in former times, to define the boundaries between different tracts of land.

THE GLORIOUS FLAVIUS RECESVINTUS, KING.

IV. Where One Person makes a Claim to Land Included within the Boundaries of Another.

Where anyone inherits or acquires land within the boundaries of another person, or, during the absence, or without the knowledge of the owner of the same, obtains possession of such land for a long period of time, or for more than the term of fifty years, even though his occupation of said property was public and notorious, he shall have no permanent title thereto; and as soon as the boundaries of said land shall have been established by the discovery of the ancient landmarks, by persons appointed to find the same, he shall restore said land so appropriated to the owner thereof. Nor shall any obligation of the owner, nor undisputed possession for a long period of time, avail against the ancient landmarks, when they are discovered. But it must be proved, if it can be ascertained, whether said land was acquired by one of the contesting parties or by the ancestors of either of them; for if such time should have elapsed that neither of said parties, nor any of their ancestors, knew who first obtained the title to or possession of said property, and the party in possession is unable to show by an instrument in writing, or by witnesses, whence the title to said premises was derived, because the fact of original possession is in doubt; whoever of said claimants is in possession of said land at the time shall have an irrevocable right to retain it. Where, however, one person seems to have been in possession of said land without the other claimant asserting any right to the same, and such possession shall be public, and apparently established by existing landmarks, and no evidence of fraud be disclosed; it is not reasonable that the title of the owner should be lost by reason of its occupation for a protracted period by another.

Where one person has obtained possession of land by force or fraud, this shall in no wise affect the rights of another claimant. If, however, one person should attempt to gain possession of property occupied by another, not through fraud or insolence, but by a judicial proceeding, if his claim is just, he shall be entitled to possession of said property. But it, unknown to the owner, he should unexpectedly attempt to gain possession of the land of the latter, the owner of the same shall have the right to accuse him of being a trespasser with violence, and, by legal proceedings, compel him to surrender said property.

V. Where any Change was made in the Boundaries of Land During the Time of the Romans, no Claim Based upon Other Boundaries shall Prevail.

Where real property, in which any person claims an interest, was disposed of before the coming of the Goths, and was transferred to the possession of another party either by sale, donation, partition, or any other transaction, whatever title or right to said property shall be proved to have been formerly conveyed by the Romans shall remain inviolable. But where a title to real property cannot be established by any certain landmarks or boundaries, the following proceeding must be observed, to wit: an examination of the premises must be made by persons selected by the consent of all parties; and the judge, for his own information, shall cause the oldest residents of the neighborhood to be sworn, that they will, without fraud, show where the boundaries of the land in question are situated; and no one shall establish a new boundary without the presence of the other party, or in the absence of one of the inspectors appointed by common consent, as aforesaid. If a freeman should violate this provision, he shall be liable for the penalty of forcible entry, as prescribed by law. Where a slave commits this offence, without the knowledge of his master, he shall receive two hundred lashes in public, but his master shall incur no liability for his act.[1]

---

[1] The intricate questions relating to the leasing, conveyance, descent, and forfeiture of real property are, as has been seen, elaborated and set forth with great skill and learning in the Visigothic Code. Not a single chapter treating of this subject is designated *Antiqua*, to indicate that it is derived from the Civil Law. And this is the more remarkable when the nomadic origin and barbarous customs of the not remote ancestors of those who enacted these important regulations, are considered. A nation of shepherds and marauders could not be supposed to be familiar with the tenures, contracts, transfers, boundaries, and torts, by which the title to landed estates is either acquired or lost; yet the Visigoths framed their laws with due consideration for the principles of equity, and the general welfare of all classes of freeborn citizens. In many respects their laws were superior to those of the Romans. Only two years by the Twelve Tables, and twenty under the Code of Justinian, were necessary to create a prescriptive right to the ownership of land. Under the Roman jurisprudence, until the population became debased by servile and barbarian marriages, no foreigner could legally hold or convey real-property. The Visigothic Code, on the other hand, carefully guarded the rights of the subject race, and prevented them from being prejudiced by the fraud or oppression of their rulers. The inferior classes under the Republic and the Empire, were practically serfs, living in a condition of abject villenage; those of corresponding station subject to the domination of the Visigoths, were often thrifty tenants of indulgent landlords, or, at the worst, were bound by exacting contracts which they had entered into of their own free will. The extreme solicitude manifested for the protection of the rights of all parties, where the title to real-property is concerned, is disclosed by the manifold precautions enjoined, and the stringent rules to be observed, in determining the existence of adverse possession. A contract for the rental of land, which would be valid in any of our courts, could easily be drawn from the laws of the Code relating to leaseholds.—[ED.

BOOK XI.

CONCERNING THE SICK AND THE DEAD, AND MERCHANTS WHO COME FROM BEYOND SEAS.

TITLE I. CONCERNING PHYSICIANS AND SICK PERSONS.

I. No Physician shall Presume to Bleed a Woman, in the Absence of her Relatives.

No physician shall presume to bleed a freeborn woman without the presence of her father, mother, brother, son, uncle, or some other relative, except urgent necessity should demand it; and where it happens that none of the above-named persons can be present, the woman must be bled in the presence of respectable neighbors or slaves, of either sex, according to the nature of her illness. If a physician should do this without the presence of any of the aforesaid persons, he shall be compelled to pay ten *solidi* to the husband or the relatives of said woman; for the reason that it is not at all improbable that, on such an occasion, wantonness may sometimes occur.[1]

II. No Physician shall Visit Persons Confined in Prison.

No physician shall presume to enter a prison when governors, tribunes, or deputies, are excluded therefrom, without being accompanied by the jailer, lest the prisoners, influenced by fear, may obtain from said physician the means wherewith to commit suicide; for should any poison be furnished or administered by physicians, under such circumstances, the course of justice would be greatly obstructed. Should any physician be guilty of this offence, he shall be liable to punishment for the same.

III. Where a Physician Treats Disease under a Contract.

Where any person demands that a physician treat him for disease, or cure his wound under a contract; after the physician has seen the wound, or diagnosed the disease, he may undertake the treatment of said sick person under such

---

[1] "*Ludibrium interdum adcrescat.*" It would appear from this precautionary measure, that the members of the medical profession, in that age, did not differ greatly from some of their brethren of to-day. The practice of medicine was not highly regarded by the Visigoths, a nation of warriors, and it was often exercised by slaves, as formerly at Rome, and subsequently by barbers and charlatans during the Middle Ages. Malpractice was a term of the broadest significance; the risks assumed by the practitioner, even in ordinary cases, were not compensated for by the fees he was entitled to receive, when successful; and the danger of damages and penalties he incurred where he lost a patient, made the profession anything but an alluring one. After rendering conscientious and assiduous services, to be considered guilty of homicide, and be surrendered to the exasperated relatives of the deceased patient, as a subject for the savage excesses of the *Lex Talionis*, was not a prospect calculated to advance the interests of medical science.

Not until three centuries later, under the Moorish domination, did the physician and the surgeon acquire the extensive knowledge, and attain the professional eminence, which made the medical colleges of the Spanish Peninsula the centre of that branch of learning, not only of Europe, but of the then known world.—[ED.

conditions as may be agreed upon, and set forth in an instrument in writing.

IV. Where a Sick Person Dies, while a Physician is Treating him under a Contract.

Where a physician undertakes the treatment of a sick person under a contract reduced to writing, he must restore said sick person to health; and, if the latter should die, the physician shall not be entitled to the compensation stipulated in said contract, and no liability shall attach to either of the parties to the same.

V. Where a Physician Removes a Cataract from the Eye.

Where a physician removes a cataract from the eye of any person, and restores the invalid to his former health, he shall be entitled to five *solidi* for his services.

VI. Where a Freeman or a Slave Dies from Being Bled.

Where a physician bleeds a patient, and the latter is greatly weakened in consequence, said physician shall be compelled to pay him forty *solidi*. If the patient should die as the result of being bled, the physician shall be delivered up to the relatives of said patient, to be disposed of at their pleasure. Where the patient is a slave, and is seriously weakened, or dies, the physician must give his master another slave of equal value, in his stead.

VII. Concerning the Compensation to be Received for the Instruction of a Student in Medicine.

Where a physician receives a slave for the purpose of instruction in medicine, he shall be entitled to twelve *solidi* by way of compensation.

VIII. No Physician shall be Imprisoned without a Hearing.

No physician shall be imprisoned without a hearing, except in case of homicide. Where he is charged with debt, he must provide a surety.

TITLE II. CONCERNING THOSE WHO DISTURB SEPULCHRES.

I. Concerning Persons who Deface or Injure Tombs.

Where any person injures a tomb; or robs a corpse; or strips it of any ornaments or clothing; if he should be freeborn, he shall be compelled to pay a pound of gold to the heirs of the deceased, and to restore the stolen property. Where there are no heirs, he shall pay the above-named sum to the royal treasury, and shall receive in addition a hundred lashes. If a slave should commit this crime, he shall receive two hundred lashes; shall be put to death by fire; and whatever he stole shall be returned.

II. Where a Coffin is Removed from a Grave.

If anyone should steal the coffin of a dead person, for any purpose of his own, he shall be forced, by order of the judge, to pay twelve *solidi* to the heirs of the deceased. If, however, a slave should commit this offence under the direction of his master, his master shall at once render satisfaction for his act. Should a slave do this of his own accord, he shall receive a hundred lashes, and shall restore to the place, and to the body of the deceased, whatever he took therefrom.

TITLE III. CONCERNING MERCHANTS WHO COME FROM BEYOND SEAS.

I. Where Foreign Merchants are Detected Selling Stolen Property

Where any foreign merchant sells gold, silver, clothing, or ornaments of any description, for a fair price, to any of our subjects, and said property should afterwards prove to have been stolen, the purchaser shall incur no liability therefor.

II. Foreign Merchants shall be Judged by their own Magistrates, and According to their own Laws.

When any legal cause of action arises between foreign merchants, it shall not be heard by any of our judges, but by their own, and it shall be decided according to their own laws.[1]

[1] This law, which grants to every foreign trader the privilege of being judged by his own magistrates, is the precursor of modern legislation establishing consular and other tribunals instituted to protect the commercial interests, and define the judicial rights, of persons transacting business in another country, and is of unknown antiquity. It is, however, at least thirteen hundred years old. A people capable of appreciating and adopting such a measure, must have had intelligent conceptions of the maxims and requirements of international law and have made no inconsiderable progress in the arts of civilization.—[ED.

III. Where a Foreign Merchant Carries Away with him, from our Kingdom, a Person whom he has Hired.

No foreign merchant shall dare to remove, to his own country, a person hired by him, and who belongs to our kingdom. Whoever attempts to do so, shall pay a pound of gold to the royal treasury, and shall receive a hundred lashes in addition.

IV. Where a Foreign Merchant takes Away a Slave for Purposes of Commerce.

If any foreign merchant should take away with him, a slave belonging to our kingdom, for the purpose of conveying his merchandise, he shall pay three *solidi* a year for his services; and, at the termination of his contract, shall restore said slave to his master.

BOOK XII.

CONCERNING THE PREVENTION OF OFFICIAL OPPRESSION, AND THE THOROUGH EXTINCTION OF HERETICAL SECTS.

TITLE I. CONCERNING THE EXERCISE OF MODERATION IN JUDICIAL DECISIONS, AND THE AVOIDING OF OPPRESSION BY THOSE INVESTED WITH AUTHORITY.

I. *Concerning the Admonition of the King, by which Judges are Ordered to Display Moderation in the Administration of Justice.*

II. *No Official, Invested with Power Over the People and Supervision Over their Acts, shall Subject them to Unnecessary Expense, or Other Impositions.*

I. Concerning the Admonition of the King, by which Judges are Ordered to Display Moderation in the Administration of Justice.

It is but proper that we, who impose necessary penalties for the misconduct of men, should render aid to the unfortunate, by means agreeable to God. We, therefore, order all judges and other officials to whom has been delegated the power of dispensing justice, and we also admonish them in the name of the omnipotent God, the exemplar of all virtues, that they diligently use their skill in the discovery of truth, in every case which is brought before them; and that they examine, with the utmost care, the claims of the parties to each action, without regard to the rank or condition of said parties; and that they moderate, in some degree, the severity of the law, where parties have lost their cases, espec ally where said parties are oppressed by poverty; for if the authority of the law were enforced to the utmost in every instance, there would be no opportunity for the exercise of mercy.

II. No Official, Invested with Power Over the People and Supervision Over their Acts, shall Subject them to Unnecessary Expense, or Other Impositions.

We provide laws for all the subjects of our kingdom who are under our sovereignty, for no other reason than the protection of their interests, and to the end that they may not be subjected to unnecessary expense or injury. For who is more concerned in the administration of justice, or who should be more familiar with it than ourselves, who, in the various affairs of life, extend the hand of assistance to our faithful subjects, and aid those whom we rule with equity? We therefore decree, by the following law, that no governor of a city, deputy, or other official, shall presume to oppress the people, for his own benefit, by means of any taxes, exactions, labors, or journeys; or shall accept unnecessary donations of grain from a city or a province; for we are well aware that when we appoint judges, we, at the same time, provide them with the means of subsistence. In like manner, we admonish governors of provinces, those in charge of the royal demesnes, and the officials of our treasury, that they have no power over private persons, and shall not in any way molest them. But where a private person has a lawsuit against any of the slaves of the Crown, the public agent, or attorney of the province, having been notified of the fact, shall cause the matter to be brought before the governor, or the judge of the district, and shall present his case, in order that the action may be legally determined, and such amends made as are equitable.

In order that proper supervision may be exercised over the royal officials in charge of our domains, we have agreed that the tax collectors and *defensores* shall be changed every year; and, as we are well aware that in consequence of this, much injury results to our people, we hereby decree that any tax collector or *defensor*, who has been elected by the bishops or the people, shall serve the full term for which he was chosen.

Where any tax collector or *defensor* has been appointed, he shall not give any present to a judge, nor shall a judge presume to accept or exact anything from him. If any judge should violate this law, he shall be deprived of his office, and shall be compelled to pay ten pounds of gold to the royal treasury. Should the priests, whom we address with God as our witness, learn of any misconduct of judges, or of other officials, and not bring the same to our notice, they shall be liable to the sentence imposed by the council, and shall be compelled to make reparation from their own property for such losses as the poor may have suffered through their silence.

TITLE II. CONCERNING THE ERADICATION OF THE ERRORS OF ALL HERETICS AND JEWS.

I. *Laws Having Been Given to True Believers, it is Now Necessary to Place Restraints upon Infidels.*

II. *Concerning the Renunciation of the Errors of all Heresies.*

III. *Concerning the Laws Promulgated on Account of the Wickedness of the Jews.*

IV. *Concerning the Extirpation of the Errors of the Jews in General.*

V *Jews shall not Celebrate the Passover According to their Custom.*

VI. *Jews shall not Contract Marriage According to their Custom.*

VII. *Jews shall not Perform the Rite of Circumcision.*

VIII. *Jews shall not Divide their Food into Clean and Unclean, According to their Custom.*

IX. *No Jew shall Subject a Christian to Torture*

X. *No Jew shall Testify Against a Christian; and Under what Circumstances the Descendants of Jews may Testify.*

XI. *No Jew shall Circumcise a Christian Slave.*

XII. *Concerning the Penalties to be Inflicted for Offences Committed by Jews.*

XIII. *Concerning Christian Slaves who are Known to have been Sold or Liberated by Jews.*

XIV *Under no Circumstances shall Christian Slaves Attach themselves to Jews, or be Admitted into their Sect.*

XV. *All Christians are Forbidden to Defend or Protect a Jew, by Either Force or Favor.*

XVI. *Memorial of the Jews Presented to the King.*

XVII. *Concerning Judaizing Christians.*

XVIII. *Concerning the Perfidy of the Jews.*

THE GLORIOUS FLAVIUS RECESVINTUS, KING.

I. Laws Having Been Given to True Believers, it is Now Necessary to Place Restraints upon Infidels.

Hitherto, we have directed our steps cautiously through the arduous paths which traverse the iniquities of the Jews; and have used moderation in the restraint of human crimes and infirmities. For it has been our manifest purpose and task, both to remove ill-founded opinions, and to prohibit what is evil, as well as to abolish what has been wrongfully done, and is abhorrent to decency and honor. As the law penetrates the secret recesses of minds conscious of guilt, so its censure corrects the depravity of morals, and prevents the perpetration of crime. And, indeed, we do not attempt to bring about this purity of soul for any other purpose than for the sake of the Church of the living God, which has invested so many different nations and peoples with the robe of immortality, and has united them to herself with the bonds of one holy religion. For the excellence of our strength and earthly glory are derived from the virtues of God, and his influence, sometimes acting through compassion, sometimes through fear of the sword of justice, prevents the commission of sin; and on one occasion diminishes crime by the practice of moderation, on another, extirpates it by an exhibition of severity. Following, not only the example of noble and illustrious races who restrained the illegal excesses of the people by leniency and rational laws, but also copying the rules and imitating the example of the Holy Fathers throughout the entire globe of the earth, we shall endeavor, as far as lies in our power, to reduce to action the precepts which we have received from them. For this reason, our relatives and subjects will know that our decrees are suitable, and dictated by honesty of purpose, in that they forbid the commission of crime, and are not opposed to the opinions of the Holy Fathers heretofore promulgated. And we are confident that we shall receive two rewards from the generosity of God: one, that we will be permitted to remain in the enjoyment of peace with our neighbors, as we are now; and the other, that, when our rule is ended, we shall receive a due acknowledgment from heaven. Thus, when, by means of the laws directed to our faithful people, this salutary remedy shall have been administered to the adherents of the Holy Faith, (as medicine is absorbed by the members of the body), and peace and charity shall everywhere prevail; confiding in the virtue of God, we shall attack his enemies, pursue his rivals, and conquer his adversaries; contending manfully, and constantly persevering; dispersing and overcoming those enemies, as dust is driven by the wind, or as mud is dried up in the fields, we shall acquire the reward of Faith; and when we shall include all people as true believers in our holy religion, and shall bring all infidels to belief in its truths, our glory shall increase, and our kingdom shall be exalted.[1]

FLAVIUS RECESVINTUS, KING.

II. Concerning the Renunciation of the Errors of all Heresies.

The eternal counsel of Almighty wisdom and Divine piety, as we understand it, and revealed to us in former ages, for the benefit of our own times, dissipated the errors of perfidious heretics, as well as abolished the false maxims of impious doctrines. Nevertheless, that such a time may not come during our lives, as that of which the representative of Divine Grace formerly said: "A time will come when persons will not desire sound doctrine, but with eager ears, and according to their desires, will seek masters for themselves; and who will not listen to the truth, but will turn to false doctrines; and, as it is proper that whatever remains in the light of the

[1] This pleasing homily, which precedes a collection of the most atrocious laws ever devised for the suppression of human thought and the persecution of heretics—with the sole exception of the rules of the Inquisition, of which it is the prototype—is extremely edifying. The confidence and assurance of a heavenly recompense, expressed by the pious king in whose name this edict was promulgated, reveals the degrading superstition of the time, and the absolute domination of the monarch by his spiritual advisers.—[ED.

Faith should be defended, by legal edicts, from the efforts of all who seek to contradict it; and that whatever ideas have arisen through the influence of error, be removed by legal proceedings; therefore, we decree that no man of whatever race or lineage, either native or foreigner, proselyte or old in faith, visitor or resident, shall openly or silently, impugn the unity of the Catholic faith; or take part in any injurious disputes affecting the truth of said faith; or countenance the same by remaining silent." No one shall attack the decrees of the Gospel, or criticise the institutions of the Church, or call in question the sacred institutions established by the ancient Fathers; no one shall treat with contempt discussions concerning points of doctrine which arise in modern assemblies; no one shall entertain any thoughts against the holy edicts or the true religion, or shall utter any words in depreciation of the same; or perfidiously cause a controversy to arise with an obstinate unbeliever; or engage in a quarrel on account of the contempt of honor exhibited by a listener. Any person who violates any of the provisions aforesaid shall be arrested; and should he be an ecclesiastic, or belong to any religious order, he shall lose his rank and dignity; shall be regarded forever as a criminal; and shall be punished by the loss of all his property. If he should belong to the laity, he shall be deprived of honor and position, and stripped of all his possessions. Every violator of this law shall be condemned to perpetual exile, unless he should be converted from his errors by the interposition of Divine mercy, when he may be suffered to remain and live in accordance with the commands of God.

FLAVIUS RECESVINTUS, KING.

III. Concerning the Laws Promulgated on Account of the Wickedness of the Jews.

The execrable errors of heretics in general, having been already prohibited and disposed of, it now becomes our duty to make special provision for some that exist in our days, and of which we are, at present, well aware. For while the virtue of God, by the sword of his Word, extirpated all other heresies, root and branch, we have to lament that the soil of our kingdom is still only defiled by the infamy of the Jews. Therefore, to the end that we may establish peace in our realm, by the spirit of God (which, indeed, seems folly to pagans, and scandal to the Jews themselves), we, who believe in the virtues of Christ, and the wisdom of God, for the sake of whose commiseration we attempt, with pious intentions, to put an end to ancient errors, that others may not arise in future ages; decree by this law, which shall be forever observed, and by the mandate of the Holy Scriptures, that our edicts, as well as those promulgated by our royal predecessors against the perfidy and persons of the Jews, shall be forever inviolate, and shall be obeyed for all time. And if anyone should violate said laws, he shall be liable for the damages provided by them, and to the punishments especially prescribed for their infraction.

FLAVIUS RECESVINTUS, KING.

IV. Concerning the Extirpation of the Errors of the Jews in General.

No Jew who has received the sacred rite of baptism shall renounce the faith of the holy Christian religion, or blaspheme said faith, in any way. No Jew shall impugn its precepts by deed or word; or speak insultingly of it either secretly or openly. No Jew shall flee to avoid being received into the Church, or conceal himself for such a purpose, after having taken to flight. No Jew shall entertain the hope of resuming his errors, or of performing the ceremonies of his infamous belief. No Jew shall entertain in his heart any perfidy against the Christian religion, and in favor of his own sect, or exhibit such perfidy by word or deed. No Jew shall attempt to infringe, or oppose, any regulations or laws of the Christians which have been published. No one shall venture to conceal a Jew who is aware of the existence of these offences which have been prohibited, or who has committed them. No one shall delay to denounce a fugitive Jew when he is found, or to reveal his hiding place. Any person who violates the provisions of the aforesaid law, shall be subjected to the punishment prescribed for the same.

V. Jews shall not Celebrate the Passover According to their Custom.

No Jew shall celebrate the Passover upon the fourteenth day of the month, nor shall perform any of the ceremonies customary at such times. Nor shall any Jew, in honor of his ancient, erroneous belief, observe any festival days, great or small; or attempt their observance; or desist from labor upon any holidays; or hereafter keep the Sabbath, or any other sacred days prescribed by his rites, or attempt to do so. Anyone detected violating this law shall be liable to the condemnation and penalty prescribed for the same.

VI. Jews shall not Contract Marriage According to their Custom.

No Jew shall marry, or defile with adultery or incest, anyone nearly related to him by blood. No Jew shall marry another within the seventh degree of relationship; nor shall he desire or practice any other nuptial ceremony than that customary among Christians. Whenever detected, he shall be punished according to law.

VII. Jews shall not Perform the Rite of Circumcision.

No Jew shall circumcise another; nor shall a person who has permitted himself to be circumcised be exempt from the operation of the law. No slave, freeborn person, or freedman, native or foreigner, shall practise or submit to this detestable operation. Whoever is proved to have voluntarily performed, or submitted to it, shall be punished with the utmost severity of the law.

VIII. Jews shall not Divide their Food into Clean and Unclean, According to their Custom.

The blessed apostle Paul said, "To the pure all things are pure," but nothing is pure to those who are defiled, because they are unbelievers; and, for this reason, the execrable life of the Jews and the vileness of their horrible belief, which is more foul than any other detestable error, must be destroyed and cast out. Therefore, no Jew shall make a distinction between food which is clean and unclean, as established by the customs and traditions of his ancient rites. No one shall perversely refuse to eat food of any kind, whose condition is proved to be good. No one shall reject one article of food, and accept another, unless the distinction be such as is considered salutary and proper by all Christians. Anyone detected in the violation of this law shall be subjected to the punishment instituted for the same.

IX. No Jew shall Subject a Christian to Torture.

We especially decree, by the following law, that it shall not be lawful for any Jew to testify against a Christian in any legal proceeding, or business transaction, even though said Christian should be of the lowest rank or a slave; nor shall a Jew prosecute a Christian, in any action at law; or sue him upon any written contract; or subject him to torture for any reason whatever. For it seems sacrilegious to prefer an infidel to him who is a believer, and to subject the members of the followers of Christ to torture inflicted by his adversaries. If, however, Jews should have causes of action among themselves, they shall have the right, under the law, to testify against each other; and to put their slaves to the torture in the presence of Christian judges.

X. No Jew shall Testify Against a Christian; and Under what Circumstances the Descendants of Jews may Testify.

If he who is convicted of having uttered a falsehood becomes infamous in the sight of all men, with how much more reason should he be excluded from giving testimony who denies the truth of the Divine Faith? Jews, whether baptized or unbaptized, are therefore forbidden to testify against Christians. The descendants of Jews, however, if they are of good morals, and adherents of the Faith, shall be permitted to give evidence among Christians; but not unless their morals and their belief shall be vouched for by either the king, a priest or a judge.

XI. No Jew shall Circumcise a Christian Slave.

It shall not be lawful for a Jew to purchase a Christian slave, or to accept of one as a gift. Should a Jew purchase such a slave or accept of him as a gift and then circumcise him, he shall lose the price of said slave, and the latter shall be free. The Jew who circumcises a Christian slave shall forfeit all his property to the king. Any slave of either sex who is unwilling to become a Jew, shall receive his or her freedom.

XII. Concerning the Penalties to be Inflicted for Offences Committed by Jews.

The following law is derived from others of great severity, which have been enacted to punish the perfidy of the Jews; and it is hereby decreed that whoever attempts to commit any of the crimes prohibited by former laws, or contained in any amendments to the same, or presumes to act in defiance of said laws, shall be either stoned to death, or burned by such of his own countrymen as may have entered into an agreement to do so. However, if the king, in his mercy, should decide to spare the life of such a criminal, he shall be delivered up as a slave to whomever the king may select, and all his property shall be given to others; and this shall be done in such a way that the culprit can never come into possession of his property again, or recover his liberty in the future.

XIII. Concerning Christian Slaves who are Known to have been Sold or Liberated by Jews.

To the most holy and blessed Agapius and Cecilius, bishops, and to the judges of their districts, as well as to other ecclesiastics and magistrates, of the provinces of Barbia, Ausgia, Sturgia, Viatula, Tutigia, Gabrus, and Epagrus, greeting: The authority of the law promulgated by our lord and predecessor, Recaredus, declaring that Christian slaves shall under no circumstances remain in the power of Jews, would be sufficient, if the depravity of the Jews had not afterwards corrupted the minds of princes, and they had not demanded and obtained benefits for themselves contrary to the principles of justice. And that we may, with the assistance of God, promulgate a law by which these frauds may hereafter be abolished, and for the reason that, in past times, the edict of said king has been nullified, we hereby decree: that if any Christian slave should be in the possession of a Jew after this law is published, whether said slave should have been set free or not, he shall have the same right as a Roman citizen. And if said slave, through any unlawful act, should have been transferred to the possession of any other person by an instrument in writing, when he should have been liberated according to law, he shall be given his liberty; the contract shall be cancelled; the price paid for him shall be returned to the vendor; and said slave shall have a right to pass his life in freedom, supported by his own labor, have his name inscribed upon the public records, and be taxed according to an equitable estimate of his property.

If any slaves should have been acquired by any just title, after the time in which the law of said king was promulgated, their masters shall have the right, until the Kalends of July, to sell, or liberate said slaves, as they choose. Any Christian slaves who have been circumcised by the Jews, at any time, or have joined their sect, shall be punished as prescribed by law. Where such slaves as we have declared to be free, are again reduced to slavery by the Jews, or are retained by them, without being emancipated; the Jews, guilty of such offences, shall be punished as in the case of freemen, where the latter are restrained of their liberty. All Jews who have been converted to the Holy Faith, shall be entitled to their share in the inheritance of their fathers.

Where sales have been made of slaves at a certain time, in the division of the same there shall be no separation of parents and children, but all shall be transferred together to the purchaser. Where a Jew has been proved to have obtained property by fraud, from the ancestors of any person, he shall be deprived of it, and it shall be forfeited to the royal treasury. Any slaves belonging to the Jews, who have been baptized, shall, with their children, be returned to their masters, and be liberated by them; and any property they may have acquired shall be given them along with their freedom. Those who have no property shall be aided by the person who sets them free, as far as he is able to do so; and said emancipated slaves shall be classed as other freedmen, and shall be taxed in proportion to the property they own.

XIV. Under no Circumstances shall Christian Slaves Attach themselves to Jews, or be Admitted into their Sect.

We provide for the health and safety of our subjects, and of all other persons within the provinces of our kingdom, when we rescue the adherents of our religion from the hands of infidels. For, by this means, the orthodox faith will be greatly exalted, when the execrable perfidy of the Jews shall no longer have power over Christians. The fatal control of Jews over Christians should therefore be abominated, and the people consecrated by the favor of God brought under the influence of Divine Love. Therefore, we promulgate the following law, to be forever obeyed, and admonish every royal officer, in all future times: that, from the first year of our reign no Jew shall be permitted to have a freeborn Christian, or a Christian slave, under his patronage, or in his service. Nor shall a Jew be allowed to employ any such person for hire, or avail himself of his services, under any pretext whatsoever. A Jew shall, however, be permitted to sell his slave, for a just price, to a Christian, under proper circumstances, anywhere he resides within the limits of our kingdom. It shall not be lawful to sell such slaves in foreign countries, unless it should be proved that said slaves reside there. Where slaves sold by Jews into foreign countries, as aforesaid, have no property of their own, the vendor shall give to said slaves such sums as, in the opinion of the purchaser, will be sufficient for supporting and clothing them; and this is provided in order that a transaction concluded under the name of purchase, may not appear to be exile.

Where a Jew wishes to free a Christian slave, he must do so in such a way that the latter may attain the rank of a Roman citizen, to wit: that, by the act of emancipation, no services shall be reserved for the benefit of any Hebrew, or of anyone else; and that said liberated slave may have the power to pass his life wherever he chooses, free from all obligation to, or association with, the Jews. If, however, any Hebrew should fraudulently sell or liberate a slave, and evidence of said illegal act should be proved at any future time, and any damage to the slave should result; where a freeborn person exposes such a fraudulent transaction, he shall be entitled to all the property of the parties, both vendor and purchaser, who perpetrated the fraud. Should a Christian be concerned in such a proceeding, he shall be given as a slave to whomever the king may direct; and where he has property, half of it shall be confiscated for the benefit of the public treasury, and the offender shall be branded with eternal infamy. Should a slave detect a fraud of this kind, he shall be given his freedom, and shall remain under the patronage of him in whose service he was until that time; and in order that exact justice may be done, the master of said slave shall receive another from the Crown in his stead, and, in addition, shall be entitled to a pound of gold from him whose deceit was exposed by the slave.

Where a Hebrew circumcises a Christian, or induces one to join his sect, or perform any of his rites, he shall be beheaded; the informer shall receive a proper reward; and the property of said Jew shall be forfeited to the royal treasury. All slaves who are known to be the issue of marriages between Christians and Jews, we hereby declare shall be made Christians. And if such slaves as have been converted to the Jewish religion should desire to remain in that perfidious belief, and and should refuse to return to the true faith, they shall be scourged, and scalped, in the presence of the assembled people, and delivered up to whomever we may select, to remain in perpetual servitude. Where the unlawful marital unions hereinbefore mentioned have already taken place, we hereby decree that the infidel party to the same shall have a right to embrace the true faith, should he or she desire to do so. Should, however, said party refuse, the marriage shall be dissolved, and the recalcitrant person shall be driven into perpetual exile. To the other provisions of this law we add the following: that whenever any Jew desires sincerely to embrace the Catholic faith, and has been purified by the holy water of baptism, he shall be entitled to retain, without molestation, all the property which he possessed at that time.

This edict we declare shall be in force, and shall be observed by all our subjects throughout our dominions, after the Kalends of July of the present year. If, after said date, a Christian slave should be found in the possession of a Jew, half the property of said Jew shall be forfeited for the benefit of the royal treasury, and said slave shall be set at liberty; nor shall any Jew have any claim to the person or property of said slave thereafter.

The aforesaid law which we, induced by piety and religion, have framed for the benefit of our people and ourselves, we hereby decree, with the aid of God, shall be forever valid. And may Christ, the Conqueror, make all our successors, guardians of this law, victorious, and confirm in the enjoyment of His kingdom those who He knows will faithfully enforce it. While we are not of the opinion that its provisions will be violated by anyone; nevertheless, should such a person exist, may he who audaciously disobeys it, or does not reverently observe it, be regarded by all men as the most infamous person of the century; may he lose his life at the moment when he forms the detestable resolution to break said law; and may he be oppressed by the accumulated mass of his sins through all eternity, inasmuch as, by his transgression, he has infringed this salutary decree. And, in the terrible time of the Day of Judgment, reserved for the coming of the Lord, may the said culprit be separated from the flock of Christ; and, placed at the left hand with the Jews, be burned with eternal fire, with the devil for his companion; in order that avenging punishment may be inflicted upon all transgressors, and that true Christians may receive a rich and eternal reward.

XV. All Christians are Forbidden to Defend or Protect a Jew, by Either Force or Favor.

To the former laws, which we, and our predecessors, have promulgated for the purpose of annihilating the perfidy of the Jews, it becomes necessary to add the following one to sanction and strengthen those which have been heretofore published. Now, after we have repudiated the profane enemies of the Holy Faith, and put an end to the wicked schemes of these perfidious wretches, it becomes necessary for us to confirm those things which have already been done, and arrange them suitably and in order; for, in the exact proportion as the skilful artificer gives form to the invention of his genius, so, in just such proportion does his work disclose the strength and beauty of his mind.

Therefore, lest the Jews should, by means of any artifice, and through their unremitting perseverance, obtain the legal sanction for their profane rites so much desired by them, we hereby decree that no person belonging to any religious order or rank whatsoever, or any of the royal officials, of high or low degree, or any individual of any station or family, or any prince, or person in authority, shall encourage any Jew, whether baptized or not baptized, to remain in the practice of his detestable faith and customs; or shall conceal the fact that he is doing so; or shall induce those who have been baptized to return to the observance of their perfidious ceremonies. No one shall attempt, under any pretext, to defend such persons in the continuance of their depravity, even should they be under his patronage. No one, for any reason, or in any manner, shall attempt by word or deed, to aid or protect such persons, either openly or secretly, in their opposition to the Holy Faith and the Christian religion.

If any bishop or other ecclesiastic should be guilty of such an offence, or if any member of the laity should be convicted of the same, he shall be excluded from the society of Christians, be excommunicated, and forfeit the fourth of all his property, which shall be confiscated for the benefit of the royal treasury. For it is eminently proper that those should be separated from the communion of the faithful, and be punished by the loss of their possessions, who reject the love of Christ, and, in the aid of His enemies, infamously attack the truth. The penalties for such offences shall remain the same as were provided in a former law by King Sisibutus, of holy memory.

XVI. Memorial of the Jews Presented to the King.

To our most pious and noble lord and master, King Recesvintus: We, Jews of the city of Toledo, who have hereto attached our signatures, or seals, call your attention to the fact that formerly we were compelled to present a memorial to King Chintilanus, of holy memory, by which we bound ourselves to uphold the Catholic faith, as, in like manner, we do now. But, whereas the perfidy born of our obstinacy, and the antipathy resulting from our ancestral errors, influenced us to such an extent that we did not then truly believe in our Lord Jesus Christ, and did not sincerely embrace the Catholic faith, therefore, now, freely and voluntarily, we promise Your Majesty for ourselves, our wives, and our children, by this our memorial, that henceforth we will observe no Jewish customs or rites whatever, and will not associate, or have any intercourse with, any unbaptized Jews. Nor will we marry any person related to us by blood, within the sixth degree, which union has been declared to be incestuous and wicked. Nor will we, or our children, or any of our posterity, at any time hereafter, contract marriage outside our sect; and both sexes shall hereafter be united in marriage according to Christian rites. We will not practise the operation of circumcision. We will not celebrate the Passover, Sabbath, and other festival days, as enjoined by the Jewish ritual. We will not make any distinction in food, according to our ancient usages. We will not observe, in any way, ceremonies prescribed by the abominable practices and habits of the Hebrews. But, with sincere faith, grateful hearts, and perfect devotion, we believe that Christ is the son of the living God, as declared by ecclesiastical and evangelical tradition; and we hereby acknowledge Him to be such, and venerate Him accordingly. Moreover, all the ceremonies enjoined by the Christian religion—whether said ceremonies relate to festivals, or to marriage and food—we will truly and exactly observe; and we will maintain the same with sincerity, without any objection or opposition thereto; and without any subterfuge on our part, by means of which we might hereafter deny our acts, return to what has been prohibited, or not completely fulfil all that we have promised. With regard to the flesh of animals which we consider unclean, if we should be unable to eat the same on account of our ancient prejudices, nevertheless, when it is cooked along with other food, we hereby promise to partake of the latter with no manifestation of disgust or horror. And if, at any time, we should be found to have transgressed, and to have violated any of the promises hereinbefore specified; or should presume to act contrary to the doctrines of the Christian faith; or if we should, in word or deed, neglect to fulfil the obligations to which we have bound ourselves, as being acceptable to the Catholic religion; we hereby swear by the Father, Son and Holy Spirit, who form one God in the Trinity, that, in case a single transgressor should be found among our people, he shall be burned, or stoned to death, either by ourselves, or by our sons. And should Your Majesty graciously grant such culprit his life, he shall at once be deprived of his freedom, so that Your Majesty may deliver him to be forever a slave to anyone whom Your Majesty may select; and Your Majesty shall have full authority to make whatever disposition of him and his property as may seem expedient; not only on account of the power attached to your royal office, but also by the authority granted by this our memorial. Made, in the name of God, at Toledo, on the Kalends of March, in the sixth year of Your Majesty's happy reign.

XVII. Concerning Judaizing Christians.

As the crime of hypocrisy should be deplored by all Christians; for the same reason it should be evident, that no person, under any circumstances, is deserving of pardon, who is proved to have renounced a good religion for a bad one. Therefore, because a cruel and astounding act of presumption should be expiated by a still more cruel punishment, we declare, by the following edict: that, whenever it has been proved that a Christian, of either sex, and especially one born of Christian parents, has practised circumcision, or any other Jewish rite, or anything else forbidden by God, he shall be put to an ignominious death by the zeal and co-operation of Catholics, under the most ingenious and excruciating tortures that can be inflicted; that he may learn how horrible and detestable that offence is, which he has so infamously perpetrated. All the property of such a person shall be confiscated for the benefit of the royal treasury, in order that his heirs and relatives may not, through consenting to his errors, be contaminated by them.

XVIII. Concerning the Perfidy of the Jews.

We learn from the Holy Scriptures, that Christ is called the Son of God, and it is but just, and consistent with Christian doctrine, that, as we present the favor of liberty to all true believers, we should suppress infidels, even to the loss of their lives; and, in order that the faith of Christ may increase in us to the utmost, the perfidious doctrines of the Jews must be destroyed to the very foundation. Therefore, in all devotion, we decree that henceforth, whenever a Jew, of either sex, renounces the perfidy of his religion, and is converted to the profession of the true Catholic faith and, repudiating the errors of his rites and ceremonies, lives his life according to the customs of the Christians, he shall be free from every burden and disability, which formerly, when attached to the Jewish faith, he would have been subject to for the public benefit; so that his privileges will increase with his freedom from those exactions which are imposed upon such as are blinded by the wickedness of their infidelity, and controlled by the inherited errors of their ancestors. For it is unjust that such persons as are known to have assumed the gentle yoke of Christ, and the light burden of his religion, through sincere conviction, should be oppressed with heavy taxation, or subjected to the pecuniary burdens imposed upon other Jews. It shall be, in every respect, lawful for all such persons who are true believers, to engage in trade, and to carry on business transactions with Christian customers; and if any Christian, not informed of the conversion of said Jews, should desire to purchase anything of them, it shall not be lawful for him to do so, until said converted Jews declare that they are Christians, and recite for him the dominical prayer or the Apostles' Creed in the presence of witnesses; and, as true followers of Christ accept or signify their willingness to partake of food used by Christians.

If any hypocrite should be found among those converted to the Holy Faith, he shall be condemned to slavery, and all his property shall be confiscated for the benefit of the royal treasury. Such Jews, however, as remain obstinate, and, in the perfidy of their hearts, refuse to embrace the Catholic religion, we decree shall undergo the following penalty, to wit: they shall not dare to go into foreign countries for the purpose of commerce; nor shall openly or secretly engage in trade with Christians, but shall only have the privilege of transacting business with one another; and they shall pay the taxes imposed upon them, as in such case provided; and shall pay to the public treasury, out of their own property, the taxes due from those Jews who have been converted. All slaves, buildings, lands, olive-orchards and whatever other real property they are found to have acquired from sales by Christians, or in any other manner whatsoever, although it may have been in their possession for many years, shall be confiscated for the benefit of the royal treasury, and the king shall have the absolute disposal of the same. Should any Jew, who remains in infidelity, dare to act contrary to this law, or to transact business with any Christian, having been reprimanded, he shall be given to the Crown, along with all his possessions, to be a slave forever.

We admonish all Christians, calling to witness the Divine Personage by whose blood we have been redeemed, that none of them presume, in any way, to transact business with such Jews as continue in the obstinacy of their perfidious belief. Where a Christian commits such an offence, if he is a person of superior rank or power, he shall pay three pounds of gold to the royal treasury. And if anyone should buy from such Jews anything that is worth more than twice what he paid for it, he shall pay out of his own property, three times the value of the same, along with the original price, to the royal treasury. If, however, a person of inferior station should be guilty, he shall receive a hundred lashes, and all the property which he is possessed of shall be given to the king, who shall have the right to dispose of any, or all of it, at his pleasure.[1]

---

[1] The translator has interpolated between this and the succeeding title, in the Castilian version, another, of nine chapters, under the head of "Concerning insults and opprobrious language." Part of it relates to false accusations of physical deformity and disease, or slander; part to assault, or attempted assault, where no apparent injury resulted; and the remainder is devoted to laws punishing those who call Christians Saracens, or assert that they have been circumcised. The moderate penalty of a hundred and fifty lashes was prescribed for the last two offences.—[ED.

TITLE III. CONCERNING NEW LAWS AGAINST THE JEWS, IN WHICH OLD ONES ARE CONFIRMED, AND NEW ONES ARE ADDED.

XIV. *The Confession of Jews; and In What Way Each One of Them, who is Converted, must Write Down the Proof of his Conversion.*

XV. *Conditions under which Jews must Make Oath, when, having been Converted, they give in their Confession of Faith.*

XVI. *Concerning the Christian Slaves of Jews, who have not Proclaimed Themselves Christians, and those who Expose Them.*

XVII. *No Jew, under any Authority whatever, shall Dare to Oppress, Punish, or Imprison a Christian, Except by Order of the King.*

XVIII. *If Slaves of Jews, not yet Converted, should Claim the Grace of Christ, they shall be Liberated.*

XIX. *Jews shall not Rule Christians under the Authority of Mayors of Towns, or of Superintendents of Estates; and Concerning the Penalties to be Imposed upon Such as Appoint them to Office.*

XX. *Where a Jew comes from Another Country into any of the Provinces of Our Kingdom, he Must, at once, Present himself before a Bishop, a Priest, or a Judge; and What shall be Done under the Circumstances.*

XXI. *How Assemblies of Jews shall Visit the Bishop on Appointed Days.*

XXII. *Where Anyone has a Jew in his Service, and a Priest Demands him, the Master shall not have a Right to Retain said Jew.*

XXIII. *All Restraint of and Control over the Jews shall be Vested in the Priesthood.*

XXIV. *Concerning the Penalties to be Imposed upon Priests and Judges who Neglect to Enforce the Laws against the Jews.*

XXV. *No Judge shall Presume to Investigate the Offences of the Jews without the Knowledge of an Ecclesiastic.*

XXVI. *Bishops shall be Immune from Punishment, when their Priests do not Inform them of Such Things as Should be Corrected.*

XXVII. *Concerning the Mercy to be Shown by Princes towards Those who have been Truly Converted to the Christian Faith.*

XXVIII. *Bishops shall Give to all Jews a Copy of this Book, which has been Published for the Purpose of Correcting heir Errors; and their Confessions and a Record of their Conversion, shall be Deposited among the Archives of the Church.*

I. Concerning Old Laws Enacted Against the Transgressions of the Jews, and the Confirmation of the Same.

The perfidy and cunning of the Jewish heresy increases in criminality, in the same proportion as attempts are made to abolish it by law. And, as we are about to promulgate new edicts for the suppression of these errors, it is now proper to first confirm those which have been enacted by our predecessors; and in order the better to adapt the same to the offences of the Jews, it is necessary for us to revise all preceding edicts; so that, in this way, the new laws being collated with the old ones, those which should be approved may be confirmed, as is fitting; and, at the same time, the new statutes may be drawn up so that they shall not conflict with those already in force, but that all may be united, and the entire body of laws made clear for the administration of justice. Thus, whenever edicts already in force may be judged worthy of confirmation, and whatever new edicts we may think it advisable to promulgate, may both become more manifest, and, in this manner, by the application of both classes of laws, the truth may be the more readily established. For example, we have found a law among those formerly promulgated, which declares that all heresy must be eradicated. It is reasonable and evident, however, that this must be added to and amended, in such a way that if anyone induced by the insanity of unbelief should treat with contempt any of its provisions, no matter to what rank or station he may belong, and should attempt to defend any perverse dogma in public, he shall be subjected to severe penance, exiled, and his property confiscated for the benefit of the king; and even if he should, at any time, renounce the errors of his perverse sect, he shall under no circumstances be permitted to return from exile; and his property shall be irrevocably held by those upon whom the king has bestowed it. Where any Jew, deluded by blind ignorance, retains the errors of his sect in his heart, and evinces a disposition to defend the same, either by word or deed, he must go to the bishop, or some priest of the district, for instruction; and the latter must explain to him the precepts of religion, and, with the consent of the metropolitan, also give him the formulas of doctrine and the rules of faith. If any heretic, after having been instructed as aforesaid, should still persist in his error, he shall be liable to the penalty imposed by a preceding law; that is to say, the one which is provided for those who publicly defend their own sect, in opposition to our religion. And we hereby especially confirm such laws as are directed against the offences of the Jews, to wit: such as have been enacted concerning the wickedness of the Jews, or for the purpose of eradicating their errors. Thus, Jews shall no longer celebrate the Passover, according to their customs; or presume to marry, as formerly; or practise circumcision; or distinguish food as clean and unclean; or presume to torture Christians, or to testify against them, and no Jew shall circumcise a Christian slave. All Christian slaves who have been either sold or set at liberty by Jews, shall at once receive their freedom unconditionally, and under no circumstances shall a Christian slave remain in the service of a Jew. Concerning the law by which all Christians are forbidden to protect a Jew, we decree that no Christian, under any circumstances, by any act or favor, shall attempt to shelter or defend a Jew; or shall presume to conceal a judaizing Christian. We, therefore, decree that the severe laws formerly promulgated to suppress the perfidy of the aforesaid Jews shall remain in force, for all time; with the exception of such as are referred to in the two following chapters, which have been found to be contradictory to the others, as well as opposed to the principles of justice, and to our ordinances; and we hereby declare, in the plenitude of our wisdom, that said laws shall remain irrevocable and forever in force, provided they in no wise conflict with such others as we may hereafter promulgate. In respect to such edicts as seem to us improper and conflicting, the following two are repugnant to reason and to our institutions; wherefore they shall, henceforth, not be observed and shall have no force or effect in law. The first of these is that whereby the detestable power of liberating Christian slaves is bestowed upon the Jews. The second we condemn, because it subjects to the same penalty those who are guilty of different offences. While there are different degrees of guilt according to the laws, the latter do not always impose different penalties, but many crimes are treated alike, and each offence is not punished according to the measure of its guilt; for it is evident that crimes of greater and less gravity should not be punished in the same manner; especially as our Lord has said in the Divine Law that the penalty shall be in proportion to the offence; and, therefore, this law which prescribes the penalty to be inflicted for the transgressions of the Jews shall be hereafter considered of no validity and effect; for the reason that God does not desire the death of His creatures or rejoice in their perdition, but wishes that they may live in Him through their redemption. Henceforth we shall devote ourselves to the restraining of all malice; to the suppression of infidelity; and to the eradication of all profane doctrines; and we shall boldly resist the attacks of our enemies, and overwhelm them with the weapons of Divine power.

II. Concerning Blasphemers Against the Holy Trinity.

If God in the Holy Scriptures, declares that whoever insults his brother is worthy of punishment, and as the sentence of Divine justice condemns him as a still greater transgressor who sins against the Holy Spirit, how much more unpardonable shall he be who, in the future, shall denounce the Saviour Himself! Therefore, if anyone should blaspheme the name of Christ, the Son of God, and speak with contempt of His holy body and blood as a sacrament, and should refuse to partake of the same, or, having partaken of it, should cast it away; or should utter any blasphemy against the Holy Trinity, that is to say, against the Father, Son, and Holy Ghost; the blasphemer shall have his head shaved, and receive a hundred lashes, by order of the priest or judge in whose diocese or district said crime was committed, and the culprit shall also be placed in chains, and be condemned to endure the misery of exile. The property of said offender shall be given to the king, and shall remain irrevocably in the possession of those upon whom he may choose to bestow it.

ERVIGIUS, KING.

III. Jews shall not Absent themselves, or Remove their Children or Slaves, to Avoid the Blessing of Baptism.

While Divine truth teaches us to seek, to investigate, and to knock at the door, that it may be opened unto us, admonishing us, at the same time, that violent men shall not inherit the kingdom of Heaven, it is evident that those will not merit Divine favor, who do not exert themselves to that end, with their entire hearts. Henceforth, where any Jew of those who have not yet been baptized, or have themselves delayed their own baptism; or have, under any pretext, neglected to send their children or slaves to the priest, in order to be baptized; or have removed their slaves in order to avoid their baptism; and the said Jew, after the lapse of one year from the promulgation of this law, shall not have been baptized; said transgressor, whoever he may be, shall receive a hundred lashes, and, having had his head shaved, shall be driven into exile. His property shall be forfeited to the king, and shall be bestowed upon whomever he may direct, as the life of said Jew has shown him to be obstinate and incorrigible.

ERVIGIUS, KING.

IV. Jews shall not Celebrate the Passover According to their Customs, or Practice Circumcision, or Induce any Christian to Renounce the Church of Christ.

If the obstinate perfidy of the Jews had observed the law, and the substance rather than the shadow of the truth, the crucifixion of the Lord of Glory would never have occurred. For our Passover is designated by the sacrifice of Christ; and if He rejoices in the circumcision of our hearts, that symbolic operation ought in no way to be performed in the flesh; for the prophet has said, "Circumcise the Lord, and remove the prepuce from your hearts." Therefore we, not regarding the shadow of truth aforesaid, but relying upon the promises of truth itself, decree that the following shall be observed: that when any Jew celebrates the Passover according to the rites of his religion, he shall receive a hundred lashes, be scalped, and be driven into perpetual exile, and his property shall be confiscated for the benefit of the royal treasury. Whoever shall circumcise either a Jew or a Christian, shall be mutilated; [1] and his property shall be confiscated for the use of the royal treasury. Should any woman presume to practise the operation of circumcision, or should present anyone to another person to be circumcised, she shall have her nose cut off, and all her property shall be given to the king. They, also, shall undergo a similar penalty who cause a Christian man or woman to renounce the faith of Christ, or induce anyone to return to the practice of the false doctrines of the Jews.

V. Jews shall not Presume to Keep the Sabbath, or Celebrate Festival Days, According to their Ritual.

The delusive phantoms of error having disappeared, it is now incumbent upon us to labor unceasingly; for what other course is open to the lovers of truth? The Lord, speaking by the mouth of His prophet, has denounced this heresy in the following terms: "My soul abhors your Passover, your Sabbath, and all your ceremonies." Wherefore, as we have been admonished by the apostle, that we should rather act accord-

---

[1] In the words of the text, "*veretri ex toto amputatione plectetur.*" The sentence will not bear translation, and, in the words of a famous writer referring to a similar case, "must be veiled in the obscurity of a learned language." While certainly to be classed under "cruel and unusual punishments," it reveals a fiendish ingenuity in adapting the penalty to the so-called offence.—[ED.

ing to the new spirit, than follow the ancient letter of the law, we hereby, in all faith and earnestness, give notice to the infidels, that if any Jew should presume to celebrate the appearance of the new moon, or the Festival of Tabernacles, or the Sabbath, or any holidays, or should observe any other rites or ceremonies of his worship, he shall receive a hundred lashes, shall have his head shaved, and shall be subjected to the misery of exile, and all his property shall be forfeited to the king; with the condition, however, that should he be converted at any time, it may be restored to him; but if not, it shall remain in the possession of those upon whom it has been bestowed.

VI. Every Jew shall Cease from Labor on Sunday, and on all Appointed Holidays.

There is no doubt that he is plainly an enemy of the Catholic religion who does not treat Sunday with due reverence. Hence, while we are pursuing those who deny or disobey our faith, we hereby decree with Divine sanction, that if any Jew, of either sex, should do any work on Christmas, or on any other sacred holiday, or on Sunday, or should spin, or weave, or perform any labor beyond that which the honorable custom of good Christians permits; such a transgressor shall have his head shaved, and shall receive a hundred lashes for his insolence; and where slaves, of either sex, are found occupied in such labors, they, also, shall be liable to the punishment aforesaid. The masters of said slaves, where they permit them to labor in this manner, shall be compelled to pay a hundred *solidi* to the royal treasury. Those days which shall be devoutly observed by the Jews, are the following, to wit: the Festival of the Holy Virgin Mary, during which the glorious Conception is celebrated; the Festivals of the Nativity and Circumcision; Holy Week and Easter; the day of the Discovery of the Cross; the Day of the Ascension; Pentecost; Sundays throughout the entire year; and all the days that are venerated by true believers in the doctrines of Christ.

VII. Jews shall not make any Distinction in their Food, According to their Custom.

The detestible Jewish custom, viler than any other superstition, dividing food into clean and unclean, accepts the former, while it rejects the latter. Whoever is convicted of the commission of the error of this practice, that is to say, who acts differently from the custom observed, under similar circumstances, by all true Christians, shall receive a hundred lashes and be scalped, by order of the judge in whose district the offence was committed. The provisions of this law shall be observed in every respect concerning drink, as well as food; and the punishment hereinbefore specified shall be inflicted upon all who abstain from the wines or other beverages of Christians. In regard to the flesh of swine, we hereby decree that no distinction shall be made on account of religious prejudice; but if any Jew should avoid such food through natural abhorrence, and not from a regard to the usages of their perverse sect, especially if their behavior, in other respects, is similar to that of Christians, and if they have embraced Christianity, and observe its rules, and are known to be sincere believers, they shall not be liable to punishment under the aforesaid law, merely because they have rejected the flesh of swine; for the reason that it appears contrary to justice, that those whom the faith of Christ has openly ennobled, should be rendered liable to punishment on account of their rejection of a single article of food.

VIII. A Jew shall not Marry a Person Nearly Related to him by Blood, or Contract Marriage without the Benediction of a Priest.

No Jew, of either sex, shall be permitted to marry a relative, either on the side of the wife or the husband, within the sixth degree, except according to the law imposed upon Christians; nor shall any Jew commit the crime of incest by marriage with a near relation. Those who violate the law by such an illicit union, shall undergo the following punishment, to wit: having been separated from one another each party shall receive a hundred lashes; they shall have their heads shaved, be subjected to severe penance, and then be driven into exile; their property shall be given to such children as they may have had by a preceding marriage—provided the latter have been in no way contaminated with the Jewish superstition, or polluted with the infamy of incestuous marriage. If, however, they should have no children, or, having them, the latter should be tainted with the Jewish error, or with the crime of incest, as aforesaid, then the property of said offender shall be forfeited to the king. The following, moreover, we direct shall be carefully observed in every respect, namely: that if any Jew, of either sex, after being converted, should desire to marry, he or she shall not be allowed to do so, unless a dowry is given, and a marriage contract entered into, as has been prescribed in the case of Christians; nor shall such ceremony be permitted, where it is not accompanied with the sacerdotal benediction within the bosom of the Church. If any Jew should marry without the benediction of the Church, as aforesaid, or should transgress, in any way, the provision of the law relating to marriage contracts, said Jew, after purification by baptism, shall be compelled to pay a hundred *solidi* to the king, or shall receive fifty lashes in public. Each of the persons aforesaid, that is to say, the husband as well as the wife, shall be liable to said penalty or fine; and the parents of said parties shall also be liable to the same punishment for their infraction of the law.

IX. Jews who Insult our Religion, while Attempting to Defend their own Sect, shall not Betake themselves Elsewhere; nor shall Anyone Shelter them while Fugitives.

If any Jew should presume to offer an insult to the Christian religion; or, by arguments, should induce anyone to abandon the Christian faith; or should defend the weakness of his own sect; or, while fleeing from the doctrines of the Christian religion, should conceal himself in any part of our kingdom; or should escape to foreign countries, for the purpose of concealment; or if anyone should offer a hiding-place to a transgressor of this law, knowing he is a fugitive; any of said parties guilty of any of the above-named offences, shall be punished with a hundred lashes, have his head shaved, and, after his property has been confiscated for the benefit of the king, shall be subjected to the miseries of slavery.

X. No Christian shall Accept a Gift from a Jew, to the Detriment of the Christian Faith.

Let him be considered as violating the rules of the Christian faith who pretends to be a defender of that faith, and, at the same time, defiles the truth by the acceptance of improper gifts; and let him hear what the Lord has said against him by the mouth of his prophet: "For the reason that you have sold the just man for silver, and the poor man for the price of your sandals, behold I will thunder over you as thunders a wagon loaded with hay; and he who is swift will lose his power of flight; and the strong man will lose his strength; and he who is brave, his courage; and he who wields the bow, shall not stand; and he who runs shall not be saved by his swiftness; and the rider shall not escape; and he who is strong of heart shall flee naked among the brave." Who, then, is meant by the just man who was sold for silver and the poor man for the price of your sandals, unless the only begotten Son of God the Father, whose innocent blood was formerly sold by the Jews for thirty pieces of silver, and is even now daily sold by those who pervert and deny the truth? And, indeed, there are certain of the people who, influenced by zeal for the faith, and by the most righteous intentions, promise to detect and punish the offences of the Jews, who are, nevertheless, corrupted by the common vice of avarice. For when, perchance, they have received gifts of some kind from these perfidious infidels, they unlawfully hold their peace, and those whom they formerly promised to expose and bring to justice, after the acceptance of a paltry bribe, they permit to go unpunished. Wherefore, we hereby decree that it shall be lawful for no Christian of whatever lineage, rank, or degree, whether he belong to the clergy, or to the laity, to receive a gift from a Jew, of either sex, or from any intermediary of the same, as a reward for acting against the faith of Christ; or to implicate himself in any other act against the interests of the Christian religion by the defence of such persons, for the sake of a reward. And if any person should be corrupted by the acceptance of any such gift, or should conceal the notorious errors of the Jews, and should interpose any obstacle whatever, in order that such wickedness may go unpunished, he shall be liable to the penalties laid down by the ancient Fathers, and shall pay double as much to the treasury as he shall have been proved to have received from the Jew.

ERVIGIUS, KING.

XI. Jews shall not Dare to Read Such Books as the Christian Faith Rejects.

To show favor to those readers whom it is not right to assist, is rather a mark of wickedness than of piety. For this reason, where any Jew reads books, or studies doctrines, in which the Christian faith is denied, or keeps or conceals such books in his house, he shall either receive a hundred lashes in public, or shall have his head shaved. Let all persons be cautious and beware of having books containing such doctrines in their possession, or of studying the same, or of even meditating upon them. And if, henceforth, anyone should attempt to repeat such an offence, he shall receive a hundred lashes, shall have his head shaved, and shall be condemned to perpetual exile; and because he has committed the offence a second time, he shall also lose his property, which shall be bestowed upon whomever the king may direct. Those shall be liable to a similar penalty, who presume to instruct children in the false doctrines contained in such books; and the teacher himself, when detected in the first transgression, shall receive a hundred lashes, and have his head shaved, and shall bind himself by a written agreement never to teach such doctrines again. If, after this, he should violate his agreement, and attempt to repeat what he had formerly renounced, all his property shall be forfeited to the king, and he himself shall receive a hundred lashes, shall have his head shaved, and be condemned to perpetual exile. All children under ten years of age, who are proved to have studied said false doctrines, shall be exempt from the penalties aforesaid. But any child over the age of ten years, who studies or meditates upon such doctrines, shall be liable to the fines and punishments hereinbefore mentioned.

XII. Christian Slaves shall not Serve, or Associate with, Jews.

It truly seems a crime of no small importance to the society of Christians, that the impious Jewish race, always rebellious against the rule of God, should have Christian slaves in their service, and, on the other hand, that an honorable adherent of the Christian religion should be humiliated in the presence of the children of infidels; that thus the body of Christ should appear to do homage to the ministers of Antichrist; and that, through a monstrous regulation, those very persons who are contending, by means of their customs, against our religion, should have the services of slaves attached to our Holy Faith subject to their impiety and errors. For which reason, we decree that henceforth the law promulgated by our glorious predecessor, Sisebutus, of holy memory, shall, in cases of this kind, remain in full force, and we hereby confirm the same except the clause by which the penalty of death is imposed; the said law being the one whereby our predecessors have placed all transgressors of the same under a perpetual curse.

No Jew shall presume to have in his possession a Christian slave; nor shall he dare to commit any breach of the provisions of this law, with this sole exception, which is sanctioned by the same, to wit: that a Jew shall have the power to liberate a Christian slave; because it is highly unworthy that those who are the adherents of a perfidious sect should be able to confer freedom upon Christians. For it is not consistent that the darkness should obscure the light, or that he who is himself a slave, should bestow the blessing of liberty; especially as this law was promulgated at the time the Jews were first summoned to conversion,.and this privilege was then conceded to them. Now, however, we declare that no Jew shall set a Christian slave at liberty, because it is contrary to this edict, and all such as are proved to have in their possession Christian slaves, are transgressors of the law;

and sufficient indulgence is shown them if they are not condemned for their transgression. Therefore this privilege is entirely denied them, for the reason that they presume to act against the rules and canons of the Church. We, however, for the sake of mercy, concede to them that from the first year of our reign, that is to say, for the space of sixty days from the Kalends of February, every Jew shall have the right to sell his Christian slaves, but not without the approval of the priests or judges having jurisdiction over the diocese, or the district to which said slaves belong, in order that the slaves who are sold may not undergo the penalty of death, and that the vendors may not, in some way, seek an opportunity for the commission of fraud, or the infliction of revenge. Therefore, when the sixtieth day from the aforesad Kalends shall have elapsed, it shall not be lawful for a Jew to have a Christian slave, or any other Christian, in his service. After that time, that is to say, the period of sixty days, if any Christian slaves should be found in the possession of a Jew, they shall be free, and shall have a right to all property which has been bestowed upon them by their master, as provided by this law; and said slaves shall be entitled to their freedom, even if it should be proved that they have been forcibly concealed by their master. All Jews who, after the expiration of the aforesaid time, presume to keep in their possession, or conceal, any Christian slaves, or, in any way whatever, attempt to evade the provisions of this law, shall forfeit half of their property to the royal treasury; or, if they are persons of inferior rank, and have not the means wherewith to make reparation, they shall each receive a hundred lashes, and have their heads shaved.

ERVIGIUS, KING.

XIII. Where a Jew Declares that he is a Christian, and, for this Reason, does not Wish to Dispose of a Christian Slave.

Where a Jew, fearing that he will lose his property, fraudulently asserts that he has been converted to Christianity, and protests that he ought not to lose his Christian slaves, for the reason that he has been leading a Christian life, it devolves upon us to provide, by these laws, that the astuteness of fraud does not prevail, on the one hand, or sincere conversion suffer injury on the other. We, therefore, decree that all Jews throughout our kingdom shall have the right conceded by a former edict, to sell their Christian slaves, from the Kalends of February, in the first year of our reign, until the approaching Kalends of April; and, should they wish to retain said slaves, they must prove themselves to be Christians, as prescribed by law. We grant to all Jews, against whom there exists no evident suspicion of perjury, the space of sixty days from the Kalends of April during the present year, during which time such as desire to be saved, and wish to unite with the Christian communion, may do so; and we direct such persons to visit the bishop of the diocese, and publish their confession of faith, to which their signatures or seals shall be attached, in which confession each Jew shall declare that he abjures all the errors of his sect, and that he will in no way again observe or embrace any of its false doctrines. Every Jew who renounces his former errors, and is converted to the holy faith of Christ, shall inscribe in his confession the Christian symbol; shall promise that he will under no circumstances return to his errors, as he would to his vomit; and shall profess that henceforth he will, in compliance with the terms of his written confession, in no way change anything which we have included in this law. And the aforesaid confession he shall make, not merely with bare words and promises, declaring one thing openly, while he secretly retains another in his heart, while his artifice, cloaked by his promises, has more control over him than the truth. Bishops and judges shall use every effort to ascertain whether said confession is genuine or not, and that those who swear to it, according to the law, do so with sincere, and not with deceitful, hearts. All who act honestly, and whose profession, together with their works, prove them to be worthy of the Holy Faith, and whose promise under oath establishes that they are devout Christians, can have the use of Christian slaves. Christian slaves shall not be subjected to the control of Jews unless the latter are openly proved to be Christians, use Christian food, and contract marriage according to Christian customs. Any of said persons, however, who, after having made confession and been sworn, thereby dedicating themselves to Christianity, as aforesaid, are found to have broken their promises by the practice of any rite of the Jewish sect; for the reason that they dared to profane the name of God, and pollute themselves with the filth of Jewish error, shall forfeit all their property to the king, shall each receive a hundred lashes, and, having had their heads shaved, shall be subjected to the miseries of exile which they have so justly deserved. All those who, obdurate of heart, and blinded by malice, neglect to make public confession of faith within the period aforesaid, or presume to have in their possession a Christian slave after the time prescribed by law has elapsed, shall be liable to the condemnation of the former law, relating to Christian slaves remaining in the service of Jews, to wit: half of their property shall be confiscated for the benefit of the royal treasury, or, should they be persons of inferior station, and not have the means to make reparation, as aforesaid, they shall each receive a hundred lashes, and have their heads shaved. All Jews who retain possession of Christian slaves, and do not deliver up said slaves within the prescribed time, shall be reduced to perpetual slavery, and belong to those upon whom the king shall see fit to bestow them.

XIV. The Confession of Jews; and In What Way Each One of Them, who is Converted, must Write Down the Proof of his Conversion.

I hereby renounce all the rites and observances of the Jewish sect, and, without reserve, express my utter abhorrence of all their ceremonies and solemnities which I have practised and kept in former times, until now; and I pledge myself that I will, hereafter, observe none of said rites or ceremonies, nor will adhere to any of my former errors; that is to say, I will not retain them in my mind, or, in any way, carry them into effect. Henceforth, renouncing all things which are condemned and prohibited by the doctrines of Christianity:—

I believe in one God, the Omnipotent Father, Maker of Heaven and earth, the Creator of all things visible and invisible, and in our Lord Jesus Christ, the only son of God, begotten by the Father before all the centuries; God of God, light of light, the true God of the true God, born not made, equal to the Father, that is to say, of the same substance as the Father, by whom all things were created both in Heaven and earth. And I believe in Him who for the sake of man, and for our salvation, descended from heaven, and, born of the Holy Spirit and the Virgin Mary, became a man in the flesh; suffered under Pontius Pilate; was crucified, dead, and buried; who arose on the third day, ascended into heaven, and sitteth at the right hand of God the Father; who shall come again in his glory to judge the living and the dead, and to whose reign there shall be no end. I believe in the Holy Spirit, the regenerator, proceeding from the Father and the Son, who spoke by the mouth of the prophets. I believe in the Holy Catholic Apostolic Church, I confess that there is but one baptism for the remission of sins, and I believe in the resurrection of the dead, and in life through all coming ages. Amen.

I sincerely believe in all the things hereinbefore written, and I promise that I will keep them faithfully, and that I will embrace them with all the affection of my soul, and, subscribing my name thereto, I promise that I will never again return to the vomit of the Jewish superstition; and that I will never practise, or retain in my heart, any of the rites or ceremonies which the Jews are accustomed to observe; wholly renouncing the Jewish sect, rejecting in its entirety the perfidy of the Jews, and abjuring whatever is contrary to the Christian faith. And, hereafter, I will always profess belief in the Holy Trinity, so that I may live as I ought, according to Christian customs, and that, avoiding in every way the company of Jews, I may always associate with honest Christians. Likewise, I promise that I will always partake of food with Christians, or accept it from them; and that I will, as a faithful and devoted Christian, frequently go to the house of God; and I also promise that I will devoutly take part in the services of Sunday, and in the festivals of martyrs, as enjoined by the Christian religion; and that I will be present with true Christians on all festival days which the Church has ordered shall be observed with love and devotion, and will participate in all the ceremonies prescribed by the Christian faith. This, the profession of my faith and belief, is made upon such and such a day.

XV. Conditions under which Jews must Make Oath, when, having been Converted, they give in their Confession of Faith.

I swear first by God the Father Omnipotent, who said, "By me shalt thou swear, and shalt not take the name of the Lord thy God in vain"; who made Heaven and earth, the sea and all that in them is; who placed a boundary to the ocean, saying, "thus far shall thou come, and here shall thy swelling waves be broken." Who also said, "Heaven is my throne, and the earth my footstool." Who cast down the first and proudest angel from Heaven; before whose eyes the entire celestial host stood trembling; whose glance dried up the waters of the abysses, and whose wrath caused the mountains to melt away. Who placed Adam, the first man, in Paradise, and ordered him not to eat of the forbidden fruit, and who, having eaten it, He cast out of Paradise, and bound him, as well as all the human race, with the fetters of disobedience; who freely accepted the sacrifice of Abel, and worthily rejected that of Cain; who received in Paradise Enoch, together with Elias, in the flesh, before their time was accomplished upon earth; who, at the time of the flood, deigned to save Noah and his wife, and their three children and their wives, with the animals, and the birds of the air, and the reptiles, whereby the race of each was preserved; who caused Shem to be born of Noah, and from him Abraham, and from Abraham the Israelites to be derived; who chose the Patriarchs and Prophets, and blessed the Patriarchs, Abraham, Isaac and Jacob. I swear by Him who made the promise to the holy Abraham, saying, "in thy seed all nations shall be blest," and gave him the symbol of circumcision, as an eternal covenant. I swear by the God who overthrew

Sodom and Gomorrah, and turned the wife of Lot, who looked backward, into a pillar of salt. I swear by Him who strove with Jacob, and, touching his thigh, caused him to become lame, saying, "thou shalt henceforth not be called Jacob, but Israel." I swear by the God who liberated Joseph from the hands of his brethren, and caused him to find favor in the eyes of Pharaoh, and by whom all Israel was saved from famine. I swear by the God who rescued Moses from the waters, and appeared to him in the burning bush, and who, by his hands, brought the ten plagues upon the Egyptians; and who liberated his Jewish people from Egyptian slavery, and caused them to traverse the Red Sea with dry feet, when the waves, contrary to their nature, stood, as a solid wall, upon either side. I swear by the God who drowned Pharaoh and his army in the Red Sea; and who, as a pillar of cloud by day, and of fire by night, guided the Hebrews in the wilderness. I swear by the God who, upon Mount Sinai, gave the law to Moses written in His own hand, upon tables of stone. I swear by the God who made the mountain of Sinai to smoke in the sight of the Children of Israel. I swear by the God who chose Aaron for His first priest, and consumed the sons of the latter with fire, in the tabernacle, because they offered strange sacrifices before the Lord. I swear by the God who, by His just judgment, caused the earth to gape and swallow up alive Dathan and Abiran. I swear by the God who caused the bitter waters to become sweet by casting twigs into the same. I swear by Him who, through Moses striking the rock with his rod, caused great torrents to gush forth, to refresh the thirsty Jewish people. I swear by Him who, for forty years, fed the Israelites in the wilderness, and preserved their clothing entire, so that it did not wear with the using. I swear by Him who declared by His irrevocable mandate, that none of the Children of Israel should enter the promised land, except Joshua-Ben-Nun, and Caleb, whom he promised and predicted should enter there; for the Israelites did not believe the word of God. I swear by Him who declared to Moses that he would raise his hand, and the Jewish people would be victorious over the Malekites. I swear by Him who ordered our fathers to cross the River

Jordan, and to take ten stones from that river as a testimony. I swear by Him who ordered all Israel, when they passed over the River Jordan, to be circumcised with knives of stone. I swear by Him who overthrew the walls of Jericho. I swear by Him who decorated David with the splendor of royalty, and rescued him from the hands of Saul, and of his son Absalom. I swear by Him who filled the temple with a cloud, and poured out His blessings therein. I swear by Him who carried up the prophet Elias in a whirlwind and a fiery chariot, from earth to the throne of glory; and by Him who, at the prayer of Elisha, and with a stroke of the garment of Elijah, divided the waters of the Jordan in twain. I swear by Him who preserved the three young men in the furnace of burning fire, before the eyes of a hostile king, He who holds the key of David, and who closes what no one shall open, and opens what no one shall close. I swear by Him who performed all miracles, and displayed all virtues and all signs, among the Hebrews, or among other nations. I swear by Him, and by the ten sacred commandments of the law. I swear by Jesus Christ, the Son of the Omnipotent Father, and by the Holy Spirit, the Paraclete, which is one of the Trinity and the true God; and by the holy resurrection of our Lord Jesus Christ, and by His ascension into Heaven, and by His glorious and terrible coming, when He shall judge the quick and the dead, showing Himself merciful to the just, and terrible to the wicked; and by the holy body and precious blood of Him who opened the eyes of the blind, and made the deaf to hear; restored paralytics to health; loosened the tongues of the dumb; healed those possessed of the devil; made the lame to run, and raised the dead; who walked upon the waters; who resurrected Lazarus, whose flesh was already decayed, restored him to life and strength, and changed sorrow into joy; who is the Creator of the world, the origin of light, the source of vigor; who illuminated the world by His birth, and redeemed it by His passion; who alone was free among the dead, and whom death could not hold; who broke into pieces the infernal gates, and, by the majesty of His presence, rescued souls from the power of hell; who, having conquered death, raised to Heaven, after His conquest of the world, that body which He had assumed upon earth; and who now sits at the right hand of the Omnipotent God, the Father, from whom He has received the eternal power of the celestial kingdom. And I swear by all the heavenly virtues, and by all the relics of the Saints and Apostles, and by the four Holy Gospels which have been placed under this my written oath upon the holy altar of Him of the sacred name, and which I touch and hold with my hands.

And all these things which I have taken care to renew in my confession, or have added thereto, which confession I have given, signed with my hand, to thee, the bishop governing this diocese, I have declared in all sincerity to have been offered, not with artifice or fraud, but in good faith, as stated in said confession. And I hereby renounce all the ceremonies of the Jewish ritual, and declare my belief in the Holy Trinity with all my heart, and promise that I will forever remain in the Faith, and will never again associate with the impious Jews; but that I will hereafter live, in all respects, according to the Christian customs, and take part in all their observances; and that I will keep, with all purity of heart, whatever concerns the practice of the Holy Faith, which has been set forth in my confession; and that I will always live according to the apostolic traditions and the canons of the Holy Church. And if I should violate the same in any respect, or dishonor the Holy Faith, or attempt to practice any Jewish rite, or deceive you, by this my confession, made under oath; or, under any pretext whatever, I should not, even unintentionally, perform the things which I have promised, as you believed, or understood that I did promise; then may there be visited upon me all the curses of the law which have been uttered by the mouth of God against those who disobey His commandments. And may there come upon me, and upon my house, and upon my children, all the plagues and afflictions of Egypt, as an example and a terror to others; and may I suffer the judgment of Dathan and Abiram, and the earth swallow me up alive. And after I have departed this life, may eternal fire receive me, delivered up to the devil and his angels; and may I, sharing the punishments of the inhabitants of Sodom and Gomorrah, be given up to be burned; and when, at last, I shall come before the tribunal of the dreaded Judge and sublime King, our Lord Jesus Christ, may I be numbered among those to whom the terrible and glorious Judge shall say, "Depart from me, ye accursed, into everlasting fire prepared for the devil and his angels." This oath was signed upon such and such a day and date.

XVI. Concerning the Christian Slaves of Jews, who have not Proclaimed Themselves Christians, and those who Expose Them.

All slaves, belonging to Hebrews, and who are members of the holy Christian communion, and who, henceforth, influenced, by their masters, do not declare themselves Christians, and rema'n under the yoke of their masters, for the reason that they have rejected the favor of liberty which was offered them, shall be doomed to perpetual slavery, and shall be given to whomever the king may select. Any person, by whose means this was exposed, if he should be the slave of a Jew, after having embraced the Christian faith, shall receive his freedom. If, however, the discovery was made by a Christian, he shall receive five *solidi* for every Christian slave, from him who is convicted of having violated this decree after its promulgation.

XVII. No Jew, under any Authority whatever, shall Dare to Oppress, Punish, or Imprison a Christian, Except by Order of the King.

No Jew shall have the power to rule, command, or restrain any Christian, except in cases where the king orders it to be done for the public benefit. If a Jew, acting under authority from any person, should presume to imprison, punish, coerce, or illtreat any Christian whomsoever, or should attempt to inflict upon him anything forbidden by law, or even what is not provided for by the laws, he shall either forfeit half of his property to the royal treasury, or, if he should not possess any property, he shall receive a hundred lashes, and have his head shaved. And where any person who is of noble rank, attempts to exercise this power over Christians, he shall be compelled to pay ten pounds of gold to the king; and where he is a person of inferior rank, he shall pay five pounds of gold. Those who have not the means wherewith to make reparation as aforesaid, shall receive a hundred lashes, and have their heads shaved.

ERVIGIUS, KING.

XVIII. If Slaves of Jews, not yet Converted, should Claim the Grace of Christ, they shall be Liberated.

The chosen apostle Paul, referring to something which happened at the time, or merely for the sake of truth, declared that Christ announced that, as we bestow liberty upon the faithful, so, also, we ought to afford infidels the opportunity to embrace eternal life. Therefore, if any slave belonging to a Jew should desire to be free from servitude, and seek the favor of Christ, no one shall retain him in bondage; no one shall oppose him in any way, or place any obstacle in his path; but, as soon as he shows himself to be a Christian, by his profession and his oath, and shall openly abandon, or reject the false doctrines of his master, he shall be at once released from slavery; and, removed, with all his property, from the control of his master, he shall fully enjoy the blessings of freedom; and the same rule which has been provided where Christian slaves have been emancipated, shall apply, in every respect, to his case.

XIX. Jews shall not Rule Christians under the Authority of Mayors of Towns, or of Superintendents of Estates; and Concerning the Penalties to be Imposed upon Such as Appoint them to Office.

Where a Jew is invested with authority or power by any member of the laity, and by its means he obtains control over a Christian family, his authority shall be at once transferred to the king, and he who accepted it shall receive a hundred lashes, have his head shaved, and forfeit half his property to the public treasury. If any bishop, priest, minister, clerk, or member of a monastic order, should invest a Jew with authority over church affairs, he shall forfeit to the public treasury as much of his own property as is equal in value to that over which he gave said Jew authority. If, however, he should have no property, he shall be sent into exile, that he may learn under the restrictions of penance, how impious it is to confer upon infidels, authority over true Christians.

XX. Where a Jew comes from Another Country into any of the Provinces of Our Kingdom, he Must, at once, Present himself before a Bishop, a Priest, or a Judge; and What shall be Done under the Circumstances.

Where a Jew, residing in a city or province of our kingdom, makes application to a bishop, priest, or judge of that diocese or district, and it appears from the testimony of ecclesiastical witnesses, that he has abandoned the observance of the Sabbath, and the practice of the rites and ceremonies usually observed by members of his sect; and that he did not make use of any of the same, while wandering hither and thither, or did not seek a hiding-place anywhere, in which to observe said rites; and that, while at home, he is known to have conferred with Christians of approved faith, partaken of food with them, and participated in the Christian communion; and that, upon such days as his ceremonies were accustomed to be practised, he resorted to the church to receive the salutary instructions of the bishops and the priests; and if said Jew asserts that he cannot remain for any length of time, on account of inevitable necessity, or press of business; then a confession of faith, to be signed by him, shall be drawn up by the priest of the parish, and the said Jew shall promise therein that, whenever, upon his journey, he finds any of his sect observing their rites or festivities, he will avoid them. And the said priest shall draw up a letter, wr tten with his own hand, directed to those ecclesiastics, in whose jurisdiction said Jew represents that he is about to travel, in order that, all suspicion of fraud being removed, said Jew whether traveling, or remaining in one locality, may not be subjected to religious restraint and discipline.

If any Jew should violate this law, authority is given to any bishop or priest of the diocese, as well as to any judge, to punish him with a hundred lashes; nor shall he be permitted to return to his home, unless he is furnished with letters from the bishop or priest of the diocese in which he was unlawfully found. In said letters the number of days shall be especially noted; that is, dating from the time when said Jew made application to the bishop aforesaid, as well as those included in his absence until the day of his return.

XXI. How Assemblies of Jews shall Visit the Bishop on Appointed Days.

Every colony of Jews, in whatever city or province they may be situated, shall visit the bishop or priest of the diocese upon the Sabbath, and upon all other festival days, when they are accustomed to celebrate their rites; they shall not be permitted to wander about on said days; and during all such festivals, when they are suspected of performing their rites, they shall under no circumstances leave their homes without the permission of the priest. Each of said Jews on every Sabbath, after having bathed, shall visit a bishop, or a priest, and receive his blessing. And in localities where there is no priest, each of them shall visit the judges, or other approved Christians, and shall associate with them openly, in such a manner that, if inquiry be made, said persons may give favorable testimony concerning their Christian behavior. Jewish women, that is to say, the wives and daughters of Jews, to the end that they may have no opportunity to commit any error or transgression upon the festival days aforesaid, when they are accustomed to practise their rites, shall act, in every respect, as may be prescribed by the bishops or the priests to their husbands when present; that, like their husbands, they may not absent themselves from ecclesiastical control, and on all the festival days observed by their sect, may associate with such respectable and devout Christian women as the priests or bishops may select. If anyone shall be proved to have violated this edict, he shall be punished with a hundred lashes, and have his head shaved. And, as priests are sometimes influenced by the execrable temptations of the flesh, it is hereby especially enjoined, that they shall not take advantage of opportunities of this kind, for the indulgence of the same. Wherefore, we decree, with all severity, that every priest shall strictly observe this law concerning Hebrew women, and shall not take advantage of any occasion by which he may be polluted with their company. And if, at any time, a priest should pervert the zeal which he should employ for the benefit of Christianity, for the purpose of indulging his licentious passions, he shall be deprived of his holy office, and be sentenced to perpetual exile.

FLAVIUS ERVIGIUS, KING.

XXII. Where Anyone has a Jew in his Service, and a Priest Demands him, the Master shall not have a Right to Retain said Jew.

Where anyone of the laity has a Hebrew man or woman in his service, or under his protection, and by the exertion of his authority deprives them of the privilege of resorting at any time, to the bishop or the priest, or prevents them from going, for the sake of instruction, to ecclesiastics, on the days appointed for that purpose, he shall be excommunicated by the bishop, and be deprived of said slave which he attempted to restrain illegally, and for every slave so restrained he shall pay three pounds of gold to the king.

XXIII. All Restraint of and Control over the Jews shall be Vested in the Priesthood.

Those who are charged with the enforcement of our laws, and the infliction of punishment upon infidels, are earnestly exhorted to fulfil the duty imposed upon them by Divine authority; for the Holy Spirit, whose truth is coextensive with the world, has said "Priests shall sit in My judgment seat, and shall judge according to My laws and precepts." We decree that, hereafter, priests shall observe whatever is included in our laws and that they shall not suffer a Jew to be protected by anyone in the practice of his rites, but that all such Jews shall be exempt from the favor of those by whom they are shielded; and that said priests shall diligently take measures to bring all Jews under the control of the Church, for the sake of their salvation, which is the duty of all Catholic ecclesiastics; and that it will be their earnest care not to grow lukewarm in the enforcement of any of our laws aforesaid.

XXIV. Concerning the Penalties to be Imposed upon Priests and Judges who Neglect to Enforce the Laws against the Jews.

The priests of our Holy Church must exercise due and pious care lest they be held responsible for the transgressions of the people. For what profit is there, where one is not punished for his own sin, but still can be punished for the sin of another? Therefore, to correct the negligence of such persons, we hereby decree that if any bishop, influenced by avarice or malice, should be lukewarm in the enforcement of the laws enacted against the Jews, to wit: that where any errors of that perfidious sect have been detected by him, or where he has received information of them, and it appears that he neglected to correct said errors, he shall be excommunicated for the space of three months, and shall forfeit a pound of gold to the royal treasury; and, if he should not have the means to make such pecuniary reparation, he shall be excommunicated for the space of six months; and, for the purpose of making amends for the negligence of said bishop, any other bishop who is zealous in the cause of God, shall have authority to correct the errors of said perfidious Jews, which the former bishop neglected to correct, as aforesaid. And if, through deceit, negligence, or lukewarmness, the other bishop should hesitate, or procrastinate, in discharging the duty imposed upon him, his inactivity shall be punished, and the errors of the perfidious Jews be corrected by order of the king. This rule shall also, in every respect, apply to, and be observed by, all other ecclesiastics, as well as bishops; that is to say, priests, deacons and clerks, upon any of whom the duty of restraining infidels has been imposed by the bishop. And all judges who are informed of such crimes, or who shall, themselves, discover them, and do not at once punish them, as prescr bed by law, shall each pay a pound of gold to the public treasury, as has been provided in the case of bishops. Nevertheless, priests, judges or other officials who have been invested with authority, shall not be liable to the aforesaid penalties, if they can prove that they were prevented, by command of the king, from proceeding against the Jews.

ERVIGIUS, KING.

XXV. No Judge shall Presume to Investigate the Offences of the Jews without the Knowledge of an Ecclesiastic.

No judge shall decide a cause involving the transgressions of the perfidious Jews, unless an ecclesiastic be present, lest, by the acceptance of a bribe, the Holy Faith of the Church be stained by avarice; but, as is frequently the case, where no ecclesiastic is present, the judge is authorized to proceed without him. If, however, the bishop should be absent, whether near at hand, or at a distance, he may leave a priest to act in his stead, who will co-operate with the judge in the enforcement of these laws, without any remuneration whatever.

XXVI. Bishops shall be Immune from Punishment, when their Priests do not Inform them of Such Things as Should be Corrected.

As soon as the priests, deacons, or other members of the clerical order, and all judges, vested with authority, throughout the different provinces of the kingdom, ascertain that a body of Jews is within their jurisdiction, they must not delay to place said Jews under coercion and restraint, as required by our laws; and all errors which said Jews are unwilling to renounce, shall be brought to the knowledge of the king and the bishop, in order that they may be corrected· and if a Jew should give information of the same to the bishop, he shall not be subject to punishment for any similar offence of which he may be guilty. No bishop shall be liable to discipline for neglect, when notice of the offence was not given him by his subordinates.

ERVIGIUS, KING.

XXVII. Concerning the Mercy to be Shown by Princes towards Those who have been Truly Converted to the Christian Faith.

The foregoing laws having been framed by us with care and diligence, and having attempted in them to adapt the punishment to the guilt of the offender, as, for instance, where we have sentenced certain of them to lose their property, and be driven into exile, we now hereby reserve the following privileges of mercy for ourselves, and our successors, to wit: that if any Jew, after having been ensnared by the devil, should come to his senses, and profess belief in the Holy Trinity; and the priests or judges of the diocese or district in which he lives, should establish the fact by their testimony; and the works of said Jew should correspond with his professions; in such cases the prerogative of mercy may be exercised by ourselves, and our successors; that is to say, after the confession and oath of said Jew has been made, and the evidence has been submitted to the king, the latter shall have authority to return his property to said Jew, and to recall him from exile. If, however, any such Jew, after having professed himself to be a Christian, should return to the vomit of his error, he shall be condemned to punishment, without any hope of pardon; and said punishment shall be proportionate to the proof of his hypocrisy, and the degree of his guilt, and whether he undergoes a capital penalty, or one of less severity, no mercy shall, under any circumstances, be shown him.

XXVIII. Bishops shall Give to all Jews a Copy of this Book, which has been Published for the Purpose of Correcting their Errors; and their Confessions and a Record of their Conversion, shall be Deposited among the Archives of the Church.

The perversity of a deceitful mind is accustomed to make use of the pretence of ignorance, when it asserts that it has no knowledge of the law, and declares that it is exempt from punishment because it is ignorant of the New Testament.

Now, for the purpose of removing this false and malicious excuse, we hereby order all bishops and priests to explain to the Jews within their jurisdiction, the decrees which we have heretofore promulgated concerning their perfidy; and also, to give them a copy of this book, which is ordinarily read to them publicly, in the congregations of the Church, and which they must always carry with them as evidence of their instruction. And if, after this book shall have been read to them publicly as aforesaid, or given into their hands, any of them should claim that he was not present when it was read, or should assert that he is ignorant of the laws contained therein, no excuse of his shall be thereafter received; but if, ever subsequently, he should be detected in the breach of any of said laws, under no circumstances shall he escape punishment for the same. And we add to this law, as being a necessary part of it that all written confessions and agreements which any Jew, at any time, has delivered to his priest, shall be carefully preserved by the latter, among the archives of his church, in order that it may be evidence against any Jew who may thereafter venture to resume the practice of his impious rites.

INDEX.

A.

B.

J.

K.

L.

M.

N.

O.

P.

S.

T.

V.

W.

THE END.

8961175R0

Made in the USA
Lexington, KY
16 March 2011